P9-DUJ-672

MACROBIOTICS . . .

"Macrobiotics does not require any change in your religion, way of thinking, or personal lifestyle. It requires only that you eat in harmony with your environment. By eating well, you will create order and balance in your daily life. Your peaceful spirit will extend to your family and community and eventually influence the whole world. Once you have experienced the true energy of food and learned how to control your health, behavior, and thoughts through cooking, you can never return to old unconscious and sensorial ways of eating. After preparing balanced whole foods meals, your physical condition will improve. Your thinking will become clear and focused. Your vision of the future will grow bright and cheerful. Careful cooking is the key to maintaining harmony with the surrounding natural world."

—Aveline Kushi

. . . ONE STEP FURTHER

In addition to teaching you how to properly cook brown rice and other traditional macrobiotic foods, Aveline Kushi takes the art of organic, natural foods cooking one step further. She adapts many taste-tempting dishes from other cuisines to her high macrobiotic standards, making food substitutions and preparation changes when necessary. The results are completely new, delicious, satisfying recipes presented together for the first time in a macrobiotic cookbook, dishes from Latin America, the Mediterranean, the Middle East, as well as North America and the Far East, that you are sure to enjoy.

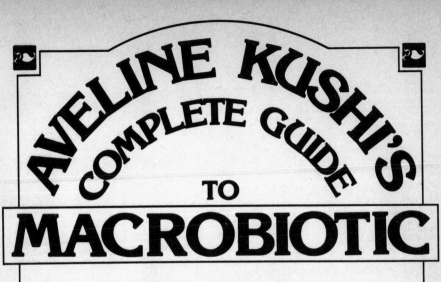

AVELINE KUSHI'S COMPLETE GUIDE TO MACROBIOTIC COOKING

For Health, Harmony, and Peace

Aveline Kushi
with
Alex Jack

Foreword by Michio Kushi

Illustrations by Aveline Kushi

WARNER BOOKS

A Warner Communications Company

Copyright © 1985 by Aveline Kushi and Alex Jack
All rights reserved.
Warner Books, Inc., 666 Fifth Avenue, New York, NY 10103

A Warner Communications Company

Printed in the United States of America
First Printing: June 1985
10 9 8 7 6 5 4 3 2 1

Book design by H. Roberts Design

Front cover photograph © 1985 by Margaret Landsman

Library of Congress Cataloging in Publication Data

Kushi, Aveline.
Aveline Kushi's Complete guide to macrobiotic cooking for health, harmony, and peace.

Bibliography: p. 390
Includes index
1. Macrobiotic diet. 2. Macrobiotic diet—Recipes.
I. Jack, Alex, 1945– . II. Title. III. Title:
Complete guide to macrobiotic cooking for health, harmony, and peace.
RM235.K86 1985 641.5'637 84-21020
ISBN 0-446-37982-4 (pbk.) (U.S.A.)
0-446-37983-2 (pbk.) (Canada)

ATTENTION: SCHOOLS AND CORPORATIONS

Warner books are available at quantity discounts with bulk purchase for educational, business, or sales promotional use. For information, please write to: Special Sales Department, Warner Books, 666 Fifth Avenue, New York, NY 10103.

ARE THERE WARNER BOOKS YOU WANT BUT CANNOT FIND IN YOUR LOCAL STORES?

You can get any Warner Books title in print. Simply send title and retail price, plus 50¢ per order and 50¢ per copy to cover mailing and handling costs for each book desired. New York State and California residents, add applicable sales tax. Enclose check or money order—no cash, please—to: Warner Books, PO Box 690, New York, NY 10019. Or send for our complete catalog of Warner Books.

CONTENTS

FOREWORD

Cooking is the highest of all the arts that humanity has invented. Cooking serves to maintain life's basic functions, both mental and physical. It can also elevate human consciousness toward endless spiritual realization. At the same time, misuse of cooking can lead to physical and psychological degeneration, threatening the eventual extinction of the human race. Cooking deals with the essence of all environmental factors, including water, fire, pressure, atmosphere, various species of plant and animal life, salt and other mineral compounds, seasonal and climatic changes, and celestial and astronomical cycles. It also affects the stages of individual development from embryonic life to childhood, maturity, and old age. Accordingly, cooking is a comprehensive art that may bring either health, happiness, and peace or sickness, misery, and destruction.

After I learned the importance of food for human destiny as well as individual life, it was one of the happiest gifts in my life that I could meet a woman who has dedicated her life to the improvement of society through the traditional art of cooking. Aveline is a woman with a simple, intuitive mind, tireless in her devotion to the common dream we share of realizing a healthy planetary community through the most peaceful method—the biological and psychological elevation of humankind.

During the thirty-five years of our married life together, she has raised five wonderful children and five beautiful grandchildren, and her insight into nature and the universe has deepened. Her understanding of food as energy has continued to grow, and her practice has become very refined, sensitive, and graceful. During this time, she has taught macrobiotic cooking to her students in North America, Europe, and Latin America. Her seminars and lectures have guided countless families toward greater health and happiness, including thousands of children who have subsequently come into this world. I myself often wonder whether I could ever have maintained my physical health and spiritual direction over the last three and a half decades without her constant support, encouragement, and companionship.

In the past, several recommended cookbooks on macrobiotic food preparation have been published. Most of these works, written by Aveline's students, were inspired by her teachings. This new cookbook, the distillation of her own experience and understanding, will benefit those who have been practicing macrobiotics for many years as well as those who are just beginning to change their way of eating in a more natural direction. This is not only a cookbook or collection of recipes; it is a revelation of Aveline's personal life describing what it was like to grow up in the Japanese countryside and the traditions and customs which form the cultural background for her own inspiration. The haiku and illustrations prefacing each chapter also contribute to making this a very special volume.

For this unique compilation, Alex Jack, who has coauthored with me *The Cancer-Prevention Diet* and *Diet for a Strong Heart*, has devoted tireless energy to expressing, precisely and eloquently, Aveline's spirit through his carefully selected words. Alex's own search for the boundless soul of humanity has taken him to Japan, India, China, Southeast Asia, Europe, and the Soviet Union. His heart is full of love for everyone, and his constantly burning flame of passion for world peace and harmony can be a model for society. Without his perseverance, this book, combining insights into the order of nature and the universe along with daily practical living, would not have been possible.

I am very grateful to Aveline and Alex for producing a book so full of love, care, and grace. I sincerely hope that it will become a daily guide and companion for individuals and families on every continent, so that the future world may recover its traditional roots, turn away from biological degeneration, and develop endlessly toward a new era of health, happiness, harmony, and peace.

—Michio Kushi

Brookline, Massachusetts
April 7, 1984

FROM AVELINE

Struggling with sickness,
the long winter now past,
I hold the budding energy
of spring close to my heart.

—Aveline Kushi
Yokota, Japan
February 1947

In 1938 I left home to attend Teacher's College in Hamada, a coastal city in southwestern Japan. After completing my studies, I returned to the mountains to teach elementary and junior high school near my home village. Some of my happiest memories go back to this time. I have saved nearly three hundred haiku which my pupils wrote. For me, their simple feeling for nature is unmatched, even by Basho and other famous poets. Some of these beautiful poems preface the chapters of this book.

The train to Hiroshima ran through our region. In August 1945, rail passengers from the south brought a rumor that something had happened in Hiroshima. In a few days the war ended. A long period of national disillusion and social disruption followed. The soldiers, young and old, came home from the South Pacific, Siberia, Manchuria, China, and many other areas. The Americans arrived, with their superior technology and Coca-Cola. Japan searched its soul.

This rootless postwar climate affected everyone deeply. I no longer had the confidence to teach and often joined with the young people in my village who were putting their energies into dancing and acting. However, I soon realized that dying for one's country could no longer be an ideal and the world was now one. I decided to devote myself to peace.

Shortly after resigning my teaching post in 1947, I experienced a sharp pain beneath my heart. From the middle of September until the following February, I remained in bed at my parents' home in Yokota. I had never been weak or sickly. On the contrary, I was very active and athletic. At college I excelled in gymnastics and the martial arts, practicing archery, lady's sword, and modern dance. My proficiency on the balance beams and jumping horse and in tumbling took me to Tokyo for the national Olympic championships in 1941, just a month before the attack on Pearl Harbor. During the war, all the young male teachers went into the army. In my school, the responsibility for teaching gymnastics to high school boys, some twice my size, fell to me. Until my illness at age twenty-two, I had always been strong and in perfect health.

As I struggled with my loss of direction in life, the lengthening winter seemed to reflect my feelings. I wrote many poems during this period of confinement, but as the weather changed, I felt new energy and life stir within me. Born in the snowy mountains, I enjoyed all seasons of the year, but early spring was always my favorite. The wild grasses begin to peek through the snow. The branches start turning a warm, purplish color. Buds begin to unfold and returning birds begin to sing. Rejoicing in the energy of spring, I wrote the poem which appears at the beginning of this chapter. I began to feel the universal spirit of creation move within me again. I felt my confusion dissolve with the last ice of the winter. I felt my appreciation for the gift of life grow with the lengthening rays of the sun.

Not long afterwards, in January 1950, I learned about George Ohsawa's world government movement. The dream of ending war and unifying all people reverberated in my heart. I went to Yokohama to visit George Ohsawa's center and decided to study macrobiotic philosophy, which utilized the energy of food as a unique tool for creating peace and harmony.

Today, none of my college friends from Hamada would ever believe that I ended up devoting much of the next three decades of my life to cooking and food preparation. In college, my nickname was Jotaro, after the young boy who tagged along after the famous sword master Miyamoto Musashi. The novel about this samurai, who lived during the time of the Tokugawa Shogun, was being serialized in the daily newspapers during the war. In the dormitory, my friends would rush downstairs every morning to read the latest installment and compare my tomboyish behavior with Jotaro's adventures.

From childhood I had always escaped from the house rather than help mother cook or do household chores. I enjoyed sports and outdoor activities and was one of the first girls in our little mountain village to ride a bicycle. Later, at school, I studied sewing and cooking but lacked confidence when I went into the kitchen. George Ohsawa taught me the importance of food, but at that time no cooking classes were given. Besides, I was much more interested in world peace activities and became the champion seller of the macrobiotic community's newspaper promoting world government and the abolition of atomic weapons. However, I noticed that my sales record went up and down depending on how I ate. When I ate simply and well, I was always able to distribute many more newspapers. People were much more attracted to my energy at those times and spontaneously came up to talk to me.

In 1951, I left Japan and sailed to America. There I met Michio Kushi, who had studied with George Ohsawa a few years earlier and was then pursuing the study of international relations at Columbia University in New York. We soon married, and for the first time I found myself in charge of a kitchen. Thus, my cooking grew out of my love for my husband and later for my children. The same sense of rhythm and balance I developed in gymnastics I now devoted to my cooking. Over the years my confidence grew as I prepared meals for my family, friends, and the young American and European students who came to study with us. Many of these men and women have gone on to become much better cooks than I, as well as excellent teachers, counselors, and pioneers in organic agriculture and the natural foods movement.

Macrobiotics does not require any change in your religion, way of thinking, or personal lifestyle. It requires only that you eat in harmony with your environment. By eating well, you will create order and balance in your daily life. Your peaceful spirit will extend to your family and community and eventually influence the whole world. Once you have experienced the true energy of food and learned how to control your health, behavior, and thoughts through cooking and eating, you will never be able to return to the old unconscious and sensorial ways of eating. After preparing balanced whole foods meals, your physical condition will improve, your thinking will become clear and focused, and your vision of the future will grow bright and cheerful. Careful cooking is the key to maintaining harmony with the surrounding natural world. But obtaining the highest quality and freshest foods is essential.

In the early 1960s, Michio and I began to devote our energy to the dream of making available whole foods to every community in this country. Food quality is the key to health and happiness. When we started Erewhon, we introduced the term "natural foods" to distinguish whole foods that have not been processed or treated with chemicals and preservatives from the commercialized, artificially processed products that destroy human health. The earth is far from universally adopting the ideal of organic whole grains and other natural foods. But I have faith that one day humanity will return to the traditional staff of life and that families will return to a more healthful way of life. Changing the quality of food on a global level is the key to ending the spread of cancer, heart disease, mental illness, and infertility in the modern world, as well as reversing the breakdown of the family, social disorder, and mistrust between nations.

It is now almost spring once again in New England. There are still patches of snow and ice on the ground, but the days are growing longer and more sunny. Today is my sixty-first birthday. In the Far East, it is said that sixty-one is the age of returning to your origins and beginning a new cycle of life. I am very happy to have written this cookbook and feel that it completes the first cycle of my life. It is not only a collection of recipes but also a celebration of my life until now.

I would like to thank my parents, my teachers, my husband, my children, my friends, my associates, and my students who have contributed over the years to my own understanding and self-development as well as to many recipes in this book. For someone like me who didn't enjoy being in the kitchen, these people have made it very easy and worthwhile. I would especially like to express my gratitude to George and Lima Ohsawa, who have inspired and guided me, and to their friend Mr. Shimizu Oritaro, who helped me come to the United States. I deeply appreciate Alex's cooperation as we wrote this book together. Without him it would never have been realized. My ability to express myself in English is limited, and he has understood my innermost spirit and provided beautiful, warmhearted explanations. It is my hope that this book will help you to create more balanced and peaceful meals. Health and energy are precious gifts. Please share your insight and understanding with others, and together let us build a world of enduring peace.

Aveline Kushi

Brookline, Massachusetts
February 27, 1984

FROM ALEX

Dad and I went to a church in Tokyo where he spoke. I played baseball outside with my Japanese friends. I broke one window and put the ball through another. That night we went to a big sukiyaki dinner.

—*Alex Jack*
Diary, August 18, 1957

The Far East has attracted me from an early age. On the eve of my twelfth birthday my father, a Unitarian minister, took me with him to an international peace conference in Japan. I quickly mastered chopsticks and enjoyed miso soup, tofu, noodles, and rice. But I couldn't stand raw fish, candied insects, and the other delicacies served at receptions and parties. One of the gastronomic highlights of the trip was discovering a Coke machine in the American Embassy, the only place in Tokyo where it could then be obtained. Ordering apple pie à la mode on my birthday was also a very sentimental occasion. While my awareness of food quality did not really develop for another decade, the journey East made a deep impression on me. In Hiroshima and Nagasaki, I met boys and girls my own age who had survived the atomic bombings. I resolved to devote myself to peace.

The opportunity to visit Asia again came in my junior year in college. In the autumn of 1965, I left for Benares, the ancient holy city on the Ganges river in India. There I studied the *Bhagavad Gita* and *Upanishads* and traveled around the country talking to Gandhi's old associates. I learned that food shapes our spiritual growth as well as our physical and mental development. I decided to experiment with the traditional diet and enjoyed rice, lentils, and chapatis, but had difficulty digesting the hot spices and curries. Growing up in cold Midwest winters did not make me a very suitable candidate for hot tropical food. That summer I returned via Japan and spent a month in Hiroshima helping atomic bomb survivors set up an arts festival. The Japanese diet was much more congenial to my temperate constitution.

When I returned home, natural foods dining proved to be more difficult. In college I was the only vegetarian in my dining hall and possibly on campus. When I went to the library I felt lucky to find a single meatless cookbook from the 1930s and gave it to the chef. She graciously prepared special dishes for me, mostly salads, soups, and casseroles. How nice it would have been at that time to have had a cookbook like this, but then so much has changed. Now there are entire vegetarian dormitories at my college!

In the spring of 1967, I returned to Asia as a reporter in Vietnam and there had an opportunity to meet leaders of the Zen Buddhist peace movement. From them I learned that the destruction of the rice fields, the importing of refined white rice from abroad, and the adoption of a European and American way of eating would eventually bring an end to traditional Southeast Asian culture and civilization. It was a situation that posed a far more tragic threat to basic values than any political or economic change. As a result of this experience, my understanding of whole foods broadened, and I began to see that food and agriculture are the keys to transforming society at all levels, from the personal to the social, from the family to the global. In the mid-1970s, my interest in natural foods led me to macrobiotics. For the last decade I have studied with Michio and Aveline Kushi and worked with them on a variety of projects.

Natural foods have now reached nearly every corner of the globe as thousands of world citizens who have studied with the Kushis and their students are bringing the message of dietary common sense and peaceful cooking methods to the planet's rich diversity of communities and homes. I am very grateful to Aveline for the opportunity to help with her cookbook. She characteristically downplays her own proficiency in the art of cooking, but everyone who has studied with her and tasted her food knows that in the kitchen she is a true Cézanne or Monet. Her ability to create colorful, festive meals with the simplest ingredients and with grace and effortlessness is legendary.

Aveline cooks almost completely by intuition. For the sake of readers who, like myself, are still attached to teaspoons, tablespoons, and measuring cups, I have helped her convert the recipes into conventional units and weights. However, like a great painter, she does not make the same dish twice in exactly the same way, but listens to her environment and lets the foods "cook" themselves. For this reason, I ask the reader's forgiveness if my own scientific approach to cooking and my limited experience in the kitchen have wreaked havoc with any of the explanations, as in my youthful enthusiasm a long time ago I broke a few windows playing ball with my Japanese friends. Some recipes from Aveline's earlier writings have been included and revised, when necessary, in light of her evolving thoughts on seasoning and refinement of procedural steps.

In addition to the Kushis, I would like to express my thanks to my parents, my sister and her family, my teachers, my friends and associates, and all others who have helped me along the way. Special thanks in preparing this volume are due to Donna Cowan, the Kushis' secretary, for her advice, encouragement, and handling manuscript queries during a trip I made to Japan for several months; Mayumi Nishimura for furnishing the fish recipes and trying out all the dressings, sauces, and dips; Richard Bourden for furnishing the basic sourdough bread recipes and Shigeko Ando for trying them out; Edward and Wendy Esko, senior counseling and cooking instructors at the Kushi Institute and authors of several macrobiotic cookbooks; Julie Coopersmith, our literary agent; Fredda Isaacson, our editor, and the staff of Warner Books; and Ann Purvis, my spiritual friend.

Alex Jack

Brookline, Massachusetts
October 19, 1984

GETTING STARTED

The first four chapters of this book present the philosophy of macrobiotic cooking. They are the starting point. The principal food in our home and most macrobiotic households is pressure-cooked brown rice. If this whole cookbook could be compressed into a single haiku, it would be the recipe for pressure-cooked brown rice in Chapter 5. Please digest this chapter thoroughly.

For those new to macrobiotics, many of the foods may be unfamiliar. There is a glossary at the back of the book to help identify possible new foods, cooking methods, or foreign terms. Most of the ingredients are available in natural foods and health food stores throughout North and South America, as well as in Europe, the Middle East, and other regions, and in a growing number of supermarkets. Some specialty items may also be available in Oriental markets or other ethnic food shops. For information on whole foods outlets in your area or mail-order sources, see Chapter 31.

Cooking is very personal. The condition of our family and their personal needs vary from those of other families. The size, thickness, and energy of foods growing in our area are slightly different from similar foods grown in other regions and under other soil and climatic conditions. Recipes are only flexible guidelines pointing in a general direction; they are not rigid formulas to be applied mechanically. The size and shape of ingredients, individual cutting techniques, the quality of cookware, the type of cooking fuel we use, water quality, and the individuality of our stoves will all affect the time and final outcome of cooking. The use of salt, oil, and other seasonings is also very subjective, and any recipe can only be an average.

Before entering the kitchen, I wash up, put on a fresh apron, and tie up my hair. I try not to wear perfume while cooking because it tends to interfere with the discrimination of aromas. Similarly, I do not listen to music or watch television while I work in the kitchen. Cooking has many unique sounds, such as the hum of the pressure cooker, the sizzle of vegetables, and the simmering of soups. It is important to develop an ear for these sounds. Each kitchen produces its own melody.

A clean, well-ordered environment is essential to fine cooking. I keep my cookware and utensils in convenient locations and clean up as I cook or just before serving the meal. There is no stack of dishes to wash afterwards, and everyone in the family rinses his or her plate and utensils. I organize the menu and schedule so the cooking flows smoothly and each course is ready simultaneously at mealtime.

The recipes in this book are designed for a typical family of from four to six people. For two persons, the recipes may be halved. Chapter 28 offers a week of typical menus for each of the four seasons and the major holidays. In Chapter 29 there is material on cooking for the single person, cooking for babies and small children, cooking for older people, making lunches for school or office, and eating well on the road. Chapter 30 discusses cooking medicinally.

The recipes in this book follow regular American measures: The teaspoon, tablespoon, cup, quart, ounce, pound, and inch. All oven and baking temperatures are in degrees Fahrenheit. Please consult the tables on pages 43–44 for converting to British imperial weights and measures, the metric system, and Centigrade baking temperatures. In some recipes, specific measures have not been indicated because the amount will depend on the size and depth of the pot or pan used, the height of layered ingredients, or the number of people served. This applies especially to cooking oil, salt or other seasoning to taste, and garnishes.

In the beginning, it is advisable to follow the recipes precisely. As you master the basic techniques, you can improvise and experiment. Eventually you will reach the stage of intuitive cooking. You will no longer be dependent on recipes, measuring cups, tablespoons, oven dials, or wall clocks. You will be able to measure ingredients, and accurately judge temperature and time intuitively, with your own common sense. You will know instinctively what foods to select for the day, how to cut and prepare them, which foods combine well with others, how long to cook each dish, how much seasoning to add and when to add it, how to adjust for the special needs of each family member or guest, and how to serve the meal in the most beautiful and appealing manner. This ability cannot be learned from a book or be thought out conceptually; it evolves naturally with experience and keeping an appreciative, peaceful mind. For example, even though you prepare brown rice daily, it will turn out differently each time. Reflecting on the taste, balance, and appearance of the meal and noting how your family feels after eating continually improve your own understanding and development.

CHAPTER 1

EAST MEETS WEST

Autumn comes.
All at once
The maple turns bright red.
—Yoshiko

CHOPSTICKS FLOATING IN A STREAM

Once upon a time, Susa-no-wo-no-mikoto, brother of the Goddess of the Sun, came down to Earth from Heaven to walk along the River Hi at Tori-Kami in the southwestern province of Izumo. Coming upon some chopsticks floating in the stream, he realized that someone was in the mountains and went to investigate. At the headwaters of the river, the young god came upon an old couple and their beautiful daughter huddled together in tears.

"Why are you weeping?" Susa-no-wo-no-mikoto asked. The terror-stricken old man and old woman told him that a ferocious dragon with eight heads lived at the top of the mountain. Each year the serpent came down to eat one of their daughters. Now only young Kushi-inada-hime remained, and as it was harvest time the dragon was sure to come again.

Susa-no-wo-no-mikoto pondered awhile and offered to slay the dragon in exchange for the young woman's hand in marriage. The parents assented. The god then instructed them to build an enclosure, set out eight barrels, fill them with strong sake, and have Kushi-inada-hime mount a platform above the barrels.

In due course, the dread serpent came down the mountain to devour his lovely victim. Drawing near the eight vats, the dragon saw the reflection of the daughter in the sake and with its eight tongues started to sip the intoxicating brew. Soon the creature fell asleep and Susa-no-wo-no-mikoto came out of hiding and cut off its eight heads. Inside the dragon's tail he found a magical sword which he presented to his sister, Ameraterasu, the Goddess of the Sun. The god married Kushi-inada-hime whose name meant Wondrous Princess of the Rice Fields. Susa-no-wo-no-mikoto was himself an agricultural deity and earlier had helped originate rice seeds, millet, barley, azuki beans, soybeans, and silkworms. The magical sword, emblem of the union of this sky god and earth maiden, was later presented to the emperor and became one of the three treasures of Japan. It has been handed down, along with the sacred mirror and sacred necklace, from one generation to the next.

GROWING UP IN JAPAN

This tale from the Kojiki, Japan's most holy scripture, holds special meaning for me because I was born and grew up in the village where these legendary events are said to have taken place. My native home is situated in mountainous country, cleared and settled by rice farmers, and the traditional way of life in which I was raised changed little over many thousands of years. The name of my village, Yokota, means "side of the rice field."

The nearest large city, Matsue, is located to the north in a region of lakes, near the Sea of Japan, about a five-hour train ride in my childhood. Today the old steam locomotives have vanished, and Matsue is a winding two-hour drive by automobile. Here Lafcadio Hearn, the great Western interpreter of mysterious and out-of-the-way Japan, became a Japanese citizen at the end of the nineteenth century, and the house where he lived with his wife and family is carefully preserved. In the opposite direction, to the south, lies Hiroshima, also formerly a five-hour ride by train.

The northern side of the mountains toward the sea and Matsue is called San-Yin (Yin Mountain). The southern side toward Hiroshima is called San-Yo (Yang Mountain). Yo is the ancient word for yang. In Chinese, yin originally meant the cloudy, dark, cold side of a peak, and yang referred to the sunny, bright, shining side. In the natural beauty of the mountains and forests, the fields and streams, we intuitively experienced yin and yang, the primordial energies of the universe. Mythology lived always in our hearts.

In this beautiful setting, village life revolved around the yearly cycle of rice. In ordinary conversation, the word for "food" or "meal" is *gohan,* which means cooked rice. When speaking about breakfast or dinner, we say, "Have you had your morning rice?" and "Did you enjoy your evening rice?" The rice cycle follows the four seasons, beginning with the preparation of the seed and sowing in spring, transplanting and cultivation of the fields in midsummer, harvesting and milling of the ripened crop in the autumn, and storage and processing into traditional grain-based products in the winter.

Our village numbered about three thousand people, and at least ninety-five percent of them were farmers. Even though I wasn't a farmer's daughter, we regularly participated in agricultural activities, and rice formed the foundation of our life. During special times, such as transplanting the tiny seedlings, neighbors customarily helped each other, and I would join the others wearing conical hats and straw sandals, in the fields. Rice planting is very strenuous and involves bending over for three, four, sometimes five hours at a time. However, we would make music and sing together, and the time would pass quickly.

My father was a textile dyer and kept a workshop in our home. Farmers traditionally cultivated silkworms and wove silk for their own clothing. They would bring the white brocade to my father for silk-screening. Since we did not have a cash economy, business transactions were handled through barter or credit. Grain served as the monetary standard until the Meiji era, and wealth was measured in units of rice. The Shogun and various lords often possessed millions of *kokus* or pounds.

The designs that my father used in making screens came from Kyoto, the old capital. Sometimes five or six overlapping designs would be imprinted on a fabric, forming an intricate and colorful pattern. Father was also accomplished in making flags, pennants, and kites. Every May 5th, Boys' Day, would find him making tall banners commemorating famous events such as the battle of Kagamusha, and our whole family would pitch in. My earliest interest in art dates from this time, and I can still vividly remember mixing sweet rice flour with colors as a base for the silk-screen dye.

My mother kept a vegetable garden and always had plenty of fresh produce for her family, which grew to include nine children. The rice that we obtained from farmers was usually about eighty percent unpolished. Polished white rice had always been favored by the aristocracy in the Far East, and following contact with the West in the nineteenth century and the growth of industrialization, farmers, merchants, and other classes consumed increasing amounts of processed foods. Occasionally we ate one hundred percent brown rice, which formed our ancestors' diet since the time of Susa-no-wo-no-mikoto and Kushi-inada-hime. By the early twentieth century, it was common, even in our remote area, to eat grain that had been partially refined. However, we rarely ever had one hundred percent white rice, as most Japanese and Chinese prefer today.

Everyday meals were simple, usually just brown rice, miso soup, and pickles prepared in the traditional manner. These were supplemented with land and sea vegetables. Sometimes we had a little fish or seafood, but we were inland mountain folk and these were considered special treats. Other animal food was rare and consisted primarily of rabbit, chicken, and wild game. In my childhood it was unheard of to eat beef. Every November, after the harvest, our village held a large trade fair for two weeks, and families from the surrounding mountains came to exchange crops, pots and pans, and other items. The highlight of the gathering was the Cow Market. The cattle were used exclusively as an energy source for farming and never consumed for food.

TRADITIONAL COOKING AND FESTIVALS

In preparing rice for our meals, Mother used well or spring water from the mountains. Traditional Japanese kitchens make use of two kinds of pots. Both are cast-iron and are placed over the fire or hung from the ceiling. Although slightly different in shape, their most distinguishing feature is the lids. To make soup, a thin wooden lid is set into the soup pot. To make rice, a heavy wooden lid is set into the rice pot. The rice lid weighed from ten to twenty pounds, and often a large stone was put on top to further increase the pressure on the cooking grain. In Buddhist temples, it often took two or three monks to lift the enormous lids over the large rice caldrons. We had a proverb taken from the kitchen referring to the disposition of eligible girls. "Rice tops" were stable, hearty, and faithful companions, while "soup tops" were restless, ailing, and fickle. Mothers advised their sons to find "rice tops" and avoid "soup tops" when selecting a bride.

After washing, the rice was put in the pot, covered with the heavy lid, and heated over a strong flame. Gradually the wood fuel was removed and replaced with a small amount of charcoal to provide a low, even heat. The rice boiled for 30 to 45 minutes, and the heavy lid was never removed until the grain was cooked. Rice that is cooked under pressure in this way is nourishing and delicious and gives a peaceful energy to all who eat it. The nearest equivalent to this traditional way of preparing rice is the modern pressure cooker. In macrobiotics, we highly recommend that everyone prepare brown rice in this manner daily. There are many other ways to prepare rice, and each has its appropriate occasion. For day-to-day strength, vitality, and serenity, pressure-cooked brown rice is the standard against which all other dishes are measured.

Traditional festivals coincided with key events in the rice calendar. At holidays, weddings, birthdays, and other special occasions, offerings of the first fruits of the field were presented to the spirits and ancestors.

Special rice dishes highlighted this cuisine and, accompanied by colorful costumes, music, and dance, contributed to joyful intervals of feasting throughout the year.

Our little mountain village had about twenty Shinto shrines and Buddhist temples. At the turn of the century, the seed of Christianity was dropped into this region. In 1923, the year I was born, a Christian church with a high steeple was built in the middle of the village, giving it a somewhat exotic atmosphere. Both my parents were devout Christians and earlier were brave enough to be the first in our area to be married in a Christian ceremony. My given name Tomoko means "God with me." Every year, at home and in church, stories from the Bible were repeated over and over, and we children came to know them by heart. Although our family was Christian, we observed the traditional holidays and festivals. In Japan, it is considered natural to observe several faiths at the same time so that religious intolerance is rare.

In preparation for New Year's, the principal holiday in Japan, we joined with everyone else in making mochi. Beginning at 6 A.M. we started pounding sweet rice with heavy wooden pestles and often worked all day until 7 P.M. Over the course of several days we made 300 to 500 pounds of mochi, a crispy, delicious sweet rice product that is fashioned into small cakes or squares and eaten in soups, stews, casseroles, and desserts during the entire month of January.

Year in and year out, rice was truly our heart. Each season revealed a new facet of this limitless treasure. When the snow started to melt, we went out to the stream to soak the best part of the harvest for seed. In the spring, the tender green shoots reflected the joyful, ascending energy we felt as flowers opened and birds returned to sing. In the crisp, cool days of autumn, golden grain stretched as far as the eye could see, promising another year of health and prosperity until the cycle was renewed in the spring.

In 1950, one of my friends returned from near Tokyo where she had studied with Sakurazawa Nyoichi. Sakurazawa had lived in Paris for many years and helped introduce Oriental medicine, judo, and flower arrangement to the West. He wrote widely on philosophy and culture and adopted George Ohsawa as his pen name. He did not oppose modern science and industry, but he saw that they would lead to widespread sickness and suffering unless based on traditional agricultural values. Ohsawa felt that modern society would destroy itself unless it returned to a more natural way of life.

During the war, when he was living in Japan, Ohsawa published anti-militaristic books and set off on a peace mission through Manchuria. The Japanese authorities imprisoned him and sentenced him to death. In July 1945, he was jailed in Nagasaki but was transferred before the atomic bombing. Released after the war, Ohsawa became active in the World Government movement. He translated *The Meeting of East and West*, by American philosopher F.S.C. Northrop, into Japanese.

My friend's report of this remarkable man touched my soul. I left home to attend his private school near Tokyo and stayed there for a year and a half. The school was known as "Maison Ignoramus" and the Student World Government Association. Its purpose was to synthesize the best in East and West and promote peace. Ohsawa called his teaching macrobiotics, which meant "Long Life" or "Great Life" and was a term that had been used by Greek philosophers beginning with Hippocrates. Ohsawa also reintroduced the traditional Far Eastern concepts of yin and yang, which had declined in use with the appearance of modern food and agriculture. At first I was put off by the vocabulary because it reminded me of organized religion. In church, everyone was preoccupied with sin; among macrobiotics, the devil was yin.

Despite the jargon, I stuck it out and about a year later had a wonderful experience which clarified the true meaning of these terms for me. I was walking alone on a beautiful hill behind the Ohsawas' house. I was surrounded by mustard greens with delicate yellow flowers and fresh wheat sprouts with green tips. As I walked in their midst on that delightful spring afternoon, I realized that all phenomena, the whole universe around us, moved according to yin and yang. The two primal energies were not opposed but complementary and combined everywhere to create a rhythmic dance. I realized this very deeply, in my heart. At that moment, it was as if I had heard the sound of a sharp crack—the sound one hears when ice cracks on a frozen pond, or when one throws a small stone against big rocks. During those few moments of deep feeling and vivid insight, joy and happiness flooded my soul.

From that time on, I understood yin and yang, the laws of beauty and truth, from the inside. Shortly afterward, George Ohsawa arranged for me to get a boat ticket to San Francisco and a bus ticket to New York, from where I hoped eventually to go to a World Government conference in Europe. I felt a bit like Lafcadio Hearn, whose niece I had come to know in college, journeying to a strange land to preserve timeless values and synthesize differing cultural traditions.

When I left Japan, modern agriculture had just begun to enter our region. Until then all planting had been organic and cultivation had been done by hand. The mature rice, along with barley, millet, azuki beans, soybeans, and other crops, had always been harvested with a sickle or small scythe. Following the war, the first tractors made their appearance, and experts from state bureaus and the university extolled the benefits of petroleum and chemicals. Patterns of food consumption changed drastically. Hot dogs, ice cream, tropical fruit, and soft drinks became popular.

Twenty-five years elapsed between the time I left for the West and was able to return home for a visit. That opportunity came in the mid-1970s when my children were grown, and I was so surprised at the differences. Farmers no longer went out to commune with their crops. It had been common for a farmer to stand meditatively amid the growing grain. Before breakfast or after dinner, they would just go out to care for and be with their crops, as they would with their children.

Now, long rubber boots had replaced sandals, and people no longer went barefoot. Farmers now wore masks and thick, protective clothing and sprayed chemicals on the fields. Tears came to my eyes as I searched in vain for the little fish, beautiful flowers, and wild grasses which had once grown between the rice stalks. The farmers' warm hearts had also disappeared. In my little village, ancestral home of Susa-no-wo-no-mikoto and Kushi-inada-hime, Lord and Lady of the Rice Fields, beef became more prized than grain.

The ancient myth had come full circle. The great eight-headed dragon had awakened to life from its slumber after many thousands of years. The destructive and chaotic stage of civilization that it symbolized had returned. Meat and sugar, dairy food and alcohol, stimulants and spices, and chemicals and artificial preservatives swept over and engulfed our land's eight major islands.

LIVING IN AMERICA

In New York I had met Michio Kushi, who had also studied with Ohsawa and had arrived in America two years earlier. He was doing graduate work at Columbia University and was active in the movement to control the spread of atomic weapons and form a peaceful federation of all the world's nations. We were soon married. Neither of us had studied cooking with the Ohsawas. In our little apartment in Manhattan we started as beginners, relying on our own intuition to guide us.

For many years, the only brown rice commercially available in the United States was called River Rice. It came from Texas and was grown with chemical fertilizers and pesticides. Still, it was all there was, and we learned to accommodate to its rather gritty texture and not so sweet, bland taste. We prepared it mainly by boiling, until Ohsawa, on one of his visits to America in the early 1960s, encouraged us to use a pressure cooker. After experimenting in Tokyo and Paris, he had found that pressure-cooked rice was much more satisfying and more efficiently prepared than rice boiled with an ordinary "soup top."

In the mid-1960s we moved to New England. To provide quality food for our first students, we started a small natural foods shop and imported traditional foods from Japan as well as organically grown local produce. The store's name, Erewhon, came from Samuel Butler's utopian novel of the same name. Looking back, it's hard to believe that when we began twenty years ago, organic brown rice, other whole grains, miso, tofu, tamari soy sauce, azuki beans, sea vegetables, sea salt, and many other basics were almost unavailable in this country.

Erewhon quickly grew from a small storefront to a chain of retail stores. In a few years, it became the largest distributor and manufacturer of natural foods on the East Coast with a fleet of delivery trucks crisscrossing New England and New York. There was also a West

Coast Erewhon. The whole foods movement developed from this tiny seed.

Our first priority was to secure a national source of organically grown whole grains, and we approached farmers in various regions of the country to try our methods. Many turned us down since the organic method required a high investment in time, labor, and patience and flew in the face of everything they had learned in modern agriculture school. A few farmers did accept the challenge though. I'll never forget visiting the Lundberg Farm in Richvale, California, and walking in the rice fields. For the first time in over twenty years I felt the energy of ripening grain, and memories from my childhood streamed into my mind. I was so exhilarated that I told the Lundberg brothers that any price would be fine if they agreed to our proposal and met our organic standards of quality. One of the Erewhon staff winced at my naive negotiating skills. But to me, rice was life itself, a priceless treasure, and any sum would have been only symbolic.

Actually, the Lundberg's were quite modest in their bargaining and readily understood the health, cultural, and spiritual benefits of the proposed change. Much of the organic brown rice now available comes from their farm and other farms in Arkansas and Louisiana which Erewhon also helped convert to organic methods. Because of the steadily increasing demand for organic brown rice in the United States and Canada, it is not yet feasible to cultivate and harvest by hand. Still, the brown rice grown in this country is very nourishing and delicious, and on a par with that available in Japan or other parts of the Far East.

In our travels over the years, Michio and I have sampled many macrobiotic meals. If the rice is cooked correctly and the taste is good, we are happy, even if other things are not so well prepared. However, if the rice is poor, the meal is not as satisfying, even if the other dishes are outstanding.

Cooking brown rice properly is both the simplest and most difficult challenge in the macrobiotic kitchen. To arrive at the point where whole grains truly become the center of the meal and thoroughly satisfy us involves a revolution in our thinking and behavior. It requires us to forget our previous way of eating and the social conditioning of the past ten, twenty, or thirty years. The art of macrobiotic cooking teaches us to subdue the inner dragon of excess, imbalance, false appetite, and poor taste.

When you have mastered the various elements that go into preparing brown rice—salt, fire, water, pressure, and a calm mind—your family will attain enduring health and happiness. You will have united yin and yang—Kushi-inada-hime and Susa-no-wo-no-mikoto. The gleaming sword of supreme judgment will stand unveiled to be passed down through your cooking, your love, and your spirit to generations without end.

CHAPTER 2

FOOD AS ENERGY

Holding the ripened rice
In both hands,
I feel a rich autumn harvest.
—Tatsuko

The morning of July 20, 1951, was beautiful and sunny. The sky and ocean met on the horizon in a symphony of blue. Fifteen days out of Tokyo, the *Colona* arrived in San Francisco, and passed beneath the magnificent Golden Gate Bridge. I was one of six passengers on the small Norwegian cargo vessel. Despite the wonderful crossing, I could not enjoy the scenery and excitement of landing. I had an intense headache and had suffered nightmares during the night before.

When he put me on the boat to America in Japan, my teacher George Ohsawa had told me to eat well and not to worry about my lack of English or specialized training. He said the universe would teach me everything I needed to know and to keep a grateful mind and appreciate all experiences, the bad along with the good. Every day during the voyage, our small group of passengers ate at the captain's table. I confined myself to some rye crackers at the table and a little roasted rice between each meal chewed in my cabin from a ten-pound supply which a friend had made especially for my trip. On board ship, another passenger, one of the Crown Prince's English teachers, encouraged me to eat more. I finally consented to have some carrots, peas, and celery that had been cooked in a rich meat stew.

That night I had bad dreams for the first time since I became macrobiotic about a year and a half before. While staying at George Ohsawa's dormitory, I had enjoyed a nice peaceful sleep each night. Some of my friends at the study house would go out and eat regular food from time to time, but I ate only what was served, and my condition became very clean. Now, passing beneath the Golden Gate Bridge, I knew that my troubles were the direct result of what I had eaten during the previous day. I realized that if our condition is not healthy, we can never become truly happy, even if our surroundings are beautiful. This valuable experience, on my first day in America, made me intensely question human nature and the quality of our lives. Since coming ashore in San Francisco, I always notice the energy of the food I am eating and correlate it with my daily health and way of thinking. It is truly the key to regaining our paradise lost.

THE INNER FIRE

On many future occasions, I experienced strong bodily reactions to various foods as well as subtle changes in perception, mood, and vitality. More and more I began to observe food as a form of energy which shapes our bodies, our emotions, our thoughts, and our spirits. The energy within us is changing all the time as a direct result of what we consume.

There are many forms of energy that we can see in food. The most basic is fire. To stay alive, our bodies must remain warm; if we become too cold, we die. Just a few degrees of temperature separate life and death. Thus, the body's energy is very much like fire, and the mouth is like a fireplace. Instead of fuel, we keep our internal fires alive with food. And as with wood, the amount and type of food determine the quality of the fire. Proper food makes for a nice steady flame that is warming, satisfying, and energizing, allowing us to engage in our other activities. Too much food dampens the inner flame, just as too much wood can kill the outer fire. Sickness is like smoke and often results from putting too much fuel in the burner. By reducing the amount of food we eat or fasting for several meals, we encourage the fire to burn normally again.

Cold foods and beverages are generally harmful to our inner fire. In the days before ice cream and ice cubes, people did not eat icy cold foods, and it was common sense to prepare most meals hot or warm. Of course, in summer cooler foods and drinks might be taken to balance the strong heat and humidity, but traditionally these were eaten only occasionally and in very small amounts.

In the Far East, it is said that a healthy person has a cool head and warm feet, while an unhealthy person has a hot head and cold feet. To check our condition, we have only to feel these two areas. In America, until recently, grandmothers and mothers used to feel their children's foreheads for a sign of their day-to-day condition. And whenever the children went out, the mothers would admonish them to keep their feet and toes warm. So the philosophy is the same as in the Far East.

BALANCING YIN AND YANG

Health is balance, the harmony of yin and yang. Health is the balance between our inner and outer environment, between mental and physical activity, between plant and animal food, between cooked and raw food, between salt and oil, and between countless other interrelated factors. Yin and yang, the universal forces of expansion and contraction, create all phenomena. On the extreme yang end of the food spectrum, meat, poultry, eggs, hard dairy foods, and refined salt are too contracted for regular consumption. On the extreme yin end, soft dairy foods, tropical fruits and vegetables, honey and sugar, coffee and other stimulants, and alcohol are too expansive for ordinary use. Between these two extremes is a central category of foods that are more balanced and appropriate for daily human consumption. These include whole grains, beans, vegetables, sea vegetables, seeds and nuts, and locally grown fruits. George Ohsawa taught us to observe the energy of food in this way, and for the last thirty-five years this compass has guided my life. Under various names and forms, the philosophy of yin and yang is found in the Bible, the Upanishads, the Buddhist sutras, and other scriptures and classics.

To balance yin and yang, we need to learn how to create, transform, and modify energy. Our body, our food, and our environment are changing forms and patterns of energy. Understanding the dynamics of change and applying it to all aspects of life to maximize our health and happiness is the goal of macrobiotics. In this way we become infinitely flexible. We are able to respond to any changing circumstances and cheerfully embrace life in all its manifestations. Energy takes many forms, and yin and yang are always found together and turning into one another. Night changes into day, winter changes into spring, and mountains turn into valleys. Our life, too, is a dance of many such polarities.

The food we eat is a reflection of the cook's condition and judgment. The quality of the food selected, the way it is cut, the length of cooking time, the amount of seasoning, how the meal is presented at the table, and its taste and flavor—all of these depend upon the cook. Day in and day out, the cook determines the basic health and well-being of the family. A cook whose own health is strong and whose judgment is sound creates food that is nourishing, satisfying, and pleasing to behold. She or he is able to modify cooking according to the changing seasons or weather, the availability or scarcity of certain items, and the personal condition and needs of her family. And she is able to do this for every meal with infinite gratitude, variation, and appeal.

COOKING WITH THE SEASONS

All food grows seasonally, and each season has a characteristic energy which is absorbed and transmitted by the food. In macrobiotic cooking, we adjust our cooking slightly with the seasons to take into account changing energy patterns within the body as well as outside in the environment. Beginning with spring, let's look briefly at the yearly cycle:

Spring—The first buds and leaves of spring usually take several weeks to peek through the snow, unfold, and open. In the same way, we can slowly modify our cooking as spring approaches. In addition to adding fresh greens to our meals, we can use more light cooking methods, such as short-time boiling, steaming, and quick sautéing. We may reduce the amount of salt and other seasonings slightly and use foods and pickles fermented for shorter periods. During the long cold winter, the energy in our bodies often freezes, but as spring approaches it begins to thaw and move upward and out. To help this process proceed smoothly, we begin using spring foods with upward energy, such as wild grasses, sprouts, and varieties of grain that have matured over the winter. Lightly fermented foods are also very helpful for releasing stagnated winter energy. Wild plants that grow in the neighborhood can be foraged. They give very strong energy and should be used only occasionally and in very small amounts. Wheat and barley have lighter energy than other grains and may be served relatively more frequently during this season. Condiments made with oil, miso, and scallions or chives are also especially enjoyable at this time of year. As the weather turns warm, it is better to balance our meals with more lightly boiled vegetables and pressed or boiled salads rather than increase our consumption of fruit.

Summer—In summer many plants ripen and reach their peak growth. At this time we can begin to use foods that have more active, expansive energy, such as leafy green vegetables, summer squashes, sweet corn, and locally grown fruits. Fresh salads can be served more frequently in summer or enjoyed in the form of marinated, pressed, or lightly boiled salads. During the hot summer months, we naturally use simpler cooking methods such as boiling and steaming, and quick sautéing, which require less time in the kitchen. Grain, noodle, bean, vegetable, and sea vegetable salads are used more often in the summer. Sushi is especially enjoyable. In hot humid weather we often lose minerals through perspiration. To replenish these nutrients, we may serve small amounts of strong condiments. Umeboshi plums and umeboshi tea are excellent for this purpose and cool off the body better than soft drinks or other cold beverages. Some dishes, such as somen or udon noodles, may be served cool or chilled, but it is better not to prepare foods or drinks icy cold. Instead, cooling effects can be created by light boiling, by shorter cooking times, and by using less salt or other seasonings. Small amounts of chilled kanten (fruit gelatin), vegetable aspics, or cool tofu, garnished with scallions, tamari soy sauce, and ginger, can be served often. Fruit salads, fresh melons, and fresh cucumbers are also very refreshing when taken in moderation at this season.

Autumn—During the late summer, energy begins to flow downward until it becomes very condensed by late autumn. The change from hot to cool weather is often sudden. To mitigate this change, we can begin to adjust our diet in late summer by including more early fall squashes and root vegetables in our meals. In autumn, food is more plentiful than at other seasons. Just as the trees produce a multitude of yellows, golds, oranges, reds, browns, and light greens, these beautiful colors are found in the cornucopia of grains, beans, squashes, root vegetables, and autumn greens, such as kale, turnip greens, daikon tops, and cabbages. Many of the foods harvested in the fall have natural preservative qualities and can be stored for several months to be used throughout the cold winter and into the spring. Millet and round vegetables, such as onions, turnips, cabbages, and squashes, may be served more frequently in the late autumn months. During the summer months, the kidneys and bladder are often overworked because of an excess intake of liquids, fruits, raw foods, and salty snack items in an attempt to balance the extreme heat. In autumn, the results of this imbalance are experienced in colds, coughs, and other sicknesses of adjustment. Stronger cooking in autumn, as well as the change in weather, starts to discharge this excess. At this season, we can begin to introduce more rich tastes and styles of cooking into our menus, such as bean stews, fried or deep-fried foods, creamy grain stews, sweet rice and *mochi*, hot *amasake*, and puréed squash soup and squash pies. Dishes can be prepared with longer cooking times and styles, such as long, slow *nishime*-style boiling, long-time sautéing, or *kinpira*-style braising. Vegetables may be cut in larger slices and chunks for longer, more slowly cooked dishes. Sea vegetable dishes can become hardier and include tempeh, dried tofu, or soybeans. In autumn, foods may start to be seasoned with a little more sea salt and a little more oil. The amount of raw foods served can be substantially reduced and dried or cooked fruits used more in preparing desserts.

Winter—The energy of winter was likened by ancient people to water or floating energy. Outside there is often a lot of water in the form of rain, snow, or ice. Also at this season there is a definite mixture of overcast, snowy, or drizzly days and clear, bright, sunshiny days. During the cold months it is important to serve warm, strong food. If we prepare cold, icy foods or a lot of raw food during these cold months, our family will soon grow out of balance with nature. Green vegetables and sprouts are not so plentiful in the winter, and we can consume primarily root and ground vegetables as well as pickles. During the winter we also prepare food with a little more salt, miso, or tamari soy sauce. More oil can also be used in winter cooking to make such dishes as deep-fried foods, tempura, long sautéed or *kinpira*-style vegetables, or hardy sea vegetable dishes. Fried grain and fried noodle dishes are especially warming in the winter. Strong miso soup and a variety of grain, bean, *seitan*, and vegetable stews are also strengthening. Longer cooking methods are used, such as *nishime* or *oden* dishes, baked bean, grain, and vegetable dishes, and long-time sautéing. Ginger can be used more frequently with stews and vegetable dishes in the winter months. Sweet rice and *mochi* are sticky and warming and can be used often.

As spring approaches, we can modify our cooking to harmonize with the renewal of growth within the earth and the stirring of movement in our own bodies. In this way we achieve balance all year-round with our natural environment.

In addition to the seasons, there is a daily pattern of change. The morning is like the spring, midday is like summer, late afternoon is like autumn, and early evening and night are like the long winter. For total balance, this daily cycle is very important. Eating foods in the season during which they grow is very important. In the case of brown rice and other whole grains, it is important that they be eaten daily as well as seasonally. The nourishing energy they provide can be compared to the earth spinning on its axis each day while at the same time traveling in a longer seasonal orbit around the sun.

By enjoying the fruits of the earth in an orderly way, we can maintain our families' health and well-being at all times.

WARM AND COOLING ENERGY

As we have seen, foods that are cooked and served warm or hot heat the body, while cold or chilled foods cool down the body's inner fire. Apart from the temperature at which foods are served, foods have a natural energy that may be described as cold, cooling, stabilizing, warm, or hot. Our internal heat changes with the quality of the foods we eat. Hot weather tends to create cold foods, and to cool off we are naturally attracted to the energy of such vegetables as cucumber, watermelon, and zucchini. Similarly, the food we enjoy most in colder weather, such as tempura, fermented food, and long-cooked stews and soups utilizing root vegetables, produces a warming effect.

While this energy is independent of the cooking temperature, cooking changes the energy of some foods from cold to warm. Salt is a good example. Heated, salt creates warmth and produces a warming effect in the body. Cold salt has a cooling effect. The energy of oil also changes when heated. Raw oil in a salad has a very different effect than when it is consumed in its sautéed form.

The use of fire, seasoning, pressure, and time all affect the energy of the food being prepared and can modify and transform its quality. The accompanying chart lists some typical foods in the macrobiotic diet and the kind of energy they create. We may use this chart to maintain or adjust our body's internal heat and maintain balance with our environment.

FOOD	HOT	WARM	CENTERING	COOL	COLD
Azuki beans			x		
Brown rice			x		
Burdock			x		
Cabbage			x		
Carrots			x		
Celery			x		
Cucumber				x	
Daikon				x	
Garlic	x				
Gingerroot	x				
Kombu					x
Kuzu					x
Lotus root					x
Lotus seeds				x	
Mustard greens		x			
Nori					x
Pearl barley				x	
Scallions	x				
Soybeans			x		
Wheat		x			

THE FIVE TASTES

Taste is another form of energy. In traditional Oriental medicine, each taste is correlated with a season at which it is predominant, a type of warming or cooling energy, and specific organs of the body which it nourishes.

Sour—A sour taste is associated with spring. Sour-tasting food contracts, shrinks, and gives quickening energy. It is especially beneficial for the liver and gallbladder. Sourdough bread, wheat, vinegar, sauerkraut, and lemon are typical sour tastes.

Bitter—A bitter or burnt taste is associated with summer and its energy is dry and dispersing. Bitter foods, which stimulate the heart and small intestine, include dandelion, burdock, black sesame seeds, and some types of corn.

Sweet—A sweet taste corresponds with late summer, and typical examples include whole grains, beans, and many vegetables, especially round vegetables, such as onions, squashes, and cabbages. Natural sweetness is a nourishing energy. It relaxes and centers the whole body, though it is especially soothing to the spleen, stomach, and pancreas. Modern refined sugar is not sweet to the taste, but pungent.

Pungent—A hot or spicy taste correlates with the tang of autumn and gives hot, dispersing energy. Pungent foods have strong upward and outward power that stimulates circulation and helps discharge material from deep inside the body toward the surface. Typical examples include scallions, daikon, ginger, and peppers. A sharp pungent taste is beneficial to the lungs and large intestines. However, foods that are too spicy, such as tropical spices, create hyperactivity, overstimulate the blood, and irritate the intestines.

Salty—A salty taste corresponds with wintertime and gives strong downward discharging energy. Good-quality salt softens a hardened condition and is good for strengthening the kidneys and bladder. Typical examples are sea vegetables, miso, umeboshi plums, and tamari soy sauce. Animal foods, which contain high amounts of sodium, are overly salty and can lead to tight kidneys, putting additional strain on the heart.

In macrobiotic cooking, we try to present a full range of tastes at every meal. The naturally sweet taste of whole grains and vegetables makes up about sixty to eighty percent of the meal. The other tastes are represented in side dishes, sauces, and condiments. Depending upon the season and family members' personal health, the meal may be modified to slightly accentuate one specific taste.

THE FIVE COLORS

Color is also a form of energy. Greenish or light blue foods, such as undyed lemons, often have a sour taste and nourish the liver and gallbladder. Reddish and orange foods, such as corn, are associated with the heart and small intestine. Yellow foods, such as millet, squash, and carrots, are particularly good for the stomach, spleen, and pancreas. White or pale foods, including barley, rice, and daikon, are beneficial for the lungs and large intestine. Sea vegetables, beans, and other dark foods strengthen the kidneys and bladder.

Color stimulates appetite and creates beauty and order, making the meal more satisfying and enjoyable. Ideally, there should be a harmonious balance of colors at the table. Since our principal food is naturally sweet whole grains and vegetables, the predominant hue is usually yellow, orange, or light brown. The other colors usually form the remaining forty to fifty percent of the meal. Bright green is extremely calming and peaceful and ideally is represented at every meal, if only in a few slices of scallion.

In cooking macrobiotically, we are extremely careful to preserve the fresh bright color of vegetables and some methods, such as *ohitashi* boiling, will bring out the food's natural color more brightly than in the uncooked state. Umeboshi plums, umeboshi vinegar, and *shiso* leaves create wonderful red and pink shades, as do red radishes sliced or whole. Not every color nor every taste need be featured in a side dish of its own. Often just a touch of color with a garnish, such as a bright green parsley sprig or a few black sesame seeds, is enough. Condiments and pickles are also very colorful and can be attractively arranged to complete the menu.

Finally, variously colored bowls, plates, and serving dishes can be used to enhance the beauty of the meal. They create harmonious patterns of light and shadow and may be chosen to complement the texture of the food they contain. Flowers, leaves, pine needles, sea shells, and other natural objects may be used for decoration to create a pleasant, happy mood. Candles, lamps, and artistic ornamentation can also be used.

THE FIVE TRANSFORMATIONS

Temperature, taste, and color are just three examples of a universal cycle of energy flow known in the Far East as the Five Transformations. Just as God or Infinity divides into yin and yang, the two primordial energies branch into five major limbs. Nature as a whole goes through five phases of development. First there is the seed, then sprouting and growth, followed by ripening and blossoming, leading to the harvest and storage, and concluding with dormancy and replanting. The seasons of the year, the hours of the day, and the periods of development in our lives all pass through these five stages. The following chart lists some of the traditional correlations. There are many other patterns of energy in our lives but they more or less follow this same sequence.

CHART OF THE FIVE TRANSFORMATIONS

5 TRANSFORMATIONS	TREE	FIRE	SOIL	METAL	WATER
5 Compacted Organs	Liver	Heart	Spleen	Lungs	Kidneys
5 Expanded Organs	Gall-bladder	Small intestine	Stomach	Large intestine	Bladder
5 Physical Roots	Eyes	Tongue	Lips	Nose	Ears
5 Physical Systems	Tissue	Blood vessels	Muscle flesh	Skin	Bones
5 Physical Branches	Nails	Body hair	Breast	Breath	Head Hair
5 Directions	East	South	Center	West	North
5 Seasons	Spring	Summer	Late summer	Autumn	Winter
5 Colors	Blue	Red	Yellow	Pale	Black
5 Tastes	Sour	Bitter	Sweet	Spicy	Salty
5 Odors	Oily-greasy	Burning	Fragrant	Fishy	Putre-fying
5 Environments	Windy	Hot	Humid	Dry	Cold
5 Emotions	Anger	Laughter	Wonder	Worry	Fear
5 Grains	Wheat	Corn	Millet	Rice	Beans

THE STANDARD MACROBIOTIC DIET

The macrobiotic approach to health is based on the traditional philosophy that food is our best medicine, together with hard work, exercise, self-reflection, and a more natural lifestyle in general. Whether we are trying to maintain the daily health of our families or relieving a serious illness, our food can be prepared simply and in a delicious, attractive way, while at the same time including a wide variety of ingredients.

For cooking, wood or gas is recommended. These types of fuel provide a steady, even heat and preserve the natural qualities of the food. Electric or microwave heat produces a chaotic vibration in the food and should be avoided whenever possible. In a temperate, four-season climate, the Standard Macrobiotic Diet, based on traditional ways of eating in both East and West, modified for modern times, includes the following categories of food:

Whole Grains—The principal food of each meal is whole cereal grain, comprising from fifty to sixty percent of the total volume of the meal. These include brown rice, millet, barley, oats, whole wheat berries, rye, buckwheat, and corn. Grain and flour products, such as whole wheat or buckwheat noodles, pasta, *seitan*, bread, bulghur, couscous, and rolled oats, may be served occasionally.

Soups—About five to ten percent (1 to 2 bowls) of daily intake may be in the form of soups. Soup broth can be made with miso or tamari soy sauce, which are prepared from naturally fermented soybeans, sea salt, and grains, to which several types of land and sea vegetables, especially *wakame* or *kombu*, may be added during cooking. The taste of soup should be mild, not too salty or too bland. Soups made with grains, beans, vegetables, and occasionally a little fish or seafood may be served from time to time.

Vegetables—About twenty-five to thirty percent of each meal should include fresh vegetables prepared in a variety of ways. Every day a balanced mixture of root, round, and leafy green vegetables should be served. Up to about one-third of the vegetables may be served raw in the form of a fresh salad or traditionally made pickles. Wild vegetables may be served in small volume and very occasionally. In temperate zones, vegetables of tropical origin are to be avoided.

Beans—A small portion (about ten percent) of daily food intake includes cooked beans or bean products, such as tofu, tempeh, and natto. These may be prepared individually or cooked together with grains, vegetables, or sea vegetables, as well as served in the form of soup.

Sea Vegetables—Seaweeds are rich in minerals and vitamins and are served daily in small volume (about five percent or 1 to 2 servings). They may be included in soups, cooked with vegetables or beans, or prepared as a small side dish.

Salt, Oil, and Seasonings—Unrefined sea salt, miso, tamari soy sauce, or umeboshi plums may be used in cooking to give a salty taste.

Unrefined dark sesame oil is the most suitable oil for daily cooking. Light sesame oil, corn oil, and occasionally other high-quality unrefined vegetable oils may also be used. Brown rice vinegar, sweet rice vinegar, and umeboshi vinegar may be used for a sour taste. Food should not have an overly salty flavor, and seasonings should be added during cooking rather than at the table. Spices, herbs, and other stimulants or aromatic substances are to be avoided. Kuzu root powder and arrowroot flour are used for gravies and sauces.

Condiments—A small amount of condiments may be used on grains, beans, or vegetables at the table. These include *gomashio* (roasted sesame salt), roasted sea vegetable powders, and tekka root vegetable mixture.

Pickles—A small amount of homemade pickles may be served each day to aid digestion. Traditionally, fermented pickles are made with a variety of root, round, ground, and leafy green vegetables and are prepared in sea salt, rice or wheat bran, tamari soy sauce, miso, or umeboshi plums. Spices, sugar, and vinegary pickles should be avoided.

Beverages—Spring or well water that is clear and pure is used for drinking, cooking, and preparing teas and other beverages. Bancha twig tea is commonly served at meals, though any other traditional tea that does not have an aromatic fragrance or stimulating effect, and is not artificially processed, may also be served. Roasted grain teas and grain coffees are also frequently enjoyed.

For those in good health, a variety of supplemental foods may also be enjoyed. For those who are ill or lacking in vitality, some of these foods may need to be avoided or reduced depending upon the individual condition. Supplemental foods include:

Animal Food—A small amount of fish or seafood may be served a few times a week, if desired. White-meat fish contains less fat than the red-meat or blue-skinned varieties, and deep ocean fish contain fewer pollutants than the freshwater varieties. Other animal food, including meat, poultry, eggs, and dairy products, are strictly avoided.

Seeds and Nuts—Roasted seeds and nuts, lightly seasoned with sea salt or tamari soy sauce, may be served occasionally as snacks. Nut butters, which are oilier, may be used very sparingly.

Fruit—Fruit may be served a few times a week, preferably cooked or naturally dried, as a dessert or snack, provided the fruit grows in the local climate zone. Fresh fruit may also be served in moderate volume during its growing season. Fruit juice is generally too concentrated for regular use, although occasional consumption in very hot weather is allowed. Tropical fruits are to be strictly avoided unless you live in the area where they grow.

Desserts—Desserts may be served several times a week and may include cookies, puddings, cakes, pies, and other dishes prepared with naturally sweet ingredients or natural sweeteners. Rice syrup, barley malt, *amasake*, and apple juice are the best sweeteners. Honey, molasses, corn syrup, carob, fructose, and all types of refined sugars and artificial sweeteners should be strictly avoided. Maple syrup may be used in recipes very sparingly.

Provided the proportion of food in each of the four main categories is generally correct and each mouthful of food is chewed thoroughly, family members may eat as much as they like, two or three meals a day. It is best to eat only when hungry and leave the table feeling satisfied but not full. Similarly, drink only when thirsty and do not consume unnecessary second and third refills. For better digestion, it is good practice not to serve food or snacks within three hours of bedtime because this puts extra strain on the intestines and kidneys. During each meal, a moment should be taken to express our gratitude to God, nature, or the universe for the gifts of the earth and to reflect on the use to which the food is put. This may take the form of grace, a moment of silence, chanting, or whatever feels appropriate and comfortable.

COOKING WITH INTUITION

The Standard Macrobiotic Diet allows broad scope for personal creativity and enjoyment and is easy to adopt. In making the transition it is important to proceed in an orderly way and not try to make the change overnight. Begin with pressure-cooked brown rice, miso soup, and a few basic vegetable, bean, and sea vegetable dishes, while at the same time diminishing in volume the foods previously eaten. Gradually introduce condiments, pickles, and naturally sweetened desserts, and vary the combinations and styles of cooking frequently so the food remains appealing and appetizing.

As you continue to prepare these foods, your own health and judgment will improve, your taste for natural food will deepen, and your ability to select the freshest items, prepare them properly, and arrange them in a beautiful meal will develop naturally. Whole grains, vegetables, and other natural foods lend themselves to endless combinations and variations. A complete meal can easily be prepared within an hour.

While cookbooks such as this can introduce you to macrobiotic food preparation, until you have actually tasted the foods and seen them prepared, you will not have a standard against which to measure your own cooking. In the beginning, it is recommended that everyone study with an experienced macrobiotic cook. Only a few cooking lessons are needed to orient you in the right direction. Every family member should be encouraged to study proper cooking and participate in some aspect of food preparation or cooking in the home. At the back of this book is a list of Macrobiotics International centers offering cooking classes as well as sources for obtaining some of the food. Most of the foods in this book are now available in natural foods stores, as well as in selected supermarkets. However, some specialty items are not so widely available, and people who live in more remote areas may prefer to order them by mail.

With experience, you will eventually reach the point where you no longer need a cookbook or teacher but can cook with your own intuition as a guide and nature and the universe as primary instructors. By listening to the sounds of food as it cooks and by observing its moving energy, colors, shapes, aromas, and tastes, you will be able to answer endless questions and participate in the creation of life itself.

CHAPTER 3

COOKWARE AND UTENSILS

The winter sky darkens.
Wood strapped to our back,
We go to the charcoal kiln.
—Fusako

Quality cookware and utensils will improve the flavor and taste of food, as well as make for more nourishing and satisfying meals. Natural materials, such as wood, glass, ceramic, or earthenware, and metals, such as cast-iron, stainless steel, or enamel-coated steel, that do not interact with food are recommended. Plastic, Teflon, and other synthetic materials, as well as aluminum and asbestos, are preferably avoided. For daily cooking, hand methods of preparation that give more calm, peaceful energy are superior to electric blenders, electric hand mills, and food processors. For parties or special occasions, modern time-saving appliances may be used for making large quantities of food.

BAKING UTENSILS

Baking sheets, muffin tins, bread pans, pie plates, and a rolling pin are essential items for baking. Steel and tin are traditionally used for baking, though glass and ceramic also give good results for some types of dishes.

BAMBOO RICE PADDLES

These thin flat spatulas come in a variety of sizes and are used for toasting grains, flours, and seeds and for serving foods. Bamboo paddles are very durable and will prove to have many uses in the kitchen.

CHOPSTICKS

Used for sautéing, deep-frying, serving, and as eating utensils. For sensitive cooking, bamboo chopsticks are best. Japanese chopsticks are tapered with pointed tips, while Chinese chopsticks have square ends.

COLANDER

A perforated metal utensil used for washing vegetables and grains and for draining cooked pasta. A fine wire mesh strainer with a handle is also very useful, especially for washing sesame seeds, millet, and other small grains.

CROCK

Crocks are earthenware containers used for preparing and aging miso or pickles. Their wide mouths offer ease in mixing, skimming, and removing ingredients. Sizes range from the ½ gallon to 20 gallons.

CUTTING BOARD

A square, rectangular, or oval-shaped board for cutting vegetables and kneading flour. Wooden boards are preferable to plastic or synthetic, but soft Oriental woods are usually not appropriate for Western climates. Cutting boards used to prepare vegetables should not be used to prepare fish or other animal food. In addition to mixing energies, animal food contains bacteria that can produce a toxic effect in plant food. Keep a separate board for seafood.

DROP TOP

A lid that fits inside the pot and rests on the contents rather than on the rim of the pot. A drop top is used for cooking some vegetable and bean dishes as well as for aging miso and making pickles. It provides a little pressure to the ingredients. In cooking, the drop top allows steam to escape. In aging and pickling, it allows some air circulation. Wood is traditionally used but metal or porcelain is also suitable for cooking.

FLAME DEFLECTOR

This light metal pad is inserted between the pressure cooker or other pot and the flame on a stove. It helps distribute heat evenly and prevent burning. A flame deflector or trivet (a three-legged metal stand) must be used when cooking with pottery. Be careful to avoid asbestos flame deflectors.

FOOD MILL

A small hand mill, usually with a raised crank, used to purée and strain grains, fruits, vegetables, baby foods, *kayu*, applesauce, and other items.

FRYING PANS

Several frying pans are essential in the natural foods kitchen. A 9-inch heavy cast-iron or enamel cast-iron frying pan is ideal for long, slow sautéing of vegetables, for *kinpira-* and *nishime-*style dishes, and for making fried rice and noodles. Cast-iron heats up slowly, holds the heat, and cooks evenly, especially over medium-low heat. A light 6- or 9-inch stainless steel frying pan is ideal for quick sautéing, for tempura, crêpes, and dry-roasting grains, seeds, nuts, and flour. Stainless steel does not hold heat or cook as evenly as cast-iron but heats up quickly and gives good results at medium to high temperatures. To clean cast-iron, wash but do not soak in hot soapy water, dry over low heat, and store uncovered to prevent rust. If food sticks after cooking, put a little hot water into the pan and let it sit until the food loosens. Then scrub the pan with a vegetable brush. To season or reseason cast-iron and prevent rusting, wash and dry the pan thoroughly. Then coat the inside with sesame oil using a paper towel or clean cloth. Add 2 to 3 tablespoons of oil to the pan, place over the heat, and rotate and tilt the pan to cover the bottom and sides with the oil. Place the frying pan in a low oven (225 to 250 degrees) for 2 to 3 hours; turn off the heat, and let the pan cool for several hours or overnight. Stainless steel is cleaned by rubbing gently with a sponge or soft cloth in warm water, using soap if desired. If burnt food sticks to the bottom, soak in warm water overnight. Be careful not to use too high a heat when cooking with stainless steel or it may warp or stain. Porcelain enamel is sometimes used to coat cast-iron or serve as the inner lining for stainless steel. Its nonporous surface will not rust but may chip or crack if left on a burner when empty. To clean porcelain, soak and wash in warm water, using soap if desired. Steel wool or scrubbies should never be used on its delicate surface.

GLASS JARS

Large glass jars are useful for storing grains, seeds, nuts, beans, sea vegetables, and other dried foods. Wood or ceramic containers, which allow air to circulate, are even better for storage but are more expensive and often hard to locate.

GRAIN MILL

A small hand mill used to grind whole grains, beans, seeds, and nuts into varying textures. Flour ground just prior to using is freshest and preserves much more of the nutrients than store-bought flour.

GRATER

A small-toothed, flat utensil made of porcelain or stainless steel used to shred or extract the juice from gingerroot and other vegetables. Porcelain is preferable, especially for medicinal use.

KEG

A large wooden container used for fermenting and aging both miso and pickles.

KNIVES

Sharp knives are essential for cutting vegetables and other ingredients. The large Oriental knife with the squared-off end and double bevel is time-tested and most efficient. Oriental knives utilize a gentle back and forth motion that preserves the natural energy of the food, while chef's knives, paring knives, and other styles usually require an up and down motion that tears and crushes the food, reducing its energy and impairing its taste. Carbon-steel knives hold a better edge than stainless steel. However, they can pit or rust, especially after contact with fruits and other acidic foods. To wash carbon-steel knives, rinse in soapy water and dry immediately. To prevent pitting, they may be scoured lightly with steel wool. To prevent rusting, brush lightly with vegetable oil after each use. A knife made of high-carbon stainless steel combines the rust-resistant properties of steel and the sharp edge of carbon. From time to time, knives should be sharpened to keep their edge. A sharpening stone or steel cylinder is customarily used. To sharpen, draw the blade of the knife at a 20-degree angle across the stone or steel in a gentle circular motion. The entire length of the blade should be sharpened to ensure even cutting. For better control, many people like to sharpen only one side of the blade. If you are right handed, sharpen only the right side; if you are left handed, sharpen only the left side. Oil the sharpening stone or rinse it in water each time before use. Stainless steel knives that are harder than stone or steel cylinders may be sharpened on the unfinished bottom of a ceramic dish. Store knives in a rack rather than together in a drawer to avoid dulling.

OIL BRUSH

A small brush used to brush oil on a frying pan, especially when oil needs to be carefully regulated for medicinal purposes. A new, clean art or paint brush may be kept for this purpose.

OIL SKIMMER

A lightly curved, fine-mesh strainer with a handle. The skimmer is used for removing bits of batter or grain from tempura frying oil.

PICKLE PRESS

A small enclosed container made of glass or other material with an adjustable screw plate used for pressing salads or making light pickles.

PRESSURE COOKERS

There are a variety of pressure cookers available. I prefer stainless steel, which maintains a steady, even vibration during cooking and is easy to clean. By contrast, aluminum scratches easily and can oxidize, leaving traces of metal in the food. Background radiation can also raise the temperature of aluminum pots, causing the food inside to spoil rapidly.

SAUCEPANS

A variety of saucepans with covers are essential for everyday cooking. A small 2-quart saucepan made of stainless steel is good for boiling small quantities of vegetables, heating up leftovers, and for serving as the top of a double boiler set inside a 4-quart saucepan. A 4-quart saucepan made of stainless steel, glass, or ceramic is useful for making soups, boiling vegetables, and preparing sauces. A large 6-quart saucepan made of enamel-coated cast-iron is ideal for long, slow cooking of grains, beans, and vegetable casseroles or for quick soups and vegetables.

SOUP POT

A heavy kettle of cast-iron, enamel-coated cast-iron, or stainless steel with a tight-fitting lid used for boiling noodles or pasta, steaming (with a rack set inside), preparing stock and large volumes of soup. Heavy cookware allows for more careful cooking. An 8-quart kettle is a good size for family use.

STEAMER

There are several types of steamers used for steaming vegetables, light grains, and other ingredients. A small metal basket that folds up when not in use can be set inside a kettle or saucepan. A bamboo steamer can be set on top of the pot.

TAMARI DISPENSER

A small glass bottle with a pouring spout is very useful in controlling the quantity of tamari soy sauce used in cooking.

TEA KETTLE

There are many types and sizes of tea kettles. At home we use a large glass kettle with a tight lid for making bancha tea. A small heat-resistant glass kettle, such as Pyrex or Corning Ware, may be used for simmering small amounts. A regular stainless steel whistling kettle is suitable for boiling water quickly for grain coffee or other beverages to which hot water is added directly.

TEA STRAINER

A small inexpensive bamboo strainer is ideal for sifting out twigs when pouring bancha or other tea from the tea kettle into cups.

TRADITIONAL POTTERY

Pottery made from clay fired in kilns at very high temperatures is the world's oldest and most natural cookware. Like the modern pressure cooker, it requires little liquid, and the pot's heavy lid keeps nutrients from escaping with the steam. Types of pottery include earthenware, stoneware, terra-cotta, porcelain, and china. Stoneware is fired at twice the temperature of earthenware, absorbs more heat, and retains fewer odors than other types of pottery. A flame deflector or trivet is necessary for cooking with pottery on top of the stove. Casserole dishes used for baking in the oven may also be made of pottery. Unglazed pottery needs to be seasoned prior to its first use. Pottery that is glazed on the inside but not the outside gives the best heat absorption. Some glazed pottery is made for purely decorative use and has a glaze that is poisonous if used in cooking, so make sure the finish is designed for cooking before using. Some vessels need to be soaked in water prior to each use, while others do not. To wash pottery, soak briefly in warm water and scrub with a vegetable brush. Avoid soap and detergents.

VEGETABLE BRUSHES

Small hand-held brushes made from natural materials tightly bound with wire. These are excellent for cleaning root vegetables and other items without bruising the skins. They may also be used to clean pots and pans.

WOODEN SPOONS, BOWLS, AND OTHER UTENSILS

Wood is an ideal material for serving dishes and cooking implements. It is a natural substance, will not scratch the surface of pots, conducts less heat than metal, will not leave a metallic taste in the food, and is aesthetically beautiful to look at and handle. Hardwoods, such as cherry, beech, maple, and boxwood, absorb food odors less easily, resist splintering, last indefinitely, and make the best serving bowls. Bamboo is excellent for rice paddles, tea strainers, and small mats used to wrap sushi or cover food. Bamboo mats allow heat to escape and air to enter so that just-cooked food will remain warm, up to an hour or more, set in a serving bowl or dish and covered with a bamboo mat. Leftovers can also be covered with these mats and will spoil much less quickly than if left uncovered or covered with plastic or foil.

WOK

A wok is a traditional deep Chinese pan set on a small stand and used to cook on top of the stove. Its inverted round shape is excellent for quick stir-frying, sautéing tempura, and deep-frying. Cast-iron gives steadier, more even heat, while stainless steel gives light, quick cooking. For ordinary family use, a 14-inch wok is usually sufficient.

CHAPTER

4

SALT, OIL, AND SEASONINGS

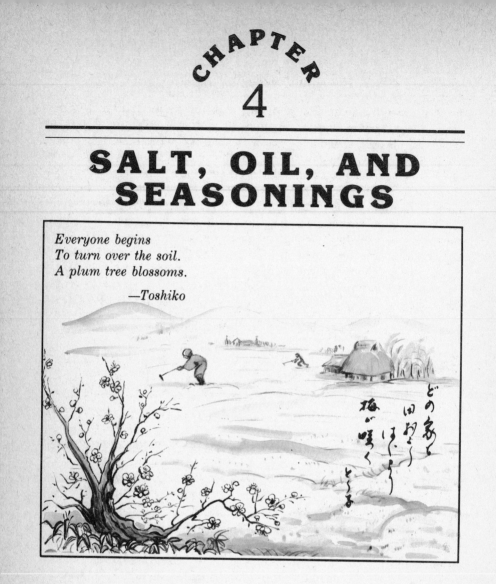

Everyone begins
To turn over the soil.
A plum tree blossoms.

—Toshiko

There are three keys to proper cooking: 1) selecting the best-quality foods and beverages; 2) learning the proper use of fuel; and 3) finding the appropriate balance of salt and oil. These factors chiefly determine our day-to-day health and happiness. In macrobiotic cooking, we regularly use unrefined sea salt for seasoning, as well as miso, tamari soy sauce, and umeboshi plums that have been salted and pickled. The main cooking oil is dark, unrefined sesame oil, although other high-quality, naturally processed unrefined vegetable oils may also be used from time to time. Brown rice vinegar, sweet brown rice vinegar, and umeboshi vinegar, as well as freshly grated gingerroot, are also used frequently to season or garnish different dishes.

SALT

Salt is essential to life. Without it, we could not live. The importance of salt has been universally recognized from ancient times. In the Bible, people with common sense are referred to as the salt of the earth. In Japan, for many centuries the Ise Shrine maintained the highest quality of salt against which all others were measured. During the feudal era in Japan, salt was considered so precious that rival warlords never interfered with the transportation of salt from the seashore to the inland and mountain regions.

When I was small, my parents would buy sea salt in 100-pound quantities, a crude type for pickling and another for cooking. In modern times, highly industrialized table salt, made from mined rock salt or refined sea salt, has largely replaced traditionally made unrefined sea salt. Many people in Japan have observed the change of salt quality. The taste of food has declined and pickles spoil much more easily today.

Unrefined sea salt is processed in several ways. Usually it is evaporated from salt water, dried in the sun, redissolved in water, filtered, reevaporated, and crystallized in gas-heated pans. Unrefined sea salt made in the traditional manner contains about 2 to 3 percent trace minerals in addition to sodium chloride and minute quantities of about sixty other elements naturally found in the ocean, including gold, silver, tin, and lead. The unrefined sea salt sold in North American natural foods stores comes primarily from European or Mexican coastal regions. The proportion of trace minerals varies according to the method of processing used, usually from about 0.5 to 3 percent. Good-quality sea salt is very delicious. When you put a little on the tip of your tongue, it should taste sweet and then gradually turn salty. The more refined the salt is, the more salty it will taste. If the salt is too coarse, the tongue will contract immediately from too much nigari remaining in it. When selecting salt, I look for a nice sweet variety, avoiding not only the more salty tasting ones but also the crude gray sea salt, which contains excess mineral compounds. If only gray sea salt is available, it can be rinsed well in cold water until the gray color is gone and dry-roasted in a heavy frying pan before using.

Commercial table salt is a highly refined product containing 99.5 percent sodium chloride. Most of the natural trace elements have been removed in processing and in their place magnesium carbonate, sodium carbonate, potassium iodide, and dextrose (a form of sugar used to stabilize the iodine) have been added. Like white bread and white rice, refined table salt depletes the valuable minerals in the body and may contribute to high blood pressure and other illnesses.

The amount of salt we need depends upon our condition and level of daily activity. It is important to find the right amount and neither underuse nor overuse salt. Too little or no salt can lead to lack of vitality, stagnated blood, and loss of clear thinking. Too much salt can produce hyperactivity, aggressive behavior, and excessive retention of fluids, which can lead to kidney troubles.

Babies and small children do not require as much salt as older children and grown-ups. For babies, we generally use no salt in cooking and make their food separately. For small children, a small amount of salt is introduced gradually. Their food may initially be cooked with that of the rest of the family and taken out and served separately just before any final seasoning is added. After the age of four, the amount of salt can be slowly increased until about the age of seven when it may approach the normal strength of seasoning for adults. Women also naturally need slightly less salt than men, and the elderly take less than those in the prime of life.

For those with a big family like mine, the way to adjust for everyone's personal salt needs is through condiments. I cook regular meals with just enough salt or other seasoning to meet everyone's basic requirement and provide an assortment of condiments at the table that may be added as desired. Ordinarily we discourage adding plain salt to food at the table. Adding seasoning to foods during cooking makes for a much more balanced and digestible dish. However, for personal adjustment, condiments containing cooked sea salt or other seasonings may be added at the table. The foremost of these is gomashio or roasted sesame salt, which may be added to whole grains, soups, vegetables, salads, and other dishes.

Over the years, my husband and I have found that the original macrobiotic style of cooking introduced to this country was much too salty for most Americans and Europeans. The climate here is much drier than that in Japan and because of early dietary habits most Westerners have grown up consuming large amounts of animal food that is high in sodium and other minerals. As a result, far less salt is required in the West than in the East. The recipes in this cookbook reflect this adjustment. The amount of sea salt, miso, tamari soy sauce, and other seasonings is only about one-fourth of that traditionally used in Japan. Compared to the standard American diet, this amount also represents just about twenty-five percent of the amount of sodium consumed by those who regularly eat meat, poultry, eggs, dairy food, and frozen, canned, and convenience foods containing large amounts of refined salt. Still, the measurements suggested in this book are only an average. The needs of your family may differ slightly and, as your cooking improves, you should learn to trust your own intuition and make slight adjustments, up or down, according to the quality of the ingredients you use, the method of cooking, the season of the year, and personal needs.

In cooking, salt is used in the following ways:

Grains—One pinch of sea salt per cup of grain is usually added when pressure-cooking or boiling. The salt makes the grain sweeter to the taste, chewier, and stronger in energy.

Soups—I usually use a very little amount of salt in the beginning of cooking, except when making soup stock, when it is added at the end. Salt is not needed in miso soups which already contain salt in the miso.

Vegetables—Salt softens vegetables and causes them to lose water. For marinating or pickling, salt may be added directly without cooking. During cooking, salt makes water boil faster. At the beginning of sautéing, steaming, and quick-boiling, I usually add a touch of sea salt to root, round, and ground vegetables. This makes them sweeter tasting, crispier, and keeps their colors bright and beautiful. However, for leafy green vegetables that are slightly bitter, such as daikon greens, mustard greens, and watercress, salt makes them even more bitter and should be avoided.

Beans—Beans are usually seasoned with plain sea salt while they are cooking. The salt should be added after the beans have cooked about seventy percent. If salt is added at the beginning of cooking, the inside and outside of the beans will cook unevenly. Usually a little more salt or other seasoning is used when cooking beans than whole grains.

Sea Vegetables—Seaweed already contains sea salt and is high in minerals. Sea vegetables are usually seasoned during cooking with tamari soy sauce. Salt makes them too salty and harsh to the taste.

Fish—A little salt sprinkled on top of baked fish will crisp it up nicely.

Fruit—A pinch of salt on fresh strawberries, melon, or other fruit will make them extra sweet and delicious.

Nuts—Roasting nuts and seeds in a little sea salt or tamari soy sauce helps to balance their naturally high oil content.

Appreciating salt is the work of a lifetime and developing a sensitivity to its effects is a barometer of our health and judgment. My teacher, George Ohsawa, used to smile and say that salt is the great magician. The cook who truly understands salt, oil, and other seasonings can control the destiny of his or her family.

MISO

Miso is a fermented food made from soybeans, usually various grains, such as brown rice or barley, sea salt, and an enzyme starter called *koji*. Miso has a sweet, rich flavor and is strengthening to the blood, stomach, and intestines. It satisfies the desire for a strong taste and gives very warm energy. There are many different types of miso. Some are sweeter tasting, some more salty, and a few pungent. Aging takes from several months to several years and greatly affects the flavor, texture, and energy of miso. For daily cooking, I usually use barley miso that has fermented for 18 to 24 months. We will look at the different misos in more detail in the chapter describing miso soup.

Traditional miso is made from the highest quality organic ingredients and aged naturally. In modern Japan, the quality of miso has declined. Most of the commercial miso now available contains chemicals, is artificially aged, and may be detrimental to health. When we started Erewhon, high-quality traditionally made miso was one of the first foods we imported from Japan. Since then, several macrobiotic friends in the United States, South America, and Europe have started miso-making companies using all local ingredients and traditional methods. We recommend these products highly.

Because of its delicious taste, miso is easy to overuse. The amount I use in cooking depends on the relative saltiness of the type of miso as well as the individual dish. For miso soup, I usually use about one teaspoon of miso per cup of liquid. As a rule of thumb, this amount may also be kept in mind when preparing grain, bean, or vegetable dishes with miso. Below are some of the ways I use miso:

Grains—Miso makes excellent sauces and gravies for grains and noodles. I occasionally use it as a substitute for salt in seasoning whole grains or in baking.

Soup—Miso is typically used for making a rich-tasting soup with a wide variety of land and sea vegetables. It is also good in broths for noodles and may be used as seasoning in grain, bean, or vegetable soups.

Vegetables—In cooking, miso is usually added at the very end of cooking. After purėeing in a little water, it is added to the pot and allowed to simmer for one to two minutes. Miso should not be boiled. Sometimes, for very slowly cooked vegetables, such as whole onions, miso is added at the beginning and allowed to seep into the vegetables during cooking. Miso may also be added at the start for baking, broiling, and barbecuing. In general, cooking with miso creates a sweeter taste than either salt or tamari soy sauce. Miso is also used for making delicious salad dressings, sauces, spreads, dips, and pickles. Small balls of miso deep-fried in sesame oil are very delicious.

Beans—Miso gives a nice sweet taste to some beans, especially kidney beans and soybeans. I also like to use miso with tofu. Pan-fried tofu sandwiches with a miso spread and tofu miso pickles are very delicious.

Sea Vegetables—Most seaweeds are seasoned with tamari soy sauce. However, *wakame* is very good with miso in soup, salads, and sauces.

Condiments—Miso is used in many condiments, such as tekka. It goes well with roasted sesame seeds, nuts, barley malt, and maple syrup. Miso may be combined with a sour taste, such as brown rice vinegar or lemon, and with a pungent taste, such as ginger or pepper.

Fish—Miso on top of broiled fish makes a nice dish. It may also be used for marinating fish or seafood.

Miso is a versatile, savory food. Once used in your cooking, it can never be forgotten.

TAMARI SOY SAUCE

Tamari soy sauce has become very popular in the West. Made from fermented soybeans, a little wheat, water, and sea salt, it is easy to use, rich-tasting, and gives strong energy. Tamari soy sauce is so tasty that a tendency can arise to add it to everything, which creates excessive thirst and a desire for liquids and sweets. This should be guarded against. In macrobiotic cooking, tamari soy sauce is usually added during cooking and not at the table. This also makes for a more digestible meal.

In Japan, soy sauce is usually referred to as *shoyu*. To distinguish naturally processed shoyu from the chemically processed variety that has spread through modern Japan, George Ohsawa selected the name *tamari*. Tamari is a liquid by-product of the miso-making process. For example, there is a famous tamari derived from 100 percent soybean miso and sea salt in the central region of Japan where the Tokagawa Shogun grew up. In recent years, a natural soy sauce has been introduced to the West called real tamari or genuine tamari. Some confusion has resulted between this product and tamari soy sauce. Real or genuine tamari is soy sauce made without wheat, similar to the by-product of the miso process. It is slightly stronger tasting than regular soy sauce and very expensive. I sometimes use this wheat-free tamari as a dipping sauce for tempura. For daily cooking, I use regular tamari soy sauce, which, because of the linguistic confusion, is also sometimes labeled as organic or natural *shoyu*. In this cookbook, all recipes calling for tamari soy sauce refer to this product.

When we started Erewhon in the early 1960s, good-quality tamari soy sauce was unavailable in this country. Even in Japan it is hard to find, as most commercial soy sauce now sold is made with chemicals, processed at abnormally high temperatures, and artificially aged. It is also made with low-quality beans, grains, and refined sea salt. After a lengthy search we finally arranged to import organic tamari soy sauce to the West. Today, even supermarkets in the United States often carry high-quality tamari soy sauce. The typical family here, in South America, or in Europe now has far better *shoyu* than the ordinary Japanese family. We are encouraging friends here to begin making tamari soy sauce from all locally grown or processed ingredients.

Tamari soy sauce may be used in a variety of ways.

Grains—Tamari soy sauce is sometimes used with whole grains in cooking. I occasionally add a touch to pressure-cooked brown rice, but more frequently I add it while cooking fried rice or fried noodles or making a kuzu sauce to put over grains. One-half teaspoon of tamari soy sauce equals about one pinch of sea salt. Two to three teaspoons of tamari soy sauce are usually sufficient to season a dish for four to six people.

Soups—Tamari soy sauce is a basic ingredient of tamari broth, dashi soup stock, and most clear soups. It may also be used as a flavoring for squash soup, onion soup, and other naturally sweet vegetable soups. For a slightly stronger taste than salt, I sometimes add it to bean and grain soups as well.

Vegetables—Tamari soy sauce is used in many ways with vegetables and is usually added at the very end of cooking and allowed to simmer for several minutes. In some styles, such as *nishime*-style boiling, a mild tamari soy sauce flavor is added at the start, especially when cooking tofu, seitan, or tempeh. It may also be used as a marinade or dressing for fresh salads, for making quick pickles, and as a dipping sauce for tempura. Tamari soy sauce's nice salty flavor goes well combined with either sour, sweet, or pungent tastes.

Beans—Tamari soy sauce gives some beans, especially yellow and black soybeans, a strong delicious taste. A touch may also be added to azuki beans while cooking. Often a little salt will be added to beans when they are seventy percent cooked, and tamari soy sauce will be added to taste at the very end and simmered a few minutes before serving.

Sea Vegetables—Most seaweeds are seasoned during cooking with tamari soy sauce, especially kombu, hiziki, and arame.

Condiments—Though not usually added to foods at the table, a few drops may be used to flavor noodles for extra taste.

Beverages—A drop of tamari soy sauce is often added to teas for a calming effect and for creating vitality. Beverages seasoned with tamari soy sauce have many medicinal applications.

Like good-quality sea salt and miso, tamari soy sauce is one of the macrobiotic cook's best friends. Please learn to use it wisely. To ensure our families' health, we should always select the highest quality foods.

UMEBOSHI PLUMS

The umeboshi plum, which somewhat resembles the apricot, grows in the colder, northern regions of Japan. The tree blossoms in early spring, giving forth beautiful flowers with soft white petals. Picked in early summer, the fruit is very acidic and will produce sickness if eaten raw. However, fermented with sea salt and special enzymes and bacteria for a year or more, umeboshi plums become transformed into very strong medicine. They have a tangy flavor, combining a sour and salty taste exquisitely. In Japan we have a saying, "Eat one umeboshi plum before taking a journey and you will have a safe trip." Umeboshi are excellent for traveling, and I always carry a small bottle of them wherever I go. One plum will usually quickly neutralize stomach upset, nausea, air sickness, or help detoxify the body from the effects of unacceptable food.

We also use umeboshi plums in regular cooking. They may be substituted for salt, miso, or tamari soy sauce in many recipes. With aging the plums become less tart and salty. I once tasted an umeboshi that had aged for twenty years. It was very mild and delicious. Customarily preserved with *shiso* (beefsteak) leaves, umeboshi have a beautiful red color and add beauty to the meal. In modern Japan, most commercially available umeboshi plums are now artificially aged and colored and made with inferior ingredients.

Although my family did not grow umeboshi trees, we had a friend who gave us many fresh plums each year. After cleaning, we would soak them in salt water for a week and dry them in the strong July sun. We then repeated this process of soaking and drying several times, until the plums were thoroughly penetrated by the salt. Then we left them for a final drying on top of a small shed in the backyard. The night dew was especially good and seemed to enhance their flavor. Finally, we packed them once again in salt water along with red-purple *shiso* leaves. Covered with rice paper, the umeboshi were left to ferment for 1 to 2 years. After they were pickled, we saved the juice or salty brine in which they were stored. This is called *ume-su* or umeboshi vinegar and has many uses.

Several years ago one natural foods distributor came out with a ready made umeboshi paste. It was smooth, the pits had been removed from the plums, and it didn't need to be ground in the *suribachi*, the traditional mortar that we use to grind sauces and dressings. The paste is very good for this purpose. However, for strong cooking and for medicinal purposes, whole umeboshi plums have much more balanced energy and are preferred.

Grain—Umeboshi are excellent with brown rice and other whole grains. A small piece of umeboshi is customarily added to the center of rice balls. They may also be pitted and eaten raw with soft rice or other grains. As a dressing, purééd umeboshi or umeboshi vinegar makes a wonderful sauce for noodles, grains, and vegetables and gives a nice mild sour taste. I occasionally cook with umeboshi instead of salt as a seasoning for grain. This gives a unique flavor and creates a different taste. I use about one-third of a plum per cup of uncooked grain. For a delicious zesty taste, a little puréed umeboshi or umeboshi paste can be spread on corn on the cob instead of butter.

Vegetables—Umeboshi are often used in sauces for vegetables. Usually I dilute the plums with a little water or soup stock and mix in scallions and roasted sesame seeds. A nice pink dressing can be made with umeboshi and tofu. Fresh vegetables may be pickled with umeboshi or *shiso* leaves.

Beverages—Umeboshi makes a good tea steeped by itself or added to bancha tea. Umeboshi tea is a traditional summertime drink. Served cool, it slakes thirst and cools off the body better than soft drinks or icy cold beverages.

OLIVES

Like umeboshi plums, olives contain a natural balance of tastes and flavors. I first discovered olives in the United States, but didn't really appreciate them until I visited southern France. There I saw how they were traditionally processed. I am especially fond of the small black olives which are used in Mediterranean cuisine. Green olives are also nice. I have not experimented very much with cooking with olives, but I enjoy them from time to time plain or as a garnish for other dishes. Olives that are not packed in vinegar or spices are less acidic and more digestible.

OILS

Quality vegetable oil is essential to health. It strengthens cells and capillaries, lowers cholesterol in the blood, and lubricates the skin and hair. High in nutrients, such as vitamins A and E, oil is flavorful and easy to digest. In the macrobiotic kitchen, unrefined naturally processed vegetable oils are used in sautéing, pan-frying, deep-frying, and frying tempura-style foods, as well as in making dressings, salads, and dips.

Vegetable oils are generally high in polyunsaturated fatty acids. This kind of fatty acid, which is also found in whole grains, beans, seeds, and some marine products, is needed by the body for proper metabolism.

Except for fish and some seafood, animal products are high in saturated fatty acids and dietary cholesterol, a waxy fat-like substance that, if taken in excess, can accumulate in arteries and around vital organs and lead to heart disease. Plant foods do not contain cholesterol. About forty percent of the modern diet is composed of fats and cholesterol. This includes the hard saturated fats in meat, poultry, eggs, and dairy food; heavy, greasy cooking fat, such as butter and lard; refined vegetable oils, such as coconut and palm oil, which are predominantly saturated in quality; and margarine, spreads, and convenience foods, which are highly processed to make them solid at room temperature.

Unrefined vegetable oils are processed in different ways and come in several grades. The highest quality are pressed at relatively low temperatures, filtered, and bottled. They appear rich and cloudy, retaining the natural aroma and flavor of the seeds from which they are extracted. Lesser qualities of unrefined vegetable oil are solvent-extracted using a highly toxic chemical derived from petroleum, which is heated at extreme temperatures. Some oils are labeled as "cold pressed" to signify that they are not chemically processed. However, this term has been used by some refined-oil manufacturers and because of the lack of a standard definition is not necessarily an indication of quality.

Refined vegetable oils may be either pressed or solvent-extracted. However, in contrast to unrefined oils, they are also usually degummed, washed in a highly caustic solution, such as lye, to remove essential fatty acids, bleached, deodorized, and sometimes winterized (chilled). In the process, the natural color, taste, aroma, and nutrients are lost, producing a bland colorless product that lasts for a long time on the shelf and in the refrigerator. The vitamins A and E, lecithin, and other nutrients stripped from natural oil are often sold back to consumers in the form of vitamin and mineral supplements. Like white bread, white rice, and refined salt, refined vegetable oil is detrimental to human health and should be strictly avoided.

Another highly refined process is hydrogenation in which vegetable oils, such as margarine, are chemically treated to solidify them at room temperatures. In hydrogenating, polyunsaturated fatty acids are saturated to various degrees. This processed oil is widely used to make potato chips and fried fast foods. Even though they may be sold in the natural foods store, I avoid soy margarine and other hydrogenated products.

Oil gives balance and satisfaction to a meal and like salt, it is easy to overuse. Too much oil destroys the taste of foods, especially naturally sweet vegetables, gives rise to both oily and dry skin conditions, and thins the blood and lymph. Unlike salt, it is hard to take too little oil if you are eating a whole grain diet, as cereals, beans, and seeds naturally contain all the polyunsaturated fatty acids needed by the body. Oil protects the skin from heat in the summer and cold in the winter. If you are sensitive to these extremes, it could be that you are not consuming enough oil or fat to properly insulate you from the elements.

The ideal way to obtain oil is from whole foods, such as roasted whole sesame seeds. Normally, for a healthy person, one or two dishes a day may be made with a little oil, such as a side dish of sautéed vegetables or sea vegetables and a sauce or dressing containing a little oil. Tempura-style or deep-frying uses very large quantities of oil. However, if properly done, tempura-style and deep-fried foods are not oily and heavy to the taste but crispy and light. Even so, I do not recommend using these strong, rich styles of cooking more than once a week. For persons who are seriously ill, we often recommend a form of the macrobiotic diet that avoids or minimizes oil, even good-quality unrefined oil, until their condition improves.

Oil creates outward, expanding energy. Only a tiny amount is needed when cooking. One or two tablespoons are enough to sauté a large pan of vegetables, noodles, or grains for the whole family. Usually, I use just enough oil to cover the bottom of the pan. For those who need to watch their oil intake very closely, oil may be brushed on the pan with a tiny brush used just for this purpose and kept very clean.

Some foods do not go well cooked together with oil. These include kombu, fall- and winter-season squashes, azuki beans, and chick-peas. To help digest oil, especially tempura-style or deep-fried food, I always serve a little grated daikon radish and sometimes fresh grated gingerroot or umeboshi plum as part of the meal. Fish and seafood are naturally oily, though white-meat fish is less fatty than red-meat or blue-skinned varieties. Nuts are also high in oil and may be roasted occasionally as snacks, or chopped and added to grains and casseroles. Nut butters are much oilier and more fattening than plain nuts and seeds and should be used very sparingly. Only the highest quality nut and seed butters should be used.

The principal vegetable oils include:

Sesame Oil—Unrefined sesame oil comes in two forms. Dark sesame oil is made from pressing roasted sesame seeds and has a wonderful smoky aroma, nutty taste, dark color, and cloudy appearance. It is a superior product and the ideal oil for everyday cooking, baking, sauces, and spreads. Light sesame oil is milder in taste, clearer in consistency, and less flavorful. It is also less expensive than dark sesame oil. I use it primarily for making large quantities of food or for delicate dishes where the strong flavor of dark sesame oil might be too much. Sesame oil is highly stable and resistant to spoiling. After opening, it should be kept tightly sealed in its bottle or other container and stored in the refrigerator or a cool, dark place.

Mustard Seed Oil—This wonderful oil is pressed from the seeds of the same plant that gives mustard green leaves. Like sesame seeds, these tiny seeds are the subject of many legends and parables, as in the New Testament. In Japan, my mother cooked with mustard seed oil frequently and it is excellent for everyday cooking. Unfortunately, it is not widely available in this country.

Corn Oil—Unrefined corn oil has a rich corn flavor and a smooth buttery consistency. Darker corn oil comes from the whole kernel, while the lighter form comes from the corn germ. After sesame oil, I use corn oil most frequently for sautéing, baking, or sauces and dressings. Corn oil should not be used for tempura or deep-frying because it foams easily.

Safflower Oil—Safflower is a very mild oil and makes nice dressings and sauces. During the war it came into popular use in Japan when sesame oil grew scarce. Safflower oil tends to spoil easily and at home we do not even use it for tempura or deep-frying.

Sunflower Oil—Sunflower oil has a pleasant taste and a clear consistency. It is very popular in the Soviet Union, Canada, and other cold northern climates. It keeps well and may be used occasionally in temperate-climate cooking instead of sesame or corn oil.

Soybean Oil—Soybean oil has a strong flavor which many people find unpleasant. Commercially, refined soy oil is widely used by the fast-food industry. Unrefined soybean oil is available in natural foods stores and may be used from time to time by those who do not mind its taste.

Olive Oil—Olive oil is the only major oil that needs no heating above room temperature or extraction under high pressure. The highest grades, obtained from the first pressings of the olives, are called extra virgin. The next grades are called virgin and then pure. These grades are obtained from the second pressings, often using chemical means. High-quality olive oil keeps well and can be stored without refrigeration for up to a year. Olive oil is mostly monosaturated in quality, which makes it heavier and more fatty than polyunsaturated oils. It is nice in salads and occasionally in cooking.

Other unrefined, naturally processed oils may also be used for variety from time to time, including peanut oil, cottonseed oil, and linseed oil.

VINEGAR

Good vinegar completely changes the taste and feeling of a food, creating a nice sour flavor. I used to use apple cider vinegar as a seasoning, but now we have wonderful organic brown rice vinegar and sweet brown rice vinegar. These make delightful sauces and dressings. Vinegar may also be used in making sushi, and in grain salads it goes very well with couscous, bulghur, and cracked wheat. It may also be combined with oil, salt, and sweet and spicy items and makes excellent pickles. I do not ordinarily use vinegar directly in cooking, except to occasionally add a touch to burdock. Nor do I use vinegar in soups, but I will sometimes add a touch to sea vegetables to soften them if they are too hard and salty. Umeboshi vinegar, the juice left over from pickling umeboshi plums, is also an excellent seasoning, and I use it sometimes from the beginning of cooking with red radishes, cauliflower, or cabbage. Umeboshi vinegar also makes lovely dressings and sauces and may be added to noodles and salads.

SAKE AND MIRIN WINE

Sake rice wine and mirin, a naturally sweet cooking wine made from sweet rice, are traditionally used for holiday cooking or other special occasions. In my village, there was a big sake factory opposite our church. My family didn't use alcohol and the first time I drank sake was in college. Sake may be used to sweeten grains, beans, sea vegetables, and vegetables, as well as combined with other ingredients in dressings and sauces. I remember mother was once cooking about 25 pounds of rice in a large kettle over the fire. She became distracted and by mistake it did not cook up completely. To save the rice, she went next door to a neighbor's and borrowed one or two cups of sake to pour over the rice to simmer it until it was done. The fermenting power of the sake enabled the rice to finish evenly and the sake taste disappeared during the cooking.

Mirin has a unique full-bodied sweet taste. It may be added to various dishes to mellow the flavor of excessively salty or overly pungent foods. Just a dash added to noodle broths, dressings, or marinades creates a subtly different taste. Mirin is available in selected natural foods stores.

GINGER

Gingerroot is an indispensable part of macrobiotic cooking. Ginger stimulates the appetite, gets circulation moving, and adds a nice pungent flavor to a meal. It can be used grated or squeezed into a juice. Just a touch of grated ginger, about ¼ teaspoon for four to six people, adds zest when it is sprinkled on top of grains, noodles, and vegetable dishes at the very end of cooking and simmered with the other ingredients for one minute or less before serving. It may also be sprinkled raw on top of the dish as a garnish. Ginger juice is much stronger and more concentrated than grated ginger. To make it, grate the gingerroot and then with your hands or a clean cloth squeeze out the juice and add it to the dish you are cooking. About ¼ teaspoon of ginger juice equals the strength of 1 teaspoon of grated ginger, so a little goes a long way. Ginger juice is often used to season soups or noodle broths. It is incorporated into the liquid completely, unlike grated ginger which remains as tiny shreds.

Ginger may also be pickled, used in condiments, and added to beverages. It has many internal and external medicinal uses.

APPROXIMATE SEASONING EQUIVALENTS

The relative saltiness of sea salt, miso, tamari soy sauce, and umeboshi plums varies depending on the particular batch or strength. Thus, equivalents can only be rough approximations.

1 pinch sea salt = ½ teaspoon tamari soy sauce
= ⅔ teaspoon miso
= ⅓ umeboshi plum
¼ teaspoon sea salt = 1½ teaspoons tamari soy sauce
= 1⅔ teaspoons miso
= 1 umeboshi plum
½ teaspoon sea salt = 1 tablespoon tamari soy sauce
= 1 tablespoon plus 1 teaspoon miso
= 2 umeboshi plums
1½ teaspoons umeboshi paste = 1 umeboshi plum
1 teaspoon umeboshi vinegar (ume-su) = ⅔ umeboshi plum
¼ teaspoon squeezed ginger juice = 1 teaspoon grated ginger
1 tablespoon brown rice vinegar = 1 tablespoon lemon juice
1 tablespoon arrowroot flour = 1 teaspoon kuzu
1¼ cups barley malt or rice syrup = ½ cup maple syrup
2¼ tablespoons barley malt or rice syrup = 1 tablespoon maple syrup
1 cake tofu = 16 ounces (for recipes in this book)

MEASUREMENTS

Liquid Measures and Volumes

3 teaspoons = 1 tablespoon
4 tablespoons = ¼ cup
5⅓ tablespoons = ⅓ cup
8 tablespoons = ½ cup
16 tablespoons = 1 cup
4 cups = 1 quart

1 tablespoon = ½ fluid ounce
2 tablespoons = 1 fluid ounce
3 tablespoons = 1½ fluid ounces
½ cup = 4 fluid ounces
1 cup = 8 fluid ounces
2 cups = 16 fluid ounces

Weights

1 ounce = 1/16 pound
4 ounces = ¼ pound
8 ounces = ½ pound
12 ounces = ¾ pound
16 ounces = 1 pound

Baking and Tempura Frying Temperatures

	Fahrenheit	Centigrade
Slow	205–275	120–150
Moderate	350–375	180–190
Hot	400–450	200–230
Tempura	345–355	175–180

Metric Equivalents

1 teaspoon = 5 grams
1 tablespoon = 15 grams
2 tablespoons = 30 grams
3 tablespoons = 44 grams
1 ounce = 28 grams
1¾ ounces = 50 grams
3½ ounces = 100 grams
8 ounces = 227 grams
1 pound = .45 kilogram

1 teaspoon = 5 milliliters
1 tablespoon = 15 milliliters
2 tablespoons = 30 milliliters
3 tablespoons = 44 milliliters
1 ounce = 30 milliliters
1 cup = 236 milliliters
1 cup = .24 liter
1 quart = .96 liter
4½ cups = 1 liter

¼ inch = 6.3 millimeters
½ inch = 12.7 millimeters
1 inch = 2.5 centimeters
3 inches = 7.6 centimeters
6 inches = 15.2 centimeters

British Imperial Equivalents

4 teaspoons = 1 tablespoon
1 fluid ounce = .96 U.S. ounce
1 quart = 1.03 U.S. dry quart
1 quart = 1.2 U.S. liquid quart

CHAPTER

5

BROWN RICE

Rice sacks!
How far are you going
On the snowy road?

—Yoshie

RICE AND EVOLUTION

On the evolutionary calendar, the earth has entered the season of Galactic Autumn. Human beings are the most developed form of life. Cooked whole grains are the ideal food. Fifty million years ago, during Galactic Summer, monkeys, chimpanzees, and other advanced species ate fruits, nuts, and seeds as their principal foods. Earlier, during Galactic Spring, dinosaurs dominated the environment and subsisted on ferns, mosses, and other primitive vegetation.

Among cereal grains, brown rice is the most balanced. Its size, shape, color, texture, and proportion of carbohydrate, fat, protein, and minerals fall in the middle of the spectrum of the seven principal grains. Wheat, barley, oats, and other grains are divided in half by a slight indentation in their kernels. Rice has no such line and is biologically the most integrated grain—our evolutionary counterpart in the plant world.

Rice is particularly soothing to the brain and nervous system, our species' most developed organs. Rice is now cultivated on every continent and may be considered humanity's universal staple.

RICE QUALITY

I always try to obtain the highest quality organic brown rice available and keep a constant supply on hand. Next best is natural or ecologically grown brown rice, cultivated with a minimum of soil additives and pesticides. I buy in bulk when possible and closely examine a handful of individual grains from the bin for consistent milling. A light green color indicates grains that have been harvested prematurely. I also check for the presence of hulls, or the dark outer sheaths which are taken off in milling. More than an occasional immature grain or husk indicates that the quality of the rice is not good. I also check for broken or chipped grains which have lost their energy and will not sprout. Rice with a conspicuous amount of dirt, pebbles, and other extraneous matter should also be avoided if possible. At home I sometimes further test the potency of the grain by placing a cup of rice in a bowl of water. If more than 1 to 2 percent of the kernels remain floating on the surface, the rice is low in vitality.

Until recently, only hulled brown rice has generally been available. Small motorized hulling machines are now available for household and community use, and some rice growers are marketing unhulled grain for this purpose. Rice that is freshly hulled just before the meal contains the maximum energy and nutrients. Though expensive, the home hulling machine will return its investment many times in improved health and consciousness.

SHORT, MEDIUM, LONG GRAIN, AND SWEET RICE

Brown rice is classified into four main varieties. *Short grain rice* is the smallest and hardiest and contains the most minerals and a high amount of gluten. It is naturally sweet to the taste and the most suitable for daily consumption. *Medium grain rice* is slightly larger and cooks up slightly softer and more moist. It too is excellent for daily consumption. *Long grain rice*, the most elongated variety, is light and fluffy when cooked. It is the type favored in the tropics and in the southern regions and sunbelt of the United States. In warm weather I occasionally prepare long grain rice for supper here in temperate New England. It can also be used in puddings and desserts. *Sweet rice*, the most glutinous variety, is high in protein and as delectable as its name implies. I occasionally prepare it for regular meals, especially mixed in with short grain rice. Usually sweet rice is reserved for making mochi, holiday dishes, and other special occasions. Sweet rice dishes and beverages are also recommended for babies, children, and nursing mothers.

STORING GRAINS

I buy rice in bulk when possible and store it at home. I usually obtain the grain at discount by ordering in large volume, and the local natural foods store often delivers the 25- or 50-pound sacks to my house at no extra charge. I keep the bags of rice in a cool, dark place, slightly raised up from the floor to prevent moisture or spilled water from seeping in. I am also careful to keep the grain away from radiators, the stove, the rear of the refrigerator, or direct sunlight.

In order to further reduce moisture and mold, grain should be stored in airtight containers. Opened bags of rice can be poured into barrels, preferably wooden ones, though plastic will do. The sacks may also be placed inside large plastic lawn bags or a new garbage pail. Smaller quantities may be kept in large glass bottles or containers. Ties, lids, or tops should be securely fastened after each use. Grains will attract mice, insects, and other small creatures, so it is important to keep the rice well protected. Sometimes tiny insect eggs get into the grain in the field or in warehousing. These eggs are virtually invisible and may not begin to hatch until the grain is stored on the kitchen shelf in its container. In this case, if the infestation is small (under ten insects per pound), the grain can be saved. Spread the grain (or flour) on a baking pan in a layer up to ¾ inch thick. Put the pans in the freezer and let them stay there 3 to 4 days at zero degrees, or heat in the oven for 30 minutes at 140 degrees. Both of these methods will destroy the insects and their eggs. Afterwards, sift the grain and place it in a freshly cleaned container.

This kind of infestation is rare. Whole grains usually keep indefinitely if properly stored. There are many stories of grains, beans, and seeds sprouting after hundreds of years. Because of atmospheric and environmental conditions, one year's harvest may differ greatly in energy and taste from the next. Rice also differs from region to region and country to country. European rice is generally a little smaller in size than American rice and requires less water in cooking. Japanese rice, often grown on soil containing volcanic ash, is usually higher in minerals and may need less seasoning. On my travels, I have collected many samples of rice and sometimes set aside an especially fine variety for special occasions.

WASHING AND SOAKING RICE

To prepare rice for cooking, I place a handful at a time on a dinner plate and pick out any visible stones, particles of soil, or heavy dust.

Then I place the rice in a pot or bowl and cover with cold water. In the bowl I gently wash the grain by stirring it with my hand in a counter-clockwise direction. Then I drain off the water. If the rice is dirty, I will repeat this step three or more times until the water becomes almost clear. I stir and rinse as quickly as possible in order to retain the grain's natural sweetness, which is reduced by absorption of moisture. Finally, I place the rice in a strainer or colander to rinse off any light dust which remains.

After washing, I usually soak the rice for 2 to 3 hours or overnight. I do this by placing the rice in the pressure cooker, adding the appropriate amount of cooking water in the recipe, and covering. Soaking makes the rice softer and more digestible. In hot weather, though, I do not soak the rice for too long a time because the rice tends to get mushy. If time does not allow, the rice may be cooked directly after washing and without soaking. Soaking is a good practice to follow and with a little planning, it will be easy to fit it into your schedule.

COOKWARE

The pressure cooker I use, as explained in Chapter 3, is made of stainless steel. For cooking, wooden utensils are superior to metal ones. They do not scratch pots and pans nor do they leave a metallic taste in the food. A small bamboo rice paddle is indispensable for removing rice from a pressure cooker. This implement is contoured to lift rice from a pan or bowl with maximum efficiency. If the grain sticks to the paddle, moisten it slightly with water. Rice paddles are inexpensive and available in most natural foods stores.

Rice and other foods are ideally served in bowls or plates made of natural materials, such as wood, glass, or clay. Plastic may be used for storage if better-quality containers are unavailable. However, the vibration of synthetic materials may affect the quality and taste of the food and should be avoided at the table. This applies especially to hot foods, which may melt the plastic.

PRESSURE-COOKING

In ancient China, Mexico, Europe, and the Middle East, grains were cooked under pressure in heavy pots or caldrons. Stones set on top of thick lids often added additional weight. Pressure, along with fire, salt, and water, was recognized as an important factor in cooking, especially as the earth's climate cooled in the current evolutionary phase.

Pressure-cooking is the quickest and most thorough way to prepare whole grains, especially brown rice. When cooked, each grain should be separate and distinct, and the rice should taste sweet. Pressure brings out this natural sweetness, and rice cooked in this way is the most digestible form of grain for daily consumption. Other foods may also be pressured-cooked from time to time, especially beans. However, pressure-cooking is very energizing, and to create balance in the meal, it is advisable to prepare the other dishes for the meal using other cooking methods. Occasionally, I mix vegetables with the grain and pressure-cook them together. However, for day-to-day meals, I prepare the vegetables separately by boiling, steaming, sautéing, or some other method.

When pressure-cooking, I am careful not to fill the pot more than half full with grain (or to 70 percent capacity, including grain and water). Above that amount, the valve may clog and the rice will not cook as it should. On rare occasions, a pot of rice may be forgotten about and left pressure-cooking on the stove for several hours. Even in this case, with the new safety model pressure cookers, the lids will not come off. Rice cooked for several hours will be hard but still edible, and the burnt grains on the bottom will easily come up off the bottom of the pot after soaking.

WATER

Water affects the quality of rice and other foods during cooking. It is important to have a source of clear, clean well or spring water. Ordinary municipal tap water, which often contains chlorine, detergent residues, and other impurities, is acceptable for washing and rinsing but may adversely affect the quality of the food during soaking and cooking. At home we order bottled spring water from a local distributor who delivers it by truck once or twice a month in large 5-gallon containers. Spring water is often available in natural foods stores and supermarkets in 1-gallon containers. Not all spring water is the same high quality, and I've found that, by changing brands, the quality of my cooking is sometimes noticeably improved. Spring water may also be collected from a stream or natural spring in the countryside or mountains. I've gathered it in an assortment of bottles and containers, and an afternoon's trek for water is good exercise as well as more economical than purchasing it at the store. In areas I'm unfamiliar with, I'm careful to make sure the water is safe and not polluted by environmental toxins.

SALT AND SEASONING

In macrobiotic cooking, the rule of thumb is to use a pinch of sea salt per cup of rice or other grain to be cooked. A pinch is an average amount held between the thumb and index finger. The taste of the rice after cooking should be neither too salty nor too bland. For a slightly saltier dish, I may, from time to time, use a three-finger pinch. For a less salty dish, half the amount will suffice.

In pressure-cooking I usually add the salt after the grain and water have heated up for 10 to 15 minutes and the water is just beginning to bubble. I add the salt just before the water starts to boil and I put the lid on the pressure cooker. If I put the salt in earlier, the water warms up too quickly, and the ingredients may cook unevenly on the inside and outside. In macrobiotic cooking, we generally add seasoning during cooking and not at the table.

As an alternative to salt, one third of an umeboshi plum may be added for each cup of uncooked rice. For variety, ½ teaspoon of tamari soy sauce may also be used as a substitute for salt. Occasionally, bancha twig tea or green tea may be used in place of spring water during cooking if a slightly stronger flavor is desired.

COOKING FUEL

Until I went to Tokyo, all of my food was cooked over a wood or charcoal fire. Even in college, the kitchen had a large wood-burning stove. Wood is the ideal energy source. It is natural, renewable, and creates food with the strongest and most peaceful energy and the most delicious taste. Unfortunately, wood is not always available or practical, especially in a modern urban environment. Wood also takes more time and effort to prepare.

I learned to cook with gas when I lived in Tokyo and New York. Modern gas stoves are very efficient and their flame is easy to adjust. Gas maintains the natural vibration of the food, and it is an excellent fuel for city dwellers. We have a gas range at home, and the Kushi Institute cooking classes use gas.

Electric ranges are very popular today but have serious limitations. Electricity produces very chaotic vibrations in food. Most people find that food cooked on an electric stove or hot plate is not nearly so appetizing as food cooked with gas. Electricity also responds far less quickly to changes in heat and is harder to adjust to the desired temperature. In consultations with cancer patients, Michio has found that about nine out of ten cook with electricity or microwave, which is the most chaotic method of all. After switching to a gas stove, these people usually experience an immediate improvement in their health and consciousness and they get more enjoyment out of their food and cooking.

Coal is another cooking fuel. It has many of the same benefits as wood. Charcoal is also suitable, but be careful to use only charcoal that has not been treated with chemicals.

TEMPERATURE

The taste and quality of rice are influenced by the intensity as well as the quality of heat. With pressure-cooking, there are several ways to vary the heat, depending on whether the rice has been soaked and the quantity of rice to be cooked.

1. If the rice is prepared without soaking, begin with low heat and let the pressure come up very gradually. This produces a calm, stable quality in the rice and a sweeter flavor. This method is also used for cooking a small amount of rice, 1 or 2 cups.

2. If the rice has soaked for several hours, start cooking with low heat and gradually increase the heat to high over 15 to 20 minutes. This method gives the rice more energy and may also be used in cooler weather or to provide more vitality.

3. If the rice has soaked for a long time or overnight, begin with high heat and reduce to low when the pressure has been up for about 10 minutes. This method is very energizing and may be used to generate warmth in extremely cold weather or in preparing for strenuous activity, such as cleaning the house or working in the garden.

PRESSURE

After the rice has pressure-cooked, I remove it from the burner. If I'm cooking a small quantity, 1 to 2 cups of raw rice, I allow the pressure to come down by itself without removing the gauge, about 15 to 20 minutes; then I open the pressure cooker before the rice gets cold. This gives the rice an even more peaceful energy and delicious taste. Also, any moisture inside will thoroughly loosen scorched or burnt grains on the bottom of the pot. If I'm cooking a medium amount of rice, 3 to 4 cups, I'll let the rice sit in the unopened pressure cooker for about 10 minutes before opening it. For large quantities, 5 cups or more, I let the rice sit only 5 minutes before opening or the rice around the sides of the pot will get wet, moist, or soggy.

Basic Brown Rice

2 cups organic brown rice
1¼ to 1½ cups spring water per cup of rice
Pinch of sea salt per cup of rice

Gently wash the rice (short- or medium-grain) and quickly place it in a pressure cooker and smooth out the surface of the rice so that it is level. Slowly add spring water down the side of the pressure cooker so that the surface of the rice remains calm and even. If time permits, soak the rice for 2 to 3 hours or longer. Put the pressure cooker on the stove, either uncovered or with the cover on untightened, and begin to cook over low heat. When the water begins to bubble (after about 10 to 15 minutes), add the sea salt. Then tighten the cover of the pressure cooker securely, and bring up slowly to full pressure. This is signified by the hissing, jiggling, and/or spinning of the gauge, depending on the model of pressure cooker used. When the pressure is up, put a metal flame deflector under the pot and turn the heat to low. Cook for 50 minutes.

When the rice is done, remove the pressure cooker from the heat and allow it to stand for at least 5 minutes before reducing the pressure and removing the cover. If you wait 10 to 15 minutes for the pressure to come down naturally before opening, the rice will be even better. This wait allows any burnt or scorched grains on the bottom to loosen.

Using a bamboo rice paddle or wooden spoon, lift the rice from the pressure cooker one spoonful at a time and smooth into a large wooden bowl. Distribute evenly the heavier, well-cooked rice at the bottom and the lighter, fluffier rice at the top. Alternating scoops in this way makes for a more balanced bowl of rice.

Rice pressure-cooked in this way will have a delicious, nutty, naturally sweet taste and will impart a very peaceful, strong feeling.

COOKING IN QUANTITY

Each cup of uncooked rice makes about three cups of cooked rice. I allow about one cup of cooked rice per person at the meal. At home, family, staff, and guests usually number from fifteen to twenty people, and I usually cook a minimum of twelve cups of raw rice at a time. The household goes through a 50-pound sack of brown rice in about two weeks.

Smaller amounts of rice (one or two cups of raw rice) take slightly more water, lower temperature, and more time than the usual three to four cups prepared for the average family of four to six persons. Otherwise the rice may become too dry. When making a moderate-to-large amount of rice (five or more cups of uncooked rice), I reduce the amount of cooking water by about ¼ to ½ cup per cup of rice and increase the cooking time by 5 to 10 minutes to about an hour. This prevents the rice from becoming too soft or mushy.

For restaurant or institutional cooking, we use another method entirely. In extremely large amounts, 15 pounds or more, it is not always easy to cook the rice evenly. Often the rice at the bottom is done before the rice on top has barely warmed up. To prevent this, boil the water in the pressure cooker first. Then add the rice and salt, mix well, and cover. When the pressure comes up, cook over low heat.

BURNT, DRY, WET, OR MUSHY RICE

If the rice is burnt or scorched on the bottom of the pressure cooker, the heat may have been too high or the grain cooked too long. In addition to letting the pressure come down naturally after cooking, the scorched grains can easily be removed by adding a little water and allowing them to soften. I save this rice for making soft rice cereal or rice *kayu* bread. The rice may also be allowed to dry for several days and then be deep-fried for a crispy snack. Scorched grains are very chewy and delicious.

If the rice is too wet, I turn the heat a little higher the next time. Mushy rice indicates the use of too much water; dry rice means there was not enough.

SERVING RICE

After the pressure has come down, I immediately remove the rice with a wooden rice paddle or wooden spoon and place in a large wooden bowl. If the rice is left in the pressure cooker, moisture will condense and cause the grains to expand, producing a wet and often tasteless dish. After putting rice in the wooden bowl, I cover the bowl with a bamboo sushi mat, which allows the rice to cool down slowly and permits air to circulate and moisture to escape. The bamboo also allows the rice to retain its essential warmth for an hour or more until it is served.

WARMING UP LEFTOVER RICE

Leftover rice will keep for several days. After the rice cools off, I transfer it to a closed container and store it in the refrigerator or in a cool, dark place. Warming up leftover rice is easy and quick. Simply place the rice in a small ceramic bowl or container and set inside a large pot. Add about ½-inch of water down the side of the pot, cover, and bring to a boil. Be careful not to get water in the bowl with the rice. This method is similar to a double boiler. After the rice has steamed for a few minutes, remove the bowl and serve. This method allows the rice to retain its sweetness and strength without becoming moist or soggy. Leftover rice may also be added directly to soups, sautéed with vegetables to make fried rice, or cooked in other ways.

OTHER VARIABLES

In addition to water, salt, fire, time, pressure, and heat, there are other factors to consider in the preparation of daily food. Celestial energies, the seasons, the climate, the weather, the vitality of the different ingredients, and our own physical and mental condition all subtly affect our cooking. In the macrobiotic kitchen, we learn to harmonize our inner and outer environments. A perfect bowl of rice reflects an enlightened heart and a peaceful, active household.

CHAPTER 6

BROWN RICE DISHES

Sunshine bathes the field.
Amid the rice stalks
A grasshopper's shadow.

—Meiko

In addition to basic pressure-cooked rice, there are a variety of brown rice dishes that I prepare for ordinary meals and special occasions. Please refer to the previous chapter for the discussion on preparing rice, including washing and soaking the grain, as well as the basic method of pressure-cooking, which is used in some of the recipes that follow.

Boiled Rice

If a pressure cooker is unavailable, the most suitable alternative is boiling. I use a cast-iron pot or ceramic vessel with a heavy lid. This extra weight on top helps to exert pressure and bring out the natural sweetness of the grain.

2 cups brown rice
2 cups spring water per cup of rice
Pinch of sea salt per cup of rice

Wash the rice and dry-roast it for several minutes in a stainless steel frying pan over low heat. Stir gently with a wooden rice paddle or spoon to prevent burning. Place the roasted rice in a pot. Add the water and salt and cover with a lid. Bring to a boil, lower the heat, and simmer for about 1 hour, or until all the water has been absorbed. Remove and serve.

Variation: For fluffier rice, put the rice in a casserole in the oven after boiling and bake at 200 to 250 degrees for about 1 hour.

Soft Rice

Soft rice is traditionally eaten for breakfast in Japan, China, and other Eastern countries. It is also taken to help relieve colds, fevers, and more serious conditions. When I was little, we had a proverb, "Prepare soft rice and serve with umeboshi," whenever anyone became sick. On rare occasions when mother was ill, my brothers and sisters and I would go to a secluded spot in the mountains and gather pure spring water for preparing this dish. We would prepare the soft rice in an earthenware pot, with plenty of this clear, clean water and a little sea salt, and heat it for a long time over low heat. Served with small slices of umeboshi (salty, pickled plums), the soft rice would nourish mother two or three times a day. After one or two days on this diet, the body's natural balance is usually restored and normal appetite and strength return.

Today, most Japanese have adopted a modern diet. Degenerative diseases and family troubles have been the unfortunate result. However, many people still eat soft rice and miso soup in the morning. I recently heard about a 109-year-old Buddhist monk who ate soft rice every day and was strong and active until he passed away.

1 cup brown rice
5 cups spring water
Pinch of sea salt

Wash the rice and pressure-cook or boil as in the basic recipes. Not all the water, however, will be absorbed. The rice should be creamy and some of the grains should still be visible after cooking. In case the water boils over while the rice is cooking, turn off the heat and allow the rice to cool off. Then turn on the heat again and continue to cook until done. Wait for the pressure to come down naturally, open the pressure cooker, and serve.

Variations: Soft rice may also be made by simmering overnight over very low heat for 5 to 8 hours. For this method, use 10 cups of water to 1 cup of rice. When making soft rice for babies or small children, be careful to omit salt or other seasoning. The juice on top of the rice from this dish is especially good for babies. Vegetables such as squash, daikon, or Chinese cabbage may be added while cooking. Also a 1-inch square of dried kombu is a nourishing source of minerals and may be included at the beginning of cooking. For variety, raisins, apricots, or other dried fruit may occasionally be added.

Miso Soft Rice

Leftover rice seasoned with miso makes another variety of delicious soft rice for the morning meal.

- 2 cups cooked brown rice
- 7 to 8 cups spring water
- 1 cup celery sliced on diagonal
- 1 6- to 8-inch strip of kombu, soaked and sliced or diced
- 4 shiitake mushrooms, soaked and sliced or diced
- Puréed barley miso
- Sliced scallions

Put the rice, water, celery, kombu, and shiitake in a pot. Bring to a boil, reduce the heat to low, and cover. Simmer for 1 hour or so, or pressure-cook for about 45 to 50 minutes. Season with puréed barley miso to taste and simmer for several minutes longer. Add the sliced scallions at the very end of the cooking time and serve hot.

Rice Cream

Like soft rice, brown rice cream makes a delicious morning cereal. It is also used medicinally and is especially recommended for persons who have difficulty swallowing or holding down food. Many cancer patients and others who have been unable to eat have been able to digest rice cream or soft rice and regain their strength and vitality.

- 1 cup brown rice
- 10 cups spring water
- Pinch of sea salt, or ⅓ umeboshi plum per cup of rice

Rinse the rice before cooking. Then, dry-roast the rice in a cast-iron or stainless steel frying pan over medium-low heat until it is golden brown and the grain releases a nutty fragrance. Transfer to a pot, add water and seasoning, and bring to a boil. Cover, lower the heat, and place a flame deflector beneath the pot. Cook about 1½ hours until half the water has evaporated. Let the rice cool and then put into medium cheesecloth or unbleached muslin. Tie the cheesecloth together to make a bag and squeeze the cream out of the pulp.

Heat the cream and then serve. Add more seasoning if needed.

The pulp is also very good to eat and can be made into a small ball and steamed with grated lotus root or carrot or mixed with whole wheat flour and deep-fried.

Variation: Garnish with scallions, chopped parsley, nori, gomashio, or roasted sunflower seeds. This dish may also be pressure-cooked starting with 5 cups of water.

Roasted Rice

When I was growing up, my favorite snack was roasted rice. In the middle of September, just before harvest, we would go to the fields and gather a small amount of raw rice. Then we roasted it with the husks still on in an earthenware pot. After roasting we took off the husks and ate the grain piping hot. Also, when traveling or taking long walks, we always carried roasted rice because it took only half as long to prepare as regular rice. Roasted rice is crispy, chewy, and delicious. Rice roasted right after picking is the food I miss the most in America. The nearest experience to eating rice straight from the field is eating just-picked corn from the garden. Each grain begins to lose some of its ripening energy as soon as it is picked. Prepared even a few hours later, the taste is very different. Once the basic roasting method is learned, a variety of appetizing grain and vegetable dishes can be prepared. This recipe is one of my favorites.

- ½ cup lotus seeds
- 2 cups brown rice
- ½ cup deep-fried cooked seitan cut into ½-inch cubes
- ½ cup quartered and sliced carrots
- ½ tablespoon minced scallion roots
- 3 cups spring water

Soak lotus seeds for 3 to 4 hours or overnight. Dry-roast the rice in a frying pan, gently stirring with a wooden paddle until golden brown and a nutty fragrance is released, about 10 to 15 minutes over low heat. Put the rice mixture and the remaining ingredients in a pressure cooker and mix well. Add the water and pressure-cook for 30 minutes. Usually no seasoning is added because the cooked seitan is prepared with tamari soy sauce. Remove the food from the pressure cooker and serve.

Variation: If the rice is not roasted, it may be soaked together with the lotus seeds.

Baked Rice

Prepared for variety, this dish has a lighter, fluffier grain.

- 1 cup brown rice
- 2½ cups spring water per cup of rice
- Pinch of sea salt per cup of rice

Wash the rice and then dry-roast it in a frying pan for a few minutes. Combine the rice, water, and salt in a pot and boil for 1 hour. Transfer the rice to a casserole dish and cover. Bake in a preheated 300-degree oven for about 1 hour. The rice should be light and moist, neither dry nor wet.

FRIED RICE

In our region of Japan, we didn't use much oil in cooking. Thus, we didn't make fried rice. After coming to New York and visiting Chinese restaurants, I started to experiment with this style of cooking. Fried rice is a wonderful way to use leftover rice, especially during the winter. Oil is constantly needed by the body in small amounts. For those in good health, fried rice may be eaten once or twice a week. You will see that both of the fried rice recipes call for chopped scallion roots as part of their ingredients. Scallion roots are the strongest part of the plant. They are very nutritious and should, therefore, never be discarded when you are chopping the vegetable. Here are two seasonal dishes.

Winter-Style Fried Rice

- 1 to 2 tablespoons dark sesame oil
- ½ cup diced or quartered celery
- 1 cup diced onion
- 1 tablespoon chopped scallion roots
- ½ cup carrots, quartered and sliced very thin, or cut into matchsticks
- ½ cup burdock, quartered and sliced very thin, or cut into matchsticks
- 1 to 2 tablespoons spring water, if the rice is dry
- 2 cups cooked brown rice
- Tamari soy sauce or sea salt
- 1 tablespoon chopped parsley or scallions and their roots

Oil and heat a frying pan; then make separate layers of the celery, onion, scallion roots, carrots, and burdock. Pour the water into the frying pan. Spoon the rice on top of the vegetables. Cover the pan and cook over low heat for 15 to 20 minutes, or until the vegetables are soft and the rice is warm. The heat should be low so the vegetables don't burn. Just before they are done, add tamari soy sauce or sea salt to taste, and the chopped parsley or scallions. Mix the rice and vegetables together. Cook for 2 to 3 minutes longer and serve.

Summer-Style Fried Rice

- 1 to 2 tablespoons dark sesame oil
- 1 cup crumbled tofu
- ½ cup diced onion
- 1 tablespoon chopped scallion roots
- 1 cup fresh corn kernels (scraped from 1 medium-sized ear of corn)
- 2 cups cooked brown rice
- 1 to 2 tablespoons tamari soy sauce or sea salt
- ½ cup chopped parsley or scallions
- Toasted nori strips

Heat a frying pan and add the oil. Add the tofu and scramble for 2 to 3 minutes. Add onion, scallion roots, corn, and rice. Cover, reduce the heat to low, and cook for 5 to 10 minutes, or until the vegetables and rice are hot. Add a little tamari soy sauce or sea salt. Cook a few minutes longer. Just before the dish is ready, add the chopped parsley or scallions. Mix the rice and vegetables well. Serve and garnish with toasted strips of nori. If you want to keep the parsley or scallions bright green, do not cook them with the rice; simply use them as a garnish.

Azuki Rice

Rice cooked with azuki beans is known as Red Rice. Traditionally in the Far East, red is the color of happiness, and these tiny red beans have always been considered lucky. We would prepare Red Rice for birthdays, graduations, and other joyful occasions. This dish is served during Shinto festivities on the first and fifteenth of every month, and it is especially delicious made with sweet rice. Medicinally, azuki beans are strengthening for the kidneys.

- ¾ cup azuki beans
- 2 cups spring water
- 3 cups brown rice
- Pinch of sea salt per cup of rice

Wash the azuki beans and boil them in about 2 cups of water for 10 to 15 minutes. The liquid should turn a beautiful red. Watch the beans carefully while they are boiling; if they are boiled too long, the color is lost. After boiling, let beans and liquid cool to lukewarm.

Wash the rice and put it in a pressure cooker. Add the beans to the rice. Add the water in which the beans boiled plus enough additional spring water to total 5 cups. Do not add the salt yet. Put the pressure cooker over low heat for 15 to 20 minutes. Add a pinch of salt per cup of rice. Turn the heat to high. Place the cover on the pressure cooker and bring to pressure. When the pressure is up, reduce the heat to medium-low. Put a flame deflector under the pressure cooker and cook the rice and beans for approximately 50 minutes. Remove the cover when the pressure is completely down. Let the rice sit for 5 minutes to loosen the rice on the bottom of the pot. Remove the rice and beans, place in a wooden bowl, and serve.

Variations: For a more digestible dish, soak the rice and beans together for 3 to 4 hours, or overnight, before cooking. Other dried beans and pulses, such as chick-peas, lentils, and kidney beans, may be cooked with rice in this way. However, the proportion of beans to rice is generally smaller, ⅛ to ⅓ cup of beans to 1 cup of rice. The amount of water is about the same, 1¼ to 1½ cups per cup of dry ingredients.

Black Soybean Rice

In some parts of Japan, black soybean rice is served on funeral days, probably because the color is associated with mourning. In other parts of the country, this dish is served on happy occasions. It makes a substantial and nutritious center of any meal.

- ½ cup black soybeans
- 2 cups brown rice
- 1¼ cups of spring water each per cup of rice and per cup of beans
- 2 teaspoons tamari soy sauce

Put the beans on a clean, damp towel and rub them to remove any dust. Do not wash the beans or the skins will come off. Dry-roast the soybeans in a frying pan for several minutes, stirring constantly to avoid burning. When the insides of the beans are slightly brown, they are roasted. Meanwhile, pick over the rice for any impurities and wash the rice. Mix the beans with the washed rice in a pressure cooker. Add the water and tamari soy sauce. Bring to a boil slowly, taking 15 to 20 minutes. Place the cover on the pressure cooker and turn on the heat. When the pressure is up, put a flame deflector under the pot, and pressure-cook for 50 minutes. When done, reduce the pressure and let sit for 5 minutes. Remove the rice and beans and serve.

❧ Gomoku (Five-Variety Rice) ❧

My mother always served this delicious rice dish on Christmas. Her gomoku included tiny red clams from a nearby lake. These clams were famous throughout the region and were considered a special treat.

- 2 cups brown rice
- 2 tablespoons diced dried lotus root
- 2 pieces diced dried tofu
- 6 medium diced shiitake mushrooms
- 2 tablespoons diced dried daikon
- 2 two-inch squares diced kombu
- 1 teaspoon finely minced scallion roots
- 1 large diced carrot
- ⅓ cup chopped seitan
- 1½ cups spring water per cup of roasted rice
- Chopped scallions or parsley for garnish

Dry-roast the rice in a frying pan, stirring gently about 10 to 15 minutes over a low heat. Soak the dried lotus root in warm water for 30 minutes. Soak the dried tofu for 10 minutes, the shiitake for 10 minutes, and the daikon and kombu for 5 minutes each. Dice these ingredients but do not mince. You will need ⅓ cup *each* of the lotus root, tofu, mushrooms, daikon, and kombu. Place roasted rice in a pressure cooker. Add all the other ingredients and mix well. Because seitan contains tamari soy sauce, additional seasoning is not needed in this recipe. (Add a pinch of sea salt per cup of rice if you do not use the seitan.) Pressure-cook for 45 to 50 minutes as for regular rice. Then remove the pot from the burner and let sit 5 minutes or longer. Reduce the pressure and remove the cover. Garnish with scallion or parsley and serve.

Variation: This dish may also be made with unroasted rice. In this case, first soak rice before cooking and use 1¼ cups of soaking water or spring water per cup of uncooked rice.

❧ Rice Salad ❧

While I was growing up, we occasionally had cold rice mixed with cooked vegetables in the summer. Chirashi sushi, as the dish was known, was made with green peas, carrots, and fried egg and had a delightful red, green, and yellow color. In America, I have come to enjoy Western-style rice salad, especially for dinner during the hot season. Here is one variety.

1 to 1½ cups quartered and thinly sliced carrots
2 cups broccoli flowerets and stems
½ cup chopped celery
3 cups cooked brown rice
2 cups cooked chick-peas
Lemon juice, about ¼ cup
1 teaspoon tamari soy sauce
Chopped parsley and lemon slices for garnish

Boil the vegetables for a short time. They should retain their crispness. Drain them and mix them with the rice and chick-peas. Sprinkle the lemon juice and tamari soy sauce over the ingredients. Mix again, garnish with parsley and lemon slices, and serve.

Variations: Other vegetables may be added or substituted, including lotus root, burdock, and pickled seitan. Tiny shrimp also go well with this dish, if desired. Instead of lemon juice, dressings can be made of 1 tablespoon sweet rice vinegar and 1 teaspoon of tamari soy sauce, or 1 tablespoon ume vinegar (or the diluted juice of 2 whole umeboshi plums), or ½ teaspoon freshly grated and squeezed gingerroot juice.

SUSHI

Sushi is now famous throughout the world. The most popular style consists of rice rolled with vegetables, fish, or pickles, wrapped in nori, and sliced into rounds. However, this is only one of four main ways to prepare this dish. In Japan, sushi is customarily served at meetings or on holidays and special occasions. These include the Ancestors Festival on August 15.

Maki-Sushi

Maki-sushi is the familiar rolled sushi. Popular varieties include nori-maki, consisting of lightly boiled carrots, scallion, and egg; kappa-maki, cucumber; and tekka-maki, raw tuna. The basic method is as follows:

1 sheet nori
1 to 2 cups cooked brown rice
1 carrot
Pinch of sea salt
2 or 3 whole scallion greens
⅛ teaspoon umeboshi paste

Toast the sheet of nori over low heat for a few seconds until it turns green. Place the nori on a flat bamboo sushi mat. Rinse your hands with water to prevent the rice from sticking and spread the rice evenly over the nori. Leave uncovered about ½ to 1 inch along the top end of the nori and from ⅛ to ¼ inch at the bottom.

Slice a carrot into long strips about ¼-inch thick. Boil the carrot strips with a pinch of salt for 2 to 3 minutes. Remove when the carrots are crisp and let cool. Cut the scallion greens into 8- to 10-inch strips and blanch in boiling water a few seconds. Place the carrot and scallion greens lengthwise about ½ to 1 inch from the bottom of the sheet of nori. Purée the umeboshi lightly and spread it along the entire length of the vegetables.

Roll the sushi mat up, pressing firmly against the rice. Make sure the vegetables are in the center of the roll. Vegetables too far to the side indicate placing them too far from the bottom edge of the nori and rice before rolling. Wet the edge of the nori slightly to seal the rolled up sushi.

To cut, moisten a sharp knife and slice the sushi roll into ½- to 1-inch-thick rounds. The knife should be moistened before each slice. The nori may tear or the rice stick to the knife if the blade is not sharp and wet.

After slicing, arrange the rounds on a platter or serving bowl. The cut side with rice and vegetables should be facing up.

Variation: Other good combinations include cucumber and umeboshi and seitan cut in long thin slices with parsley or watercress (either fresh or boiled). Mixing in sweet rice (about 10 to 30 percent) with regular brown rice makes a sushi that holds together very nicely. Instead of rice, cooked buckwheat noodles may be used as a bed. Simply lay flat in long rows and prepare as above.

Nigiri Sushi

Nigiri means "clasping" and sushi prepared in this style is made by placing vegetables or seafood on top of small balls of cooked rice and tying together with strips of nori. Sashimi, or raw fish, such as snapper, tuna, or octopus, is often prepared in this way. My favorites are boiled broccoli and seitan. The nori is cut into long thin strips with scissors. When served, the nori appears vertically around the rice and topping.

Chirashi Sushi

Chirashi sushi is much like Western rice salad. Vegetables are boiled separately, including carrots cut in matchsticks or cubes, green peas lightly cooked to retain their bright color, and corn on the cob, which is cut off the cob after boiling. Combine the vegetables with cooked brown rice and a pinch of sea salt and marinate with a little brown rice vinegar. If desired, a touch of maple syrup may be added for a sweet taste. Also, sweet rice may be used with or instead of regular rice. Mix the vegetables and rice together and serve like tossed salad.

Garnish with very thinly sliced scallions and nori. Scallops and shrimp may be added to this dish, if desired.

Kitsune Sushi

Kitsune means "fox" and according to legend, foxes love fried tofu. Fox-style sushi is made by deep-frying tofu that is 1½ to 2 inches square. After deep-frying, cover the tofu with water and boil with a touch of tamari soy sauce for 5 to 10 minutes. Cut the tofu in half diagonally to obtain two triangular pieces. Use a spoon to scoop out the soft inner part of the tofu from the base of the triangle. Stuff the hollowed out tofu with rice salad or rice mixed with brown rice vinegar. Serve on end so the peak of the triangle is up.

RICE BALLS

Rice balls are one of the most basic, easy-to-make, and satisfying foods. You can eat them with your hands; they are a meal in themselves, convenient for traveling, and a perfect dish for any occasion.

In the Japanese countryside, rice balls are prepared for everyone in the fields during planting and harvest. At these times, farmers spend all day hard at work and cannot afford to take off much time for lunch. Neighbors join together on these occasions, as many hands make light work. A cooking area is set up near the fields, and many mothers and daughters gather to prepare rice balls for the whole community. A girl who can make a rice ball quickly and without wasting a single grain is thought of as a very good prospective daughter-in-law. Much matchmaking goes on at these times. By lunchtime, hundreds of rice balls are piled up neatly on trays or in lacquer boxes for the hungry workers in the fields. In our dirty clothing, we would all relax on the banks of the paddies, eat lunch together, and have a happy time.

When I was a child we took rice balls along during hikes in the mountains. Each of us wrapped five or six of them in a large bamboo leaf and tied them up with a scarf which we slung over our shoulder. At the start of the journey, the weight was a little heavy. At the end, only the scarf was left. We also used bamboo leaves to fashion cups to drink from when we came to mountain springs.

In this country, I associate rice balls with the founding of Erewhon. When we first came to Boston in 1965, we rented a tiny shop on Newbury Street. One half of the shop was stocked with miso, umeboshi plums, tamari soy sauce, and other high-quality natural foods. In the other half, Michio began giving lectures. On Thursdays, I always made rice balls and gave them to Michio's students, who numbered only five or six at the beginning. This was the way we started macrobiotics in Boston.

Today, rice balls have become very popular among macrobiotic people all over the world. Children take them to school for lunch. Parents take them to work. Celebrities take them to banquets. For picnics or traveling, rice balls make a tasty, convenient meal. They keep fresh for a few days without refrigeration and there is no need for plates or utensils to eat them. They leave no residue so there is nothing to clean up. They are energizing, balanced, and tasty. They can be made with a variety of ingredients, including leftovers, and come in many shapes, sizes, and textures. Rice balls are truly ecological fare, the macrobiotic alternative to fast food.

Basic Rice Balls

- 1 sheet nori
- 1 cup cooked brown rice
- ½ to 1 umeboshi plum

Toast a thin sheet of nori by holding the shiny side about 10 to 12 inches over a low flame. Rotate for 3 to 5 seconds, or until the color changes from black to green. Fold the nori in half and tear it into two pieces. Fold and tear again. There should now be four pieces, 3 inches square. Add a pinch of salt to a dish of water and use it to wet your hands. Form a handful of rice into a solid ball. Press a hole in the center with your thumb and place a small piece of umeboshi inside. Then close the hole and press the ball together again until it is solid. Cover the rice ball with nori, one piece at a time, until it sticks. Dampen your hands occasionally to prevent the rice and nori from sticking to them but do not use too much water.

Variations: Rice can be made into triangles instead of balls by cupping your hands into a V-shape. Balls or triangles can be rolled in toasted sesame seeds and eaten without nori. Small pieces of salt or bran pickles, vegetables, pickled fish, or other condiments can be inserted inside instead of the umeboshi. Instead of nori sheets around the outside, use roasted crushed sesame seeds, shiso leaves, pickled rice leaves, dried wakame sheets, or the leaves of a green leafy vegetable.

Rice with Other Grains

Brown rice blends well with other grains and this is an excellent way to include them in the meal. Barley pressure-cooked with rice is especially light, and I enjoy combining them in hot weather. Fresh corn kernels (scraped off the cob) mixed with rice also makes a refreshing late summer or early autumn meal. Millet cooked with rice is also tasty but slightly dry. Adding more water or preparing a sauce to serve over the millet makes this dish more appetizing. Wheat berries with rice are a delicious way to prepare wheat in its whole form. By itself, wheat is difficult to digest; with rice it is chewy and satisfying. Rye, too, is rarely cooked alone and goes well with rice, barley, or oats.

The usual proportion for cooking rice with other grains is 3 parts rice to 1 part other grain, a pinch of sea salt per cup of grain, and 1¼ to 1½ cups of spring water per cup of combined grain.

The following recipe combines rice, wheat berries, and chick-peas and may be followed for other combinations.

½ cup dried chick-peas
¼ cup dried wheat berries
2 cups brown rice
1¼ cups of spring water per cup of grains and beans combined
Pinch of sea salt per cup of grain and beans combined

Wash the chick-peas and wheat berries separately and soak them individually overnight. The next day, discard soaking water. Wash the rice and put it in a pressure-cooker. Add the chick-peas and wheat berries to the rice and mix thoroughly. Add the water. Do not cover or add salt yet. Put the pot over low heat for 15 to 20 minutes. Then add the seasoning and put the cover on the pressure cooker. Turn the heat to high and bring up to pressure. When pressure is up, reduce the heat to medium-low and put a flame deflector under the pot. Pressure-cook for 50 minutes. Reduce the pressure as for plain rice, remove the cover, and let sit for 4 to 5 minutes. Remove the cooked grains and beans and transfer to a wooden bowl for serving.

Brown Rice with Corn on the Cob

2 cups brown rice
1 cup fresh corn kernels (scraped from 2 medium-sized ears of corn)
1¼ to 1½ cups spring water per cup of rice
Pinch of sea salt per cup of rice

Wash the rice and put it in a pressure cooker. Add the corn and water. Mix well. Do not add the salt yet. Pressure-cook, following the directions for plain brown rice (page 51).

RICE WITH SEEDS, NUTS, AND OTHER INGREDIENTS

I am especially fond of rice cooked with lotus seeds. These are large, cream-colored, and look somewhat like chick-peas. They have a mild taste and give a chewy texture to a dish. Be sure they are thoroughly soaked so they are properly softened.

Almonds and walnut pieces go well with rice, as do shiso leaves, the salty pickled leaves with which umeboshi plums are aged. Bancha twig tea may occasionally be substituted for spring water. It gives a strong soothing flavor.

Brown Rice and Lotus Seeds

- 2 cups brown rice
- ½ cup lotus seeds, soaked for 3 to 4 hours
- 1¼ to 1½ cups spring water per cup of combined grain
- Pinch of sea salt per cup of rice

Wash the rice and put it in a pressure cooker. Add the soaked lotus seeds and water. Put the pot over low heat for 15 to 20 minutes. Add the sea salt and turn the heat to high. Put the cover on the pressure cooker and bring to pressure. Cook in the same way as for plain brown rice (page 51).

Brown Rice with Almonds

- ½ cup almonds
- 2 cups brown rice
- 1¼ to 1½ cups of water per cup of rice
- Pinch of sea salt per cup of rice
- Parsley sprig or chopped chives for garnish

Put the almonds in a small amount of water and boil them for 2 to 3 minutes. Remove and drain. Remove the skins and put the almonds in a pressure cooker. Wash the rice and add it to the pot with the almonds. Mix the rice and almonds together so the nuts are evenly distributed. Add the water and put the pot over low heat for 15 to 20 minutes. Add the sea salt and cover the pot. Bring to pressure and cook as for plain brown rice (page 51) for about 50 minutes. Before serving, garnish with a sprig of parsley or a few chopped chives.

Variation: Walnut pieces may be substituted for the almonds, but they don't need to be parboiled or skinned.

Brown Rice with Shiso Leaves

2 cups brown rice
1¼ to 1½ cups spring water per cup of rice
Pinch of sea salt per cup of rice
¼ cup finely minced shiso leaves

Wash the rice. Pressure-cook the rice in the regular way. When the rice is done, remove it and put it in a wooden bowl. Mix in the finely minced shiso leaves so they are evenly distributed through the rice.

Brown Rice and Bancha Tea

2 cups brown rice
1¼ to 1½ cups cooled bancha tea per cup of rice
1 teaspoon tamari soy sauce
Pinch of sea salt per cup of rice
Chopped scallions, parsley, or other greens for garnish

Wash the rice and put it in a pressure cooker. Add the bancha tea. Put the pot over low heat for 15 to 20 minutes. Add the tamari soy sauce and sea salt. Cover and bring to pressure. Cook in the regular way, serve, and garnish, if desired, with chopped scallions, parsley sprigs or any other greens.

Spanish Paella

I normally don't enjoy rice cooked with animal food. On a recent visit to Spain, some friends took Michio and me to a restaurant in Barcelona. They ordered paella, a traditional Spanish rice casserole which can be made with seafood. The paella came with shrimp, clams, and several small fish, and we were both pleasantly surprised at its delicious taste. A little red saffron powder was used to take away the smell of the fish. The following is a basic vegetarian paella.

1 medium-sized carrot
2 cups dry-roasted brown rice
½ cup cooked seitan, cut into 1-inch chunks
½ cup lotus seeds, soaked
½ cup deep-fried tempeh or tofu
2 tablespoons finely chopped scallion roots
3⅓ cups spring water
Fresh ginger juice
Chopped parsley or scallions for garnish

Slice the carrots into chunks using the rolling method of cutting in which the chunks are the same size but different shapes. Put all ingredients into a pressure cooker and mix well. After the pressure is up, cook for 30 minutes. As the rice is already roasted, longer cooking time under pressure is not necessary. Bring the pressure down and remove the cover.

Remove the rice to a wooden bowl and mix in a little fresh ginger juice. Garnish with chopped parsley or scallions and serve.

SWEET RICE AND MOCHI

Sweet rice is more glutinous than regular rice and is eaten plain, combined with other grains, or made into mochi, amasake, sake, or other special foods and beverages. I occasionally add a small amount of sweet rice to regular short-grain rice for our daily meals.

Mochi is sweet rice served in cakes or squares. They are made by first pounding cooked sweet rice with a heavy wooden pestle, fashioning the rice into smaller units, and allowing them to dry. In Japan, mochi is eaten throughout the month of January in celebration of the new year. When I was teaching, my pupils would return to class after the holidays with gifts of mochi for their teacher. Their presents consisted of 5 to 10 tasty sweet rice cakes wrapped up in gaily colored paper. We would all sample the mochi at a school party, and each student's mochi would have a slightly different taste and texture.

Similarly, each region in Japan has its own way of preparing mochi. Some prefer mochi in clear soup. Others make it with seafood or sweeten it with rice syrup to make a snack or dessert. In Tokyo, pan-frying or baking mochi with tamari soy sauce and ginger was popular. My family's style was very simple. We usually ate it with nori, a little bonito fish flakes, a bit of daikon radish, and scallions. Another favorite of mine was *sakura mochi*. This is a soft sweet rice patty wrapped in cherry blossom leaves, similar to the way stuffed grape leaves are made in Greece.

Mochi is also customarily eaten during holidays. On January 4, the Buddhist monks festival, we made mochi with *kinako*, or yellow soy flour, and everyone refrained from eating any animal food on this day.

On January 15, the Pine Tree Festival is observed. Much as is done here at Christmas, families select a small pine tree which they place outside instead of inside their house. We would build bonfires in the snow and cook mochi on long sticks like toasting marshmallows in the West.

On May 3, Girls' Day, mochi is prepared with mugwort and white rice. This is called Green Mochi because of the distinctive hue produced by this herb. We also made Red Mochi on this day by adding dry, red-colored saffron to sweet rice.

On May 5, Boys' Day, we combined mochi with rice flour to make special dumplings. We wrapped these patties very attractively in bamboo leaves. After steaming and boiling the dumplings, we dipped them either in juice from grated ginger and tamari soy sauce or in rice syrup or barley malt for a sweet taste.

July 7 is the evening of the Star Festival, celebrating the annual reunion of two mythological lovers in the Milky Way. On this night we set up a special table under the stars and set out mochi, dumplings, origami (folded color paper designs), small bamboo cups, and a small circle of animals fashioned from garden vegetables. We made these birds and mammals from cucumbers, yellow squash, and eggplant and used chopsticks for their legs. After offering prayers before this table, we shared the food in honor of this celestial event.

On August 15, Ancestors Festival, we served sweet rice plain or in dumplings using kinako soy flour. Regular mochi is too heavy to eat at this time of year.

Sweet Rice

1 cup sweet rice
1 cup spring water per cup of rice
Pinch of sea salt per cup of rice

Wash the rice and put it in a pressure cooker. Add the water and salt and cook following basic brown rice recipe (page 51).

Mochi

Mochi is growing in popularity in the United States and Canada and is available in frozen form in selected natural foods stores. It is also very easy to prepare at home. Either way, it can be stored in the refrigerator, taken out, sliced as needed, and heated up in a few minutes.

2 cups sweet brown rice
1 to 1¼ cups spring water per cup of rice
Pinch of sea salt per cup of rice

Wash the sweet rice and soak preferably several hours or overnight. Pressure-cook following basic brown rice recipe (page 51). When done, pound the rice in a wooden bowl with a heavy pestle or mallet until all the grains are crushed and sticky and the texture is smooth. Wet the pestle occasionally to prevent the rice from sticking to it. Good mochi takes 30 minutes or more of pounding.

Form the rice into small balls, cakes, or squares or spread in one large rectangular piece, about ½ to 1 inch thick, on an oiled or floured baking sheet. Allow to dry for 1 to 2 days. Store covered in the refrigerator or keep in a cool, dry room.

To serve, cut into bite-sized pieces. Roast the pieces in a dry skillet for about 5 minutes on each side. The cakes or squares will puff up when done and may be slightly browned on the outside.

Mochi may also be steamed, baked, sautéed in oil, deep-fried, or added to soups and stews. Mochi may be eaten plain or served with a variety of toppings, including tamari soy sauce or rice syrup.

❧ Ohagi ❧

Ohagi are balls of lightly pounded sweet rice coated with nuts, seeds, or purēed beans or vegetables. *Ohagi* are simpler to prepare than mochi. They make a delicious snack, attractive picnic fare, or delectable party treat.

2 cups sweet rice
1¼ cups spring water per cup of rice
Pinch of sea salt per cup of rice

Prepare the rice as in the pressure-cooked basic brown rice recipe on page 51. Pound after cooking as in making mochi above, but only until the grains are half broken. This takes about 20 minutes or more. Form the dough into small balls and roll in various coatings. My favorites include ground sesame seeds, ground roasted walnuts, azuki beans with a little rice syrup, purēed chestnuts, kinako soy flour, and squash purēe. Arrange the different rice balls attractively on a tray or platter and serve.

❧ Sweet Rice Dumplings ❧

2 cups sweet rice flour
1 cup boiling spring water

Put the flour in a mixing bowl. Add the water and mix. Knead for about 5 minutes; then shape the dumplings into any form you wish, keeping the thickness at about ½ inch. Drop into boiling water. When the dumplings rise to the surface they are done. Serve with clear soup, miso soup, or coat like ohagi with kinako or other toppings.

❧ Sweet Rice with Chestnuts ❧

I have wonderful memories from my childhood of going into the mountains in the autumn and picking fresh chestnuts. Like other girls and boys around the world, we delighted in roasting them over the fire, shelling them, and eating them hot. Chestnuts are very sweet and blend well with rice. They can also be used in making desserts. Dried chestnuts are available year-round.

2 cups sweet rice
½ cup dried chestnuts
1¼ to 1½ cups spring water per cup of rice
Pinch of sea salt per cup of rice

Wash the rice. Wash the dried chestnuts after sorting out any discolored ones. Dry-roast the chestnuts in a frying pan over low heat for several minutes, stirring and moving the chestnuts around constantly to roast them evenly and to prevent them from burning. Combine the rice and chestnuts in a pressure cooker and cook as for basic brown rice (page 000).

Variation: Instead of roasting, the dried chestnuts may be soaked overnight to soften them and make them more digestible. Fresh chestnuts may also be used. Shell after roasting. Azuki beans make a nice addition to this basic recipe. Simply cook ½ cup azuki beans in water for about 20 minutes or soak the beans overnight. Combine with the rice and chestnuts and cook as above.

Wild Rice

In New York, I discovered wild rice and really enjoyed its fluffiness and natural flavor. At the time there was no organic brown rice available, and this traditional hand-picked grain of the native people here was deeply appreciated. When cooked, wild rice has an almost floury consistency. I like it alone or in combination with brown rice (about ⅓ cup wild rice to 1 cup brown rice). Wild rice is nice in summertime in a salad with corn, green peas, and cucumber. The following is a basic recipe.

2 cups wild rice
2 cups spring water per cup of wild rice
Pinch of sea salt per cup of wild rice
Drop of sesame oil (optional)

Dry-roast the wild rice in a frying pan for about 5 minutes, or until it browns and gives off a nice aroma. Put the rice in a pot with the water, salt, and a drop of sesame oil for flavor, if desired. Turn heat to high and then lower when the mixture comes to a boil. Simmer for 45 minutes. Take off the heat, scoop the rice into a wooden bowl, and serve.

Variation: Wild rice may also be pressure-cooked using 1½ cups of water instead of 2 cups. Follow the regular method of pressure-cooking, but cook for only 30 minutes after the pressure is up as the grain is very light to begin with. Wild rice may also be combined with brown rice. Use ⅓ cup of wild rice per cup of brown rice.

CHAPTER 7

WHOLE GRAINS

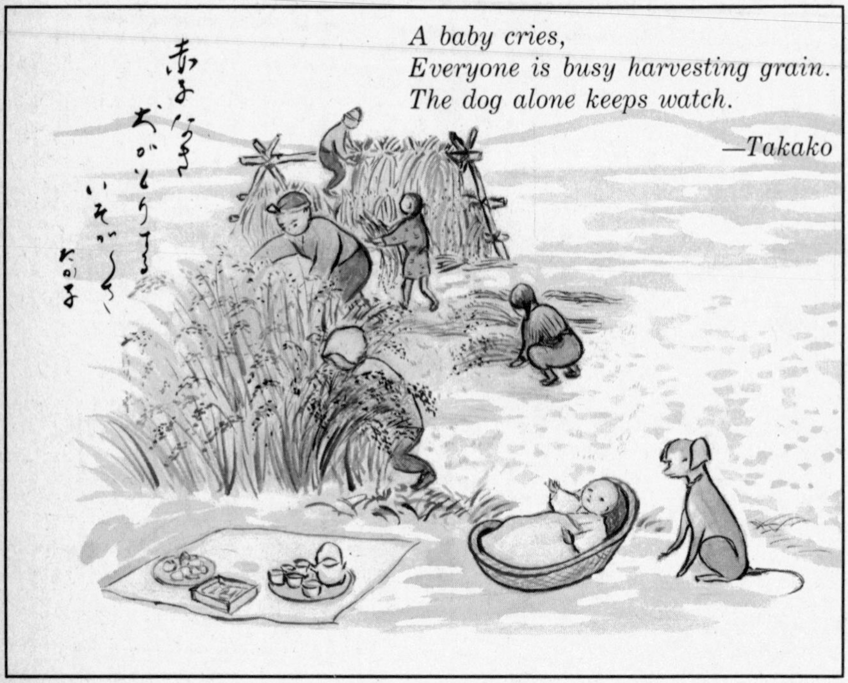

A baby cries,
Everyone is busy harvesting grain.
The dog alone keeps watch.

—Takako

Whole cereal grains make up from fifty to sixty percent of the macrobiotic diet by volume and are the center of every meal. Each grain has its own personality, and the natural foods cook soon becomes familiar with its special qualities, uses, and effects. Grains supply the body with a steady, even source of energy. For proper digestion, they are eaten whole. In the last two chapters, we discussed how to prepare brown rice. In this chapter we will cover barley, millet, oats, wheat, rye, buckwheat, and corn. There are also wild grasses and regional grains, such as amaranth, that can be eaten daily and prepared in a variety of ways.

Flour products and naturally processed grains make up a second category of food prepared from whole grains. These include seitan, fu, noodles, pasta, bread, crackers, and baked products—all of which will be discussed in subsequent chapters—and cracked wheat, bulghur, rolled oats, Scotch oats, corn grits, rye flakes, couscous, and other forms of grain that have been milled, mechanically cut, or partially refined. I occasionally prepare these flour and cracked grain products for variety or enjoyment. Unlike whole grains, their natural energy has been diminished by processing, so I use them only occasionally and as complements to grain in whole form at the meal.

The third and most fragmented category of grains includes white flour, polished rice, and other grain products that have been refined, bleached, or artificially preserved and enriched. White bread, for instance, has been stripped of the bran, the outermost protective layer of fiber, and the germ, the innermost kernel from which the wheat stalk sprouts and the root descends. These foods are lifeless and are avoided in the macrobiotic kitchen.

BARLEY

Barley is one of the world's oldest grains and has been cultivated for thousands of years in both the East and West. It was the staple of Egypt under the pharaohs, ancient Greece and Rome, the Holy Land during Bible days, and Tibet. Barley is chewy, extremely easy to digest, and nourishing. Hippocrates, the Father of Western Medicine, recommended barley soup to restore health and vitality and modified its strength according to the specific illness. Jesus distributed whole meal barley bread at the Sermon on the Mountain and at the Last Supper.

In the Far East, pearl barley is traditionally eaten to dissolve excess protein and fat from animal food consumption and to clean up blemishes on the skin. This smaller, whiter, more compact variety of barley is available in some natural foods stores and, like wild rice, is relatively expensive. *Pearl* barley is not to be confused with *pearled* barley, a milled form of the grain from which most of the vitamins and minerals have been removed. For ordinary, everyday use, *hulled* barley is recommended and is the barley most commonly stocked in natural foods stores.

By itself, barley is somewhat bland in taste and is usually added to soups, stews, or casseroles or cooked with rice or other grains. Its chewiness enhances the texture of dishes and produces a light, cooling effect, especially during the summer and warmer months. Barley can also be added to vegetable dishes, used as a stuffing for squashes or cabbages, and added in whole form to bread, muffins, and other baked goods. Toasted barley is ground into flour to make hearty bread and pastries. When roasted with the hulls and boiled in water, barley makes a delicious tea, which, in Japan, we call *mugi cha*.

Pressure-Cooked Barley

2 cups barley
1¼ to 1½ cups spring water per cup of barley
Pinch of sea salt per cup of barley

Wash the barley and, if time permits, soak it for 4 to 8 hours. Put the barley in a pressure cooker, add the water, and cook the same as for basic brown rice (page 51).

Variation: Barley can also be boiled using 2 cups of water to 1 cup of grain. Leftover barley can be fried like rice with scallions, mushrooms, and other vegetables and is especially crispy.

Soft Barley

This dish makes an appetizing morning cereal.

1 cup barley
4 to 5 cups spring water
Pinch of sea salt
Chopped scallions, parsley, nori squares, or *gomashio* for garnish

Combine all the ingredients in a pot and boil for 1¼ to 1½ hours. Garnish as desired and serve hot.

Barley and Brown Rice

1 cup barley, soaked
2 cups brown rice
1¼ to 1½ cups spring water per cup of grain
Pinch of sea salt per cup of grain

Soak the barley for several hours. Wash the rice. Put the grains in a pressure cooker and cook the same as for basic brown rice (page 51).

MILLET

Millet is eaten across northern regions of China, Korea, and Japan and in some parts of Europe and Africa. There are many varieties. Those grown in the United States and Canada are primarily yellow in color. Millet's small grains are round and compact but fluff up when cooked, producing a light, attractive dish. Because it grows in colder northern climates, millet is very warming to the body and most beneficial consumed in late summer or autumn. Millet can be eaten plain, though it is somewhat dry, so is usually topped with a gravy, sauce, or served mixed with lentils or with azuki beans. Millet may also be added to soups, stews, salads, breads, used in stuffings and croquettes, or pounded and shaped into loaves or cakes and baked. Medicinally, millet is good for stomach, spleen, and pancreatic conditions. To bring out its delicious, nutty flavor when preparing millet, I sometimes dry-roast the grain in a frying pan for about 5 minutes, or until it is slightly golden. Millet is also enjoyable unroasted.

Boiled Millet

2 cups millet
2½ cups boiling water per cup of millet
Pinch of sea salt per cup of millet

Wash the millet. Lightly dry-roast in a frying pan and stir quickly but gently to prevent burning. When the aroma is released, add the boiling water and salt. Bring to a boil again, cover, lower the heat, and simmer for 30 to 35 minutes.

Variation: Roast the millet with a little sesame oil or sauté onions for 3 to 5 minutes over low heat. Then add the millet and sauté for another 3 to 5 minutes. Add the boiling water and cook as above.

Note: By itself, millet is often not pressure-cooked because of its light consistency. However, for a softer, well-cooked dish, it may be pressure-cooked for about 35 minutes. Mixed in small proportions with other grains, such as rice, barley, or oats, millet may be cooked under pressure, and it goes well, cooked under pressure, with hard squash.

Soft Millet

This makes a nice creamy breakfast cereal.

1 cup millet
4 cups boiling spring water
Pinch of sea salt per cup of millet
Chopped scallions, parsley, toasted nori, or *gomashio* for garnish

Cook as in the basic boiled millet recipe above but do not dry-roast the millet. Garnish as desired.

Baked Millet with Squash

This is a delicious, naturally sweet dish for autumn or winter. Its deep yellow color and firm texture make for a satisfying main course.

- 2 cups millet
- 2 cups diced winter squash
- 1½ to 1¾ cups spring water per cup of millet
- Pinch of sea salt per cup of millet

Wash the millet and dry-roast in a frying pan until golden. Wash and dice the squash. Put the millet and squash into a pressure cooker. Add the water and sea salt. Cover and bring to pressure. Pressure-cook over a flame deflector for 15 to 20 minutes. Remove the pot from the heat and let the pressure come down. Transfer the pressure-cooked ingredients to a covered baking dish and bake in a preheated 350-degree oven for 30 to 40 minutes. When done, the millet and squash should be firm like corn bread. Cut into squares and serve hot.

Pressure-Cooked Millet Gomoku

- 2 cups millet
- Kernels from 2 to 3 ears fresh sweet corn
- ½ cup diced carrots
- ¼ cup diced burdock
- ½ cup diced celery
- ½ cup diced onions
- ½ cup diced cooked seitan
- 3 cups spring water
- Chopped parsley for garnish

Wash the millet. Dry-roast millet in a frying pan for a few minutes until it is golden brown. Put the millet and vegetables in a pressure cooker. Add water. (Salt is not necessary as there is tamari soy sauce in the cooked *seitan.*) Cover the pressure cooker and place over medium-high heat. Bring up to pressure. When the pressure is up, reduce the heat to medium-low and put a flame deflector under the pot. Cook for 15 minutes. Remove the pot from heat and let the pressure come down naturally. Remove the cover and transfer the millet and vegetables to a bowl. Garnish with chopped parsley and serve.

Variation: Scallops or shrimps may be added to this dish, as well as a little grated fresh ginger.

OATS

Oats spread across northern Europe with the Roman legions and are the staple grain in Ireland, Scotland, and northern England. They are grown as supplemental food in other parts of the world. In Japan we called oat husks *karasamugi* or "crow's wheat" because their distinctive shape resembles a crow.

Oats have more fat than other grains and produce a warming energy. They cook up soft and are a popular morning cereal among hardworking people. The stamina they provide contributed to the spirit of the American frontier.

In the natural foods store, oats come in three forms: whole oats from which only the outer husks have been removed; Scotch oats that have been steamed and steel-cut into pieces; and rolled oats that have been steamed and passed through rollers. Whole oats are creamy and delicious and preferred for everyday use, even though they take longer to prepare. Scotch oats are usually dry-roasted before cooking and very chewy but have less vitality than whole oats because they have been mechanically split. Rolled oats, the common oatmeal eaten today, are very soothing and tasty and, like Scotch oats, may be used occasionally as a change of pace. The instant oatmeal sold in supermarkets should be avoided. Aside from morning cereal, oats can be added to soups, stews, breads, or vegetable-grain dishes. Oat flour is especially sweet and keeps fresher longer than whole wheat. Oats make excellent cookies, puddings, and pastries.

Whole Oatmeal

1 cup whole oats
5 to 6 cups spring water
Pinch of sea salt per cup of oats

Wash the oats, soak for several hours or overnight, put them in a pot. Then add the water and salt, cover, and bring to a boil. Reduce the heat and simmer over low heat for several hours, or overnight until water is absorbed. Use a flame deflector to prevent burning. Dulse flakes make a nice garnish.

Variation: Cooking time can be reduced by pressure-cooking instead of boiling. Follow the basic brown rice recipe (page 51).

Scotch Oats

1 cup Scotch oats
3 cups spring water
Pinch of sea salt per cup of oats
Chopped scallions, parsley, toasted nori, and sunflower or sesame seeds for garnish

Wash the oats and dry-roast them in a frying pan for 5 to 10 minutes, stirring to prevent them from burning. In a separate pot, bring the water to a boil and add the roasted oats and salt. Bring back to a boil, reduce the heat to low, cover the pot, and put a flame deflector beneath the pot. Simmer for 20 to 30 minutes, or until the water is absorbed. Garnish as desired.

Rolled Oats

1 cup rolled oats
Pinch of sea salt per cup of oats
3 cups boiling spring water
Dulse, sesame seeds, or gomashio for garnish

Add the oats and salt to the pot of boiling water, return to a boil, then reduce the heat, and cover. Insert a flame deflector under the pot and simmer for 20 to 30 minutes, or until the oats are creamy. Garnish with dulse, sesame seeds, or gomashio.

Variation: For a sweet taste, add a small handful of raisins or currants to the oats and cook as above.

WHEAT

Wheat is native to Europe, Asia, and the Middle East. In antiquity, it was scarcer than barley and other grains and used on holidays or special occasions, except by the wealthy who could afford to eat it every day. Today, wheat is cultivated around the world and has surpassed rice as the chief cereal crop. In whole form, wheat is hard and needs to be chewed well. We always soak it, and after soaking it becomes soft and sweet. It also takes longer to cook than other whole grains. Bulghur, cracked wheat, and other partially processed forms are more digestible and easier to prepare. In flour form, wheat is consumed as pasta, noodles, breads, and bread products.

Wheat is classified according to its protein content and season of growth. *Hard wheat* contains higher levels of gluten (cereal protein) than soft wheat and is grown primarily for making bread. *Soft wheat* contains more carbohydrate and is used for making pastries or mixing with harder flours. *Spring wheat* refers to grain planted in the spring and harvested in the autumn and may be either hard or soft. Similarly, *winter wheat* is sown in the fall, sprouts beneath the snow in winter, and is reaped in spring. One type of spring wheat is *pastry wheat* which is low in gluten and used for making pastry and crackers. Another type of wheat is called *durum.* It is low in gluten and is used for making noodles and pasta. Wheat is also identified by its color, such as red, white, silver, or gold.

Although I occasionally make bulghur, couscous, or other cracked wheat dishes, I prefer to cook wheat in its whole form. Combined with brown rice or azuki beans, whole wheat berries are especially delicious and chewy. Whenever anyone asks me to recommend a form of exercise, I tell them to chew cooked whole wheat berries. Chewing stimulates all the muscles of the body and gives power to the intestines, as well as alkalizing the complex carbohydrates in the grain for proper digestion. According to the *Yellow Emperor's Classic of Internal Medicine*, the ancient medical text of China, wheat is good for relieving liver conditions.

Whole Wheat Berries

2 cups wheat berries
1¼ to 1½ cups spring water per cup of wheat berries
Pinch of sea salt per cup of wheat berries

Wash the wheat berries and cook following basic brown rice recipe (page 51) or boiled rice (page 54). Wheat will usually take longer to cook than rice. Soaking the berries for 3 to 5 hours before cooking reduces the cooking time and makes a softer, more digestible dish.

Variation: Combine 1 part wheat berries and 3 parts brown rice or other grain. Another tasty combination is 3 parts wheat berries and 1 part azuki beans.

Bulghur

Bulghur is whole wheat that has been partially boiled, dried, and ground. It is popular in Greece, the Balkan countries, North Africa, and the Middle East. In the summer, bulghur makes a fluffy grain for salads or sandwich fillings and creates a light feeling.

1 cup bulghur
2 to 2½ cups of boiling spring water
Pinch of sea salt per cup of bulghur
Chopped parsley for garnish

Put the bulghur in a pot and add the boiling water and sea salt. Bring to a boil, cover, reduce the heat to low, and simmer for 15 to 20 minutes. Garnish with chopped parsley.

Variation: Bulghur is often cooked together with vegetables. A tasty combination is 1 small diced onion, ½ cup diced carrots, and ¼ cup diced celery. Cook the vegetables together with the bulghur and mix them when cooked.

Couscous

Couscous is another popular Middle Eastern dish. It is made from wheat that has been refined and cracked but not bleached. Because it loses nutritional value in processing, couscous should be used very sparingly. I use it for an occasional summer salad and for a delicious light cake.

1 cup couscous
Pinch of sea salt

Place the couscous in a steamer, add a pinch of salt, cover, and steam for 5 to 10 minutes.

RYE

Rye is a staple of Scandinavia and other northern regions of Europe and Asia. Like wheat, it is rarely consumed in whole form: It is used primarily as flour to make rye bread, crackers, or other baked products. Rye also is used to make whiskey. Since its texture is on the hard side, rye requires thorough chewing and is good exercise for the whole body. In Boston, I have experimented cooking whole rye with brown rice or with root vegetables and found it very delicious.

Basic Rye

2 cups rye
1¼ to 1½ cups spring water per cup of rye
Pinch of sea salt per cup of rye

Cook in the same way as for basic pressure-cooked brown rice (page 51) or boil with 2 cups of water.

Variation: For a chewier brown rice, add 1 part rye to 3 parts rice. Rye may also be dry-roasted in a frying pan for a few minutes prior to cooking to make it more digestible. Soaking for several hours or overnight also softens this grain.

Rye and Vegetables

2 cups rye
5 cups spring water
1 cup diced carrots
1 medium-sized onion, peeled and diced
1 ear fresh corn
Sea salt
1 bunch parsley or watercress
1 umeboshi plum
1 tablespoon grated gingerroot (optional)

Wash the rye and dry-roast it in a frying pan for about 5 minutes. Put the roasted rye in a pressure cooker, add 2 cups of water, and pressure-cook for 45 minutes. Boil the carrots, onion, and corn on the cob for 1 minute with 2 pinches of sea salt to bring out their natural sweetness. Dip the parsley or watercress into a saucepan of boiling water for 1 minute, but do not add salt or these greens will become more bitter. Drain and chop the parsley or watercress. Scrape the kernels from the corn cob and add them to the rye in the pressure cooker. Add the onions and carrots, and place the greens on top. Dissolve the sliced umeboshi in a little water and add it to the grain and vegetables. Grated gingerroot may also be added for flavoring. Mix well and serve as a salad in a large bowl.

BUCKWHEAT

Buckwheat is the traditional staple in Siberia, Manchuria, Russia, Poland, and other parts of Europe and Central Asia. Its kernels are called groats, and it is eaten in whole form or in coarse or fine granules, which are roasted and called *kasha*. In Japan, buckwheat has been eaten for centuries in the form of noodles called *soba*.

In Japan, buckwheat grew on the mountainsides in my region, and I recall its distinctive triangular-shaped kernels, beautiful white flowers, red stalks, and green leaves swaying in the breeze. Since it flourishes in nearly any soil, among rocks, and in cold climates, buckwheat is the hardiest of the cereal grasses. It is extremely warming to the body and provides reservoirs of energy and stamina in the winter and cold weather. George Ohsawa once advised me, "If you want a studious child, don't give him buckwheat." Prior to the birth of one of my children, I remember craving the rich, deep taste of buckwheat. This child turned out to be very active like the dashing and dancing Cossacks whose staple is this hardy grain.

In the natural foods store, buckwheat is sold in roasted and unroasted varieties. The roasted type needs only 3 to 5 minutes further roasting, while the unroasted variety takes about 10 minutes. I select whole groats over cracked groats, but if only granules are available I prefer the coarser variety to the finer one. At home I especially enjoy cooking buckwheat in gomoku-style with 5 to 6 vegetables, such as celery, burdock, green peas, and onions with kombu and shiitake. Buckwheat is also used in traditional Jewish cooking to make knishes and *kasha varnitchkes* and can be added to soups, cooked with other grains, and milled into flour for rich-tasting pancakes and muffins.

Medicinally, buckwheat helps eliminate excess water from the body. It is especially warming in the autumn and winter. However, in the summer it may be enjoyed in salads with fresh celery, onions, or other vegetables together with boiled fresh corn kernels. Because of its strengthening qualities, we limit how much we give to children, who usually already have a surplus of energy.

❧ Kasha ❧

1 cup buckwheat groats
2 cups boiling spring water
Pinch of sea salt per cup of buckwheat
Chopped scallions or parsley for garnish

Wash the buckwheat and dry-roast it in a frying pan for several minutes. Put the grain in a pot and add the boiling water and salt. Bring to a boil, lower the heat, and simmer for 20 to 30 minutes, or until the water has been absorbed. Garnish with chopped scallions or parsley and serve.

Variation: Cook the buckwheat with sautéed cabbage and carrots or with raw onion and chopped parsley.

❧ Creamy Buckwheat Cereal ❧

A hardy cereal for cold winter mornings.

1 cup buckwheat groats
5 cups cold spring water
Pinch of sea salt per cup of buckwheat
Chopped scallions, parsley, toasted nori, or roasted sesame seeds for garnish

Wash and dry-roast the buckwheat. (For a creamy cereal, do not roast.) Put the buckwheat in a pot and add the cold water and sea salt. Bring to a boil, cover, and reduce the heat to low. Simmer over a flame deflector for about 30 minutes. Garnish as desired and serve hot.

Buckwheat Salad

1 cup buckwheat groats
2 cups spring water plus the juice from the sauerkraut
Pinch of sea salt
2 tablespoons finely chopped parsley
1 cup steamed, chopped kale
1 cup chopped, drained sauerkraut

Wash the buckwheat and dry-roast it for several minutes in a frying pan. Bring the water and the drained sauerkraut juice to a boil. Add the buckwheat and salt to the boiling liquid. Cover and cook for 20 minutes.

Sauté finely chopped parsley in a very small amount of water. Mix the parsley with the buckwheat. Mix in the steamed, chopped kale and chopped sauerkraut. Add the dressing below.

Variation: Add 4 ounces of sautéed or fried tempeh for an even richer taste and texture.

Dressing

¼ cup tamari soy sauce
1 teaspoon squeezed gingerroot juice

Pour the dressing over buckwheat salad and mix in. Transfer to a salad bowl and serve.

Creamy Buckwheat Dumplings

1 cup buckwheat flour
2 cups cold spring water
Pinch of sea salt
Dark or light sesame oil
Grated fresh ginger, chopped scallions, and toasted nori for garnish

Mix the buckwheat flour, cold water, and salt together to make a light batter. Heat the sesame oil (1½ to 2 inches in depth) in a deep-fat fryer and add the batter by tablespoons to the hot oil. Be careful not to crowd pan. Deep-fry until puffed and crispy and the dumplings rise to the surface. Remove the dumplings with a slotted spoon and drain them on paper towels. Serve, garnished with ginger, scallions, and nori.

Quick Buckwheat Dish

In Japan we call this dish *Sobagaki.* It is enjoyed on brisk winter mornings and after returning from the cold outdoors.

2 cups buckwheat flour
1 cup boiling spring water per cup of buckwheat flour
Pinch of sea salt per cup of buckwheat flour
Dashi
Grated fresh ginger, chopped scallions, and toasted nori for garnish

Dry-roast the buckwheat flour in a frying pan for a few minutes. Pour the boiling water over the flour and mix for 2 to 3 minutes, or until the water is completely absorbed. Add the salt. Serve with dashi and garnish as desired.

CORN

The hybrid corn available today is very different in quality from native Indian corn. Traditional open-pollinated or standard varieties of corn were smaller (often only a few inches long), more compact, and hardier than the commercial, artificially developed strains that make up 99 percent of the corn grown in the United States today. Indian corn also grew in a variety of colors: red, blue, white, and yellow. In macrobiotic cooking, we usually prepare corn as a vegetable side dish rather than as the central grain of the meal. However, open-pollinated varieties of corn are starting to make a comeback. Seeds for backyard planting are now available from several organic seed companies, and true, robust Indian corn may once again become a staple on this continent in the future.

There are five basic types of corn: *sweet corn*, the kind most commonly eaten today; *dent corn*, the whole yellow corn with indented crowns available in natural foods stores and the corn from which most cornmeal is made; *flour corn*, a starchy variety favored in Latin American cooking; *flint corn*, another field corn high in starch used in Latin cuisine; and *popcorn*, the movie theater staple akin to ancient wild and early domesticated corn.

When I was a child, we used to grow corn around the edge of the garden and like the Indians we prepared it by soaking the dried kernels in water and adding wood ash. The wood ash (from hardwood, not paper or other printed or pulpy material) helps to soften the hulls and contributes calcium and other alkaline nutrients to the grain.

In America, fresh corn from the field is the native food I enjoy the most. It is a wonderful summer treat, and I like to prepare it baked or boiled.

In Latin America, corn is still the staple grain, and there are many wonderful dishes made from whole corn along with beans, squash, and sea vegetables. In Venezuela several years ago, I was first introduced to *arepas*, oval cakes made from white corn dough, and they reminded me of mochi, the pounded sweet rice cakes we make in Japan.

Aside from whole corn preparations, such as arepas or tortillas, corn is milled into flour or cornmeal and can be baked into muffins, cakes, and bread. Medicinally, corn is good for strengthening the heart and circulatory system. The Indians also went on corn fasts for spiritual development. Corn husks can be saved for adding a sweet taste to soup stock. Corn silk, the golden strands inside the husk, can be dried and steeped in hot water to brew a tea that is good for strengthening the kidneys.

Whole Corn

2 cups whole dried corn kernels, preferably dent corn
4 cups spring water
1 cup sifted wood ash
Pinch of sea salt

Soak the corn overnight. Put the corn kernels in a pressure cooker. Add the wood ash and 2 cups of water. Cover, turn the heat to high, and bring up to pressure. When the pressure is up, reduce the heat to medium-low. Put a flame deflector under the pot and pressure-cook for 1 hour. Remove from the heat and allow the pressure to come down naturally. When the pressure is completely down, remove the cover, and transfer the corn to a strainer or colander. Rinse all the wood ashes thoroughly from the corn. Put the corn into a clean pressure cooker and add the sea salt and the remaining 2 cups of water. Pressure-cook again for 1 hour. When cooked, remove from the heat, and transfer to a serving bowl. Use in soups, vegetable dishes, or salads.

Baked Corn on the Cob

This traditional method of baking the corn in its husk makes for a sweeter and more delicious corn on the cob than either boiling or steaming.

Put 4 to 8 ears of fresh corn, in their husks, on a baking sheet and bake in a preheated 350-degree oven for 30 minutes. The silk and husks will retain the corn's natural juices during baking. When done, remove the husks and silk and serve hot.

Instead of butter, margarine, salt, or pepper, we use umeboshi plums to season corn. Simply purée 1 or 2 pickled plums in a suribachi with a little water or a little corn oil, if desired, or use ready-made umeboshi paste, and apply lightly to the corn. The umeboshi gives a salty taste. It is strong, so don't use too much.

Basic Corn Dough

Dough made from dry whole corn kernels taken from corn on the cob is the basis for tortillas, arepas, empanadas, and other traditional

Indian corn dishes. In Spanish corn dough is called *masa*. Flour, flint, or cracked corn available from Latin American markets is recommended for this preparation. Leftover dough will keep for about a week in the refrigerator. As it ages, the dough begins to sour and lends itself for use in making corn doughnuts and other naturally sweetened foods. If pink or red spots appear, the dough has spoiled. I learned the basic method for making corn dough and some of the following recipes from Anna Troconis and Maritza Rojas, two macrobiotic friends from Venezuela who have taught traditional cooking with corn at the Kushi Institute. The basic recipe will yield about 1½ to 2 pounds of corn dough.

- 4 cups whole dry corn kernels
- 1 cup sifted wood ash tied in a muslin bag
- 8 to 10 cups spring water

Put the corn, ashes, and water in a pot and pressure-cook for 20 minutes. Drain the water after cooking and wash corn thoroughly to remove any residue from the wood ash. Use at least four changes of water. The loosened skins of the corn should float off in the rinsing water. If they don't, add more ash and cook for 10 to 15 minutes longer.

After rinsing off the wood ash, return the corn to the cooker. Add fresh water to cover and pressure-cook for 50 to 60 minutes longer.

Remove the corn from the cooker and let cool completely. Grind the corn in a hand grinder (do not use a blender) and knead for 10 to 15 minutes by hand. Add water for consistency and sea salt to taste. Use in one of the following recipes.

Arepas

These delicious corn dough balls are the traditional staple in many parts of Latin America and are eaten instead of wheat bread. They can be made plain or stuffed with a variety of ingredients.

- 1½ pounds corn dough
- ¼ teaspoon sea salt
- Spring water
- Sesame oil, preferably dark

Crumble the dough and add the salt. Knead with a small amount of water until soft and the consistency of bread dough. If you use too much liquid, add more dough or let it dry for a few minutes in the open air. Form the dough into 6 to 8 fist-sized balls. Brush a cast-iron frying pan with dark sesame oil. Flatten the arepas into ovals. Cook for 2 to 3 minutes on each side, or until a crust forms. Then bake in a preheated 350-degree oven for 20 minutes, or until the arepas begin to puff up. They are done when they make a hollow, popping sound when tapped.

Variations: Arepas can also be made without baking by pan-frying for 10 minutes in a covered frying pan over a low heat. Then uncover, turn up the heat, and cook for an additional 15 minutes. For variety, try adding 2 cups of sesame seeds or chopped sautéed vegetables to the dough and knead thoroughly. Fancier arepas can also be made by serving with a tofu, tempeh, or miso-tahini spread.

Tacos and Tostadas

Tortillas, the thin flat corn cakes, are the staple of Mexican cooking. They are used to make tacos, which are folded tortillas filled with beans and trimmings, and tostadas, which are flat tortillas. This recipe makes 10 to 12 tortillas.

2 pounds corn dough
Sea salt
Spring water
Corn oil for deep-frying

Crumble the dough and knead it for a few minutes, adding a small amount of water for consistency and salt to taste. Moisten your hands and use a wet square of cotton fabric to help mold the dough. Form the dough into balls and then flatten them into thin circles about 5 inches across. Deep-fry both sides in oil for 1 to 2 minutes by twirling with two forks. Lay on paper towels to drain off any excess oil and keep warm in a slow oven until served.

The Mexicans traditionally eat tacos and tostadas with black beans or pinto beans. Cook 1½ to 2 cups of dried beans following the basic recipe on page 257–258 and then mash in a pot or suribachi, adding a little water if necessary. The beans should be on the moist side. In addition to beans, good fillings include pickled tofu, seitan, or rice with vegetables. Garnishes of shredded lettuce, diced onions, chopped *arame* or *hiziki* can be added. The hot sauces and relishes used in Central America are not appropriate to our temperate climate and are best avoided. For a pungent taste, chopped scallions or a ginger sauce will do nicely.

Empanadas

Empanadas are similar to tacos and tostadas except that the filling is inserted into the tortillas before they are deep-fried. Simply place the beans or other ingredients on the circular dough, fold over, and press the edges together with your fingers or a fork. Deep-fry each side for about 4 to 5 minutes and drain on paper towels.

Bollos Polones

These stuffed corn balls are boiled. They are especially good for those whose intake of oil is restricted.

- 2 pounds corn dough
- ¼ teaspoon sea salt
- 8 cups spring water
- Parsley or chopped scallions for garnish

Moisten your hands and knead the dough for a few minutes, adding the salt and a little water to moisten. Form into 10 to 12 fist-sized balls. Make a hole in the middle of each ball and insert the filling (such as beans, *seitan*, vegetables, or fish). Close the hole, using more dough if necessary, turning ball clockwise with your thumb in the middle. Bring the water to a boil in a large pot. Put the balls in and cook for 20 minutes. Garnish with parsley or chopped scallions. Serve with a miso sauce, a carrot sauce, or other topping.

Polenta

Polenta is popular in Italy and southern Europe as well as Latin America.

- 1 6-inch piece kombu
- 1 carrot, diced
- 1 onion, peeled and diced
- 1½ cups dried kidney beans
- 8 ounces seitan (optional)
- 4½ cups spring water
- Tamari soy sauce to taste
- 14 fresh ears of corn on the cob
- ½ teaspoon sea salt, if no seitan is used

Put the kombu, vegetables, and beans in a pressure cooker. Add the water and salt and cook under pressure for 45 minutes, or until the consistency is thick. Add tamari soy sauce to taste. Scrape the kernels from the corn and grind them in a hand mill (not a blender). Make a layer of half the corn in an oiled baking dish; then cover with a layer of bean and vegetable mixture. Cover with remaining corn. Bake in a preheated 350-degree oven for 1 to 1¼ hours.

CHAPTER 8

NOODLES AND PASTA

Rotating the mill stones,
I grind flour
With my mother.

—*Yoshie*

Noodles are delicious, offer endless variety, and are more digestible than flour prepared in baked form. In Japan, noodles are a way of life. There are restaurants that serve only noodles. Some serve only *soba*, the hardy buckwheat noodles that have been enjoyed in the Far East for centuries. These restaurants are called *sobaya* or *soba* houses. Others serve only *udon*, or whole wheat noodles, and are called *udonaya*. Vendors sell homemade noodles from pushcarts on the street corners, and some of them play flutes to attract customers.

Today, most noodles and pasta in the East and West are made with refined flour, chemical preservatives, and other artificial ingredients and are produced by automated machinery. In the United States, the

Food and Drug Administration has ruled that most products sold as noodles must contain eggs. Traditional Oriental noodles are exempt from this classification. During the last two decades, the international macrobiotic movement has made available high-quality noodles and pasta made from whole cereal grains. These products are suitable for regular use and include *soba, udon,* and other noodles imported from Japan and a variety of whole wheat spaghetti noodles, elbows, shells, spirals, and other Western-style pasta.

A TRADITIONAL NEW YEAR'S EVE

In my mind, soba is always associated with New Year's Eve. When I was growing up, it was the custom for children to help their parents prepare noodles from freshly milled buckwheat flour, a small amount of whole wheat flour, sea salt, and cold mountain water. The preparations would start early in the morning, when we began to knead the dough beneath small newly made straw tatami mats. We would do this with our feet, much like stepping on grapes to prepare wine. We had a saying in the countryside, "Noodles and maidens improve with kneading."

After the dough was soft, we rolled it out on a large wooden cutting table that was about three feet square. The rolling sticks were about 1 inch thick and made a clicking sound. Whenever we heard this sound we always knew someone was making noodles. After rolling and pressing, the dough was cut into thin strips with a heavy rectangular knife. Expert noodle-makers made very thin dough like pizza and fine, narrow noodles. We were not so skilled and often made thick, obi-style noodles named after the wide sash traditionally worn around the waist by the Japanese.

After being cut into long lengths, the noodles were placed in a large kettle to cook over a strong wood fire. If the fire wasn't strong enough, the soba got mushy, and if there wasn't enough water, the noodles would turn into dumplings. By contrast, mochi, made by cooking pounded sweet rice, required a very gentle low flame. The different applications of heat gave rise to another common saying, "When boiling soba, we ask the devil to make fire, but when cooking mochi we ask an angel."

When the noodles were boiled, we added a touch of icy cold water from the mountain springs to the kettle to stop the boiling completely. When the water boiled again, we added more cold water. By the start of the fourth boil, the soba was perfectly cooked. The cold water made the noodles crispy and chewy and lighter in texture. This is called the "shocking" method and can be duplicated in a modern kitchen over gas heat. In this way we made 25 to 50 pounds of soba on the cold, frosty last day of December. After cooling off, the noodles were washed and stacked by handfuls in large bamboo storage boxes.

At midnight the temple bell in our village pealed 108 times to welcome in the new year. At this late hour, traditional families throughout Japan celebrated the happy occasion with delicious homemade soba. It was served rewarmed in a hot broth or cold with a strong sauce on the side. On New Year's morning we feasted on mochi, which had also been prepared in large quantities during the waning days of the previous year. Thus, buckwheat and sweet rice, the strongest and sweetest of the grains, were made side by side—a perfect example of balancing different energies, harmonizing yin and yang, unifying devil and angel.

FAMILIES OF NOODLES

Soba comes in many varieties and is classified according to its percentage of buckwheat flour. Forty percent soba includes forty percent buckwheat and sixty percent whole wheat. Fifty percent soba is made up of equal amounts of both flours. Either one of these sobas is fine for regular use. The soba we prepared in Japan on New Year's Eve was about seventy to eighty percent buckwheat. One hundred percent soba is the strongest, most expensive, and a superior food for very cold weather or strenuous activity. Another strong variety is *jinenjo soba*, mixed with flour from the long Japanese mountain potato. For summertime, light thin *ito soba* is good with a cold broth.

Udon is the second major family of Japanese noodles; it is made with whole wheat flour and sometimes a small amount of unbleached or sifted white flour. Udon noodles are wider and thicker than soba and because they are less energizing they are enjoyed more in the warmer months. Both types of noodles may be eaten year-round. The method for making udon is similar to that of soba.

Other Far Eastern noodles include *somen*, slender whole wheat noodles about half as thick as udon; *saifun*, clear cellophane noodles made from mung bean threads and used in making sukiyaki; *maifun*, rice flour noodles; *ramen*, either udon or soba that has been deep-fried; and various green noodles made with flour combined with mugwort, artichoke, or green tea.

Soba is traditionally served in one of six ways.

1. *Kama-age* is soba that is "picked up from the pot." Without rinsing them under cold water, the noodles are served hot along with some of the broth they are cooked in. Soba broth by itself is called *soba yu*. This broth is often served in Japan instead of tea and is a nice thick beverage.

2. *Zaru-soba* is soba prepared in individual bamboo baskets or strainers. The noodles are first cooked all together in a large pot; then the noodles are put into small baskets that are dipped in boiling water for a minute or two to reheat them. Individual bowls of broth are prepared for the noodles to be dipped into or for pouring over the noodles at the table.

3. *Kake-soba* is "swimming" soba, reheated and served in a broth that is different from the liquid it was originally cooked in.

4. *Yaki-soba* is fried soba, cooked and served with tofu, onions, carrots, celery, or other vegetables.

5. *Churashi sushi soba* is chilled soba served salad-style with such vegetable combinations as fresh corn kernels, green peas, carrots and cucumbers or with celery, sauerkraut, and scallions.

6. *Nori-maki soba* is soba prepared with vegetables or seafood, wrapped in nori, and served sushi-style in sliced rounds.

Both soba and udon create warm energy. Udon is generally topped with a rich sauce that contains a variety of items, while soba is often enjoyed with only a simple broth. This is another example of natural balance in the traditional kitchen. Light soba broths include kombu stock, shiitake mushroom stock, or a combination of the two. For a stronger flavor, dried daikon, onions and carrots, or bonito fish flakes may be added to one of these basic broths. Combining carrots, onions, shiitake mushrooms, and dried daikon, and sometimes fried tofu, produces a richer stew-like sauce that goes especially well with udon. A kuzu sauce is often enjoyed with fried noodles.

Garnishes are very important on top of noodles. Simple ones include toasted nori, sliced scallions, roasted sesame seeds, or a drop of dark sesame oil. Japanese also traditionally put dried mixed condiments over noodles on occasion, including *gomi*, *sichimi*, and *etomi*. *Mi* means taste. *Go* means five, *shichi* means seven, and *eto* means nine. These numbers refer to the number of ingredients in the condiment. There is also a medicinal condiment called *yakumi*. These condiments often include dried hot pepper and have a sharp taste. They give balance to a meal, but we must be very careful to use them only occasionally and very sparingly.

Please learn the basic techniques for cooking noodles and in moderation enjoy this versatile food. Oriental noodles already contain salt so no additional seasoning needs to be added during cooking.

Noodles and Broth

Noodles

6 to 8 cups spring water
1 8-ounce package soba or udon noodles

Broth

1 piece kombu, 2 to 3 inches long
4 cups spring water
2 dried shiitake mushrooms
2 to 3 tablespoons tamari soy sauce
Chopped scallions, chives, or toasted nori for garnish

Bring the cooking water to a boil. Add the noodles and return to a boil. After about 10 minutes check to see if they are done by breaking the end of one noodle. Buckwheat cooks faster than whole wheat and thinner noodles faster than thicker. For buckwheat, you can use the shocking method. If the inside and outside are the same color, the noodles are ready. If even a tiny bit of the inside is a different shade, the noodles need to cook longer. When done, remove the noodles from pot, drain, and rinse thoroughly with cold water to stop them from cooking and to prevent clumping. The noodle cooking water can be saved for soup stock and for adding to flour to make bread.

To make the broth, put the kombu in a pot and add fresh water. Soak the shiitake mushrooms, cut off and discard their stems, and slice the mushrooms. Add them to the pot. Bring to boil, lower the heat, and simmer for 3 to 5 minutes. Remove the kombu and shiitake and save them for other dishes. Add tamari soy sauce to taste to the pot and cook for 3 to 5 minutes. Put the cooked noodles into the broth to warm them, but do not let them boil. When hot, remove the noodles and serve immediately with a little broth. Garnish with scallions, chives, or toasted nori.

Variations: A little grated fresh ginger may be added to the broth. The kombu and shiitake may be left in the broth and served with the noodles if desired. Dried daikon, carrots and onions, or bonito fish flakes also make good additions. The noodles are also customarily enjoyed with cooked seitan, fu, tofu, natto, or tempeh.

❧ Fried Noodles ❧

4 cups spring water
1 8-ounce package soba or udon noodles
1 tablespoon dark sesame oil
2 cups shredded cabbage
1 to 2 tablespoons tamari soy sauce
½ cup sliced scallions

Boil the noodles as in the previous recipe, rinse them under cold water, and drain. Oil the frying pan and add the cabbage. Put the cooked noodles on top of the cabbage, cover the pan, and cook over low heat for 5 to 7 minutes, or until the noodles are warm. Add the tamari soy sauce and mix the noodles and vegetables well. Do not stir the ingredients together until this time; they should be left to cook peacefully until the very end. Cook for several minutes longer and add the scallions at the very end. Serve hot or cold.

Variations: Many combinations of vegetables may be used, including carrots and onions, scallions and mushrooms, and cabbage and tofu. Hard root vegetables take longer to cook and they should be sautéed in the oiled frying pan before the noodles are added. Add the soft vegetables just before sprinkling on the tamari soy sauce.

Soba with Jinenjo

Pieces of this long mountain potato make an especially strengthening bowl of soba in the winter.

- 1 8-ounce package of soba noodles
- 5 to 6 cups broth
- 1 cup grated jinenjo
- Chopped scallions for garnish

Cook the noodles and the broth as in the basic noodle recipe. Warm the noodles in the broth for a few minutes. Put 1 tablespoon of grated jinenjo on each individual serving on top of the noodles and broth. Garnish with scallions and serve hot.

Cold Somen Noodles

These thin white noodles often come packaged in five individually tied bundles. One bundle makes 3 small bowls of noodles. Somen take less time to cook than soba or udon because they are slender. Be careful not to overcook the noodles or they will become soggy. This dish is a favorite in the summertime.

- 3 bundles, or 8 ounces somen noodles
- 3 cups broth, chilled
- Grated fresh ginger, toasted nori, or sliced scallions for garnish

Prepare noodles and broth as in the basic recipe above. Refrigerate the broth or chill it with ice cubes. Ladle the broth into individual serving bowls and add a little grated fresh ginger, toasted nori, or sliced scallions as a garnish if desired. Serve the noodles and broth separately.

Variations: Another method is to place ice cubes in a large serving dish and set the cooked somen on top of them. After the noodles have chilled, serve in small individual bowls with broth and garnish or set the serving dish with the noodles and ice on the table and let everyone serve themselves. Soba and udon can also be served chilled in this way. Instead of broth, a dip can be made. Each serving should be served separately and include 1 tablespoon tamari soy sauce, 1 tablespoon mirin, and 4 tablespoons *kombu* stock.

❧ Spaghetti ❧

Whenever I visit Italy, I enjoy the wonderful taste and texture of spaghetti, even though its quality has changed lately. The original whole grain pasta of Italy, including Sicily, has long since given way to refined flour pasta and a cuisine based on tomatoes, peppers, eggplants, and other foods of tropical origin that came into southern Europe following the exploration of South America. The deep orange carrot sauce below is better suited to our temperate environment than tomato sauce. It is so delicious that many of our friends do not even notice the difference. Tamari soy sauce and other macrobiotic condiments can also be enjoyed with pasta. When traveling to Florence, Rome, or even a local Italian restaurant, I bring along a small supply.

Unlike Oriental noodles, Western-style pasta is made with little seasoning, so always be sure to add a pinch of sea salt to the cooking water.

- 1 quart spring water
- 8 ounces whole wheat spaghetti
- Pinch of sea salt

Boil the water and add the noodles and salt. Bring the water back to a boil, lower the heat to medium, and cook for about 10 minutes, or until done. Rinse the noodles under cold water to stop further cooking and to prevent clumping.

❧ Basic Spaghetti Sauce ❧

- 1 small beet, including greens
- 4 to 5 carrots
- 1 green pepper
- 4 celery stalks
- Dark sesame oil
- 4 chopped onions
- 2 tablespoons miso

Chop the beet greens and dice the beets. Slice the carrots, green pepper, and celery. Pressure-cook together for 20 minutes or boil for 45 minutes. Sauté the onions in a little sesame oil in a frying pan until the onion is translucent. Then add to the other vegetables. Mash all vegetables in a suribachi or use a food mill or blender. Add the diluted miso (rice miso is nice for this dish) and simmer for 5 minutes. Taste to see if you have enough miso. Serve over whole wheat spaghetti or other pasta.

Variations: For Italian spaghetti, add a pinch of dried oregano and a pinch of dried basil. Sautéed mushrooms and/or *seitan* chunks may be added for a richer sauce. Cooked tofu cubes give the taste and appearance of cheese to this dish. Up to 2 tablespoons of tahini may be added to make a creamier sauce.

❧ Baked Lasagne with Tofu ❧

- 1 teaspoon dark sesame oil
- ½ cup shelled fresh green peas
- Kernels from 1 ear of fresh corn
- ½ cup peeled and diced onion
- 1 pound tofu
- 1 teaspoon tamari soy sauce
- 12 whole wheat lasagne noodles, 8 to 10 inches long

Sauté the peas, corn, and onion in the sesame oil in a frying pan for about 5 minutes, or until almost tender. Mash tofu in a suribachi or bowl and add to the vegetables. Sprinkle the tamari soy sauce over the ingredients, mix well, and cook for 1 to 2 minutes longer. Cook the noodles separately in a large pot, following the basic noodle recipe, page 94. Rinse and drain. Place a layer of cooked lasagne on the bottom of a baking dish. Alternate layers of vegetables and tofu with layers of noodles, ending with a layer of noodles. Cover baking dish and bake for 20 to 25 minutes in a preheated 350-degree oven. When done, the noodles should be crunchy around the edges. Remove and serve with the light carrot sauce in the previous recipe or a mild kuzu-tamari sauce.

Variations: Use other vegetables, seitan, or tempeh for layering with the noodles. Large whole wheat shells or spirals may be used instead of lasagne.

CHAPTER 9

SEITAN AND FU

After a golden harvest,
Winter wheat gives
A beautiful green.

—Yoshiko

Seitan is a whole wheat product cooked in a broth of *kombu*, tamari soy sauce, and water. It has a rich, dynamic taste and lends itself to a variety of dishes ranging from cutlets to soups, salads, and layered casseroles. Similar in taste and texture to meat, seitan was developed by Zen Buddhist cooks in China and Japan and used instead of chicken and pork. Made from separating the starch and bran from the gluten (cereal protein) in whole wheat flour, seitan is also known as wheat gluten or wheat meat. In this country, wheat meat patties have become very popular served as grainburgers and make an ideal substitute for hamburger or other animal food entrées. In Europe, wheat gluten often forms a part of the traditional diet and is usually made with a little oil.

High in protein, seitan creates strength and vitality and is quite filling. It can be made at home with whole wheat flour from hard spring or hard red winter wheat, although spring wheat has a softer texture and is often preferred. Although part of the traditional tempura cuisine of Japan, seitan was not used much in the countryside where I grew up, and I really first started making it in the United States. Now it's a regular part of our diet, and we have it in our household two or three times a week. Because it is cooked in a tamari soy sauce broth, seitan doesn't need additional seasoning. For variety, however, a little grated fresh ginger can be added. On holidays and for parties, I occasionally add fresh mint or other herbs to enhance its flavor.

Wheat meat is also available precooked in many natural foods stores, usually in 8- or 16-ounce packages. At the store I always check the ingredients, avoiding packaged seitan that does not use high-quality natural tamari soy sauce or that contains garlic or strong spices. To prepare, simply warm up the ready-made seitan for 5 to 10 minutes by pan-frying, steaming, boiling, or baking. Seitan will keep fresh for about a week in a closed container in the refrigerator.

In the following recipes calling for *cooked* seitan, either homemade or store-bought wheat meat can be used. Those specifying *uncooked* seitan call for homemade gluten dough that has not been boiled with kombu and tamari soy sauce. Making seitan at home takes less than half an hour and makes for a fresher dish than using the store-bought variety.

Homemade Seitan

- 3½ pounds organic whole wheat flour
- 8 to 9 cups warm spring water
- ¼ to ⅓ cup tamari soy sauce
- 1 teaspoon grated fresh ginger (optional)

Put the flour in a large bowl and gently add the warm water. Stir with your hand until the consistency resembles oatmeal or cookie batter. Knead for 3 to 5 minutes, or until flour is mixed thoroughly with water.

Ideally, the mixture should now sit for 2 to 3 hours or overnight. The longer it sits, the less stiff it becomes and the easier to separate the starch and the protein. However, a faster method is to cover the dough with warm water after the initial kneading and let sit for a minimum of 5 to 10 minutes. Knead again in the soaking water for 1 minute. Pour off the cloudy water and save.

Put the glutinous mixture in a large strainer and put strainer inside a large bowl or pot. Pour over cold water to cover and knead the gluten in the strainer. The starch and bran (reddish outer coating) of the wheat will wash out while you are kneading. (It is customary to save the first rinse water containing the starch and bran. See below.) Repeat the rinsing and kneading process in the strainer and pot until all the starch and bran are washed off. Alternate between cold and hot water when rinsing and kneading the gluten. Always start and finish with cold water to contract the gluten. The gluten should form a sticky mass after two or three cycles.

Separate the gluten into 5 or 6 pieces and form them into balls. Drop the balls into 6 cups of boiling water and boil for 5 minutes, or until the balls float to the surface. Use chopsticks to loosen the balls if they stick to the bottom of the pot. Remove the balls from the pot and let them cool for a few minutes. Add a 3-inch piece of kombu to the boiling water, return gluten balls to the pot, add the tamari soy sauce and, if desired, 1 teaspoon grated fresh ginger. Bring to a boil, lower the heat and cook for 45 to 60 minutes. Serve hot, or use in one of the recipes below. Leftover seitan may be stored in a closed container with a little liquid from the pot. Save the rest of the kombu tamari broth for soup or noodles.

The water containing the washed off starch and bran can be saved to use as a thickener for soups, stews, gravies, puddings, and sauces or used as a starter for sourdough bread.

The sediment in the water can also be used by itself. Allow it to stand in a jar. The starch and bran will settle to the bottom and the clear water at the top can be poured off. Put the sediment on a baking sheet and let dry. After the moisture has evaporated, the starchy mixture will harden and can be used like *kuzu*. Store in a jar and break off small pieces for diluting in water to use as a thickener.

Instead of boiling the seitan, it may be deep-fried. This makes for a much softer dish, but because of the large amount of oil used it should be prepared only occasionally. After alternating between cold and hot water as explained above, squeeze out all water remaining in the sticky gluten. In a deep-fryer or saucepan, add dark sesame oil to a depth of about 1½ to 2 inches. Divide the gluten into 12 pieces and again squeeze out any remaining liquid. If the dough is too moist, coat with extra flour or arrowroot flour. After oil is heated to proper temperature (see chapter on tempura-style and deep-fried foods), stretch and flatten pieces of dough by hand and deep-fry in hot oil for 2 to 3 minutes until nicely brown. Deep-fry two pieces at a time, remove and add another couple of pieces. After all pieces have been cooked, blot out excess oil from seitan by patting with a dry paper towel or rinse with hot water. In another saucepan, cover the deep-fried seitan with spring water, add ⅓ cup of tamari soy sauce, and cook for 5 to 10 minutes.

The recipe above makes about 1½ pounds of seitan and will serve from 6 to 8 people.

Seitan Kinpira

2 tablespoons dark sesame oil
½ cup celery sliced diagonally
½ cup burdock cut into matchsticks
1½ cups carrots cut into matchsticks
1 cup seitan, cooked and diced

Heat the oil in a frying pan. Add the celery, burdock, and carrots and place the cooked seitan on top. Simmer, covered, over low heat for about 5 to 10 minutes. Uncover and mix well. If the seitan is not done, add 1 to 2 tablespoons of water, cover, and cook for another 5 to 10 minutes.

❧ Sautéed Seitan and Onions ❧

- 2 tablespoons dark sesame oil
- 4 cups onions sliced into rings
- 2 cups cooked seitan, sliced
- Chopped parsley for garnish

Heat the oil in a frying pan. Add the onions. Put the sliced seitan on top of the onions. Cover and simmer over low heat until the onions are translucent and become very sweet, about 30 minutes. The juice in the seitan slices will filter down into the onions and bring out their natural sweetness. Mix and simmer for 3 to 5 minutes longer. Garnish with chopped parsley and serve.

Variation: To keep the onions crispy, put the seitan in pan first and put the onions on top. Cover, lower the heat, simmer for 3 to 5 minutes; then mix, and serve.

❧ Seitan and Sauerkraut ❧

- 2 cups cooked seitan cut in chunks or slices
- ½ cup sauerkraut juice from the drained sauerkraut
- 1 cup drained sauerkraut
- Chopped scallions for garnish

Put the seitan and sauerkraut juice in a saucepan and cook for 5 minutes. Put the sauerkraut on top. Cover and simmer over low heat for about 5 minutes, or until all the ingredients are warm and the sauerkraut flavor goes into the seitan. Garnish with chopped scallions and serve.

❧ Seitan with Vegetables and Kuzu Sauce ❧

- Spring water
- 2 cups diced onions
- 2 cups sweet corn kernels
- ½ cup diced celery
- 1 cup cubed cooked seitan
- 1 tablespoon kuzu
- 1 cup shelled fresh green peas

Pour 1 inch of water into a pot and bring it to a boil. Add the onions, corn, celery, and seitan. Cover and simmer for 3 to 5 minutes. Dilute the tablespoon of kuzu in ½ cup water. Reduce the heat and add the kuzu, stirring constantly to prevent lumping. While mixing in the kuzu, also add the green peas. Cook the kuzu until it becomes translucent, about 3 to 5 minutes. Transfer to a serving dish and serve.

Variation: Use green pepper instead of celery for a more pungent taste.

Deep-Fried Seitan and Vegetables

- 1 cup seitan cut into large chunks or 1-inch balls
- 1 strip kombu, 6 to 8 inches long, soaked and sliced
- 2 to 3 shiitake mushrooms, soaked and sliced
- ½ cup celery cut into thick diagonals
- 1 cup daikon cut into thick quarters
- 1 cup carrots cut into chunks
- ½ cup burdock cut into thick diagonals
- ½ cup lotus root cut into thick quarters
- Spring water
- ½ to 1 teaspoon grated fresh ginger

First deep-fry the seitan (see p. 100). Put the kombu in a pressure cooker. Add the shiitake mushrooms, celery, daikon, carrots, burdock, and lotus root. Place the deep-fried and cooked seitan on top. Add 4 to 5 cups water to just cover the ingredients. Pressure-cook for 5 to 10 minutes. Remove and serve.

If boiling instead of pressure-cooking, cover and boil for 40 to 45 minutes. The water should have a light salt taste. Add 1 to 2 teaspoons tamari soy sauce to season, if desired. Garnish with ½ to 1 teaspoon grated fresh ginger and let boil for 1 more minute before serving.

Variation: The recipe can also be used for seitan that has not been deep-fried. Kuzu may be added to thicken the mixture and so can about ½ cup of gluten water saved from the seitan-making process.

Seitan Croquettes

- 10 2-inch-long pieces burdock
- 10 2-inch-long pieces carrot
- Spring water
- Pinch of sea salt
- 2 cups uncooked seitan (gluten)
- Dark sesame oil
- 1 strip kombu, 6 to 8 inches long, soaked and sliced
- 2 tablespoons tamari soy sauce
- 1 cup diced onion
- Seitan starch water from making seitan or 1 tablespoon kuzu
- ½ teaspoon grated fresh ginger
- Chopped parsley for garnish

Boil the burdock and carrot pieces in ½ cup of water for 5 minutes. Add a pinch of sea salt. Strain the burdock and carrots and save the water for later use.

Separate the seitan into 10 equal-sized pieces. Wrap one piece of uncooked seitan around both 1 piece of burdock and 1 piece of carrot. Deep-fry in a pan containing at least 1 inch of dark sesame oil until golden brown. Remove from the oil and drain on paper towels.

Put the kombu in a heavy pot. Place the fried gluten on top of the kombu. Add water, including the juice from the burdock and carrots, to cover the gluten. Add the tamari soy sauce. This mixture should be slightly salty to the taste. Bring to a boil. Cover and reduce the heat to low. Simmer for about 25 to 30 minutes.

Add the diced onion to the pot. Add about ½ cup seitan starch water saved from making seitan to thicken the cooking water or 1 tablespoon of kuzu. This will make a thick sauce. Simmer for about 10 to 15 minutes. At the end, ½ teaspoon of grated fresh ginger may be added and cooked for 1 minute. Garnish with chopped parsley and serve.

Seitan Stew

- 1 strip kombu, soaked and sliced
- 1 cup onions cut into ¼-inch-thick half moons
- ½ cup celery cut into ¼-inch-thick diagonals
- 1 cup carrots cut in chunks
- 1 to 1½ cups cooked seitan, cut into chunks
- 3 to 4 cups kombu-tamari water from cooking seitan
- ½ to 1½ cups starch-bran water from cooking seitan
- Chopped scallions or parsley for garnish

Put the kombu in a pot. Add the onions, celery, carrots, and seitan. Pour in the kombu-tamari cooking water and bring to a boil. Cover and lower the heat. Simmer until all the vegetables are soft, about 30 to 40 minutes. Add the starch-bran water or 1 tablespoon of kuzu to thicken and stir well. Let simmer for another 15-20 minutes. Garnish with chopped scallions or parsley and serve.

Variation: A half cup of soaked barley goes very well in a stew.

Wheat Meat Burger

This recipe makes enough for 1 or 2 servings.

4 ounces cooked seitan, sliced in patties
1 teaspoon dark sesame oil
Whole wheat bun or sesame seed roll

Pan-fry the cooked seitan for 5 to 10 minutes. Place in bun or roll and serve with sautéed onion slices, sauerkraut, lettuce, miso-tahini spread, or other trimmings.

Sweet and Sour Seitan

This dynamic dish, combining several tastes and flavors, makes a tasty appetizer or side dish.

2 cups cooked seitan, sliced
1 cup burdock cut in chunks
1 cup apple juice
3 cups seitan-tamari cooking water
3 to 4 tablespoons kuzu
Brown rice vinegar
¼ cup chopped scallions

Put the seitan, burdock, apple juice, and seitan cooking water in a pot. Bring to a boil. Cover and lower the heat to medium-low. Simmer until the burdock is soft. Reduce the heat to low and add the diluted kuzu and a small amount of brown rice vinegar. Simmer for 2 to 3 minutes. When done place in a serving bowl and mix in the chopped scallions. Serve hot.

FU

Fu is a wheat gluten product similar to seitan but toasted, steamed, and dried. Light in consistency, fu absorbs liquid and expands several times in volume when cooked. Like seitan, it is easy to digest and gives energy. Fu can be enjoyed plain, garnished with grated fresh ginger and toasted black sesame seeds, or added to miso soup or tamari soy sauce broth, stews, salads, or cooked together with vegetables.

At home, fu can be made using the basic method for preparing seitan, page 100. Then gently toast in a moderately hot oven for a few minutes. After cooling, lightly steam to allow the fu to puff up. Cut into rounds and let dry in a cool place. Store in an airtight container.

Dried fu is available in several forms in natural foods stores or Oriental markets: flat strips, large doughnut-shaped rounds, and small rounds. A good quality 100-percent whole wheat product is *kurunafu*, which has a natural light brown color. We asked a Japanese food company to make whole wheat fu available to North American natural foods stores. It came out a little dark, but the taste is good and I recommend it. Oriental food stores often carry a very white refined fu. It is attractively cut in fancy shapes, such as flowers, but contains artificial color and should be avoided.

To prepare dried fu, soak for 5 to 10 minutes in hot water until softened and press out any excess water by squeezing between the palms of your hands; then slice into cubes or bite-sized pieces and add to miso soup, or boil, sauté, steam, bake, or deep-fry for your favorite dish.

Fu and Broccoli in a Broth

1 strip kombu, soaked
4 to 5 cups spring water
1 cup fu, soaked and sliced
1 cup broccoli flowerets and stems
Tamari soy sauce

Put the kombu and water in a pot and bring to a boil. Cover and lower the heat to medium-low. Simmer for about 10 minutes. Remove the kombu, drain, and set aside for future use. Add the fu to the water and simmer for 5 minutes. Add the broccoli and simmer until done. The broccoli should be bright green when done. When the broccoli is just about done, season with a little tamari soy sauce and simmer for 2 to 3 minutes longer. Transfer to individual serving bowls and serve while hot.

CHAPTER 10

BREADS AND BAKED GOODS

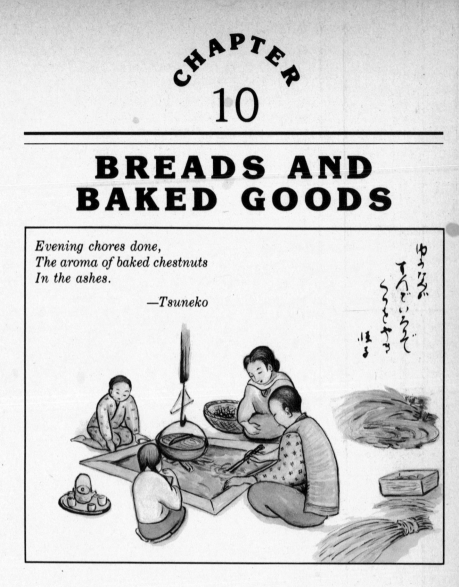

Evening chores done,
The aroma of baked chestnuts
In the ashes.

—Tsuneko

In the West whole grains have traditionally been made into flour and consumed in the form of bread. In the Far East, baking was uncommon until very recently. Since childhood I had read many stories in the Bible about bread. But like most families, we didn't have an oven, and I didn't taste bread until I went away to college. After the war, when cornmeal became plentiful, we experimented with baking and cooking with this grain but our efforts didn't turn out so well. At George Ohsawa's study house, I was introduced to whole wheat bread which was often served on holidays and birthdays.

Through Ohsawa's influence, the modern natural foods movement started in Europe and naturally fermented bread made from organic stone-ground whole wheat flour reappeared. During the last century, white flour had almost entirely replaced whole wheat, and modern bread was customarily made with refined salt, sugar, and various additives. In Belgium, Pierre Gevaert and his family set up Lima Bakery, named in honor of George Ohsawa's wife, Lima. Their wonderful sourdough bread, made in the style of traditional European village bakers, has become world renowned.

At the Lima Bakery, Pierre gave Michio and me a tour of the bread-making process step by step. The bakery's delicious sourdough loaf is large, round, and beautiful, and many times since then I have brought it home. One of our young American friends visited the Gevaerts and learned their techniques. When he came back to New England he started the Baldwin Hill Bakery in 1975. The bakery's large round loaf, made with organically grown whole wheat flour, deep well water, and sea salt, is baked in a wood-fired brick oven and has become the standard for naturally fermented bread on the East Coast. I very much enjoy traditionally made bread like this. It doesn't spoil easily and when it hardens, it can be put in the oven for a few minutes to freshen. With a little umeboshi plum, peanut butter, sauerkraut, or sandwich filling, it is very nourishing, almost a meal in itself.

In Amsterdam, we visited the wonderful bakery at Manna Foods. Adalbert Nelissen explained to us that in the old days bread was sometimes hung on a rope to age. Naturally fermented bread like this kept all year-round without spoiling or producing mold. Whenever any was needed, a loaf was taken down, soaked in cold water, and reheated in the oven. Like wine, the longer fermented bread is aged, the better its taste and flavor. The process reminded me of noodle-makers in Japan who say that dried soba or udon noodles improve with aging.

Another wonderful bread is whole grain pumpernickel rye. In the early 1970s, a couple from West Berlin came to Boston to attend an East West Foundation seminar and stayed with us. They gave Michio and me a special pumpernickel loaf made with all-natural ingredients in the time-honored manner. It was exceptionally sweet and could be enjoyed as a sandwich between slices of other bread! I have never forgotten its taste and whenever I visit Germany I search for it, though so far without success.

In macrobiotic cooking, we do not recommend preparing yeasted breads for regular use. Traditionally made breads have been baked for thousands of years leavened only with proper kneading, wild yeast in the air, or a sourdough starter. Only when whole wheat flour became refined into white flour, stripping the grain of the bran and germ, did the baking industry develop yeast to put a little life back into commercial bread.

The difference between yeasting and fermentation needs to be clearly understood. Yeasts (wild or cultivated) feed on natural sugars present in the wheat and produce alcohol and carbonic gas which cause the dough to rise. A risen loaf will absorb heat more easily than an unrisen loaf. A risen loaf will be more thoroughly cooked inside and will be more tender—qualities essential for consumption and digestibility. Fermentation takes place through the work of bacteria which break down essential nutrients in the wheat into a form that is more easily assimilated. This process may be called predigestion and is similar to the effect of eating miso or other fermented foods. Ideally, bread both rises and ferments. Natural sourdough combines both of these steps. Finally, it is important to thoroughly chew each mouthful of bread, even of the best sourdough quality. Chewing is the last step in predigestion and without it much of the nutrients will still be unavailable to our bodies. Once Michio was giving a consultation to the owner of a modern bakery. He told the man to reduce his own consumption of flour products. Even good-quality bread, taken in excess, tends to produce mucus in the body and is less energizing than grain consumed in whole form. This is another reason for thorough chewing. Mixing the dry, baked flour with saliva causes less mucus to build up in the body. Bread low in quality, made with refined ingredients, stagnates in the intestines, thins the blood, and can lead to a decline in vitality. The man replied that he and his family never ate their own bread because of the chemicals and additives it contained. I was so sad when I heard this story. He did not understand that his own health and the health of society are inseparable.

WHOLE WHEAT BREAD

Wheat is the most popular grain for making bread. It is light, chewy, naturally sweet to the taste, and retains moisture well. The basic recipe for two medium-sized loaves follows, along with comments on the major factors that go into bread-making.

- 8 cups organic stone-ground whole wheat flour
- ¼ to ½ teaspoon sea salt
- Spring water

Combine flour and salt in a large bowl. Add enough water to make a pliable dough, approximately 1 cup or less of liquid per cup of dry ingredients. Add more flour if too moist or more water if too dry, until workable consistency is obtained. Knead on board or counter for 10 minutes or more. Place dough in a bowl lightly oiled with sesame oil and set aside in a cool spot for 8 to 12 hours to ferment. Cover with damp cheesecloth or hand towel during this time. The dough will naturally rise by attracting wild yeast in the air. After the dough has initially risen, knead it again for several minutes until soft. Form into desired shapes and put in 2 oiled bread pans. Set pans in a warm spot, again cover with cheesecloth or towel, and let sit for 2 more hours. After the second rising, make several slits on top of the dough with a knife. Bake in a preheated oven at 300 to 350 degrees for 1 to 2 hours until done.

Flour—The gluten (protein factor) content of the wheat is the key to the natural leavening, or rising, of bread. The colder the climate, the higher the gluten. Hard red winter wheat from Canada makes one of the best bread flours. Hard spring wheat is also excellent. Pastry flour is usually used for pancakes and pastries but can be added in small quantities to bread for a lighter consistency. Durum wheat is used in pasta, and white wheat, also low in gluten, is used for breakfast cereals. The freshness of the flour is also very important. Oxidation starts after milling and, within as little as five days, nutrients such as vitamin E in the flour may be lost. White flour needs no refrigeration because it has no life. Organic-quality flour is also essential and gives a more delicious and nourishing loaf.

Milling—Flour is traditionally made by grinding whole wheat berries with millstones at a very slow speed and a cool temperature. This process preserves the precious wheat germ, allows the grain to ferment naturally, and retains the normal acidity and oxidation levels of the whole grain. Modern hammer mills and cylinder mills pound the wheat at high temperatures, crushing the germ and bran and causing the grain's natural oil to turn rancid immediately. Refined flour is then subjected to aging with caustic substances, such as alum, chalk, methyl bromide, ammonium carbonate, and nitrogen trichloride, and treated with preservatives, bleaches, and whiteners. Altogether about 90 nutrients are lost in refining and only four are required to be returned in enriching. The rest are sold back to the consumer in the form of vitamin and mineral supplements. At the natural foods store, I buy only 100-percent organically grown stone-ground whole wheat flour. Fresh flour can also be made at home with whole wheat berries and a small stone hand mill.

If the grain is hard, grinding may break it instead of ripping it. To prevent this, moisten the grain about 3 to 4 hours before grinding by spraying a little water on it, or steam it for 2 minutes and let stand about 2 hours before grinding. Generally North American wheats are much drier than the softer European grains. In grinding, the best texture is powdery, more like cornmeal than sand. If your hand mill grinds slowly, this texture can be obtained in one grinding. However, if the hand mill is fast, it may be necessary to do two grindings, the first rough and the second fine. However, if the flour is too finely ground, the bread will have a cake-like texture. If too coarse, it won't leaven properly. All flour should be refrigerated and bought fresh or ground at home in small quantities and only as needed.

Water—Water contributes to the sweetness of the loaf. Good-quality spring or well water is preferable to chemically treated tap water or distilled water. The water that noodles are cooked in is also very good and contributes a unique flavor to a loaf. Soft water produces a soft and sticky dough. To harden it, use a little extra salt. Hard water toughens the gluten and retards fermentation. To soften first boil the water.

The amount of water used in any recipe will vary from flour to flour, depending on its ability to absorb moisture. In general, when making dough, it is preferable to add water rather than flour during the kneading process. Doing so keeps your bowl, hands, and working surface cleaner, contributes to stickier gluten, and prevents dryness. Thus, to get the right consistency, that of an earlobe, reserve a portion of the water in any given recipe and add it gradually throughout the kneading process as needed. The right consistency is obtained when the dough does not stick too much to the bowl and after kneading well is capable of being stretched without immediately breaking.

Seasoning—Salt aids fermentation, helps the crust form, retains moisture content in the loaf, and improves the bread's taste. Unrefined sea salt, which is high in trace minerals, makes the best-quality bread. The fresher the flour, the more salt it can absorb. The amount of seasoning will vary depending on the ingredients, the season of the year, and personal taste. I generally use very little salt, about ¼ teaspoon per loaf. Some people prefer more, so please adjust accordingly. Miso may be used in place of salt—it produces a light, sweet-tasting bread.

Natural Starters—Wild yeast in the air is sufficient to start whole wheat flour rising. If properly kneaded and moistened, the dough will naturally ferment and expand without the need of any other ingredients. Traditionally, a sour-tasting starter was sometimes added to the dough to enhance flavor and taste. (In the next recipe, we will look at sourdough bread.)

Oil—Oil is not necessary, either, for making good bread. In fact, it makes for heavier loaves that spoil much more quickly. Occasionally a little oil may be added to the batter if desired for a more tender crust and to help keep the bread from drying out. One to 2 tablespoons per loaf are plenty. Sesame oil gives bread a nice nutty taste. Corn oil is buttery and has a mellow aroma. Olive oil gives a light taste and fresh bouquet.

Yeast and Sweeteners—Brewer's yeast is an expansive substance. Taken in excess, it can bloat the abdomen, cause indigestion, and clog the intestines. Yeasted breads spoil much more quickly than unyeasted breads. Traditionally, breads are made without yeast. However, for party breads or a quick-rising whole wheat loaf, granulated yeast that is free of BHA and other additives may be used occasionally. Only a small amount need be mixed into the batter. A traditional leavening agent called *barm* is sometimes used by natural foods bakers. Barm is a by-product of the brewing process and gives a slightly bitter, hop-like taste. One cup of barm equals 1 teaspoon of yeast. Sweeteners such as sugar, honey, or maple syrup are also completely unnecessary since fermented bread is naturally sweet. However, for extra sweet breads on holidays a little amasake, rice syrup, or barley malt may be added. Some natural bakers also use diastatic malt, which adds a nutty flavor and bloom to the crust. This is available at brewing supply stores or can be made at home by drying and pulverizing sprouted barley. Only a tiny amount is added to the dough. A little freshly grated ginger juice can also be used to quicken fermentation, about ⅓ teaspoon per loaf.

Kneading—After mixing the basic ingredients, water is worked into the flour and kneaded into a pliable dough. For naturally fermented bread, a wooden board or surface that is slightly wet works best. For a yeasted dough, an oiled or floured surface is better. It is important to keep your hands damp and clean while kneading. Stickiness can tear and harm the gluten. The dough should be kneaded for a minimum of 10 minutes, at least 300 to 350 times. When done, it should be resilient to the touch, springing back when poked. The dough should not stay firm in a ball but expand and ooze when held. Keeping a calm, peaceful mind is very important when kneading or the dough will absorb and transmit the negative energy of the baker.

The purpose of kneading is to make the gluten in the flour stick together and to bring air into the dough. In kneading, tension in the dough is also built up. When we knead too much at one time, however, the dough will become too tense and break apart instead of binding together. We recognize this problem when the surface of the dough starts to tear apart. Richard Bourdon, the master baker at Manna Foods in Amsterdam, recommends the following technique: Once the ingredients are mixed together, start kneading by gently folding over the dough for approximately 5 minutes or until you notice it starting to tear or becoming too sticky. Then let it rest for 5 minutes. Repeat both kneading and resting four more times (altogether five times over a period of 50 minutes). Kneading should be done gently and not by using much strength.

Proofing—After kneading, the dough should be set aside to ferment for several hours. This is called proofing. Place the kneaded dough in a lightly oiled bowl and cover with several layers of damp cheesecloth or a hand towel. The bowl with naturally fermented dough should be placed in a cool spot, between 45 and 65 degrees, but not in the refrigerator.

However, if the dough is too cold during proofing, the fermentation and rising will be very slow. The slower the fermentation, usually the better the aroma. The taste and the quality of the bread are generally not affected by temperature. To reduce the proofing time, especially with sourdough breads, the dough may be placed in a warmer environment, between 72 and 78 degrees. However, too high a temperature will cause the dough to ferment too quickly, rise too high, or become overly sour. In summer, it may need to be proofed at night. The amount of proofing will vary with the ingredients, the weather, the altitude, and other factors. Generally the dough should be proofed for 8 to 12 hours. Dough prepared in the morning and baked in the evening usually turns out better than dough proofed in the evening and baked in the morning. Dough also rises better on sunny days than rainy ones and during the full moon than at other times of the month.

When proofing lasts too long, the pH level of the dough becomes too high, causing too much tension on the gluten. This prevents the bread from gaining in volume during the second stage of proofing which is called shaping. We can recognize this afterwards when the dough does not rise much in the oven and the taste of the bread is too sour. Also, there will be a tear or a crack on top or on the side of the bread as if the bread were lifting its hat. Too short a proofing period causes the bread to lie flat in the mold during shaping instead of rising and keeping its rough shape on top. This problem can be identified when a big tear or crack forms in the middle on top of the bread, though the taste will be less sour. The right balance between proofing and shaping produces a nicely rounded, well-risen bread that shows no cracks and tastes just right. This balance can be learned only by experience.

Shaping—After the dough has proofed and risen for the first time, knead it for a few minutes until it is soft; then form it into the desired shapes, and put it in oiled bread pans. I am fond of round shapes but rectangular or square shapes are fine, too. Tin, steel, and glass make the best baking pans. Ceramic and cast-iron do not work as well. After shaping and placing in the pans, the dough should be set aside to rise a second time. Put the bread pans in a warm place, cover them with a cloth or light towel, and let sit for a couple more hours. To speed up the process, the pans may be put in a very low oven, under 145 degrees, for about half an hour.

Baking—After the second rising, make several slits in the top of the dough with a sharp knife. This allows steam to escape while baking and prevents a hard crust. The slits are usually shallow but may be made up to half the depth of the loaf. For rectangular loaves, one long cross cut down the length of the loaf may be made. For round loaves, a spoke-like pattern will do. The pans are then placed in a preheated oven and baked at 300 to 350 degrees for 1 to 2 hours if baking fermented bread; 45 minutes to 1 hour for yeasted bread. For even baking, use the middle rack and set the pans in at least 1 to 2 inches from the sides. Baking time will vary, depending on the ingredients, the type of pan used, the size of the loaf, moisture content, and altitude. The bread is done when the crust turns medium dark and the sides of the loaf pull away from the pan. Thumping the bottom of the bread should also produce a hollow sound.

You can practice identifying the difference in sound by taking out a bread that has baked for 20 minutes and hitting it on the bottom like a drum, and then taking it out after an hour and hitting it again.

Once the bread has cooled, cut one slice and examine the crumb. It should be spongy and not sticky. No threads of gluten should be visible. If you gently press your thumb into the bread, it should not produce a hole but spring back to its original shape. The taste should resemble neither raw flour nor noodles.

In order to give the loaf a chance to form better in the oven, develop a thinner crust, and a nicer color, Richard Bourdon recommends a special steaming method. For this, preheat the oven to 500 degrees and put in an empty shallow cookie sheet or similar tray. Place the loaf of bread separately in the oven, and then pour some hot water in the cookie sheet to create steam. Close the door and lower the temperature to 400 degrees. Bake at 400 degrees for 20 minutes and then reduce the temperature to 325 and bake for about 50 more minutes.

Cooling and Storing—When the bread is baked, remove it from the oven, lightly rub the surface with a little oil for luster, if desired, and cool on a bread rack.

The best way of storing naturally fermented or sourdough bread is in the open air in a paper bag. If the bread is kept in a plastic bag, airtight box, or other moist environment, mold will easily form. If the bread is allowed to dry out, it can be kept a very long time, even up to a year. Before using, moisture may be added by steaming the entire loaf or individual slices of the loaf in a vegetable steamer. It will taste like freshly baked bread. It is not necessary to keep the bread in a refrigerator or freeze it. If kept in the open air, it will mature and the taste will become even richer. If stored in the refrigerator, the bread's taste will become dull.

Baking Hints—A perfect loaf of bread depends on harmonizing many factors and takes experience. Bread may be judged by its crumb, or soft inside portion, and the crust, or hard outside part. A tacky crumb may be caused by insufficient leavening, too rapid fermentation, or too low an oven temperature. A crumbly crumb results from using too much liquid, not enough kneading, too low an oven temperature, or over-long proofing. A crumb with large holes and textures is a sign of too much leavening, too little salt, not enough mixing of ingredients, or failure to punch down the dough adequately when kneading. A crumb that is too dense can be the result of too much leavening, a weak sourdough starter, too much salt, too hot an oven, not enough proofing, overkneading, or too quick fermentation. Crust that is overly thick can mean that the oven was too low or the loaf did not bake long enough. A tough crust results when moisture becomes trapped beneath the crust and hardens when cooling. Cracks or blisters on the crust signify too much liquid, too hot an oven, or too weak a dough. A pale crust can indicate too low an oven temperature or placing the bread too low in the oven. Too dark a crust is produced by too high an oven temperature or excessive sweeteners or other energizers. When bread bulges out of the pan, too much dough was put in the pan to begin with or the dough lacked enough salt. Bread that turns stale rapidly has often risen too fast after the dough was first kneaded, or the dough was allowed to become too warm, not enough salt was added, the flour was too soft, the water was insufficient, or the oven temperature was too low.

COMBINING WHEAT WITH OTHER GRAINS

Whole grains other than wheat are low in gluten and do not leaven breads very well. They do make excellent unleavened flat breads, such as corn tortillas. Combined with whole wheat in small quantities, other grains give bread a variety of delicious flavors and different textures. They can be added in flour form or cooked as whole grains. Softly cooked grains that are left to sour slightly for about three days make a wonderful leavening agent. Usually only 10 to 20 percent of other grains or flour are combined with whole wheat.

Barley—Barley flour gives a dense, moist, cake-like consistency to bread. The flour may be dry-roasted first for a nuttier taste. Cooked leftover barley gives a nice chewy texture.

Brown Rice—Rice flour gives a nice nutty flavor and crispness to bread. Sweet rice flour makes for a sticky texture and is used more in pastries. Softly cooked brown rice, mixed with a little whole wheat flour, makes a wonderful loaf called rice kayu bread.

Buckwheat—Buckwheat flour is heavy, dense, and more popular in pancakes and waffles than in bread. However, it retains moisture well and may be used in small quantities for an extra hearty loaf.

Corn—Cornmeal has a sweet flavor, coarse consistency, and crumbly texture. It retains more water than wheat. White corn has a sweeter taste than yellow corn, but yellow corn is more delicate. Fresh corn from the cob added to dough makes a delicious, beautiful loaf.

Millet—Millet flour gives a fine, cake-like quality to bread as well as a beautiful color.

Oats—Oat flour has a rich, sweet taste. It is the oiliest of the grains and makes for a chewy, moist loaf.

Rye—Rye and pumpernickel breads are famous around the world. Usually about 50 to 60 percent rye flour is combined with whole wheat flour to make rye bread.

Besides grains, other ingredients may be added to bread. For holidays and special occasions, wonderful seed and nut breads can be made with sesame seeds, sunflower seeds, chopped walnuts, and other nuts. Carrots, onions, squashes, zucchini, apples, raisins, and other vegetables and fruits may also be added from time to time for a uniquely different loaf.

SOURDOUGH BREAD

Traditional whole grain bread is often fermented with a sour starter. This starter can be made at home by combining whole wheat flour and cool spring water into a batter, which is then set aside to ferment for a few days. Excellent starters can also be made with cooked whole grains that have turned slightly sour to the taste over three days, with noodle cooking water that has set and slightly soured, or with starch water that is left over from making seitan and fermented in a warm place for 3 to 4 days. Sour starters may also be used to make pancakes, waffles, and muffins as well as bread. The proportion of flour to water may vary depending upon the quality of the ingredients, the season, and other factors.

I am grateful to Richard Bourdon, the baker at Manna Foods in Holland, for the basic sourdough recipe, as well as the variations that follow for raisin bread, barley bread, and sesame bread. He is really dedicated to his art. We have had excellent results in our kitchen at home with his methods.

The procedure for making sourdough bread is divided into four stages: 1) making a dough and allowing spontaneous fermentation to happen, 2) taking a small amount of this dough and producing a starter, 3) making the sourdough with the starter, and 4) baking bread with the sourdough. The entire process is relatively simple but takes place over 5 days, so you should plan accordingly. Once the starter is made it can be stored and used for making additional loaves over the course of 2½ days. A delicious non-sour, naturally fermented bread can also be made in 2½ days using only Step 1. This makes 1 loaf. Multiply the ingredients proportionately if you wish to bake in larger volumes.

Step 1: Spontaneously Fermented Bread

24 ounces whole wheat flour
12 ounces whole wheat pastry flour
3 cups spring water
1 teaspoon sea salt

Mix together all the ingredients in a bowl and knead into a dough (see instructions on setting aside water, page 110, and kneading, page 112). Pastry flour is added to the whole wheat in a volume of 1 to 2 parts in order to provide sufficient starch to ferment.

Cover the kneaded dough with a damp cheesecloth or hand towel and let sit overnight on a bread board. The second morning fold over the dough a few times and cover until evening. To keep the dough from sticking to the cloth on subsequent kneadings, you may wish to sprinkle with a little water after kneading or use a plant mister to keep it moist. In the evening fold over the dough a few times more and set aside for the next morning. Repeat the third morning and set aside until noon. Shape the dough, put it into an oiled mold, and let sit at room temperature (but not lower than 42 degrees) until evening. At this time it should have gained in volume about one-third of its bulk.

Two tablespoons of this dough are now used to make the sourdough starter in Step 2 below. The rest of the dough may be used to make regular whole wheat bread by transferring to an oiled baking dish and baking at 400 degrees for 20 minutes and then reducing the temperature to 325 and baking for about 50 more minutes.

This spontaneously fermented loaf, like those in the basic whole wheat bread recipe, will be nicely fermented but not highly risen since the wild yeasts in the air have not yet developed very much. To obtain naturally fermented bread that rises well, we need to make the starter in Step 2.

Step 2: Making the Starter

2 tablespoons dough set aside from Step 1
1 cup whole wheat flour
Enough water to make a thick batter

Dissolve the 2 tablespoons of naturally fermented dough in a small amount of water. Add 1 cup of whole wheat flour and mix in enough water to produce a thick batter. After about 4 minutes of vigorous mixing, cover and set aside in a glass jar at room temperature (not under 42 degrees) for 24 hours, mixing occasionally. During this time the wild yeasts and bacteria need air to reproduce themselves. At the end of this period, the batter should smell slightly sour and fruity. On the tongue it should fizz a bit. If these qualities are absent, wait a few more hours. The jar may be placed in a warmer place, such as a bowl with warm water, until it is ready. If starting from scratch in Step 1, the starter should now be ready in the middle of day 4.

Step 3: Making Sourdough from Starter

- 1 cup whole wheat flour
- 3 tablespoons starter from Step 2
- ⅔ cup spring water

In the evening (of day 4 if starting from Step 1), mix all the ingredients and knead well. The dough should have the texture of an earlobe. Put the dough in a jar whose volume is at least double the size of the dough, cover, and set aside in a warm place, about 72 degrees. Next morning (day 5) the sourdough should have risen about twice its original volume. If not, set in a warmer place for about an hour and a half or the rest of the day if necessary. If it has not doubled in height by this time, discard this batch and start Step 3 over again using a fresh 3 tablespoons of starter. If the new batch does not rise, something is wrong and you must start all over again from Step 1. However, if and when it does rise, the sourdough is ready to be used in the basic sourdough bread recipe in Step 4 or in the other recipes that follow.

If you wish to bake more often, dissolve 1 tablespoon of the sourdough in one half cup of water and then add flour until you have a thin, pancake-like batter. Keep this batter refrigerated until the next time you want to bake bread. It will keep for about 1 month. The night before you plan to bake bread, follow Step 3, using the batter as a starter.

Step 4: Basic Sourdough Bread

- 16 ounces whole wheat flour
- 4 ounces whole wheat pastry flour
- ¾ to 1 cup warm spring water (approximately 100 degrees)
- 4½ tablespoons sourdough from Step 3
- 1 teaspoon sea salt

If you started the process at Step 1, you should now be working on the morning or afternoon of day 5. Mix all ingredients, keeping aside some water as explained in basic breadmaking instructions and knead well following the basic instructions on kneading. Cover and set aside in a warm place, ideally between 72 and 78 degrees, for an hour and a half. Shape into a loaf and put into an oiled baking tin. Cover and set in a warm place until the dough has risen about two-thirds in bulk, about 4 hours later. Preheat the oven to 500 degrees and in the oven place an empty shallow cookie sheet or similar tray. Place the shaped loaf in the oven separately and then pour some hot water in the cookie sheet to create steam. Close the door and lower the temperature to 400 degrees. Bake at 400 degrees for 20 minutes and then reduce the temperature to 325 and bake for about 50 more minutes. Yield: 1 loaf.

Raisin Bread

- 1 pound whole wheat flour
- 1¼ cups warm spring water (approximately 100 degrees)
- 3½ ounces sourdough
- ½ tablespoon sea salt
- 4 ounces soaked raisins

Mix all the ingredients together except the raisins. (See Step 3 in the Sourdough Bread recipe for making the sourdough.) Knead mixture following the basic instructions on kneading. At the last stage of the kneading process, add the raisins. They should be warm, at room temperature. Cover and set aside in a warm place, ideally between 72 and 78 degrees, for an hour and a half. Shape into a loaf and put into an oiled baking tin. Cover and set in a warm place until the dough has risen about two-thirds in bulk, about 4 hours later. Bake in a preheated 400-degree oven for 20 minutes and then reduce the temperature to 325 and bake for about 50 more minutes until done. Yield: 1 loaf.

Variation: This bread can be made without sourdough by following the basic method for spontaneously fermented bread (see Step 1 in the Sourdough recipe). In this case, add the raisins one hour before shaping and putting into the baking mold. Several ounces of chopped nuts may also be added to the basic recipe for variety if desired.

Barley Bread

- 18½ ounces whole wheat flour
- 5¼ ounces sourdough
- ½ tablespoon sea salt
- 10½ to 11 ounces warm spring water (approximately 100 degrees)
- 1⅓ tablespoons light or dark sesame oil
- 1½ ounces toasted sesame seeds
- 4½ ounces cooked barley

Mix flour, sourdough (see Step 3 in basic Sourdough Bread recipe), salt, water, and oil and knead following basic instructions on kneading. At the last stage of the kneading process, add sesame seeds and barley. Cover and set in a warm place, ideally between 72 and 78 degrees, for an hour and a half. Shape into a loaf and put into an oiled baking tin. Cover and set in a warm place until the dough has risen about two-thirds in bulk, about 4 hours later. Bake in a preheated 400-degree oven for 20 minutes and then reduce the temperature to 325 and bake for about 50 more minutes. Yield: 1 loaf.

Variation: This bread can be made without sourdough by following the basic method for spontaneously fermented bread (see Step 1 of Sourdough Bread recipe). In this case, add the barley and sesame seeds one hour before shaping and putting into a mold.

❧ Sesame Bread ❧

18 ounces whole wheat flour
12 ounces warm spring water (approximately 100 degrees)
3 ounces sourdough
½ tablespoon sea salt
10½ ounces toasted sesame seeds

Mix all the ingredients except the sesame seeds together (see Step 3 in Sourdough Bread recipe for sourdough). Knead following basic kneading instructions. Add the sesame seeds at the last stage of the kneading process. Cover and set aside in a warm place, ideally between 72 and 78 degrees, for an hour and a half. Shape into a loaf and put into an oiled baking tin. Cover and set aside in a warm place until the dough has risen about two-thirds in bulk, about 4 hours later. Bake in a preheated 400-degree oven for 20 minutes and then reduce the temperature to 325 and bake for about 50 more minutes. Yield: 1 loaf.

Variation: This bread can be made without sourdough by following the basic method for spontaneously fermented bread (see Step 1 of Sourdough Bread recipe). In this case, add the sesame seeds one hour before shaping and putting into the mold.

❧ Rye Bread ❧

Rye is harder than other grains and requires thorough chewing when prepared in whole form. Prepared into flour and mixed with whole wheat, it makes a very distinctive, digestible bread. The following recipe makes 2 medium-sized loaves.

5 cups whole wheat flour
3 cups rye flour
½ teaspoon sea salt
Spring water, about 4 cups

Combine the two flours and salt and mix well. Gradually add enough water to form a ball of dough, about 4 cups altogether. Knead for 10 to 15 minutes, about 350 times, adding a little more flour from time to time to prevent the dough from sticking. Oil two bread pans, divide the dough in half, and shape into two loaves. Put the loaves in the pans and make shallow cuts in the top of each loaf. Brush the loaves lightly with oil and cover them with a warm damp cloth or hand towel. Set aside in a warm place to rise for about 8 to 12 hours. Bake in a preheated 300-degree oven for half an hour; then raise the oven temperature to 350 degrees and bake for another 1¼ hours.

Variations: If desired, 2 tablespoons of sesame or other unrefined oil may be added to this basic recipe. For a sourdough rye bread, add ¼ cup of starter and reduce the volume of water to about 3 cups or less. For flavoring, a few caraway seeds may be added to the dough.

Corn Bread

Corn bread has a nice corn taste, crumbly texture, and yellow color. I used to make it frequently but now prefer arepas and other baked products using whole corn rather than corn flour.

- 2 cups cornmeal
- 2 cups boiling spring water
- ½ teaspoon sea salt
- 1 teaspoon corn oil
- 1 cup whole wheat flour
- ¼ cup chopped roasted walnuts

Scald the cornmeal in 2 cups of boiling water. Add the salt and oil to the whole wheat flour and then mix with the scalded cornmeal. Add the chopped nuts and enough additional water to make a thick batter. Pour into an oiled 9- by 5-inch baking pan and bake in a preheated 350-degree oven until the top of the cornbread is lightly browned, about 30 to 40 minutes. Cut into thick slices or squares and serve.

Variation: For a sweeter corn bread, add a little barley malt or rice syrup. Corn muffins can be made from this same recipe. Bake 30 to 40 minutes at 400 degrees. Yield: One dozen muffins.

Rice Kayu Bread

Kayu is the Japanese word for grain that has cooked for a long time until it is soft and creamy. For this recipe, the soft rice recipe in the rice chapter can be used for the softly cooked rice (page 55). George Ohsawa originated this wonderful bread, and it is very popular in macrobiotic households around the world. Leftover rice or other grains may be softened a little and used in the basic recipe. The combination of rice and wheat is a true marriage of East and West. Please enjoy and introduce it to your friends.

- 2 cups whole wheat flour
- ⅛ to ¼ teaspoon sea salt
- 2 cups softly cooked brown rice

Mix the flour and sea salt together. Add the soft rice and form the dough into a ball. Knead the dough about 350 to 400 times. While kneading, a little more flour may be sprinkled on the dough to prevent it from sticking. If the rice is soft enough, additional water will not be required. If regular pressure-cooked rice is used, add a little water to form the ball of dough. Oil an 8-inch-square pan with a little sesame oil and lightly dust the pan with flour. This will prevent the bread from sticking to the pan. Shape the dough into a loaf shape and place it in the pan. Lightly press the dough down around the edges to form a rounded loaf. With a sharp knife, make a shallow slit in the top center of the dough. Place a clean, damp towel on top of the dough to keep out the dust. Place the loaf in a warm place, such as a pilot-lit oven or near a warm radiator. Let the dough sit for about 8 to 10 hours, occasionally moistening the damp towel with warm water as it dries out. After the dough has risen, bake in a preheated 200- to 250-degree oven for about 30 minutes. Then raise the oven temperature to 350 degrees and bake for another 1 to 1¼ hours. When the bread is done, remove and place on a rack to cool.

Variation: A few raisins or roasted seeds may be worked into the dough for a slightly sweeter or crunchier bread.

Miso Bread

Miso enhances natural fermentation and produces a sweet-tasting, light loaf. This recipe yields 2 loaves.

8 cups whole wheat flour
2 to 3 tablespoons miso
3 cups spring water

Put the flour in a mixing bowl. Purée miso with a little water and add to the flour. Mix the ingredients together and knead for about 10 minutes, or until a smooth elastic texture is obtained. Put the dough in a lightly oiled bowl and cover with a damp cloth. Allow the dough to stand in a warm place overnight. The next day, knead the dough again for a few minutes and form into 2 loaves. Heat the bread pans in the oven and then brush them with oil. Place loaves in pans and cover them with a damp cloth. Allow to rise in a warm place for 2 to 4 hours. Place in a cold oven and bake at 350 degrees for 1¼ hours. Place a pan of cold water on the lower rack in the oven to ensure even baking.

Variations: Add only half of the miso and proceed as above. Before forming the dough into loaves, spread the dough to a 1-inch thickness the length of the bread pans. Spread the remainder of the miso on top of the dough, roll up and place in the pan. Bake as above. When the bread is sliced, the miso layer will form an attractive spiral. For a richer-tasting bread, spread a thin layer of tahini over the miso layer.

❧ Sprouted Wheat Bread ❧

Sprouted bread is light, chewy, and more like a dessert than a bread. Delicious sprouted wheat bread is distributed by Essene and other natural foods bakeries. The following recipe is from a cooking column in *East West Journal* by Rebecca Theurer Wood, one of my students and an excellent macrobiotic cooking instructor and natural baker living in Colorado.

- 7 cups whole wheat berries
- Spring water
- Pinch of sea salt

Wash the wheat berries and soak them overnight in a 1-gallon glass jar. Strain out the water the next morning (and save for soup stock or other use). Rinse and strain the wheat berries again in the evening. Repeat this procedure for 2 to 3 days, or until the wheat sprouts and is 1 inch in height. Then grind the sprouts as finely as possible in a meat grinder or hand stone mill but not a blender or food mill. Grind twice if necessary. Mix the ground sprouts and salt and place in a lightly oiled shallow casserole dish or pan. Cover and bake in a preheated 200-degree oven for 4 hours, or until the bread shrinks from the sides of the pan. The cover may be taken off for the last 20 minutes of cooking.

Variation: Sprouted rye may be added to or substituted for wheat. Minced onions, ground sesame seeds, and other ingredients may be added, if desired.

❧ Blueberry-Corn Muffins ❧

- 1 cup whole wheat pastry flour
- 1 cup toasted corn flour or cornmeal
- ¼ cup rice flour
- ½ teaspoon sea salt
- 2 cups apple juice
- 1 cup fresh blueberries

Mix the flours and salt together. Add the apple juice and blueberries and form into a batter. Let sit for a couple of hours, covered with a damp cloth, in a warm place. Stir the batter briefly and ladle into oiled muffin tins. Bake in a preheated 350-degree oven for 30 minutes, or until done.

Variations: Other fruits, nuts, and seeds may be added to the batter. Cranberries, raisins, currants, walnuts, sesame seeds, and sunflower seeds are popular.

Whole Grain Crackers

½ cup cracked wheat
½ cup whole wheat flour
½ teaspoon sea salt
Spring water
½ to 1 cup roasted sesame seeds
1 teaspoon grated orange rind

Soak cracked wheat for 1 hour. Sift the flour and salt together and add them to the cracked wheat and sesame seeds using enough water to obtain a sticky dough. Add the grated orange rind. Dust a baking sheet with cornmeal and spread the dough to about a ⅛-inch thickness. Dip your fingers in water from time to time to spread it out smoothly without sticking. Score batter with a knife, if desired. Bake for 15 minutes in a preheated 450-degree oven. Cut or break the crackers apart when done.

Buckwheat Pancakes with Strawberry-Kuzu Sauce

Buckwheat flour in pancakes, waffles, and muffins is rich-tasting, light in texture, and very easy to digest. I am very fond of 100-percent buckwheat pancakes, but most people prefer them combined with whole wheat.

Pancakes

1 cup buckwheat flour
1 cup whole wheat pastry flour
2 tablespoons light sesame oil
1 cup amasake
¼ teaspoon sea salt
Spring water

Combine the dry ingredients. Add the oil, amasake, and salt. (Amasake that has aged a few days and turned slightly sour is best.) Add enough water to create the desired consistency for pancakes. Mix very well with a spoon or wisk. Cover the batter with cheesecloth and let sit in a warm place overnight so that it begins to ferment. This will help the pancakes to rise and become lighter. In the morning, oil a pancake griddle or skillet lightly with light sesame oil. When the griddle is hot, spoon a small amount of batter to form a round cake. Fry one side until small air bubbles start to form on the top side of the pancake. Turn the pancake over and fry the other side until golden brown. Be careful not to cook over too high a heat or the pancakes will burn. Keep the pancakes warm in a slow oven until ready to serve with strawberry-kuzu sauce below.

Strawberry-Kuzu Sauce

3 cups strawberries
3 cups spring water
Pinch of sea salt
3 to 4 tablespoons kuzu

Wash and hull the strawberries and slice them in half. Put the strawberries in the water and bring to a boil. Reduce the heat to medium-low. Add the salt, cover, and simmer for 5 to 10 minutes, or until the strawberries are soft. Dilute the kuzu in a little cold water and add it to the strawberries. Stir constantly to avoid lumping. Simmer until thick, 3 to 5 minutes. Spoon over pancakes and serve hot.

Variations: If the sauce is not sweet enough, a small amount of rice syrup or barley malt may be added. Other kinds of fresh fruit in season, such as apples, pears, cherries, peaches, and blueberries, can be used instead of strawberries. Dried fruit may be used, too, but it must be soaked, chopped, and cooked longer than fresh fruit. This batter may also be used to make waffles.

French Crêpes

Crêpes are a nice light way to consume flour and can be filled with a variety of vegetables, fruits, or applesauce. Like bread and pancake batter, crêpes are better if the batter is made the night before and left to sit until morning.

2 cups whole wheat pastry flour
2 cups spring water
¼ teaspoon sea salt
Dark sesame oil, as needed

Mix the ingredients well and whip in a blender or with an egg beater. This will make a lighter batter. Pour a small amount of batter onto a hot, lightly oiled frying pan or griddle. Smooth out with the back of a spoon in a circular shape. The crêpes should be very thin. Cook until done but be careful not to burn them. Fill with your favorite filling, roll up, and fasten with toothpicks. Yields approximately 6 crêpes.

Whole Wheat Pizza

This pizza, made with all natural ingredients, may be enjoyed for a party or other special occasion. This recipe yields two 13-inch pizzas.

Pizza Crust

2½ cups whole wheat pastry flour
½ teaspoon sea salt
1 tablespoon dark sesame oil
1 cup spring water

Put 2 cups of the flour in a bowl and mix in the salt. Add the oil and water and work into the flour mixture with your hands. Beat the dough until smooth and elastic. Add the remainder of the flour to make a stiff dough. Turn out onto a floured board and knead until smooth. Let stand for 15 minutes. Using half the dough at a time, roll into a circle and transfer to an oiled 13-inch pizza pan. Gently pull and stretch dough to fit pan and turn the edges under to obtain a thicker edge. Spread the filling over the dough and bake in a preheated 375-degree oven for 30 minutes, or until the edges are slightly browned. Serve hot.

Pizza Filling

- Dark sesame oil
- ½ cup minced onions
- ½ cup chopped celery
- 1 cup parsnips cut in large slices
- 2 cups carrots cut in large slices
- ½ cup spring water
- Pinch of sea salt
- 1 to 2 tablespoons barley miso
- Drop of ginger juice or pinch of grated fresh ginger
- ½ cup sliced green pepper
- ½ cup sliced scallions
- 1 cup cubed tofu

Heat a pressure cooker and brush it with oil and add the vegetables in the following order: onion, celery, parsnips, and carrots. Sauté each vegetable briefly before adding the next. Add the water and salt, cover, and bring to pressure. Cook for 15 minutes. Purée the vegetables and blend with miso and ginger. Heat a frying pan and brush it with oil. Lightly sauté the pepper and scallions. Blend with the puréed vegetables and spread the filling over the pizza dough. Arrange the tofu cubes attractively on top just before baking the pizza.

CHAPTER 11

SOUPS

Pounding miso!
Outside
The bright half moon.
—Yoshiko
みそつきや
外は明るい
半月だ
芳子

Our daily meals mirror our evolutionary development. If we eat foods of the proper quality and in the correct amounts and sequence, we may fulfill our biological potential. We will grow strong in body and mind and pass our vitality, life, and spirit on to the next generation. If our way of eating is unbalanced or chaotic, we will lose our health, and our family will decline.

At the table we start with soup, a replica of the ancient sea in which life began. The ideal soup contains a small amount of sea vegetables as well as miso or tamari soy sauce, which simulate the salty composition of the ocean from which primitive life evolved. In the middle of the meal come land vegetables. We eat these according to the natural order, from the most contracted to the most expanded, from yang to yin. First we take the more compact root vegetables, followed by ground and stem vegetables, and finally leafy greens and occasionally fresh salad.

At the end of the meal, corresponding with the primate phase of development, there may be seasonal fruits, nuts, or seeds. Of course, throughout the meal, we eat whole grains, the food by which we first secured our health and human understanding.

A bowl of soup is soothing, relaxing, and stimulates the appetite. I feel we renew our life daily by returning to this primordial source. Soup creates the atmosphere for the entire meal. Ideally, its taste, aroma, color, and texture complement the courses that follow. In macrobiotic cooking, we learn to see the whole in each part and to see each part in relation to the whole. If the meal as a whole is rich and nourishing, or contains many courses, I will introduce it with a simple miso soup or a clear soup made from kombu or shiitake mushroom stock. If the meal is on the light side, I may make a thick miso soup, an appetizing vegetable, bean, or grain soup, or a hearty stew.

The same principle of balance applies to other considerations in preparing soup. In cold weather, I naturally prepare more warming soups, include heavier ingredients, such as root vegetables, with a little more miso, salt, or other seasoning added. In hot weather, I make more cooling soups, use lighter ingredients, such as leafy vegetables, and slightly reduce the seasoning. If the soup has a naturally sweet flavor, such as squash soup does, the rest of the meal may emphasize other tastes. If the soup does not include miso, I may use miso to season one of the other dishes in the meal.

If the soup is a bean or pulse soup, I generally avoid serving beans and other high-protein foods in the rest of the meal. If the main vegetables in the meal are cooked together, the soup may have a single creamy vegetable taste. If the vegetables are prepared separately as side dishes, I may make a mixed vegetable soup, combining several ingredients. If the vegetables in the soup are cubed or diced, I will usually cut the vegetables in the rest of the meal in large rounds or chunks, and vice versa.

The variety of soups we can prepare in the macrobiotic kitchen is virtually limitless. I have selected several dozen of my favorites. Some are simple, mild, and easy to make. Others have many ingredients, are strong tasting, and take a while to prepare. Each has its appropriate season and occasion. By learning how to make balance with soup, our meal begins on a harmonious note and contributes to deep feelings of enjoyment, satisfaction, and wholeness.

MISO SOUPS

Miso is a smooth, dark purée made from soybeans, fermented barley or rice, and sea salt which have aged together over a period of several months to several years. Miso is very sweet and delicious and can be used in making soups, aging pickles, preparing sauces and spreads, and for occasional seasoning in place of salt in cooking. Miso contains living enzymes that aid digestion, strengthen the blood, and provide a nutritious balance of complex carbohydrates, essential oils, protein, vitamins, and minerals. According to legend, miso was a gift from the gods to ensure humanity's health, longevity, and happiness. Miso has been an important food in the Far East since the beginning of civilization and is now becoming popular in the West.

When I first came to the United States, high-quality natural miso was unavailable. When we were living in New York, we ordered a keg of miso once or twice a year from Japan for our family's daily use. Later, Erewhon began to import miso on a large scale, and it became a staple in natural foods and health food stores across the country. In the last few years, macrobiotic pioneers have started miso companies in North Carolina, western Massachusetts, and elsewhere to provide delicious miso from organically grown North American grains and beans.

In Japan, miso consumption has sharply fallen during the last thirty years. Except for a handful of families who still make miso in the traditional way, commercial miso in Japan is now usually made with chemicals, preservatives, and sugar, and the aging process is artificially speeded up from one to two years to two to three months. Interest in miso and traditional methods of miso-making have recently been revived. In 1981, Japan's National Cancer Center reported results of a nationwide medical study showing that people who ate miso soup every day had lower rates of cancer and heart disease and suffered less from every other unnatural cause of death. This finding conformed with traditional Oriental medicine and folk wisdom which valued miso as the supreme medicine for the prevention and relief of disease.

When I was growing up, we had miso soup twice a day. In the morning, Mother made it more simply with just spring water as a base. In the evening, she prepared a richer soup, often with a stock base and occasionally added fish. In our Brookline, Massachusetts, home, we have light miso soup for breakfast every morning. For lunch and dinner, we often have a rich miso soup, noodles with tamari soy sauce broth, or one of the other fine vegetable, bean, or grain soups described in this chapter. At least one small bowl of miso soup with wakame is recommended each day. Among macrobiotic families, miso soup has become an effective and inexpensive natural form of health insurance.

Miso comes in several varieties and its taste differs widely according to the quality of its ingredients, the length of time it has aged, and the method of preparation. In general, barley miso (also known by its Japanese name of *mugi miso*) is the sweetest and most suitable for daily cooking. There is a one-hundred-percent soybean miso called *hatcho miso*, which is strong tasting and good for making long-time pickles, for making condiments such as tekka, and for regular use in soup as well. A lighter brown rice miso (or *genmai miso*) is good for occasional use in summer. Two or three of these misos may also be mixed. There are also red, white, and yellow misos, which are usually aged for only several months. Light tasting, these misos are used primarily with fish dishes.

Natto miso, made from lightly fermented soybeans and ginger, is a spicy condiment.

In making miso soup and for regular cooking, I use a barley miso that has aged for at least eighteen months and preferably for two to three years. Of course, I am careful to be sure that the miso is organic in quality and contains no chemicals or additives. In the natural foods store, miso sold in bulk is usually preferable to miso sold in sealed containers. The latter have been pasteurized, thereby reducing the beneficial enzymes and bacteria that aid digestion.

A powdered miso is available for use while traveling. If circumstances permit, instant miso should be cooked for a few minutes in water rather than steeped like a tea bag. At home, it is better to use regular miso for daily cooking. Miso can also be made at home with a grain starter called *koji*, which contains a special bacteria that enables the soybeans to ferment. Koji is available now in many natural foods stores. Please see my book *How to Cook with Miso* (Japan Publications, 1978) for instructions on making miso at home.

In general, the vegetables for miso soup should be very well cooked. Ideally, they melt in the mouth and after thorough chewing can be swallowed simultaneously with the broth. Because miso contains living microorganisms that aid digestion, the soup should be simmered over low to medium heat for 3 to 5 minutes, but not boiled, after the miso purée is added.

Miso may be enjoyed the year-round, although the varieties, ingredients, and cooking methods may change with the seasons. Miso broth by itself is very satisfying on practically any occasion. To enjoy its simplicity, I make it plain, diluting the miso in spring water, and just adding a touch of sea vegetables and perhaps a contrasting garnish.

A second way is the layered method in which several kinds of vegetables are layered in the pot according to yin and yang with the softest on the bottom and the hardest on top. Cold water is added almost to cover; then the vegetables are cooked until tender and the miso added at the end. Just before adding the miso, additional water or soup stock may be added to bring the volume of liquid up substantially. The vegetables lose their layered texture if initially cooked in too much water. After this preliminary period of cooking, further liquid may be introduced.

A third method of making miso soup involves sautéing the vegetables first in a little sesame oil to remove the vegetables' sharp, raw taste. Water is then added and the vegetables are cooked as in the other methods. The miso is added just before the end of the cooking time. Sautéing makes a richer tasting soup that is very delicious and especially nourishing in the wintertime.

On rare occasions, I may add fish or seafood to miso to make a very energizing dish. Vitality can also be created by adding mochi, tofu, fried tofu, seitan, or tempeh squares or cubes to miso soup. In the long run, vegetable protein provides more endurance than animal protein, and I prefer to use it in cooking.

I use about 1 teaspoon of miso per cup of water or stock in the soup, but this depends on the saltiness of the miso. The concentrated miso is puréed in about three or four times the volume of water (for example, 1 tablespoon of water to 1 teaspoon of miso, before being added to the water in the pot). Because miso is so sweet and delicious, it is easy to overuse it. This produces a craving for liquid, fruits, or sweets to balance the miso's strong salty content. The taste of miso soup should be neither too salty nor too bland. In making quick or basic miso soup, I use a small stainless steel saucepan. For heavier soups and stews, I use a cast-iron or ceramic pot or large kettle. I am careful to leave the ladle used to transfer the soup into individual serving bowls in an empty dish by the pot in between servings.

The recipes that follow are just a few of the dozens of delicious miso soups that can be prepared in the macrobiotic kitchen.

Basic Miso Soup

- 1 3-inch piece dried wakame
- 1 cup thinly sliced onions
- 1 quart spring water
- 1¼ to 1½ tablespoons miso
- Chopped scallions, parsley, ginger, or watercress for garnish

Rinse the wakame in cold water for 3 to 5 minutes and slice it into ½-inch pieces. Put wakame and onions in a pot and add the water. Bring to a boil, lower the heat, and simmer for 10 to 20 minutes, or until tender. Reduce the heat to very low but not boiling or bubbling. Put the miso in a bowl or suribachi. Add ¼ cup of the broth from the pot and purée until miso is completely dissolved in the liquid. Add the puréed miso to the soup. Simmer for 3 to 5 minutes and serve. Garnish with scallions, parsley, ginger, or watercress.

Miso Soup with Daikon and Tofu

In Japan, farming families have daikon miso soup frequently throughout the fall and winter. The taste of this root vegetable complements miso. When cooked in soup, it becomes soft without losing its shape. Tofu is also soft-textured and harmonizes perfectly in the miso.

- 1½ cups daikon, cut into ½-inch pieces
- 1 quart spring water
- Several 3-inch pieces of wakame
- 1 cup tofu cut into 1-inch squares
- 3 teaspoons miso
- 1 scallion, chopped for garnish

Add the daikon to the water and cook for 5 minutes. Meanwhile, soak the wakame for 3 to 5 minutes and then chop it into small pieces. Add the wakame and tofu squares to the pot, bring to a boil, and simmer until the tofu expands and rises to the top. Put the miso in a bowl or suribachi, add ¼ cup of the broth from the pot, and purée. Blend the miso purée with the soup and simmer for 3 minutes. Garnish with chopped scallion and serve.

Variation: For variety, this soup may also be made without either the daikon or tofu.

Miso Soup with Rice and Scallions

This makes a hearty wintertime breakfast that will keep you warm all day.

- 1 3-inch piece dried wakame
- 2 cups sliced scallions and scallion roots
- 1 quart spring water
- 2 cups cooked brown rice
- 1¼ to 1½ tablespoons miso
- 1 scallion, sliced for garnish

Rinse off the wakame quickly and soak it until it is soft. Remove the wakame from the soaking water and cut it into ½-inch pieces. Put the 2 cups of scallions and the wakame in a pot and add water to cover. Bring to a rapid boil. Add the rice and remaining water. Cover the pot and simmer gently for 10 minutes. Put the miso in a bowl and add ¼ cup of the broth from the pot and purée. Add the purée to soup and simmer for a few minutes. Garnish with the sliced scallion and serve.

Miso Soup with Millet and Squash

- ½ cup millet
- ½ cup sliced celery
- 1 cup sliced onions
- 1 cup cubed but not peeled butternut squash
- 1 quart spring water
- 1¼ to 1½ tablespoons miso
- 1 sheet nori, toasted for garnish
- Chopped parsley for garnish

Wash the millet and dry-roast it in a frying pan. In a pot, layer the vegetables, starting with the celery, then the onions, and squash on top. Spread millet evenly over the top of the layered vegetables. Carefully add water to just below the level of the squash. Cook covered over medium heat, adding water gradually as the millet expands. Do not stir. After the millet becomes very soft, about 25 to 30 minutes, add the rest of the water. Bring to a boil; then lower the heat. Mix the miso with a small amount of the broth from the pot and purée. Add the puréed miso to the soup a couple of minutes before serving. Garnish with nori cut in small strips, and parsley.

Variation: Other grains, such as barley, rice, buckwheat, oats, or cracked wheat, may be substituted for the millet.

Celery Miso Soup

Celery is not usually grown in Japan. When I came to America, I was happy to discover that this popular vegetable is very much at home in miso.

- ½ cup celery cut into 1-inch pieces
- ½ cup thinly sliced onions
- 1 teaspoon dark sesame oil
- 1 quart spring water
- 1¼ to 1½ tablespoons miso
- 1 sheet nori, toasted for garnish

Sauté the celery and onions in the oil. Add enough water or stock to cover the vegetables and bring to a boil. Add the remaining liquid, cover the pot, and cook until vegetables become tender. Put the miso in a bowl and add ¼ cup of the broth from the pot and purée. Add the purée to the pot and simmer for a few minutes. Garnish with nori cut in small strips or squares and serve.

Creamy Onion Miso Soup

The whole onions in this soup open up to look like delicate lotus blossoms and become tender enough to melt in your mouth.

- 3 tablespoons diced onion
- 1 teaspoon dark sesame oil
- 6 whole medium-sized onions, peeled
- 1 quart spring water
- 3 tablespoons whole wheat flour
- 1¼ to 1½ tablespoons miso
- 1 teaspoon minced fresh parsley

Sauté the diced onion in the oil. Make three vertical slashes from the top and halfway down each whole onion. Place them cut side down over the sautéed onions. Cover the whole onions with 3 cups of water (saving 1 cup) and simmer until the onions are soft but not so soft that they are falling apart, about 20 to 30 minutes. While onions are simmering, toast the flour in remaining oil until brown, then let cool. Mix the flour with remaining 1 cup of water to make a paste. Stir into the soup and cook until thick, stirring gently to avoid breaking the onions. Put the miso in a bowl and add ¼ cup of the broth from the pot and purée. Add the purée to the soup and continue to simmer for a few minutes, or until ready to serve. Garnish with the minced parsley.

Variation: This soup may also be made with kombu stock. In this case, omit the oil and flour.

Miso Soup with Sesame Seeds and Broccoli

The rich flavor of sesame makes this a favorite in our household.

- 1 large broccoli stalk
- 1 teaspoon dark sesame oil
- 1 quart spring water
- ½ cup toasted sesame seeds
- 1¼ to 1½ tablespoons miso

Separate the top of the broccoli from the stem and cut it into flowerets. Slice the stem into 1-inch-thick pieces. Sauté the broccoli stems in the oil. Add water to cover the vegetable and bring to a boil. Add all but ½ cup of the remaining water and cover the pot. Bring to a boil, lower the heat, and simmer until the broccoli stems are soft. To keep the broccoli flowerets green, pour the remaining ½ cup of water into a separate pan and boil, uncovered, until their color begins to deepen. Add the cooking water to soup but set the broccoli flowerets aside. Thoroughly grind the sesame seeds in a suribachi. Add the miso to the suribachi with the ground sesame seeds; then add ½ cup of the broth from the pot and purée. Add the purée to the soup and simmer for a few minutes. Serve, floating a few broccoli flowerets in each bowl.

Mochi Miso Soup

- 1 quart spring water
- 1 cup sliced Chinese cabbage
- 1¼ to 1½ tablespoons miso
- Several pieces of dry pan-fried or baked mochi
- 1 sheet toasted nori, cut into 1-inch squares
- 1 cup sliced scallions

Bring the water to a boil and add the Chinese cabbage. Lower the heat and simmer until the cabbage is just about done, about 3 to 5 minutes. Turn the heat to low and add the miso puréed in a little broth.

Simmer for 2 minutes longer. Pour the hot soup over 1 or 2 pieces of pan-fried or baked mochi. Garnish with the nori squares and scallions and serve.

Fu Miso Soup

Fu are dried wheat gluten cakes or sheets. They are very delicious in soup or broth with noodles. If the wakame soaking water is salty do not use in the soup. However, if the soaking water is not salty include it in the liquid for this soup.

- ¼ cup wakame, washed, soaked, and sliced
- 1 cup daikon cut in rectangles
- 1 cup dried fu, soaked and sliced
- 5 to 6 cups spring water including reserved wakame soaking liquid, if desired
- 2 tablespoons miso
- ¼ teaspoon grated fresh ginger (optional)
- 1 scallion, sliced for garnish

Put the wakame, daikon, and fu in a pot and add the water. Bring to a boil, cover, and reduce the heat to low. Simmer until the daikon is soft, 30 to 40 minutes. Reduce the heat to very low and add the miso puréed in a little broth. Simmer for several minutes and, if you wish, add ¼ teaspoon of grated fresh ginger and simmer a few moments longer. Pour into serving bowls, garnish with a few sliced scallions, and serve.

Miso Soup with Okara and Dried Daikon

Okara is the coarse soybean pulp left over when tofu is made at home. It is very delicious in soups but should not be cooked too long so as to preserve its taste.

- ½ cup dried daikon
- 3 cups spring water
- 1 shiitake mushroom
- 1 8-inch strip kombu, soaked and sliced
- ½ cup okara
- 2 tablespoons miso
- Sliced scallions for garnish

Soak the dried daikon in 1½ cups of water. Soak the shiitake in ½ cup of water and soak the kombu in 1 cup of water. After 5 to 10 minutes of soaking, drain the daikon, shiitake, and kombu and put the soaking water into a pot. Slice the daikon thinly and add it to the pot. Then slice the shiitake and kombu and add them to the pot. Bring to a boil, cover, reduce the heat to low, and simmer until the daikon is done, about 30 minutes. Reduce the heat to very low and add the okara and miso to the soup stock. (The okara may be sautéed in a little sesame oil before being added, if desired.) Simmer the soup for 1 to 2 minutes longer. Serve garnished with sliced scallions.

Jinenjo Miso Soup

Jinenjo is a long mountain potato native to Japan. It is available in some natural foods stores. This miso soup should be simply made with basic miso soup containing just sea vegetables, miso, and water so the jinenjo may be tasted.

1 tablespoon grated jinenjo
1 cup hot basic miso soup
Sliced scallions for garnish

Put the grated jinenjo in a soup bowl. Pour the hot miso soup over the jinenjo. Garnish with sliced scallions and serve.

CLEAR SOUPS AND SOUP STOCK

Clear soup is simple and elegant—a visual delight. In Japan we call it *osumashi*, meaning clear water or pond. It is made from kombu and vegetable or shiitake mushroom stock and usually contains a small square of tofu, one or two slices of carrot cut into flower shapes, a radish square, or some other beautifully prepared vegetable, and a little ginger, scallion, or parsley as a garnish.

Clear soup is mild in taste, soft in texture, and creates a feeling of tranquility and anticipation. It is customarily served on holidays and on formal occasions where there are many courses in the meal.

Tamari soy sauce is generally not used as seasoning in clear soup because it gives a dark color. However, if desired, a touch of soy sauce may be used at the end of cooking. Tamari broth itself can be made by adding tamari soy sauce to soup stock; it is commonly served with noodles.

Kombu Soup Stock

Kombu is a wide, thick, dark green sea vegetable that is high in calcium and other minerals. The unique flavor complements many vegetable and animal foods. Kombu stock is the most popular stock in macrobiotic cooking. In traditional Japanese cooking it is known as *dashi*.

1 3-inch piece kombu, or kelp if unavailable

1 quart spring water

Dust the sand off the kombu but be careful to leave the white powder undisturbed. For a rich taste, soak the kombu for 5 minutes before cooking. Put the kombu into water and heat. The length of time the kombu remains in the stock is determined by its quality. If the kombu is very thick, such as the finest varieties available in natural foods stores or Oriental specialty shops, remove it from the stock just before the water boils and save it for another dish. Such strong, thick kombu should not be used in the soup since it will have to cook for a long time to become tender and it will absorb too much taste from the other vegetables. However, if the kombu is thin or ordinary kelp is used in its place, leave the sea vegetable in the stock to provide adequate flavor. Cook for another 5 to 10 minutes. Kombu stock is used for clear soup or as a broth for other soups.

Dried Shiitake Mushroom Stock

These dried mushrooms are very delicious and are used medicinally to balance heavy animal food consumption. Shiitake are not recommended for regular use by persons with weak conditions. Those in good health may have a small amount of shiitake (a few slices) every day. These dried mushrooms blend well with kombu and may be combined to make a stock for clear soup.

2 medium-sized dried shiitake mushrooms

1 quart spring water

Soak the mushrooms in the water for 5 minutes. Remove them and slice them into small pieces. Remove and discard the mushroom stem, which is fibrous and often contains sand. Return the mushrooms to the water again and bring to a boil. Lower the heat and simmer for 5 minutes. The shiitake may be left in the stock or saved for another dish.

Vegetable Stock

Vegetable stock can be made from carrots, onions, sometimes just a touch of burdock, and other naturally sweet vegetables. It may also be made from wilted vegetables or vegetable parts that are not ordinarily eaten. These include cabbage hearts, pea pods, corn husks, vegetable cores, tough outer leaves, and squash peelings. (I avoid greens that lend a bitter taste, such as carrot tops, spinach, or Swiss chard.) I save these odds and ends in a container and, when enough accumulate, I make a delicious stock. After cooking, some of the stock vegetables can be prepared separately as a tasty side dish. Simply recook with a little tamari soy sauce. Add kombu and shiitake, if desired.

Vegetable parts, cut into small pieces
Spring water to cover

Boil for 5 to 10 minutes and remove the vegetables.

❧ Dried Vegetable Stock ❧

For a sweeter stock, I use dried vegetables, such as dried daikon, or dried root vegetables, such as carrot or turnip.

½ cup dried vegetables
5 cups spring water

Wash and then soak the vegetables in the water for 5 minutes. Bring to a boil and cook for 3 minutes. Remove the vegetables and save them for a side dish. Use the stock for soup.

❧ Grain Soup Stock ❧

This is a favorite in some Zen monasteries.

½ cup brown rice, barley, or other grain
1 quart cold spring water

Dry-roast the grain; then put it in a pot and add the cold water. Bring to a boil and cook for 2 to 3 minutes. Use the stock for soup and save the grain for later use in bread, tempura, or baked dishes.

❧ Fish Stock ❧

Fish heads and bones can also be saved for stock. Simply tie the fish parts in cheesecloth, put in water, and boil for a few minutes. Fish parts can also be boiled directly in water and removed from the stock by straining through a cheesecloth after boiling. Fish stock may be used for vegetable or grain soups.

Bonito Stock

Bonito fish flakes are also commonly used in the Far East to make soup stock. Good bonito has no fishy smell and harmonizes well with vegetables. Ideally, I obtain smoked bonito fish which I shave myself rather than using the prepared flakes. To prepare, add 3 tablespoons of fresh shaved bonito flakes to kombu stock. Just before the water boils, remove the kombu and bonito shavings and boil for 1 minute. Remove from the heat and strain. The bonito flakes may be served with the kombu as a side dish.

Clear Soup

This basic clear soup may be made with one of the soup stocks described above.

- 1 quart kombu or other soup stock
- 1 carrot cut into flower shapes
- 1 cup tofu cut into ½-inch squares
- 1 bunch watercress, thinly sliced
- ½ sheet nori, cut in small squares for garnish
- Grated fresh ginger or ginger juice to taste for garnish

Slice and boil the vegetables separately for a few minutes, or until tender. Boil the tofu in the kombu stock for 1 to 2 minutes, or until it comes to the top. (Cooked in this way, the tofu is quite tender. If cooked too long, tofu becomes rubbery.) Put 1 to 2 pieces of boiled carrot and about a spoonful of sliced watercress into each individual serving bowl. Pour the hot kombu stock into each cup over the vegetables and add 1 or 2 tofu squares. The color of the vegetables should be bright. The color will fade if they are cooked together. Garnish with nori and grated fresh ginger or ginger juice and serve.

Variations: Instead of carrots, other vegetables such as broccoli, cauliflower, celery, parsnips, Chinese cabbage, mushrooms, pumpkin, or winter squash may be used. Bread crumbs, dried or deep-fried, make an excellent garnish for all of these clear soups.

Clear Broth with Taro Potato

Taro is a small potato which has a thick, hairy skin. It is also known as *albi*. It is generally too expansive for regular use but may be eaten occasionally, especially in warmer months. Its light delicate taste goes well with clear soup.

6 to 8 small taro potatoes
1 strip kombu, 6 to 8 inches long, soaked
4 to 5 cups spring water
Tamari soy sauce
Sliced scallions for garnish
1 sheet nori, toasted and cut into strips for garnish

Peel and wash the taro and slice them in half. Put the kombu and water in a pot and bring to a boil. Cover, reduce the heat to medium-low, and simmer for 5 to 7 minutes. Remove the kombu and set aside for use in another dish. Add the taro and simmer until soft. Reduce the heat to low and lightly season the soup with tamari soy sauce. Simmer about 5 minutes longer. Pour the soup into individual bowls and add 3 to 4 slices of taro. Garnish each bowl with a few sliced scallions and several strips of toasted nori. Serve hot.

Clear Soup with Deep-Fried Vegetable Balls

Grate carrot or other vegetables and mix with whole wheat flour and a little sea salt. Form into balls and deep-fry in dark sesame oil. Place 1 or 2 balls in each individual soup bowl and pour soup stock over them. Garnish with parsley, nori, and a touch of ginger and serve. You may also use roasted bread crumbs in this soup instead of fried balls.

Clear Soup with Seafood

To make a clear soup with seafood, add several clams or small shrimps to the basic clear soup recipe. Boil the seafood in the stock to make a nice red color and add to other vegetables in individual bowls. A slice of mushroom may also be added to each bowl to balance the strong taste of the seafood.

Tamari Soy Sauce Broth

This soup is similar to clear soup but has a stronger taste and darker appearance. At home we use it very often to enjoy the full taste of tamari soy sauce. Tamari broth is especially delicious with noodles or whole wheat pasta.

2 shiitake mushrooms
4 cups spring water
1 3-inch piece kombu
2 cakes tofu, cubed
2 to 3 tablespoons tamari soy sauce
¼ cup sliced scallions for garnish
1 sheet nori, toasted and cut into strips for garnish

Soak the shiitake mushrooms for 10 to 20 minutes; drain, and reserve water. Discard the stems. Put the kombu and shiitake in the water (plus the soaking water) and boil for 3 to 4 minutes. Remove the kombu and shiitake and save for another recipe. Add the tofu and boil until the tofu comes to the surface. Do not boil the tofu too long or it will become hard. Tofu in soup is best enjoyed soft. Add the tamari soy sauce and simmer for 2 to 3 minutes. Garnish with scallions and nori.

VEGETABLE SOUPS

Vegetable soups are simple and easy to prepare. They can be made plain by using only one type of vegetable or mixed by combining several vegetables. Single vegetable soups, such as celery soup, carrot soup, or squash soup, may be made in several ways. One way is to cook the sliced vegetable until it is soft and its juices flavor the entire soup.

The country-style method is to blend the vegetable in its liquid completely by cooking the vegetable first until it is tender and then puréeing it in a hand food mill or liquefying it in a suribachi. Adding diluted kuzu or other natural vegetable starch, such as arrowroot flour, makes this soup even more creamy and delicious.

Mixed vegetables also provide a tasty, full-bodied soup. Suggestions are given in the recipe at the end of this section.

Squash or Pumpkin Soup

This naturally sweet soup is popular at our home throughout the autumn and winter. Be sure to make enough for seconds.

1 medium-sized buttercup squash, butternut squash, or Hokkaido pumpkin
4 to 5 cups spring water
¼ to ½ teaspoon sea salt
Toasted nori, cut into 1-inch squares for garnish
Chopped parsley or sliced scallions for garnish

Wash the squash and remove the skin and seeds. (These can be saved for roasting or cutting into matchsticks, combining with tempura batter, and deep-frying.) Cut the squash into large chunks; you should have 4 to 5 cups. Put the squash in a pot and add the water and a pinch of sea salt. Bring to a boil. Cover, lower the heat, and simmer until the squash is soft, about 40 minutes to an hour. Pour the squash and cooking water into a hand food mill and purée. Return the puréed squash to the pot, season with the remaining sea salt, and simmer for several minutes. Pour the soup into individual serving bowls and garnish with a few squares of toasted nori and chopped parsley.

Celery Soup

5 to 6 cups kombu stock
2 cups diced celery
1 cup diced onions
⅛ teaspoon sea salt
⅓ cup brown rice flour
Tamari soy sauce to taste
Sliced scallions or sliced toasted nori for garnish

Put the stock, celery, and onions in a pot. Add a pinch of salt and bring to a boil. Reduce the heat to low, cover, and simmer for 15 to 20 minutes. Mix the flour with a small amount of water until no lumps remain. Slowly add the flour paste to the vegetables and broth, stirring constantly to prevent lumping. Add remaining salt and tamari soy sauce to taste. Simmer for 15 to 20 minutes over low flame. Garnish with scallions or nori and serve.

Carrot Soup

This delicious, sweet-tasting soup is cooling and I especially enjoy it during the summer.

3 cups grated carrots
1 cup minced onions
5 to 6 cups spring water
¼ teaspoon sea salt
Sliced scallions or sliced toasted nori for garnish

Put the carrots and onions in a pot. Add water and a pinch of salt. Bring to a boil, reduce the heat to low, cover, and simmer for 20 to 25 minutes. Add remaining sea salt and simmer for another 10 to 15 minutes. Garnish with scallions or nori and serve.

Variation: For a creamier soup, dice the carrots and purée them with the onions in a hand food mill after the initial cooking.

Cauliflower Soup

1 head cauliflower
4 to 5 cups spring water
Pinch of sea salt
½ cup carrots, cut into flower shapes for garnish
Chopped parsley for garnish
1 sheet nori, toasted and cut into strips for garnish

Wash the cauliflower and cut it into chunks. Put the cauliflower and water into a pot. Add a pinch of sea salt and bring to a boil. Reduce the heat to medium-low and cover. Simmer until the cauliflower is very soft. Purée the cauliflower in a hand food mill and return to the pot with all of the cooking water. Parboil the carrot flowers in a separate pot. Remove and drain. Season the cauliflower soup with a little sea salt and simmer several minutes longer. Pour the soup into individual serving bowls and garnish with 2 carrot flowers, a little chopped parsley, and a few strips of toasted nori.

Mixed Vegetable Soup

Some vegetables go well together in soups and stews and some don't. Cooking foods together is a little like arranging a symphony: Until you have experience with the violin, flute, and horn, you shouldn't try to conduct the whole orchestra. Generally, colors, textures, and tastes tend to fade and dissolve when mixed together. For example, radish and parsnip have very strong tastes and should be used sparingly or in minute quantities in combination with other vegetables. When cooking different vegetables together, I usually prepare them in different quantities, shapes, and sizes to give the dish variety, enhance flavor, and create texture.

In addition to this recipe, other good vegetable combinations for soup include carrots, onions, cabbage, and broccoli; corn, onions, and carrots; corn and cabbage; daikon, burdock, celery, Chinese cabbage, and a small albi or taro potato.

¼ cup celery sliced diagonally
2 cups diced onions
1 cup carrots cut into matchsticks
½ cup burdock cut into matchsticks
5 to 8 cups spring water
1 teaspoon sea salt
1 tablespoon kuzu, diluted
Sliced scallions and toasted nori strips for garnish

Put the vegetables in a pot, starting with celery, then the onions, carrots, and burdock. Pour in 3 to 4 cups of water. Bring to a boil, lower the heat, and simmer until the vegetables become soft, about 35 to 40 minutes. Add 1 teaspoon of salt. Add 2 to 4 more cups of water, adjust the seasoning to taste, bring to a boil, and add 1 level tablespoon of diluted kuzu powder to thicken the soup. Lower the heat and simmer for 2 to 3 minutes, stirring to prevent lumping. Pour the soup into serving bowls and garnish with scallions and nori.

BEAN SOUPS

Everyone enjoys the rich taste of soup made with beans, pulses, or legumes. The soft, well-cooked beans, attractively presented with a little garnish, create a substantial dish. With whole grain bread or a bowl of grain, bean soups make a hearty, family-style meal.

❧ Lentil Soup ❧

- 1 cup dried lentils
- 2 onions, diced
- 1 carrot, diced
- 1 small burdock, diced
- 1 quart spring water
- ¼ to ½ teaspoon sea salt
- 1 tablespoon chopped parsley
- Tamari soy sauce (optional)

Wash the lentils and drain them. Layer vegetables in a pot, starting with onions, then the carrot and the burdock. Spread the lentils on top. Add the water and pinch of salt. Bring to a boil, reduce the heat to low, cover, and simmer for 45 minutes. Add the chopped parsley and remaining salt. Simmer for 20 minutes longer and serve. Tamari soy sauce may be added for flavor.

Variation: The vegetables may be sautéed first and then cooked with lentils as above.

❧ Azuki Bean Soup ❧

- 1-inch square dried kombu
- 1 cup dried azuki beans
- 1 quart spring water
- 1 medium-sized onion, peeled and sliced
- ½ cup sliced carrots
- ¼ to ½ teaspoon sea salt
- Tamari soy sauce (optional)
- Sliced scallions or chopped parsley for garnish

Soak the kombu for 5 minutes and slice. Wash the beans; then put them in a pot and add the water. Bring to a boil, lower the heat, and simmer for 1¼ hours, or until the beans are about 80 percent done. Put the onion slices on the bottom of another pot; then add the carrots, azuki beans, and kombu. Add the salt. Cook for 20 to 25 minutes, or until the vegetables are soft. At the very end, add tamari soy sauce to taste, if desired. Garnish with scallions or parsley and serve.

Variation: Instead of carrots and onion, winter squash may be used. This soup is especially recommended for persons with weak kidneys, spleen, pancreas, or liver.

Chick-Pea Soup

- 1 3-inch piece kombu
- 1 cup dried chick-peas, soaked overnight
- 4 to 5 cups spring water, including reserved chick-pea soaking water
- 1 onion, peeled and diced
- 1 carrot, diced
- 1 burdock, quartered
- ¼ to ½ teaspoon sea salt
- Sliced scallions, chopped parsley, or toasted bread cubes for garnish

Put the kombu, chick-peas, and water in a pressure cooker and cook for 1 to 1½ hours. Bring the pressure down. Transfer the bean mixture to another pot. Add the vegetables and salt. Cook for 20 to 25 minutes over medium-low heat. Garnish with scallions, parsley, or bread cubes.

Variation: A delicious cool chick-pea soup can be made by puréeing 3 cups of cooked chick-peas in a little cooking liquid or spring water. Marinate ½ cup shredded carrots, ½ cup cucumbers sliced into matchsticks, and ¼ cup chopped chives or scallions with a few drops of tamari soy sauce and let sit for 30 minutes. Place 1 tablespoon of marinated vegetables on top of each bowl of chick-pea soup and garnish with 2 to 3 toasted or deep-fried bread cubes.

GRAIN SOUPS

Each grain has a unique, rich taste. With a few simple side dishes, grain soup cooked with vegetables makes an enjoyable luncheon or light evening meal. Soup or stew is an excellent way to use leftover grain.

Barley Soup

¼ cup dried lentils
1 celery stalk, sliced diagonally
3 onions, peeled and diced
1 carrot, sliced
1 cup cooked barley
5 to 6 cups spring water
¼ to ½ teaspoon sea salt
Tamari soy sauce (optional)
Toasted nori squares or chopped parsley for garnish

Wash the lentils and drain them. Layer the vegetables in a pot, starting with the celery on the bottom, then the onion, carrot, lentils, and barley on top. Add just enough water to cover and bring to a boil. Add sea salt just before boiling. Lower the heat and simmer until the vegetables are tender. Check the taste. Add a drop of tamari soy sauce for flavor, if desired, and garnish with nori or parsley and serve.

Brown Rice Soup

3 shiitake mushrooms
1 3-inch piece kombu
1 quart spring water
2 cups cooked brown rice
¼ cup dried celery
1 to 2 tablespoons tamari soy sauce
Sliced scallions for garnish

Boil the mushrooms and kombu in the water for 2 to 3 minutes. Remove them and cut them into thin strips or pieces. Return them to the water, add the rice, and bring the mixture to a boil. Lower the heat and cook for 30 to 40 minutes. Add the celery and simmer for 5 minutes. Add tamari soy sauce to taste and simmer for 5 minutes longer. Garnish with scallions and serve.

Variation: Miso may be added for a wonderful, warming soup.

Buckwheat Soup

Sesame oil
1 onion, peeled and diced
½ cup buckwheat, dry-roasted
5 to 6 cups spring water
Pinch of sea salt
Tamari soy sauce to taste
½ cup minced parsley for garnish

Brush a small amount of dark sesame oil over the bottom of a pot. Sauté the onion until it is translucent. Add the buckwheat, water, and salt. Bring to a boil, cover, lower the heat, and simmer for 25 to 30 minutes. Season with tamari soy sauce and simmer 10 minutes longer. Garnish with minced parsley and serve.

Variation: For a richer, more dynamic soup, add carrots, cabbage, or a variety of other vegetables.

Fresh Corn Soup

- 4 ears fresh corn
- 1 celery stalk, diced
- 2 onions, peeled and diced
- 5 to 6 cups spring water or kombu stock
- ¼ teaspoon sea salt
- Tamari soy sauce (optional)
- Chopped parsley, watercress, scallions, or toasted nori for garnish

Strip the kernels from the corn with a knife. Put the celery, onions, and corn in a pot. Add the water and a pinch of salt. Bring to a boil, lower the heat, cover, and simmer until the celery and corn are soft. Add the remaining salt and tamari soy sauce to taste, if desired. Serve with chopped parsley, watercress, scallions, or toasted nori as a garnish.

CHAPTER

12

PREPARING AND CUTTING VEGETABLES

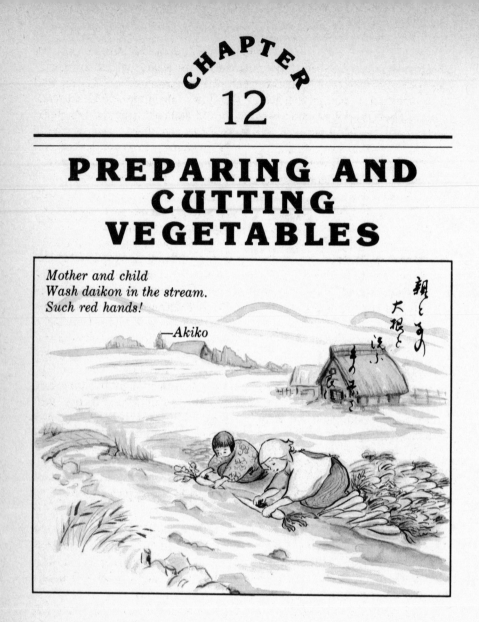

Mother and child
Wash daikon in the stream.
Such red hands!
—Akiko

Whole grains and vegetables naturally complement one another. If we eat animal food, we require simply a vegetable side dish or a salad. However, if we eat primarily grains, we naturally develop a taste for a wide variety of vegetables prepared in different styles to make a nourishing and satisfying meal. In the standard macrobiotic diet, vegetables make up about twenty-five to thirty percent of each meal by volume of food consumed. Grains and vegetables complement one another in many ways. Grains and beans come in limited varieties, while the number of vegetables is almost unlimited. Grains and beans take many months to grow, while vegetables often develop in only a few weeks. Grains and beans take a long time to cook and are primarily boiled or pressure-cooked. Vegetables may be prepared quickly as well as slowly, and can be used in fresh raw salads, pickled, sautéed, steamed, baked, and broiled as well as boiled and cooked under pressure.

In selecting vegetables it is important to see clearly their growing energy as well as to be familiar with their shapes, aromas, tastes, and textures. From childhood, I helped out in my family's garden and learned to appreciate these natural qualities. I saw how vegetables grew, what plants they flourished with, and how the seasons and elements affected them. At home we grew nearly all our own vegetables, including Chinese cabbage, burdock, scallions, string beans, kidney beans, carrots, daikon, squash, bok choy, peppers, cabbage, mustard greens, cucumbers, summer squash, parsley, and albi potato. The vegetable we purchased regularly in large quantities at the village's one vegetable store or from neighboring farmers was daikon, which we pickled. During the war, while I was teaching fifth grade, my class grew potatoes in the garden at school and won first prize at the autumn fair. Some of my fondest memories go back to gardening. I can recall standing with my mother in the garden, when I was about five years old, watching the sun sink in the distant mountain valley.

Later, I had difficulty preparing some Western vegetables because I had not seen them in their natural setting. My understanding of Belgian endive, for example, was very shallow. Then, on a trip to Belgium, I saw the endive in its own environment and I began to appreciate it from the heart and my cooking improved whenever I used it.

HARVESTING AND CLEANING VEGETABLES

Early morning is the ideal time to pick vegetables for daily use from the garden. Vegetables that have rested all night are cooler, calmer, and better to the taste than those harvested later in the day. Cucumbers, for instance, are very sweet when they are picked before sunrise but are bitter if picked at the end of the day.

As much as possible, I clean vegetables in the garden, removing dirt from the roots and peeling off the outer leaves. This replenishes the soil, and I bring less dust into the kitchen. If you wash them with only tap water, it is important to use only cold water because hot or warm water depletes vegetables of vitamins and minerals. The produce should be washed quickly. Soaking contributes to spoilage. The preferred method indoors is to dip the vegetable completely under water in a pot or bucket. Organic vegetables contain many tiny insects, insect eggs, snails, and other small forms of life that are not adequately rinsed off by just washing under the tap. Root vegetables should be thoroughly scrubbed with a natural bristle vegetable brush, which is commonly available in the natural foods store. Scrubbing should be firm but gentle, so that the skin is not broken. Leafy greens do not need scrubbing but should be submerged completely in water and each leaf rinsed separately. Leeks are among the most difficult vegetables to clean because dirt can get into the inner layers of the stalk. Sometimes I cut the leek in half lengthwise and wash under water to loosen the soil inside. Cleaning vegetables thoroughly is very important: it prevents a gritty taste and removes small organisms.

If I am not using the vegetables that day, I leave the soil on the plants and do not wash or clean them. This helps preserve them. If the vegetables are not organic, I add a teaspoon of sea salt to the wash water and rinse well to help eliminate some of the chemicals.

STORE-BOUGHT VEGETABLES

Compared to chemically grown food, organic food is usually smaller, less glossy, and more uniform in size and shape. In most natural foods stores, organic produce is clearly marked and certified. However, one way to tell the difference is to examine the shape and size of the vegetables or fruits. Organic produce is usually well proportioned and symmetrical. The leaves are generally the same length and shape. In contrast, chemically grown produce is often lopsided and the leaves are irregular. In organic plants, the core is located directly at the center, while the core in inorganic plants is off center. For example, a carrot grown with chemicals, when cut, will have a core that swerves sharply to one side. A carrot grown with animal fertilizer will often have a core that veers slightly. A carrot cultivated with natural mulch will have a perfectly centered core. Naturally, these degrees of balance will be absorbed and conveyed to those who eat them.

When shopping at a store for organic produce, I look for vegetables or fruit that are fresh looking, have beautiful color, and a nice shape. I select those that are neither too big nor too small nor distorted in shape. Produce that is dull in color, limp, or soft is lacking in vitality, less tasty, and will spoil more quickly.

In selecting greens, I avoid those that are turning yellow. This shows they were picked too late, have aged, or have been stored in too warm a temperature. Yellowing leaves are stale and musty to the taste. In selecting root and stalk vegetables, I check the ends for long fibers. These show toughness. Aging is also revealed by browning and hardening at the bottoms of stem vegetables. In selecting round and ground vegetables as well as fruits, wrinkles and soft spots reflect dryness on the inside and a loss of moisture. I prefer to pick out produce that is not prepackaged or tied in bunches, both of which can encourage spoilage.

At home I immediately cut out and discard any bad spots before storing. The rest of the vegetable is perfectly fine to use. Removing yellowing leaves or other aging parts prevents spoilage from spreading. If possible, vegetables and fruits should be stored at home slightly separated from one another, as their pressure on each other can increase rotting. Squashes are especially susceptible to this. In Japan we used to store root vegetables outside during the winter under piles of rice hulls. This kept them warm and fresh in the fields until they were used. At home we also dried daikon and hung it up on the porch. As the time passed, it became very sweet and delicious, with a taste resembling dried apricots. There are many traditional ways to store and preserve foods naturally. For example, lotus root and gingerroot keep well in a small box of sand. In the refrigerator they collect moisture and spoil more rapidly.

Leafy greens and other soft varieties are best refrigerated until they are used. I keep them separately in closed brown paper bags. In the refrigerator plastic bags collect moisture; paper bags allow the produce to breathe and retain their freshness.

CUTTING VEGETABLES

Vegetables may be cut in an almost infinite variety of shapes, sizes, and thicknesses. Attractively cut vegetables enhance the beauty and enjoyment of a meal. Cooking synthesizes many arts, and cutting may be compared to living sculpture.

The choice of cutting method depends on the natural energy of the vegetable itself, the overall menu and balance of the dishes to be served, and the amount of time available for cooking. Thinly sliced vegetables cook more quickly than thickly sliced ones. Root vegetables keep their shape and may be cut in many ways, while greens shrink in volume during cooking and do not offer as much variety in appearance. Dishes in the meal should complement one another in shape. If the vegetables in the soup are cubed or diced, then a side dish might contain vegetables cut in large rounds or vice versa. When cooking many vegetables together, I will often cut them in various shapes and sizes to give the dish variety. However, each individual type of vegetable should be cut into the same-sized pieces to ensure even cooking.

There are about a dozen ways of cutting vegetables we use regularly in macrobiotic cooking. All styles are fine and should be alternated frequently for variety. The traditional Japanese name for each cutting style is given at the end in parentheses.

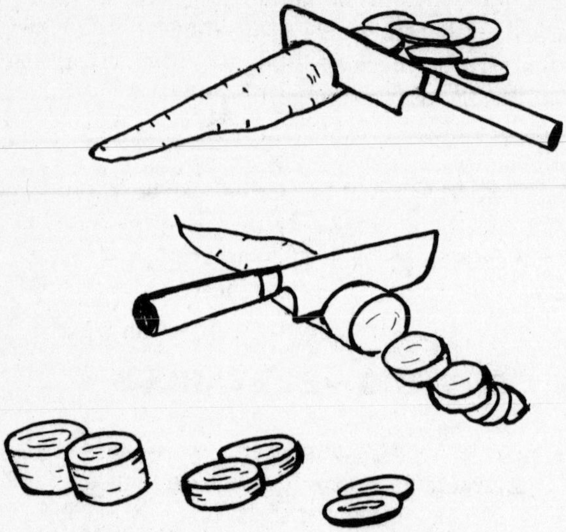

Rounds—Cut the vegetables into thin or thick rounds. (*Wagiri*)

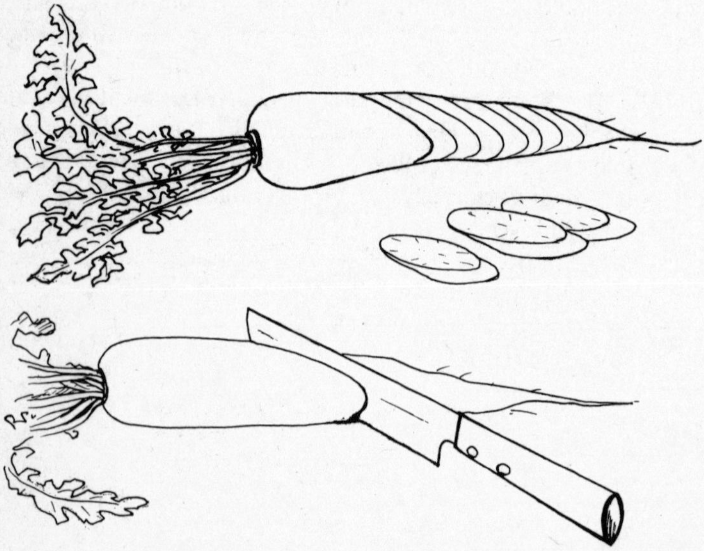

Diagonal—Slice vegetables on the diagonal by holding knife at an angle. The angle of the blade determines the length of the pieces. (*Hasu-giri*)

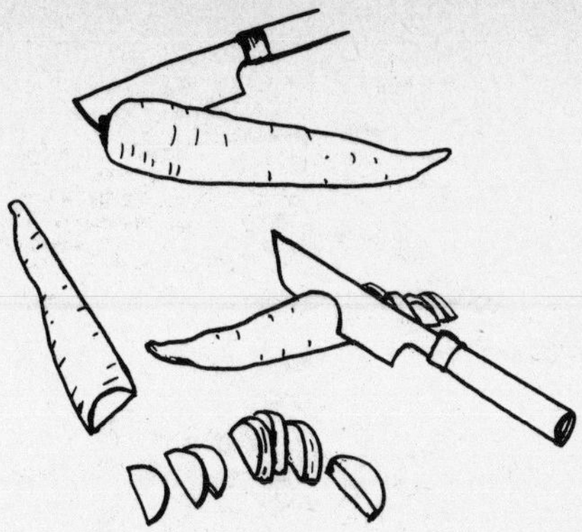

Half Moons—Cut the vegetables lengthwise through the middle into 2 halves. Then cut each half crosswise into thin rounds. (*Hangetsu*)

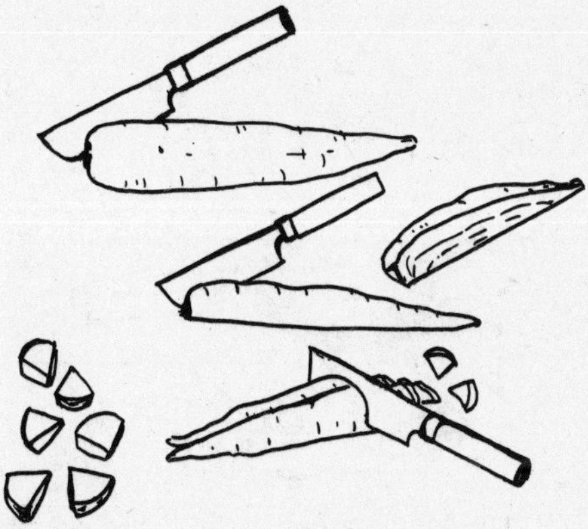

Quarters—Slice the vegetables lengthwise into halves. Then cut each half down the center again. Slice the quarters crosswise thinly as for rounds if too long. (*Ichyo-gata*)

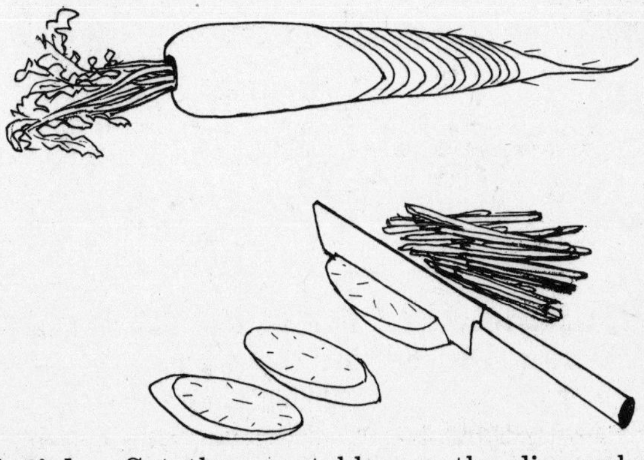

Matchsticks—Cut the vegetables on the diagonal and then slice each diagonal piece into thin matchsticks. (*Sen-giri*)

Irregular or Rolling Style—Cut the vegetables on a diagonal, rotating vegetables toward you 90 degrees after each cut. The pieces will be the same size but irregularly shaped. (*Ran-giri* and *Mawashi-giri*)

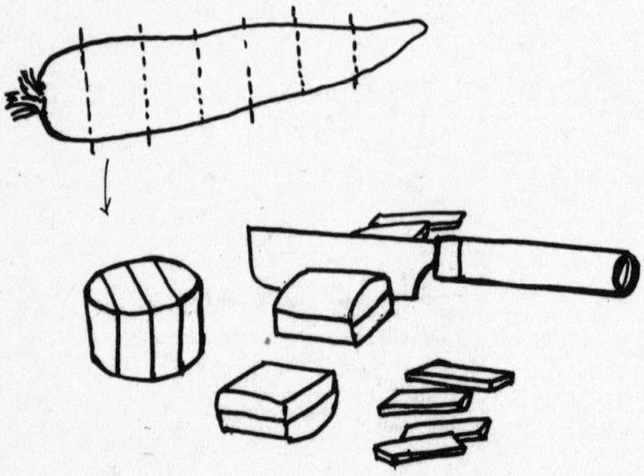

Rectangles—Cut the vegetables into large rounds 1 to 2 inches thick. Stand each round on its head and cut into 4 to 5 pieces ¼ to ⅓ inch thick. Then cut each section into thin rectangles. (*Tanzaku*)

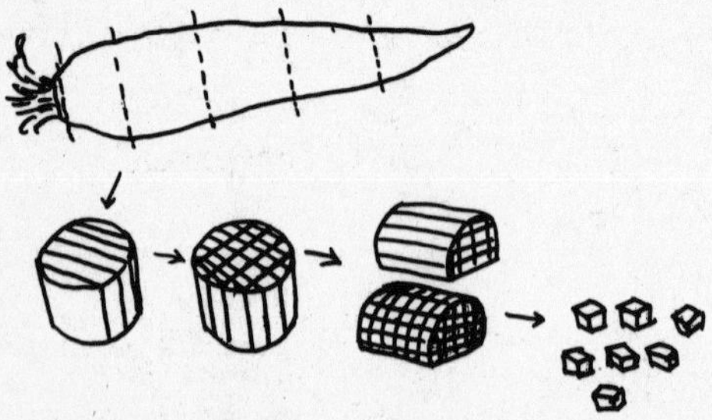

Dicing—First cut vegetables into 1- to 2-inch chunks. Stand each chunk on end and cut into ¼- to ½-inch cubes by cutting vertically, then horizontally, then crosswise. When dicing onions, cut the onion in half horizontally. Then cut thin parallel slices vertically leaving the onion attached to the root base. Then slice in opposite direction toward the base. Finally dice the root base into small pieces. (*Sainome*)

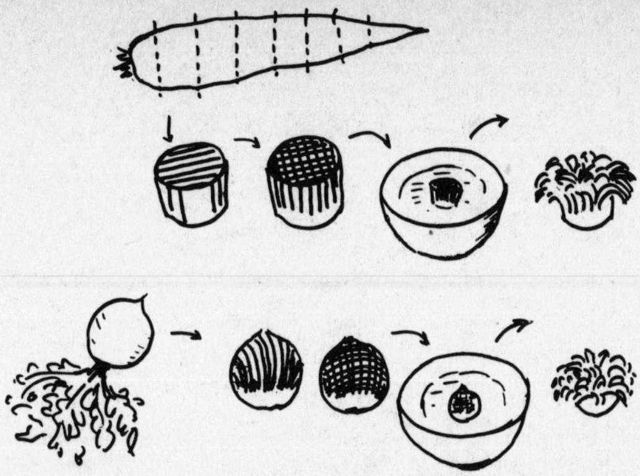

Chrysanthemums—Cut the vegetables into rounds 1 to 1½ inches thick. Leaving the base of each round attached, cut several slices across each round. Then turn the rounds 90 degrees and cut in opposite direction to the same depth. To open the flowers soak cut pieces in cold water. (*Kiku-gata*)

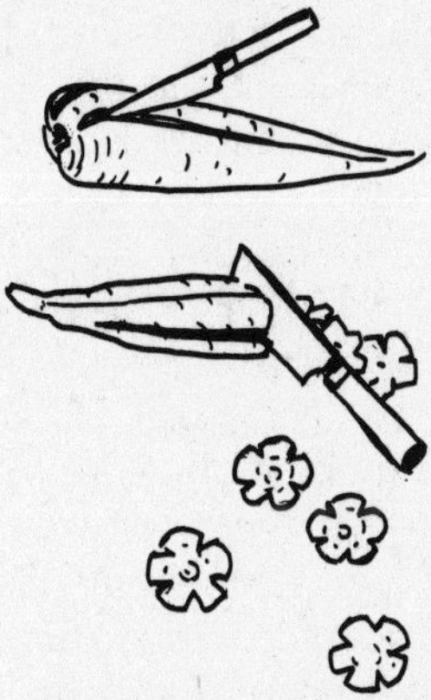

Flower Shapes—Cut 4 or 5 grooves around the vegetables lengthwise at equal distances. Then slice into thin rounds. (*Hana-gata*)

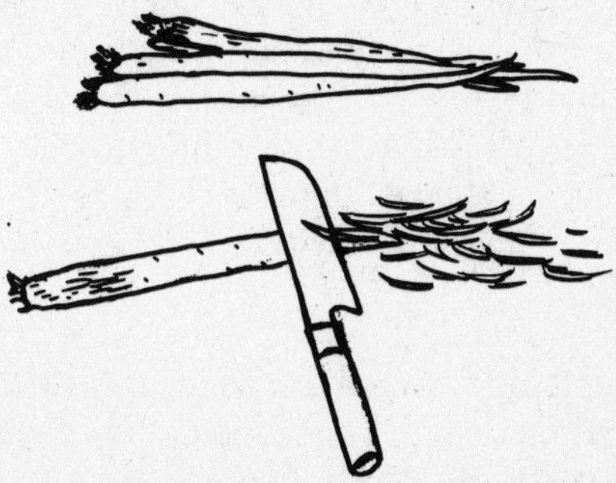

Shaving—Shave root vegetables from the bottom like sharpening a pencil. Rotate vegetable slightly during shaving. Altering the angle of the knife makes for thinner or thicker shavings. (*Sasagaki*)

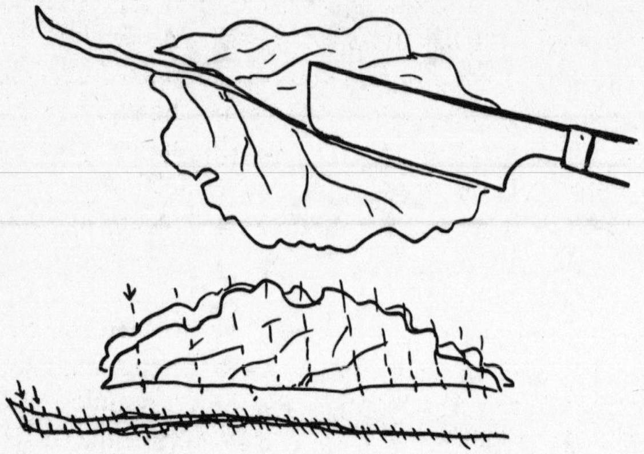

Slicing Greens—Place 2 to 3 leaves on top of one another. Cut through the center along the spine of the leaves. Cut each halved leaf either straight or on the diagonal into strips ⅛ to ¼ inch thick and then chop the spine very finely.

In addition to cutting, I also like to prepare vegetables whole. A vegetable cooked in its entirety provides whole energy. Squash, of course, is often cooked in this way, but I also enjoy whole cooked onions, whole carrots, whole endives, and other whole vegetables on occasion.

When cutting, start with a good vegetable knife. I prefer one with a large square or rectangular blade made of stainless steel or carbon steel. Keeping the knife sharp is essential for good cutting and a natural whetstone is a good investment. Also, a clean cutting board, preferably of wood, is necessary. If you prepare fish or other animal food, keep a separate knife and cutting board for that purpose. Otherwise the heavy vibrations of animal food will affect the materials used in the preparation of vegetable-quality food. After cutting each type of vegetable, I wash the vegetable knife before proceeding to the next type. Among different vegetables, it is also important to minimize the mixing of vibrations prior to cooking. After cutting, I keep each sliced vegetable on a separate plate.

When cutting, slide the front part of the blade through the vegetable using the whole length of the blade. The stroke should be smooth, fluid, and natural. Avoid sawing or pushing down on the blade. I try to be firm but gentle in slicing and proceed in a calm, orderly manner. Vegetables that are cut in a disorderly or chaotic fashion will transmit that energy to those who eat them. Food is alive and from field to dinner table should be treated with respect.

COOKING STYLES

We can create different tastes and effects with the same vegetable depending on the style of cooking we choose. When planning a menu, it is important to visualize the completed meal. As in building a house or designing a dress, we need a visual image or pattern to guide us, even though improvisations may be made along the way. By varying our cooking style, we can often use some of the same foods for breakfast, lunch, and dinner without their becoming repetitive.

There are eight main styles of food preparation, including vegetable preparation:

Uncooked—In a temperate climate about two-thirds of our daily vegetables should be cooked. Cooking facilitates digestion and gives stronger energy. The other one-third may be consumed uncooked in the form of raw salads or pickled vegetables. In a more tropical environment, a slightly higher percentage of raw foods may be eaten.

Steaming—Steamed food has a light taste and cooks quickly with less water retention. Cauliflower and broccoli, for example, steam to a crisp texture in just a few minutes and keep their bright natural color. Other vegetables, such as carrots or onions, can be steamed whole or in large slices. Steaming is also good in making couscous, heating mochi, or warming up leftover grains.

The basic method of steaming is to put ½ inch of cold water in a pot. Insert a small metal vegetable steamer inside the pot or an Oriental wooden steamer on top of the pot. Place the vegetables in the steamer along with a pinch of sea salt to bring out their natural sweetness. Cover and bring the water to a boil. Steam for 5 to 10 minutes, or until tender, depending on the size and thickness of the vegetables. Unless served mixed, it is preferable to steam each individual type of vegetable separately. The same water can be used for each but let it cool down to allow the next vegetable to heat evenly. Leftover steaming water may be saved for soup stock or used in a sauce. For those who need to avoid or reduce salt or other seasoning, steaming is an ideal way to prepare a small side dish.

If you don't have a steamer, simply put ¼ inch of water in the bottom of a pot and then add the vegetables and seasoning. Bring to a boil, lower the heat to medium, and simmer until done.

A third method is to put ¼ to ½ inch of cold water in a pot, and insert a small ceramic dish containing the vegetables or other food. Cover the pot and steam until done. This is similar to a double boiler and is a good method to rewarm rice and other grains.

When steaming, be careful not to overcook the vegetables. They should be slightly crispy and will continue to cook from the heat they have already absorbed even when the heat under the pot is turned off.

To keep their bright color, rinse the vegetables quickly under cold water but do not cover them with a bamboo sushi mat until they are cool or they will turn a dull color.

Boiling—Boiling is one of the most basic methods of cooking vegetables and should be used at least once daily. Boiling is very versatile and, depending on the method, can take a short time or a long time and can create quick energy or slow, steady energy. When boiling, I usually use only ¼ to 1 inch of water in the pot; if there are a lot of ingredients, I add enough water to come up about halfway. It is not necessary to fill the pot with water and submerge the vegetables completely. There are four traditional methods of boiling in Japanese cuisine:

Ohitashi Style—This word means "dipping" the vegetables in boiling water and is similar to blanching. Ohitashi is the method I prefer for cooking leafy greens. First, I put about 1 inch of water into a pot and bring it to a strong boil. Then I dip the greens in the boiling water for about 15 to 30 seconds and take them out quickly. Root vegetables, if sliced very thinly, can also be cooked in this way, for a slightly longer time. Ohitashi makes for vegetables with fresh deep colors and a nice crispy taste.

Nishime Style—Vegetables prepared in this tender country home style are cut in large sizes and are cooked slowly for a long time over low heat. The steam in the pot allows the ingredients to cook in their own juices, so little water is usually needed. Seasoning may or may not be added in the beginning. When done, the vegetables are very juicy and are often served together with their cooking liquid. Nishime-style cooking produces very strong, calm energy. Oden is an example of this style. Nishime-style vegetables are warming and often given to sick persons to restore their vitality as well as enjoyed by those in good health.

Nitsuke and Kinpira Styles—Nitsuke boiling involves an intermediate amount of time, neither too short nor too long. If the vegetables are very soft, they can even be cooked in their own juice without water. Also the natural juice from the vegetables can be cooked down at the end or retained and served with the vegetable. Kinpira style is a combination of sautéing and boiling and similar to braising. It is used primarily in cooking root vegetables. First, the carrots, burdock, or other vegetables are sliced thinly and sautéed in a lightly oiled frying pan for 2 to 3 minutes. (Oil may be omitted for those who need to avoid or reduce oil.) Then water is added to half cover the vegetables or lightly cover the bottom of the pan. The vegetables are cooked until they are 80 percent done. Tamari soy sauce is added to taste, the frying pan is recovered, and the vegetables are cooked for another 2 to 3 minutes. Finally, the cover is removed, and the excess liquid is cooked off. Arame and hiziki sea vegetables are frequently cooked in this way along with carrots, onions, tempeh, and tofu.

Sukiyaki and Nabe Styles—Sukiyaki means "garden fork" and refers to a traditional Japanese one-dish meal prepared in a cast-iron frying pan, which is then boiled in a broth and served with a dip. In modern Japan, sukiyaki usually includes meat. In macrobiotic cooking, we make sukiyaki with all vegetables, noodles, tofu, tempeh, or sometimes seafood. Nabe refers to ceramic pot cooking that is prepared at the table rather than in the kitchen. Actually foods are often precooked and then rewarmed at the table in a colorful earthenware casserole dish along with a light tamari soy sauce, miso, or kuzu broth. Sukiyaki is often boiled in the broth at the table and is an example of nabe-style cooking.

Sautéing—Sautéing vegetables in oil makes them delicious and crispy and is a quick method. Soft vegetables, leafy vegetables, and thinly sliced root vegetables, as well as sprouts, green peas, and corn, may all be sautéed.

First cut the vegetables into thin slices, matchsticks, or shavings. Brush a warm frying pan with a small amount of light or dark unrefined sesame oil. Prewarming the pan will prevent sticking. Be careful not to use too much oil. One teaspoon is usually adequate for a side dish for several people and 1 to 2 tablespoons for a frying pan full of vegetables for the whole family. Heat the oil and when it is warm and begins to sizzle, add the vegetables and a pinch of sea salt. The salt will bring out the natural sweetness of the vegetables. If the vegetables sizzle gently when they are added to the pan, then the oil is the right temperature for sautéing. From the beginning occasionally stir the vegetables gently with chopsticks or another wooden implement. There is no need for vigorous stirring or constant mixing. Cooking time will depend on the type, size, and thickness of ingredients. Sauté the vegetables for about 5 minutes over medium heat; reduce heat to low and continue sautéing for another 10 minutes, or until the color of the vegetables has changed and their aroma is released. Just before the end of cooking, season to taste with tamari soy sauce or sea salt and sauté for another 2 to 3 minutes.

The *kinpira* method, described above under boiling, combines sautéing and boiling and is an excellent way to prepare root vegetables.

The Chinese sauté vegetables quickly in a wok using a small amount of oil, high heat, and continuous stirring. This method of sautéing is called *stir-frying* and may also be done in a frying pan. I have used a wok on occasion and found that it makes for delicious, crispy vegetables and for even cooking. I prefer a wok of cast-iron, though stainless steel or enamel-coated steel are also good.

Another variation on sautéing is *pan-frying*, in which the vegetables are cooked in a little oil for a long time over low heat, with little stirring or mixing. The vegetables are usually cut in large slices and turned over midway through cooking. Large slices of tofu are often cooked in this way.

Sautéing may also be done without oil by using a little water instead, about 2 to 3 tablespoons.

Broiling—Broiling gives vegetables a distinctive, slightly burnt, charcoal, or bitter flavor. Occasionally at home we have vegetable shish kebabs consisting of onions, summer squash, green pepper, tempeh, and seitan slices or squares artfully arranged on skewers and broiled. Broiling allows soft vegetables to keep their shape without becoming mushy.

Baking—Baking is the method most commonly used to prepare winter squashes, as well as casseroles, hiziki rolls, and corn on the cob. When my children were small, they enjoyed carrots baked whole over carrots prepared in other ways. Baking requires longer cooking but gives extra strength and flavor. In most other cooking methods, such as boiling, energy goes from the bottom of the pot to the top. In baking, vegetables absorb energy evenly and radiate it from the center.

Pressure-Cooking—Because whole grains and sometimes beans are pressure-cooked, I ordinarily prepare vegetables in other styles. Occasionally, when time is a factor, pressure-cooking vegetables allows root vegetables to be cooked in 3 to 5 minutes. Also, when mixed together with either grains or beans, vegetables may be pressure-cooked for variety. At such times, vegetables may be pressure-cooked in large pieces or sometimes whole. Pressure-cooking generally makes a sweeter dish but can create a bitter taste if the vegetables are overcooked.

Tempura-Style and Deep-Frying—These unique techniques create rich-tasting, dynamic food. Although not suitable for the everyday menu since they involve large amounts of oil, tempura-style or deep-frying creates vegetables that are delicious and crispy and that provide quick energy. Greens, beans, sea vegetables, and most vegetables can be prepared in this way.

SEASONING VEGETABLES

In macrobiotic cooking, sea salt, miso, tamari soy sauce, or other seasoning is added during cooking rather than at the table. The choice of seasoning and the time at which it is added to the food during cooking vary depending upon the individual recipe and style of cooking. In steaming, ohitashi boiling, sautéing, baking, pressure-cooking, and tempura-style and deep-frying, seasoning is usually added at the beginning. In nitsuke and sometimes nishime boiling, a pinch of sea salt is added at the beginning and most of the seasoning, in the form of tamari soy sauce, is added 3 to 4 minutes before the end of the cooking time. This is called the "hiding" method of using salt. In other dishes, seasoning may be added gradually during cooking.

CHAPTER

13

ROOT VEGETABLES

The rising moon
Outlines the shape
Of dried radishes on the porch.
—Aiko
えんがハに
干大根や
月のかげ

Root vegetables grow underground. They provide very stabilizing energy, focus the thinking, and strengthen the will. Root vegetables include carrots, parsnips, burdock, daikon radish, red radish, turnips, rutabaga, albi potato, jinenjo potato, and lotus root. Each root vegetable has a distinctive color, and care must be taken not to scrape off the skin while washing. After gently but firmly scrubbing off the dust, I remove any black or spoiled spots on the vegetable with a knife. I am also careful to retain small hairs and roots rather than trim them off because they transmit strong energy from the soil to the plants. There are many ways to prepare root vegetables. They may be cooked for a short time or a long time, made to give a light taste or a strong taste, and prepared raw or grated as a garnish for other dishes. Their firmness lends to many varieties of cutting. They may be prepared separately as side dishes or combined with grains, beans, or sea vegetables.

Root vegetables are easy to store and usually keep for a long time in a cool, dark place. They may also be dried, pickled, or preserved in other ways for use all year-round.

CARROTS

Carrots are the most popular root vegetable. They have a nice hard shape, keep for a long time, give a beautiful touch of orange color to a meal, and satisfy the desire for a naturally sweet taste. Carrots may be prepared in many ways, including raw, boiled, steamed, baked, sautéed, and deep-fried, and they go well with many other foods. Carrots are available most seasons of the year and will keep the whole winter if soft, fresh, and young. Carrot tops may be prepared separately and make a bright green side dish. Carrots are good for alleviating eye and liver conditions.

Raw Carrots

Carrots may be enjoyed raw, especially during the summertime. One tablespoon of grated carrots gives a beautiful color and freshness to salads. They may also be shaved or cut into matchsticks and marinated with salad dressing, tamari soy sauce and brown rice vinegar, barley miso, or a little sea salt for quick pickles. Carrot juice is enjoyable on occasion in hot weather. However, it is better served at room temperature than cold. Small raw carrots make nice chewable toys for babies when they are teething. As a condiment or garnish, carrots add a beautiful touch of color.

Carrots in Soup

Carrots go well in soups. By itself, carrot soup, made from grated, ground, or puréed carrots, is thick and delicious. Adding ten percent onions will make the carrots even sweeter. Carrots are often added to miso soup, to vegetable soups, and to koi koku, a special medicinal soup made with burdock and carp, as a substitute for burdock.

Baked Carrots

Whole baked carrots are delicious and give a unique flavor and energy. I prepare them fish-style by laying out the carrots on a baking sheet and lightly cutting fish scales or X's on their top surface. If the carrots are hard, I add a little water and cover them with aluminum foil or cook them in a covered casserole dish. Then I bake them in a moderate oven for 45 to 60 minutes, or until they are tender. Children like the deep sweet taste of carrots cooked in this way, even children who don't usually like carrots. If you want to add a fish's eye, inset a green pea in one end.

Boiled Carrots and Onions

Carrots and onions together make a very sweet combination. There are many combinations and styles. Here are four I use frequently.

Ohitashi-Style Boiling #1

Slice the vegetables thinly. Pour 1 inch of water into a saucepan and bring it to a strong boil. Put the onions in the boiling water for 1 minute and then remove them. Then put carrots in the boiling water and cook for 2 to 3 minutes. Remove the carrots. A pinch of sea salt at the start will make the onions and carrots sweeter tasting. The juice remaining in the pan should also be sweet. Add a little kuzu to make a sauce. Pour the kuzu sauce over the carrots and onions. Serve salad-style with bright fresh greens to create a beautiful, enjoyable dish.

Ohitashi-Style Boiling #2

Prepare the vegetables in the same way as #1, but vary the shape of the carrots by cutting them into matchsticks, half moons, or flower shapes. In addition to carrots and onions, add fresh corn kernels to the boiling water for about 1 minute. Garnish with parsley.

Nishime-Style Boiling #1

Cut carrots free-style into irregular-shaped pieces. Use the onions whole. Put a little sesame oil in the bottom of a pot. Put the onions on one side and the carrots on the other, or arrange the carrots in between the onions. Add water to come about halfway up the vegetables, add a pinch of sea salt, and cook, covered, for 10 to 15 minutes or until tender.

Nishime-Style Boiling #2

Put two 1-inch-square pieces of dried kombu into a saucepan. Add 2 to 3 sliced onions. Cut 4 to 5 medium-sized carrots into about 4 chunks each and put the chunks on top of the onions and kombu. Add water to cover the onions and sprinkle ½ teaspoon of sea salt over the vegetables.

Cover and cook over medium heat for about 10 minutes. When the carrots are soft, the dish is done. At the end, mix everything together so the onion juice covers the carrots. Remove the kombu and save it for another recipe. If the kombu is soft, it may be sliced thinly and served alongside the carrots. To thicken the remaining juice, add about ½ teaspoon of kuzu, stir for a few minutes, and pour the sauce over the carrots and onions. Instead of kombu, 1 teaspoon of sesame oil may be brushed over the bottom of the pot before cooking.

Carrots and Sea Vegetables

Carrots go well with sea vegetables. With arame, I usually cut carrots into matchsticks. With hiziki, I also cut them into matchsticks or other sizes. With wakame, I use big chunks of carrots and add the wakame after the carrots have become soft. With kombu, I use large slices and often roll the carrots up in the kombu. With mekabu, I use big chunks of carrots.

Carrots and Burdock

Carrots and burdock cooked together kinpira-style is a favorite macrobiotic dish. The usual recipe calls for two parts carrots to one part burdock, cut into matchsticks. Sauté the burdock first in a little oil for 2 to 3 minutes; then add the carrots and sauté for 2 to 3 minutes longer. Add water to half cover vegetables and a little tamari soy sauce. Cook until almost tender. Add more seasoning to taste and a little grated fresh ginger, and cook off the remaining liquid.

Carrots and burdock may also be cooked nishime-style. Cut both vegetables into big chunks and boil in a little water. When half cooked, add a small amount of tamari soy sauce. Cook until almost tender, add seasoning to taste, and serve with the juice or cook off the remaining liquid. Garnish with roasted sesame seeds.

Carrots and Cabbage

This is another excellent combination. One way to prepare it is to slice the carrots very thin and slice the cabbage slightly more thickly. Put the carrots in the pot and add just enough water to cover them. If the carrots are hard, I use cold water. If they are soft, I use boiling water. When the carrots are half cooked, I lay the cabbage on top of them. After the cabbage is soft, I mix the vegetables together, add a little sea salt, and transfer them quickly to a serving bowl to keep them crispy. As a variation, the carrots may be sautéed in a little oil before they are boiled.

Another method is to slice the carrots in big pieces and the cabbage in wedges. Put the carrots on one side of a pot and cabbage on the other. Half cover with water, sprinkle with a little sea salt, bring to boil, cover, and cook until tender.

PARSNIPS

Parsnips have a softer texture than carrots and a stronger taste. They are also very sweet and delicious and give a meal a creamy white color. While parsnips can be combined with onions or carrots, I enjoy their unique flavor and texture by itself. Cut in half-moon shapes and boiled or steamed for a few minutes, parsnips are very crispy. My favorite parsnip dishes are parsnip soup and parsnip pie. Parsnip pie is made by boiling parsnips for a few minutes with a pinch of salt, then mashing the parsnips, and putting them in an open-face whole wheat pie crust. Bake in a moderate oven for 30 to 40 minutes. Garnish with parsley sprigs and black sesame seeds and serve hot. Baked parsnips, made in the same way as baked carrots, are also delicious. To keep the fresh white color, I serve them with a sauce made of clear soup stock, a little kuzu, and a touch of grated fresh ginger.

BURDOCK

This long, thin brown root vegetable has a firm texture and gives very strong energy. Although eaten year-round, burdock is especially warming in winter. In Japan, we grew burdock in our garden at home. It was cultivated in raised hill beds like daikon and albi in order to make harvesting easier. In many regions, burdock also grows wild and is more strengthening than the domesticated variety. Here in New England we've foraged for wild burdock many times.

Burdock can be prepared in many styles, including boiling, sautéing, and deep-frying. Used in small amounts, it goes well with other root vegetables, grains, beans, and with kombu, but it does not combine well with other sea vegetables that have a dark color. In boiled salads, burdock goes well with a rice vinegar taste. Another typical dish is *koi koku,* the carp and burdock soup traditionally given to nursing mothers and very weak persons to increase their vitality. Even someone who doesn't like fish will enjoy this rich taste.

Kinpira-Style Burdock

One of the most common ways of preparing burdock is to cook it kinpira-style with other root vegetables. In Japan, kinpira vegetables are prepared often. They also are traditionally served on holidays and special occasions, and their strong energy helps to balance sake which is also consumed at these times.

- 2 pieces dried tofu
- 1 teaspoon dark sesame oil
- 1 cup burdock shaved or cut into matchsticks
- 2 cups carrots cut into matchsticks
- Spring water
- Tamari soy sauce

Put the dried tofu in warm or hot water and soak for 3 to 4 minutes. Rinse in cold water. Remove and squeeze out any excess water. Slice the tofu into rectangular shapes. Heat the oil in a frying pan. Add the burdock to the pan and sauté for 2 to 3 minutes. Add the carrots and dried tofu and sauté for 2 to 3 minutes. Pour in enough water to about half cover the vegetables. Add a small amount of tamari soy sauce. Bring to a boil, reduce the heat to low, cover, and simmer for about 30 minutes, or until all the liquid has evaporated.

Variations: Fresh sliced lotus root may be substituted for the burdock in this dish to create a different taste. Other good kinpira combinations are turnips and carrots; carrots and cabbage; parsnips and onions; onions, carrots, and turnips; and celery and parsley stems. The dried tofu may be omitted or fresh tofu or tempeh used instead. For those who wish to avoid oil, sauté with 1 to 2 tablespoons of water instead and boil over high heat to keep the vegetables crispy. A light kuzu sauce, seasoned with tamari soy sauce, goes well over this dish.

DAIKON

White radish (daikon) is the most popular vegetable in Japan, and Japanese cooking is impossible to imagine without it. There are many types of daikon and many styles of preparation for it. The big juicy radishes, which grow up to a foot or more in length and several inches in diameter, are sweet to the taste and are harvested year-round. The smaller, thinner daikon, which resemble carrots in shape, grow more quickly and have a strong, pungent taste. My mother grew the small variety in the garden for daily use and bought the larger kind from neighboring farmers for pickling.

When I was growing up in Japan, breakfast traditionally consisted of rice, miso soup (with daikon), grated daikon, toasted nori, and daikon pickles. For lunch we usually had rice and daikon when we came home at midday. Daikon greens are also edible, and we frequently had these pickled together with the daikon root. They give a nice salty taste and are enjoyed the year-round. As children we ate so much daikon that one of the games we would play was to imitate Buddhist monks and chant "*daikon no nita, daikon no nita*" and bang a bowl with a chopstick.

"*Daikon no nita wa kuan wan wan*" means "no more daikon," and we would sing this refrain daikon-in-cheek. But year by year I have come to appreciate daikon's special energy and taste and recommend that everyone always keep it in stock.

Cooked or raw, daikon aids in the digestion of whole grains and vegetables. It also helps eliminate excess water and animal fats from the body and has a wide range of medicinal uses.

Raw and Grated Daikon

The big, sweeter variety of radish may be used to make a quick salad. Simply slice and serve with a little umeboshi vinegar, lemon, or tamari soy sauce and brown rice vinegar. Garnish with sliced carrots for color.

Grated daikon is traditionally used as a condiment or accompaniment for mochi, tempura, sashimi, and other fish or seafood. When served with animal food, it is usually mixed with a little grated ginger. To prepare, grate 1 cup of daikon and put it in a serving bowl or individual dipping dishes. Pour several drops of tamari soy sauce in the center of the daikon. Garnish with a few sliced scallions. Each person can then take from between a teaspoon and a tablespoon of daikon and put 1 to 2 drops of tamari soy sauce on it when eating. With deep-fried foods, we usually eat a little more grated daikon than with other dishes.

Daikon in Soups

Daikon goes very well with miso soup. Basic miso soup is usually made with sliced daikon and wakame. This soup is said to be especially good for neutralizing the aftereffects of consuming beer or sake.

Boiled Daikon

As a side dish, daikon may be boiled in large slices and served with a sauce, with miso, or with toasted black sesame seeds. The following is a typical recipe.

- 2 8-inch strips kombu, soaked and sliced into ¼- to ½-inch rectangles
- 1 medium-sized daikon, cut into ½-inch rounds (3 to 4 cups)
- Spring water
- 1 to 2 teaspoons miso

Put the kombu on bottom of the pot. Layer the daikon on top of kombu. Add water to half cover the daikon and bring it to a boil. Cover, reduce the heat to low, and simmer until the daikon is translucent and soft, about 30 to 40 minutes. Season with miso diluted in a little of the cooking liquid and cook for 5 to 10 minutes longer. The dish should be sweet, not salty, to the taste. If overcooked, it may become bitter.

Nishime-Style Daikon with Vegetables

This delicious country-style stew can be made with countless combinations. However, daikon is the most basic ingredient.

- 2 strips kombu, 6-inches long, soaked and sliced into 1-inch squares
- 1 cup celery cut in big chunks
- 1 cup albi potatoes, cut in 1- to 2-inch-thick slices
- 1 cup daikon, quartered and sliced 1-inch thick
- 1 cup carrots cut into chunks using the rolling method
- ½ cup burdock sliced on the diagonal
- Spring water
- 1 to 2 teaspoons tamari soy sauce

Put the kombu on the bottom of a heavy pot. Layer vegetables in the following order: celery, albi, daikon, carrots, and burdock. Add water to just cover the daikon. Bring to a boil. Reduce the heat to low, cover, and simmer until the vegetables are almost done. Add a little tamari soy sauce and continue to simmer until the vegetables are soft and all of the liquid has evaporated. Just before the water is completely gone, shake the pot up and down to mix the vegetables and to thoroughly coat the vegetables with the cooking liquid.

Variations: The combinations of ingredients may be changed to create new, delicious-tasting dishes. I often include several of the following: lotus root, tempeh, deep-fried tofu, turnips, rutabagas, parsnips, celery, onions, dried tofu, shiitake mushrooms, and soybeans. If there is no kombu on hand, wakame may be substituted.

Dried Daikon

Dried daikon is very sweet and goes well with many other foods. After shredding, it is customarily put on rice mats to dry outside in the sun for several days to several weeks. We also sliced it into rounds, threaded the rounds through the middle with rice straw, and hung the daikon up to dry on the porch. To prepare dried daikon, soak it in cold water for 5 minutes, slice, and then boil, steam, or use raw in salad with a little tamari soy sauce and brown rice vinegar.

RED RADISHES

Red radishes give a very beautiful red color to a meal, have appealing round shapes, and are good for salads and as a garnish. They have many of the same nutritional qualities as the smaller varieties of daikon but usually taste sharper and more pungent. Red radishes are easy to grow and lend themselves to cutting into fancy shapes and designs. Together with their tops, they may be pickled or cooked whole with a little umeboshi vinegar. Red radish is also very beneficial to digestion and may be substituted for daikon in any recipe if the latter is unobtainable.

Red Radishes and Kuzu Sauce

1 3- to 6-inch piece kombu
10 whole red radishes, tops removed
Spring water
3 whole umeboshi plums
1 teaspoon shiso leaves from the umeboshi plums
1 to 2 teaspoons diluted kuzu
Sliced scallions or boiled parsley sprigs for garnish

Put the kombu on the bottom of a pot and add the whole radishes. Add water to almost cover them. Add the whole umeboshi plums, but remove the shiso leaves in which the plums were pickled and save for salads or pickling. Cook for about 30 to 40 minutes, over low heat. Remove the radishes and put them into a bowl. Strain out the kombu, umeboshi plum pits, and shiso leaves from the cooking liquid. Thicken the liquid with 1 to 2 teaspoons of diluted kuzu and simmer for several minutes. Pour the kuzu sauce over radishes. Garnish with sliced scallions or with sprigs of boiled parsley. Slice the shiso leaves and put them at the side of the bowl with the radishes.

Variation: For a less salty taste, use only 1 umeboshi plum.

TURNIPS

Turnips are excellent for making quick pickles. They may also be sliced thinly for pressed salad, sliced thickly for soups and stews, and boiled or steamed as a small side dish served alone or combined with tofu, seitan, or fish.

RUTABAGAS

This large yellow root vegetable belongs to the turnip family. We did not have rutabaga in Japan while I was growing up but it is native to Europe and Asia and is now grown in the Western Hemisphere. I especially enjoy it when it has been pickled for a few days in tamari soy sauce. Rutabaga is also very sweet and delicious boiled by itself or cooked together with carrots or onions. The degree of sweetness depends on the quality of the rutabaga.

TARO POTATOES

Taro or albi potatoes are hairy tubers of tropical and semitropical origin. The large ones, sometimes as big as coconuts, grow in more southern regions, while small ones are produced in Japan and more northern climates. Traditionally, taros are prepared with their stalks and leaves, cut into large slices, and cooked nishime-style with other root vegetables. In temperate zones, we do not recommend regular use of taro or other potatoes, including white potatoes, sweet potatoes, and yams. However, taro may be included occasionally in summer in small amounts in soups, nishime dishes, or stews and are very delicious. One popular method is called *kinukatzugi* or "dressed with clothing style" and involves cooking the sliced taros with their skin on in a little boiling water. After they become soft, push out the center of the slices with your finger and the skin will drop off. The fluffy inner white part is then eaten. Medicinally, taro is used externally in macrobiotic home care as compresses to help discharge mucus and toxins from the body. Taro is available in Latin American and Oriental food stores as well as some natural foods shops.

Taro Stew

- 1 to 2 strips kombu, soaked and cut into 1- to 2-inch cubes
- 4 shiitake mushrooms, soaked, stems removed, and quartered
- 2 cups taro potato cut in 2-inch chunks
- 1 cup lotus root quartered and sliced ⅛-inch thin
- 16 ounces deep-fried tofu, cut into 1- to 2-inch cubes
- Spring water
- 1 to 2 teaspoons tamari soy sauce
- 1 to 2 teaspoons kuzu
- Sliced scallions for garnish

Put the kombu and shiitake on the bottom of a heavy pot. Add the taro, lotus, and tofu. Cover with water and bring to a boil. Reduce the heat and cook until the vegetables are soft, about 30 to 40 minutes. Add the tamari soy sauce and cook for several minutes longer. Dilute the kuzu with a little water and add it to the pot to thicken the juices. Serve garnished with sliced scallions.

JINENJO MOUNTAIN POTATO

This nice soft potato grows deep underground, has a long shape, and may reach several feet in length. In my region in Japan, it grew wild as well as cultivated, and friends and relatives would often bring us *yamaimo* (wild growing mountain potato) from the forest, or we would obtain it from farmers and woodcutters. Jinenjo gives very strong energy and is especially warming in the winter. Traditionally, it is also said to be good for restoring sexual vitality.

Jinenjo is usually eaten raw in very small amounts. It is sticky like natto or cheese. To prepare it, grate 1 to 2 tablespoons of jinenjo, add a pinch of grated fresh ginger, and add a couple drops of tamari soy sauce. Serve with a few small squares of toasted nori. Jinenjo may also be sliced and eaten raw, marinated with brown rice vinegar and tamari soy sauce.

Grated and added to miso soup or tamari soy sauce broth, jinenjo alters the taste of a dish completely. Use about 1 teaspoon per cup. It is also very good eaten with soba noodles. Add to the broth about 1 tablespoon of grated jinenjo for each bowl and pour on top of the noodles. There is also a type of soba made with jinenjo. Mochi pounded with a little jinenjo mixed in, about 5 percent by volume, keeps it soft longer.

Nishime-style, jinenjo may be boiled in large slices and seasoned with a little tamari soy sauce. It may also be added to oden- or nabe-style dishes and consumed directly from the common pot at the table.

LOTUS ROOT

Lotus root is one of the most precious vegetables. The root of a variety of water lily, it grows in deep mud in still ponds and to harvest it, you need high boots. It is freshest taken in late autumn to winter. At other times of the year, lotus root is usually prepared in dried form. Fresh lotus may be sliced into many wonderful shapes, and its hollow inner chambers may be filled or stuffed with other foods. Medicinally, lotus root is very good for the lungs, helps relieve coughing and internal bleeding, and assists in draining mucus from the sinuses. It may be applied externally as a compress, as well as eaten, or ground into a powder and prepared as a tea.

For salads, lotus root may be sliced very thin and marinated raw for a couple of hours with rice vinegar, tamari soy sauce, and mirin. Nishime-style, lotus root may be boiled in large chunks together with daikon or shiitake mushroom. In large slices, lotus root is also good cooked with azuki beans. Kinpira-style, lotus root may be sautéed and simmered in a little water like carrots or burdock. Sliced fine, lotus root is often cooked together with arame or hiziki sea vegetables. Deep-fried as lotus balls, or prepared in tempura-style, lotus root is also very delicious and rich tasting.

Lotus Root Stuffed with Miso

In this dish, miso fills the hollow chambers of the lotus. When sliced into sections, the contrast of the lotus root with the miso forms an exquisite design.

1 lotus root
1 to 2 tablespoons miso
½ teaspoon grated fresh ginger
2 tablespoons tahini
2 teaspoons minced parsley
Whole wheat flour
Tempura batter
Dark sesame oil

Wash the lotus root and boil it whole for 5 to 10 minutes in a small amount of water. Remove from the water and cut off the ends. In a shallow dish blend the miso, ginger, tahini, and parsley. Gently pound one end of the lotus into the miso mixture until the miso fills the hollow chambers of the lotus. Put the lotus on a dish and set aside for 1 hour. During this time the miso mixture will draw out the liquid from the lotus. Roll lotus in this liquid. Then roll lotus in whole wheat flour. Then dip the whole lotus into a tempura batter made from whole wheat flour, arrowroot flour, or kuzu. Deep-fry the lotus in hot oil for 3 to 5 minutes, or until the batter becomes a nice brown. Drain and, when cool, cut into thin slices. Since this is a very strong combination, 1 or 2 slices are sufficient per person.

GINGERROOT

Ginger is a light golden root with a knobby shape. It is very strong, has a spicy taste, and gives nice warm energy. It is used to relieve digestive troubles and improve circulation. Only a small amount is needed, usually ¼ teaspoon or less of grated fresh ginger or a few drops of ginger juice, to garnish a soup, casserole, vegetable, or grain dish. Cooked, ginger also makes a wonderful condiment with kombu and stimulates the appetite. Ginger is also used in sigure miso condiment, koi koku soup, and sometimes as a garnish for miso soup, tamari broth, with cold tofu in the summer, seitan, tempura, and oily foods, such as fish and seafood. I sometimes add a little grated fresh ginger to hiziki and arame, either cooked together at the very end for a few minutes or as a garnish. It is also nice with fried rice or fried noodles. Just grate and mix in at the end of the cooking time. We also often add just a touch of ginger to medicinal teas, such as ume-sho-bancha, kuzu drink, or lotus root tea. Externally, ginger is also used in making a compress to place over the kidneys, intestines, or other area to stimulate circulation and to help relieve pain. To extract ginger from the gingerroot for cooking or for medicinal purposes, I use a small-toothed, flat grater made of porcelain or stainless steel. This implement pulverizes the root into small shreds. Porcelain is preferable for grating, especially for medicinal use. To make ginger juice, simply squeeze the grated ginger with your hand or in a cotton cloth. Ginger juice is stronger than grated ginger: About ¼ teaspoon of juice equals 1 teaspoon of grated fresh ginger. Gingerroot will keep for a long period of time if stored in a little container of sand rather than in the refrigerator where it tends to mold after about a week.

Ginger-Kombu Condiment

- Several thumb-size knobs fresh gingerroot (do not peel)
- 1 medium-sized strip kombu
- Tamari soy sauce
- Spring water
- Roasted sesame seeds for garnish

Combine the ginger, kombu, and a little tamari soy sauce with water to cover the ginger. Boil for 45 to 60 minutes. For a less salty condiment, dilute the tamari soy sauce with 50 percent water. Serve the ginger thinly sliced and garnish with roasted sesame seeds.

BEETS

I first tasted beets in Paris in the 1950s. They had been boiled, sliced, and were served cold in a salad. I enjoyed them very much and have used beets in this way since then. Beet greens and dark purple or red beet stems are also very delicious, especially when they are sautéed. Because of their strong color, beets are usually cooked alone. Borscht, the traditional beet soup of Russia and Eastern Europe, is also very delicious, served hot or cold in the summer. Instead of sour cream, it can be garnished with a dollop of creamy tofu.

CHAPTER 14

GROUND VEGETABLES

Flutes and drums.
Children and adults flock
To the harvest festival.
—Toshiko

Ground vegetables can be divided into three major categories: round vegetables, stem and climbing vegetables, and tropical vegetables. We shall look at each type.

ROUND VEGETABLES

The family of round vegetables includes onions, cabbage, fall- and winter-season squashes, cauliflower, and broccoli. These plants grow very near the ground, and their taste is usually sweeter than root vegetables, which grow beneath the ground, or green and white leafy vegetables, which grow above the ground. Medicinally, round vegetables are particularly beneficial to the stomach, spleen, and pancreas.

ONIONS

I use onions daily in cooking. They have a very strong, pungent taste when eaten raw, but they become sweet when cooked. There are endless ways to prepare onions, alone or with other foods. They may be prepared uncooked, pickled, boiled, steamed, sautéed, broiled, or tempura-style and deep-fried. Onions go well with root vegetables, fried noodles, fried rice, tofu, and tempeh. They are also good cooked with sea vegetables, providing a sweeter flavor to arame or hiziki. Onions keep fresh for a long time and store easily. If an inside layer spoils, I cut it out and, after washing, use the rest of the onion which is good. The sweet, peaceful energy of onions is good for infants and young children. Cooked with squash and carrots, onions are highly recommended for people with diabetes who must watch their intake of simple sugars.

Raw Onions

Raw onions can be used in salads or for making pickles. They stimulate the appetite, especially in the summer when we are not so hungry. In salads, red onions are much milder and sweeter than other types. I am fond of diced onion in buckwheat salad. Another good combination is onions and wakame in lightly boiled salad with lemon dressing. The green part of the onions may also be used. If tough, slice very fine and use as a garnish. To pickle, slice the onions thinly and marinate them with tamari soy sauce for 30 to 60 minutes before serving.

Onions in Soups

Onions go well in miso soup. Combined with wakame and tofu, they cook quickly and taste sweet. Whole small onions are good in vegetable, bean, and grain soups. French onion soup is also very delicious.

Boiled Onions

Onions boiled quickly and served with peas, carrots, cabbage, or other greens make a wonderful dish. The onions provide a beautiful white color and a fresh, sweet, and slightly pungent taste. After slicing thinly, dip the onions in boiling water for 1 minute ohitashi-style, braise for 2 to 3 minutes with oil and water kinpira-style, or cook in about ½ inch of water for 5 to 7 minutes nishime-style. Whole or cut into large pieces, onions may also be steamed for a few minutes.

Whole Onions and Miso

All five of my children love this dish. When they were little they called it *o hehe no onions,* which means "smiling onions." Whenever they saw this dish, they began to smile at each other.

- 6 whole medium-sized onions
- 1 to 2 8-inch strips kombu, soaked for 4 to 5 minutes
- Spring water
- 1 to 1½ tablespoons miso
- 1 to 2 teaspoons kuzu (optional)
- Finely chopped parsley

Make 6 to 8 shallow cuts in each onion to give them the appearance of being sectioned, but don't cut too deeply. The slices will allow the onions to open up like flowers while they are cooking. Put the whole onions on top of the kombu in a pot. Add water to half cover the onions. Pour miso puréed in a little water on top of the onions. Cover the pot and bring to a boil. Lower the heat and simmer until the onions are soft and translucent, about 30 minutes. If there is too much liquid remaining in the pot, thicken it with 1 to 2 teaspoons of kuzu after removing the onions. Pour the kuzu sauce or the plain cooking liquid over the onions. Garnish with chopped parsley.

Variation: Brush 1 to 2 teaspoons of sesame oil on the bottom of the pot instead of using the kombu.

GARLIC AND SHALLOTS

Garlic has a much stronger flavor than onions. In Korea, small amounts of garlic are traditionally used with fried vegetables to create a hot taste and to stimulate circulation. It is used in making pickles. I have made pickles also with shallots, using a fifty-fifty combination of tamari soy sauce and apple cider vinegar, which makes them a little sweet.

CABBAGE

Cabbages are naturally sweet and go well in salads, soups, and mixed vegetable dishes. There are many types: soft, hard, red, green, Savoy. When preparing cabbage, I always make use of the whole vegetable. The hard core can be cut very fine and saved for soup and stock if not used in salads or cooking. I first tasted red cabbage in New Hampshire. Red cabbage may be used in salads or sautéed quickly, with a pinch of sea salt at the end of cooking to bring out its sweet flavor.

Soft, green cabbages are good for making boiled salad. I shred them into ⅛- to ¼-inch-thick slices and boil the slices in a little water for a few minutes. They may be served with a sour, sweet, or salty sauce. One of our young friends made baked whole cabbage stuffed with couscous and it was unique. It is prepared by putting fluffy soaked couscous between the cabbage leaves. A little diced green pepper may be added for flavor. Cabbage rolls also make a fancy holiday dish. (See my recipe in the tempeh chapter.) Tofu, seitan, arame, or hiziki may also be used in this way.

Boiled Cabbage with Sesame and Umeboshi Sauce

- 4 cups thinly sliced cabbage
- 2 cups spring water
- 2 teaspoons kuzu
- 1 to 2 umeboshi plums
- 1 tablespoon sesame seeds

Boil the cabbage just until it is a bright, colorful green, about 2 to 3 minutes. Drain the cabbage but save the boiling water. Make a sauce with the boiling water, the kuzu, and umeboshi plums. Pour the sauce over the cabbage. Wash the sesame seeds and roast until golden brown. Put the seeds on a chopping board and chop. Sprinkle the chopped seeds on top of the cabbage.

Variations: A little grated fresh ginger may also be added to the sauce. Another good topping is a mixture of ½ teaspoon of purėed miso, 1 tablespoon of brown rice vinegar, and a few sesame seeds.

Steamed Chinese Vegetables

- Spring water
- 2 cups thinly sliced cabbage
- 1 cup thinly sliced onions
- ½ cup thinly sliced celery
- Sea salt
- 2 to 4 teaspoons chopped parsley
- 1 sheet nori, toasted and cut into squares for garnish

Put a little water in a frying pan. Add the vegetables, cover the pan, and steam the vegetables. When the water starts to evaporate, add just a little more water and a small amount of sea salt, about a pinch or two. The salt will draw water out of the vegetables. Gently move the vegetables around with chopsticks or a wooden utensil to help them cook and use high heat to help keep the vegetables crisp. When the vegetables are cooked add a little chopped parsley. The vegetables should cook altogether only about 2 to 3 minutes and be almost raw and crispy. Transfer to a bowl and serve with a garnish of toasted nori.

Sautéed Cabbage, Celery, and Carrots

Dark sesame oil
2 cups thinly sliced cabbage
1 cup carrots cut into matchsticks
½ cup celery thinly sliced on a diagonal
Pinch of sea salt

Heat a small amount of dark sesame oil in a frying pan. Keep the heat high to keep the vegetables crispy. Add the cabbage and sauté for 1 to 2 minutes. Add the carrots and celery and sauté for 3 to 4 minutes longer moving the vegetables constantly with chopsticks or a wooden spoon to sauté them evenly. The salt is added at the very end of cooking. When done, the vegetables should be crisp and brightly colored.

SAUERKRAUT

Hard cabbages are generally used to make sauerkraut. In Japan, we made a quick sauerkraut by slicing the cabbage, mixing it with sea salt, and pressing it overnight or for a few days. It was very crispy. Several years ago, in Germany, I tasted a traditional sauerkraut. It was sweet and delicious, not too strong or sour. In Europe, sauerkraut is eaten with dark bread but also goes well with kasha, celery, and tempeh. The sauerkraut loses some of its sour taste if it is cooked. When preparing, I usually add a little sauerkraut juice to kasha or tempeh and then mix in the sauerkraut at the very end of cooking. See the pickle chapter for a homemade sauerkraut recipe.

CAULIFLOWER

Cauliflower is a nice peaceful vegetable. It should not be cooked too long or it will lose its sweet taste, beautiful color, crispy texture, and flowery shape, though for children it may be cooked until soft. I usually just cut to the beginning of the stem and open the flowers by hand to prevent them from crumbling. The finely chopped stalk and leaves also may be cooked. Together with red radish, broccoli, or other greens, raw or pickled cauliflower makes a nice appetizer. There are many kinds of sauces, dips, and spreads I serve with boiled cauliflower, including umeboshi vinegar sauce and roasted sesame seeds. Cauliflower may also be pickled, whole or in slices, with tamari soy sauce and rice vinegar, for about 2 weeks. In tempura, cauliflower is very delicious and beautiful.

Boiled Cauliflower and Broccoli

Spring water
2 cups cauliflower flowerets and stems
2 cups broccoli flowerets and stems
Tamari soy sauce
Grated fresh ginger
Fresh lemon juice

Put a very small amount of water in a pot and bring it to a boil. Add the cauliflower, cover, and boil until it is done, about 5 minutes. The cauliflower should be soft but not so cooked that it falls apart. Remove the cauliflower and transfer it to a bowl. Add broccoli to the same water and boil for 3 to 4 minutes, or until done. It should be bright green when cooked. Remove the broccoli and arrange it in the bowl so that the cauliflower is surrounded by a ring of bright green broccoli. Mix a small amount of water, tamari soy sauce, grated fresh ginger, and fresh lemon juice together to make a thin sauce. Pour the sauce over the cauliflower and broccoli after each person has been served. A teaspoon is enough for each serving.

BROCCOLI

Broccoli has a beautiful shape, texture, and bright green color. It can be marinated for quick salads and pickles, boiled, steamed, sautéed, or cooked tempura-style and is especially good with fried noodles, fried rice, and mixed vegetables. When sautéing, cook separately and then mix with other vegetables at the end to prevent bruising. Medicinally, broccoli is good for the lungs, stomach, and spleen.

If the stalk is hard, I peel the outside fibrous layer and use just the inside. The stalk may be kept for soups and stocks or making pickles. If cooking the stem and stalk together, I usually cook the stalk first, after slicing it thinly, and add the upper stem and flowers 2 or 3 minutes from the end of the cooking time, and serve with a sauce. There are many sauces to choose from, including tamari soy sauce and grated fresh ginger, umeboshi sauce, and roasted sesame seeds.

The most common way to make broccoli is to slice and simmer it for 3 to 5 minutes in a covered pot with a little water and a pinch of sea salt. Be careful not to overcook it or the broccoli will lose its bright color. Broccoli may also be dipped in boiling water ohitashi-style for 1 to 2 minutes or steamed.

Very often dining out in Italy I order broccoli with spaghetti and am served a whole broccoli, uncut, that comes looking like a big fish. It is very crispy and delicious.

❧ Broccoli and Tofu Cream Dressing ❧

- 1 head broccoli, cut into flowerets and stems
- 16 ounces tofu
- 2 to 3 umeboshi plums

Simmer the broccoli in a little water until done, about 2 to 3 minutes. The vegetable should be slightly crisp and bright green in color. Put the tofu between two cutting boards and press out the liquid for about 15 to 30 minutes, or squeeze out the water by placing the tofu in a cotton cloth. Purée the pitted umeboshi in a suribachi. Add the tofu and grind until smooth and creamy. Mix thoroughly. Mix the tofu cream and broccoli together.

BRUSSELS SPROUTS, KOHLRABI, AND FENNEL

When I first saw brussels sprouts in the garden, I was surprised to see how branch-like they grew. Brussels sprouts can be prepared sliced but because of their small size they are usually boiled or steamed whole without salt which tends to increase their slightly bitter taste. Cook for only a few minutes to retain their deep green color. Cutting a shallow cross on the bottom of the brussels sprouts' fibrous stem makes for more even cooking.

Kohlrabi and fennel are two unique-looking vegetables. Like other round vegetables, they may be boiled or steamed and served with a sauce. I have not yet experimented with them very much myself.

FALL- AND WINTER-SEASON SQUASHES

Hard round squashes have a strong sweet taste and we enjoy them very very much. They have a beautiful pleasing shape, golden color, and make for a very satisfying meal. Since we had few squashes in our region in Japan, we ate mostly a variety native to Cambodia which was not so sweet. Only when I came to America did I really discover this wonderful food.

The style of preparation depends on the type and thickness of the squash, and this will influence the amount of water used and the time needed for cooking. Usually when boiling, steaming, or pressure-cooking squash, I don't use oil. It doesn't go well with the squash's natural taste. However, baked squash may be lightly oiled on the inside or outside, if desired.

I generally find squash more enjoyable when it is prepared by itself, but it can be cooked with a variety of other foods. For seasoning I enjoy a plain salt taste, although tamari soy sauce and, occasionally, miso may also be used. I always leave the squash's skin on when cooking. It is usually edible and very nutritious and delicious. However, if the squash is not organic in quality, it may be washed in salt water and the skin may be removed after cooking, if desired.

Medicinally, squash is very calming and soothing to the body. Prepared with a small piece of kombu and with azuki beans, squash is especially strengthening in autumn.

After rinsing the squash in cold water, I scrape it gently with a vegetable brush. The hard stalk may be removed with a knife before it is cooked or it will soften and pull out easily after cooking. For baking I usually cut the squash in half and remove the seeds before cooking. These may be saved for roasting separately. For boiling, steaming, or pressure-cooking, I usually slice the squash in big 1- to 2-inch slices or wedges. When pressure-cooking, it is important not to overcook the squash or it will become too strong and lose its light, sweet taste. After pressure is up, 3 to 5 minutes is usually enough.

Acorn squash is small, round, and dark green to black. It is easy to slice, has a nice sweet taste, and is usually baked.

Buttercup squash is my favorite. It is round in shape but flat at the ends, dark green to black in color, and small to medium sized. It is very sweet and gives a stronger, fuller flavor than most other varieties. In addition to baking it, I enjoy buttercup in soups and stews, with soft rice in the morning, and in squash pie.

Butternut squash is more oblong in shape and has a pale skin. It is often available earlier in the season than other squashes. It is very sweet and delicious and may be used in many ways. Whole, I like to bake it fish-style with slight scales or X's carved on each half.

Hokkaido pumpkin takes its name from the northernmost island of Japan, where it is widely cultivated. Actually it was originally developed in western Massachusetts by Dr. William Clark, an early twentieth-century agricultural pioneer, whose motto, "Boys, be ambitious," is famous throughout Japan. Hokkaido is a large orange- or red-skinned squash that is very delicious.

Hubbard squash is another large variety and comes in shades of blue, green, and red. It is tasty stuffed and baked and is the squash to serve for a lot of company. Its skin is not eaten.

Pumpkin is good in pies and can be added to vegetable dishes. It is usually not as sweet as other varieties of squash. Its skin is not eaten but its seeds are very delicious roasted and flavored with a little tamari soy sauce.

Squash in Soup

Squash soup is very delicious, golden in color, and makes a wonderful first course for any meal. I make it often in autumn and winter with buttercup, butternut, or Hokkaido. For garnish I add a few sliced scallions, parsley, or black nori. Sliced squash also goes well with miso soup. It is also good with millet soup, with a few onions mixed in.

Squash with Grains

Squash is excellent pressure-cooked with millet. I use 1¼ cups of water per cup of millet and squash and a pinch of sea salt per cup of ingredients. If the squash is very hard, I may add extra water. After pressure-cooking, the squash-millet mixture may be pressed by hand into a loaf or cake shape and baked on a baking sheet covered with tin foil. Squash-millet loaf is a hearty dish and very popular so be sure to make enough.

When pressure-cooking squash with brown rice, extra water is usually not needed. Most enjoyable is squash with soft rice. To prepare it, combine 1 cup of leftover cooked rice, 2 cups of spring water (or 3 if you like it very soft), a cup of buttercup or butternut squash cut into big chunks, and a pinch or two of sea salt. Pressure-cook for 10 to 20 minutes.

Baked Butternut Squash and Onions

- 3 cups butternut squash cut into large chunks
- 2 cups spring water
- 1 cup onions sliced in half moons
- 1 strip kombu, about 6 inches long
- 2 to 3 tablespoons kuzu
- Tamari soy sauce

Put the sliced squash in a baking dish. Add a few drops of water to the squash to keep it moist while cooking. Cover the baking dish and bake in a preheated 350-degree oven for about 35 to 40 minutes, or until it is almost done. Pour the water into a pot and add the onions and kombu. Bring to a boil, reduce the heat to low, cover, and simmer for about 15 minutes. Reduce the heat to very low. Remove the kombu from the pot and set it aside for future use. Dilute the kuzu in a little cold water and stir it into the water and onions. Bring to a boil, stirring constantly to avoid lumping. Reduce the heat to low and season lightly with tamari soy sauce. Simmer for about 5 minutes. Pour the hot kuzu sauce over the baked squash, cover, and bake for several minutes longer.

Baked Buttercup Squash

1 buttercup squash
Parsley sprigs for garnish

Wash the squash and cut in half horizontally. Put the squash halves upside down on an aluminum foil–covered baking sheet. One or two drops of sesame oil may be rubbed on the outside skin to keep the squash from cracking. A pinch of salt may be rubbed on the inside of the squash to help bring out its natural sweetness. Bake in a preheated 375- to 400-degree oven for about 45 to 50 minutes. When the squash is about 75 percent done, turn it over to allow the moisture on the inside to evaporate. The squash will also slightly brown around the edges at this time. If salt has not been used initially, a touch of tamari soy sauce may be brushed over the inside at this time. Return the squash to the oven to bake for another 15 to 20 minutes, or until tender. The outer layer, including the skin, should be soft. When done, remove the squash from the oven, slice it into triangles or other shapes, and serve garnished with a few sprigs of bright green parsley.

Stuffed Hubbard Squash

One Thanksgiving while living in New York, I decided to prepare a turkey for some guests. I had never even tasted turkey, and when I tried to buy one in Queens I was told they had all been sold. I didn't know they had to be ordered in advance. This gave me a good excuse since I usually don't prepare animal food.

Several years later, in 1966, when we had moved to the Boston area, I was driving in Concord one beautiful autumn day and passed several farm stands piled high with squash and pumpkins. I was impressed at how similar to turkey the large Hubbard squash looked. At the next stand I jumped out of the car with my children and picked out the one that looked most like a turkey and brought it home.

To prepare it, I carefully cut off a section of the top like a jack-o'-lantern and set it aside. After taking out the seeds, I stuffed the squash with whole wheat bread crumbs, including some that were deep-fried, minced onions, celery, and parsley, all mixed together with a few bay leaves and 3 to 4 pinches of sea salt. Then I put the top section back on and popped it in the oven. I baked it, covered, at a high heat for about 1 hour, and served it with a tamari soy sauce and kuzu sauce.

For decoration I fashioned mock turkey wings with brown oak leaves and branches. I put onions around the bottom of the serving platter to represent eggs and arranged some watercress and parsley for a nest. A few red radishes and carrots, cut in flower shapes, completed the decoration. Everyone enjoyed it tremendously, and squash turkey became a traditional dish in our family, among many macrobiotic families at Thanksgiving, and at Erewhon parties. I later improved upon the stuffing by adding roasted buckwheat (kasha) and a little grated fresh ginger to the sauce.

STEM AND CLIMBING VEGETABLES

Stem and climbing vegetables tend to be elongated in shape, grow quickly, ripen by early summer, and give light, upward energy.

Cucumber

Cucumber is a typical summer vegetable, very cooling and usually eaten raw. It grew around the edge of my mother's garden and produced very tall, beautiful yellow flowers. To help it along, we would tie it to bamboo trellises with rice stalks. Fresh from the garden, cucumber would be eaten sliced and sprinkled with a little salt. We would also prepare it by adding a little salt, squeezing out the water, slicing, and marinating it for a short time in tamari soy sauce and rice vinegar. Cucumbers are also very delicious in salads with umeboshi or sliced shiso leaves. Cucumber juice helps elimination and is very good for the skin. The ends can be saved and rubbed on the skin for a healthier complexion.

We made our pickled cucumbers fresh by slicing the vegetables into rounds or cutting them lengthwise and pressing them for a few hours in a little salt. If the cucumbers were too hard, we sliced them, removed the seeds, dried the slices under the sun, added salt and then pressed them. In Japan, cucumbers are also sometimes pickled with miso or with the residue left from making sake wine, after first pickling with salt.

Cucumbers may also be cooked by shaving and sautéing them in a little sesame oil. For seasoning, I add a little diluted miso on top. Another traditional cucumber dish is kappa-maki sushi. Kappa is a mythical animal that has a human shape but lives in the water. According to folk legend, the kappa likes cucumber a lot. One of the kappa's characteristics is a dish on its head. When the dish dries out from leaving the water too long, the kappa dies.

Summer Squashes

Zucchini, sliced or whole, is very delicious served with a miso sauce on top. It can be boiled, steamed, baked, sautéed, or barbecued. I enjoy pan-frying the small zucchinis in a little sesame oil and topping them with diluted miso.

Yellow summer squash can be cooked in ways similar to zucchini. I enjoy it baked fish-style cut in half lengthwise. It is also good in shish kebab and goes well covered with a miso sauce.

Patty pan squash is often called star squash because of its distinctive shape and shiny white color. Boiling or steaming it with a pinch of salt brings out the juice. I like to serve star squash with a creamy sauce made from kuzu, a little tamari soy sauce, and grated fresh ginger.

Baked Zucchini with Miso-Ginger Sauce

- 2 to 3 medium-sized zucchini
- Dark sesame oil
- 1 teaspoon barley miso
- ¼ teaspoon grated fresh ginger
- Spring water
- Parsley sprigs for garnish

Wash the zucchini and slice them in half lengthwise. Slice off the stem ends. Using a knife, make light diagonal slashes in the skin of the squash like this: / / / / /. Then make shallow diagonal slices in the opposite direction to create a crisscross effect like this: X X X X X. Oil a baking dish or baking sheet and also lightly oil the skin of the zucchini. Put the zucchini on the oiled dish. Bake for about 20 minutes in a preheated 375-degree oven.

Put the miso in a suribachi and add the ginger. Purée, adding a small amount of water to make a smooth, creamy sauce. Lightly brush the miso-ginger sauce on top of the zucchini slices and bake for about 10 to 15 minutes longer. Remove from the oven and arrange the slices on a platter. Garnish with sprigs of parsley. The slices can be cut into 2- to 3-inch lengths before serving.

FRESH BEANS AND PEAS

We grew fresh beans of many colors and shapes at home. I would often bring them to my mother in a basket or large cooking apron. Shelling beans and taking peas out of the pods were the children's responsibility. In addition to the usual string beans, we had very long beans, often a foot or more in length. To prepare them, we snapped off the ends, sliced the long beans into smaller sections, and boiled them for a few minutes but not too long or their color would fade. If the beans were tough, we would cook them nishime-style for a longer time and add a light tamari soy sauce taste. A typical sauce for string beans would be made from tofu, mashed very well for 10 to 15 minutes, with a little umeboshi or sea salt to taste. The sauce would be poured over the beans and the dish served immediately. Other times we would serve fresh beans with ground roasted sesame seeds and a little tamari soy sauce.

Snow peas cook up very sweet when they are boiled for a short time and they add a nice green color to a meal. They also go well when sliced and mixed in a salad. Occasionally we would season them with a little tamari soy sauce or rice vinegar. Snow peas may also be cooked Chinese-style with cabbage, onions, and sprouts. Slice, add a pinch of sea salt, and sauté each vegetable for 1 to 2 minutes; then mix together.

Green peas make a bright topping for many dishes. After shelling, I boil them in a little water for a few minutes with a touch of sea salt. The inside part of the pod is also edible. Chirashi sushi salad is a typical dish with green peas. Mixed together with brown rice, couscous, or other grains, they make a nice summer salad. I sometimes use boiled green peas to garnish soups or stews.

Boiled String Beans and Almonds

4 cups string beans
Spring water
1 cup whole almonds, slivered and roasted
Tamari soy sauce or sea salt

Wash the beans and remove the hard stem at one end. Slice the beans on the diagonal. Put about ½ inch of water in a pot and bring to a boil. Drop the beans into the water and reduce the heat to low. Cover the pot and simmer for about 5 to 10 minutes. Add the almonds and a little tamari soy sauce or sea salt and simmer for about 5 minutes longer.

Variation: These beans can also be sautéed in a little dark sesame oil for a slightly different flavor. Instead of cooking the almonds and beans together, the nuts may be ground fine, mixed with tamari soy sauce or tamari soy sauce and rice vinegar and mixed with the string beans after cooking as a sauce. Roasted sesame seeds may be added as a garnish.

Sautéed Snow Peas and Chinese Cabbage

Dark sesame oil
2 cups Chinese cabbage sliced diagonally
Kuzu
Spring water
Sea salt
1 cup snow peas, stems removed

Heat a small amount of sesame oil in a frying pan. Keep the heat high to keep the vegetables crisp. Add the cabbage to the skillet and sauté for 1 to 2 minutes. Mix a small amount of kuzu with a little water and pour the sauce over the cabbage. Add a little sea salt to season. Stir constantly. At the very end, add snow peas and mix for no more than one minute and serve.

TROPICAL VEGETABLES

Most tropical and semitropical vegetables are not appropriate for regular use in temperate zones, even though they now grow there or are eaten on hot, humid days. Maybe in ten thousand years, when they have fully adjusted to our soil and climatic conditions, these foods will produce more harmonious effects, but now they are too weakening, thin the blood, and can contribute to illness. On special occasions, a very tiny amount may be eaten as a condiment or garnish. But please be very careful. Violations of ecological order are the main causes of chronic disease in modern times.

Eggplant is so much bigger in the United States than in Japan. At home we enjoyed its beautiful purple flower, smooth shiny color, and long shape. Since becoming macrobiotic, I have stopped preparing this lovely tropical vegetable. Once or twice I have enjoyed it sautéed or baked for a long time and served with a miso sauce.

Green pepper is also southern in origin but is relatively small in size. On hot summer days I use it occasionally in small quantities to spice up a salad or a grain or vegetable dish. Sautéed with fried noodles or fried rice, a few slices or diced squares of green pepper are plenty. Baked stuffed green pepper with miso is enjoyable once or twice in the summer.

Chili peppers and other hot peppers are much stronger than green pepper. I have experimented with adding minced red pepper to kinpira-style vegetables in my cooking classes. I find it is really too hot to enjoy.

Tomatoes came to my area of Japan in the early 1930s. I was in the fourth grade when my mother started to grow them. Like most of the family, I didn't like the taste at first and could eat only the yellow tomatoes. In Japan tomatoes were eaten like fruit. On a hot summer day we would peel the skin and eat the inside sprinkled with a little salt. We never used them as a vegetable at the table or combined them with other foods. After becoming macrobiotic, I stopped eating tomatoes in this climate altogether. At restaurants I always order spaghetti plain, and at home I cook it with carrot sauce rather than tomato paste.

Potatoes also grew in our garden at home. We raised a very small variety and were careful of the sprouts, which are dangerous to eat. In college my whole dorm became sick one night from eating a nice fluffy potato dish. Externally, we use potato in macrobiotic home care for helping to discharge excess protein and fat from the body. However, we do not recommend eating white potatoes, sweet potatoes, or yams in this environment. Occasionally in summer, we prepare the small hairy taro variety.

Asparagus is a primitive fern-like plant. It has a unique taste and, after tough ends are removed, may be boiled or steamed until crispy and served with a nice sauce made of tamari soy sauce, a little grated fresh ginger, and roasted sesame seeds. It is not for regular use but for once in a while.

CHAPTER
15

GREEN LEAFY VEGETABLES

Hita, hita—
The sound of picking watercress
In the shallow stream.

—Yoshiko

Green is a color of peace, and green leafy vegetables make for a more peaceful mind, family, and home. Leafy vegetables are soft and tender and need to be treated with sensitivity and care. They usually cook quickly, making balance with longer-cooking whole grains and beans. They give an upward, rising energy and are very tasty. Most greens take only 1 to 2 minutes or less to cook and can be prepared when the other dishes have finished cooking and the meal is about to begin.

Among greens, some are hard and fibrous like kale and daikon tops. While hard greens take a little longer to prepare and may lose some of their nice color, they are very important to digestion and should be eaten daily. The softer types may also be eaten frequently.

Greens are more delicate than round, ground, or root vegetables and must be washed very gently. I use plenty of cool water in a pan or sink and quickly submerge the greens and rinse each leaf individually of dust, sand, and soil. If not properly washed, greens may leave a gritty taste in the mouth.

There are several ways to cut greens. Because they are so sensitive to being cut with metal, I prefer to tear them by hand if possible, especially the softer varieties. Many greens are better cooked whole and sliced after they are cooked.

Greens give a soft, fresh taste to fresh salads, boiled salads, and pressed salads. They may also be pickled raw in thin slices or in big leaves.

The most common method of preparing greens is to boil them ohitashi-style, dipping them in a small amount of boiling water for a few seconds or a few minutes. When ¼ to ½ inch of water is bubbling in a saucepan, dip the greens in and move them around with a pair of chopsticks so they cook evenly. For soft greens, this takes just a few seconds and a minute may be too long. Use high heat. For hard greens, 3 to 5 minutes or more may be needed, depending on the vegetable. For most greens, I add a pinch of sea salt at the very end when the greens have almost finished boiling. This brings out their natural sweetness and helps to keep their color bright. Adding salt at the beginning makes greens too watery. For mustard greens, daikon greens, turnip or radish greens, watercress, dandelion greens, and carrot tops, I do not use any salt as it makes these greens taste bitter. I usually dip the whole leaves and slice them when they are done to retain vitamins and minerals and keep the flavor. If there are several bunches of greens to be cooked or a large quantity, I often divide them into small handfuls and dip them one at a time. Greens go well with many sauces as well as with roasted sesame seeds or a little gomashio.

Some greens, such as scallions, have small roots. These are very nutritious and should always be used. If they are too fibrous to use with the leaves, I save and mince them to add to soup, stews, or sea vegetables.

Greens may also be steamed, sautéed, or deep-fried. Tempura-style green leaves are very delicious, light, and crunchy.

KALE

Kale has a rich sweet taste and is very tender when cooked. It is one of the hardiest greens and survives under the snow during the winter. Winter and spring, kale is usually more tender and I appreciate its strong energy more at these seasons than in summer or autumn.

I usually boil the sliced stems first with a pinch of sea salt for about 3 to 5 minutes; then I dip the leaves in boiling water for 1 to 3 minutes, depending on their thickness. The leaves may also be put on top of the stems and cooked at the same time. Boiled kale goes well with umeboshi vinegar or a tofu dressing.

To sauté kale, I chop the stem very fine and sauté it in a little sesame oil. Then I sauté the greens and finally add a little salt at the end. Lemon, miso, or rice vinegar make good sauces with kale cooked in this way.

Steamed Kale and Carrots

Spring water
1 cup carrots sliced in rounds
4 cups washed and thinly sliced kale

Put a small amount of water in a pot. Put a steamer in the pot and put the carrots in the steamer. Bring to a boil, cover, and steam until the carrots are done. They should be slightly crisp. Remove the carrots and put them in a bowl. Put the kale in the steamer and steam for a few minutes, or until done. The kale should be bright green and slightly crisp. Remove the kale and mix it with the steamed carrots.

COLLARD GREENS

We didn't have collards when I was growing up in Japan, but I have come to enjoy them very much. They are sweeter than kale, soft and tender, and have a very peaceful taste. Collards are traditional to native American and black American cooking.

Steamed Collard Greens with Tamari-Vinegar Sauce

Spring water
3 cups thinly sliced collard greens
Tamari soy sauce
Brown rice vinegar

Put a small amount of water in a pot and bring to a boil. Put a steamer in the pot. Set the collards in the steamer and steam for several minutes, or until done. The greens should be bright green and slightly crisp. Remove them and put them in a serving dish. Mix a small amount of tamari soy sauce, brown rice vinegar, and water together to make a sauce. Pour 1 teaspoon of sauce over each serving of collard greens.

BOK CHOY

Bok choy is basic to Chinese cooking. Its long white stalk is not so sweet, but its plain taste blends well with strong foods, such as fried tofu, fish, or a little green pepper. Bok choy is usually sautéed. A kuzu sauce may be added at the end.

CHINESE CABBAGE

Chinese cabbage is called *haku-sai* or "white leafy vegetable" in Japan. After daikon it was the next most common vegetable in our home. It has a nice, soft condensed shape, a very simple taste, and can be prepared in many styles and combinations. Chinese cabbage's white leaves are very pretty served with green leafy vegetables. It also keeps well and like other green and white vegetables is good for the liver and lungs.

Boiling brings out Chinese cabbage's light sweet taste and juiciness. It can be added to salads, soups, or mixed vegetables and cooked a short or long time. In pressed salad, I sprinkle alternate leaves of Chinese cabbage with salt. At other times I insert sliced kombu in between. The salt brings out the vegetable's juice, and the kombu absorbs it, giving the cabbage a slight sea vegetable taste.

My mother bought Chinese cabbage in 100-pound quantities for use in making big pickles. We washed the cabbages, cut them in halves or quarters lengthwise, added salt or salt with rice bran, and aged them for a long time. After 1 to 2 months, we could enjoy them on a cold winter day. In Korea, Chinese cabbages are used to make a spicy pickle called *kim-chi.* In Seoul, the capital of South Korea, I once had a chance to see the traditional way of aging kim-chi underground. The taste is very hot but zesty and delicious. While the other people in our group dined on lots of animal food, Michio and I happily survived on only rice and kim-chi. During the war many of my pupils made poems referring to "sak sak," the sound made by chewing Chinese cabbage pickles.

As a side dish by itself, I ordinarily boil the cabbage ohitashi-style. I take each leaf off separately, dip in the water for 1 minute, and then slice it after it is cooked. Chinese cabbage may also be boiled nishime-style for a little longer time with root vegetables. Chinese cabbage is also good occasionally in miso soup, in soup stock, wrapped around carrots, tied with nori strips, and added to yudofu. Chinese cabbage is nice served with a tamari-ginger sauce and garnished with a few scallion slices.

I also enjoy Chinese cabbage sautéed. It may be stir-fried in a little sesame oil with sprouts, fried noodles, fried rice, onions, tofu, tempeh, or dried tofu.

Chinese Cabbage with Tamari-Lemon Sauce

Spring water
4 cups thinly sliced Chinese cabbage
2 to 3 teaspoons fresh lemon juice
2 to 3 tablespoons tamari soy sauce

Put about ½ inch of water in a pot and bring to a boil. Add the Chinese cabbage, cover, and simmer for 1 to 2 minutes. Stir occasionally to cook the cabbage evenly. Remove the vegetable when tender and drain. It should be brightly colored and slightly crisp. For the sauce, combine the lemon juice, ½ cup of water, and tamari soy sauce and mix. Serve the sauce and Chinese cabbage separately and pour a teaspoon on each serving before eating.

Chinese Cabbage Rolls

Spring water
5 Chinese cabbage leaves
1 carrot, cut lengthwise into ½-inch-thick strips
Umeboshi plums

Put about ½ inch of water in a pot and bring to a boil. Put the cabbage leaves in the boiling water, cover, and boil for 2 to 3 minutes. Remove, drain, and allow the leaves to cool. Put the carrot strips in the boiling water, cover, and boil for 1 to 2 minutes. Remove, drain, and let cool. Save the cooking water to make a kuzu sauce to pour over the cabbage or use it later in another dish or for soup.

Cut about ¼ inch of the hard base of the cabbage leaves off where they were attached to the core of the cabbage head. Lay one or two strips of carrot across each cabbage leaf so that they span the width of the leaf. Starting from the base of the leaf, roll up the carrot tightly inside the cabbage leaf to create a cylinder. Slice the cylinder into several equal-sized rolls. Place on a plate with the carrot side up. Place a small dot of umeboshi plum or paste on top of each individual roll. Repeat with the remaining leaves and carrot strips.

Variation: For a different taste and appearance, boiled watercress or other greens may be placed in the center of the rolls.

ESCAROLE

Escarole is easy to grow and mother always had some in the garden. It is softer than Chinese cabbage and the stem is not so tough. Escarole is a little bitter, though, and is better prepared without salt. The subject of many poems, it is often called "water grass" in Japan.

MUSTARD GREENS

Mustard greens are another vegetable I ate during my childhood. Like kale it thrives under the snow during winter and in the spring quickly shoots up from the ground to the air as a symbol of spring energy. It is very sweet, strong, and hearty. Mustard seed oil processed from this plant is often used in daily cooking in Japan. Mustard's beautiful yellow flowers always bloomed just before planting time. A typical sight in Japan during early spring is misty fields with bright yellow mustard flowers. I prepare mustard greens by boiling them ohitashi-style for 1 to 3 minutes. I don't use salt since it creates a slightly bitter taste in these greens. Mustard greens are very enjoyable served with a light vinegar taste or a ginger-tamari soy sauce.

Boiled Mustard Greens with Tamari-Ginger Sauce

4 cups thinly sliced mustard greens
¼ cup spring water
¼ cup tamari soy sauce
½ teaspoon grated fresh ginger

Put ¼ inch of water in a pot and bring it to a boil. Drop in the mustard greens and cook for several minutes, or until done. Mix often to cook the greens evenly, making sure to bring the greens from the bottom of the pot up to the top. When done the greens should be bright green and slightly crisp. For the sauce, mix the water, tamari soy sauce, and fresh grated ginger together. Serve the greens with a spoonful of sauce over each serving.

DAIKON GREENS

The beautiful big leaves of the daikon plant are edible. Though often removed from the plant at the store and a little on the tough side, I recommend them highly. When cooked, they are very chewy and strengthening and have a slightly pungent taste. To soften them, I cook the daikon tops together with a little diluted miso for a relatively long time, about 10 to 15 minutes. They also go well sautéed with fried tofu. For quick pickles, we dry the leaves for 1 to 2 days and press them with salt. Long-time pickles are often made with daikon that is just dry enough for the end of the radish and the top of the radish to touch when bent. These radishes are pickled with the leaves on top and may be aged 2 to 3 years to give very strong energy. Daikon leaves have many traditional medicinal uses and are used in macrobiotic home care for preparing hip baths to relieve stagnation in the lower abdominal region and sex organs. Red radish tops are also very energizing and can be cooked like other greens.

❧ Daikon Greens and Kombu ❧

- Light sesame oil
- 1 pound fresh tofu, cut into 6 pieces
- 2 strips kombu, 6 to 8 inches long, soaked for 2 to 3 minutes
- 1 medium-sized daikon (about 10 inches long) with greens, sliced into 1- to 2-inch lengths
- Spring water
- 1 to 2 tablespoons tamari soy sauce

Lightly pan-fry the tofu or deep-fry with light sesame oil until both sides are brown. Slice the kombu into 1½-inch squares. Put the kombu on the bottom of a heavy pot. Put the daikon on top of the kombu and cover with the fried tofu. Add 2 cups of water, bring to a boil, cover, and reduce the heat to medium-low. Simmer for 30 to 40 minutes. Add the daikon greens and a little tamari soy sauce. Steam the greens for several minutes. Do not stir and do not cook the greens too long. They should be bright green.

TURNIP GREENS

Turnip greens are softer than daikon greens and can be cooked together with turnips. When making pickles, I often include whole turnips and their greens together, pressed with salt. The beautiful purple of the turnips and green of the leaves make a colorful combination.

❧ Turnip Greens with Sesame-Tamari Sauce ❧

- Spring water
- 3 cups sliced turnip greens
- 2 tablespoons roasted sesame seeds
- Tamari soy sauce

Put ¼ to ½ inch of water in a pot and bring to a boil. Add the turnip greens, cover, and boil for 2 to 3 minutes. Stir occasionally to cook the greens evenly. Put the roasted sesame seeds in a suribachi and grind slightly. Add a little tamari soy sauce and water to make a thin sauce with a slight salty taste. Either mix the sauce in with the greens or let each person add the sauce at the table.

SPINACH

Spinach is soft, easy to grow, and cooks quickly. It may be used fresh in salads or boiled by dipping for a few seconds in hot water. Its dark color and astringent taste do not lend themselves to soups and combinations with other vegetables. Spinach contains a very strong acid and is not recommended for weak or sick people. We use spinach only occasionally in macrobiotic cooking.

LETTUCE

There are many kinds of lettuce including iceberg, romaine, and Boston. In Japan, we fed lettuce to our rabbits and occasionally ate it raw with a little tamari soy sauce, umeboshi, or roasted sesame seeds. (The first time I saw a half head of big lettuce served on a plate in a New York restaurant I was shocked. I felt like a rabbit!) In addition to salads, lettuce leaves are good for decorating special dishes. Lettuce can also be cooked but turns dark when boiled.

SWISS CHARD

Chard is a little on the acidic side and not recommended for daily use. It can be eaten raw in salads or boiled and served with a little miso or rice vinegar sauce.

WATERCRESS

It is a joy to see watercress growing in a pond or along the side of a stream in the high mountains. It grows through the icy snows of winter and is especially nice in early spring. We often picked it at this season and brought it home. Watercress can be used in salads and has a rather pungent, slightly bitter taste. A creamy sesame seed or tofu dressing goes well with a watercress salad. Boil or sauté it for a few seconds. This helps to take the edge off the flavor and brightens its beautiful green color. Usually I just let it touch the bottom of a hot pan or dip it quickly in and out of the bubbling water. Salt brings out the bitter taste of the vegetable and is better avoided. In the summer, watercress goes very well sautéed with corn and tofu, scrambled egg style, and is usually mixed in at the very end. Raw or cooked, watercress may also be added to soups or sushi.

Boiled Watercress

---

2 bunches watercress — Spring water

Wash the watercress very well. Put ¼ to ½ inch of water in a pot and bring it to a boil. Put about one-fourth of the watercress in the water and cook for about 30 to 40 seconds, moving it around with chopsticks to make sure it cooks evenly. Remove the watercress, drain, and allow it to cool. Repeat with the remaining watercress, cooking about one-quarter of it at a time. After cooking, draining, and cooling all of the watercress, slice and place it on a plate or in a serving bowl.

❧ Watercress Rolls ❧

- 2 bunches watercress
- 3 sheets nori
- 3 tablespoons tamari soy sauce
- 3 tablespoons spring water
- ½ teaspoon grated fresh ginger

Wash the watercress very well. Put about ½ inch of water in a pot and bring it to a boil. Dip one-fourth of the watercress at a time in the bubbling water for 30 to 40 seconds, moving it around several times to cook it evenly. Remove the watercress, drain, and let it cool. Toast the nori. Divide the watercress into three equal portions. Place the watercress on top of each of the sheets of nori and roll up tightly into a cylinder. Slice each cylinder in half. Then slice each half into 3 to 4 equal bite-sized rolls. Place rolls on their sides so that the bright green shows and arrange them on a plate or serving platter. Make a dip or sauce by mixing the tamari soy sauce, water, and ginger together. Dip the watercress rolls into the sauce when eating.

PARSLEY

Parsley, with its bright green color and strong taste, is one of my favorite garnishes. I mostly use the curly leaf variety, although the flat-leaf variety is also good. It may also be eaten as a small side dish or be added to other foods including soups, salads, and casseroles. It goes especially well with yellow or orange foods, such as squash, millet, or corn. To cook it, I dip it in boiling water for 1 second and then remove it. The parsley then turns an even brighter green. The stems are a little fibrous and can be boiled or sautéed a little longer than the leaves.

❧ Parsley with Ginger Sauce ❧

- Spring water
- 1 bunch parsley
- Pinch of sea salt
- 1 teaspoon tamari soy sauce
- ¼ teaspoon grated fresh ginger
- Roasted sesame seeds (optional)

Put ¼ inch of water in a pot and bring to a boil. Add the parsley and a pinch of sea salt. Cook the parsley for a few seconds, remove, and let it cool. Reserve the water. After cooking, chop the parsley very fine. To make the sauce, combine the tamari soy sauce, ginger, and a little of the parsley water. Pour the sauce over the parsley and serve. A tablespoon of roasted sesame seeds may be sprinkled on top, if desired.

CARROT GREENS

Carrot greens have a nice strong taste like parsley. They are sometimes a little hard, though, and may need to cook longer, which will make them lose some of their bright color. Carrot tops were one of my children's favorite dishes when they were growing up. I also like to sauté carrot greens with a little miso or tamari soy sauce added at the end. The miso sweetens them, and this combination may be eaten as a condiment. To prevent a bitter taste, I use no salt when cooking these greens.

Carrot Tops with Sesame Seeds

1 bunch carrot tops
½ cup sesame seeds
1 to 2 teaspoons tamari soy sauce

Wash the carrot tops and chop them very fine. Wash the seeds and dry-roast them in a frying pan. Put the roasted seeds in a suribachi and grind until about half crushed, adding a little tamari soy sauce. The taste should not be salty. Quickly boil or sauté the carrot tops for about 3 to 4 minutes. Add to the crushed seeds and mix.

SCALLIONS

Scallions are one of my favorite garnishes, providing a wonderful pungent taste and nice warm energy. They stimulate the appetite and go well on top of noodles, rice, soups, stews, grains, and beans. If scallions become old and dried out, simply put them back in the soil and they will start to grow again. The Tokyo area is famous for its deep-rooted scallions, which are cultivated in raised hillbeds. The root part of these scallions is very sweet and good in sukiyaki. Scallion roots should always be used and never discarded. They are the strongest part of the plant. Scallions may also be sautéed or boiled for a few seconds.

Scallions with Miso Sauce

Spring water
1 bunch whole scallions
Roasted sesame seeds for garnish
½ to 1 teaspoon barley miso
Lemon juice or brown rice vinegar
Tahini

Put ½ inch of water in a pot and bring it to a boil. Add whole scallions and cook for about 30 seconds. The white part of the scallions may take a few seconds longer to cook. These may be cut off and cooked separately from the green tops, if desired. Move the scallions around occasionally to cook them evenly. Remove the scallions, drain, and let them cool. Slice into 1-inch pieces. Place on a plate and garnish with roasted sesame seeds. Combine the miso, lemon juice, spring water, and tahini to make a sauce. The dressing should be on the thick side, not soupy. Dip the scallions into the sauce when eating.

Variations: Sea salt or tamari soy sauce may be used in place of miso. Also instead of miso, you can use roasted sesame seeds, crushed in a suribachi with a little salt or tamari soy sauce, and sprinkled over the scallions.

CHIVES

Chives are much stronger than scallions and combined with a little miso they make a nice condiment. They can also be boiled for 1 second, sliced, and served with a dip.

LEEKS

Leeks are much bigger than scallions and chives and not so pungent. When cooked they become sweet and creamy. Leeks are difficult to wash. I usually cut them in half lengthwise and rinse well under cold water the inside layers where the soil collects. I enjoy boiled leeks, cut fine or in big slices. They may also be sautéed or deep-fried and become very soft and sweet. Leeks make an excellent soup and may also be added in small amounts to other soups. Cooked together with a little miso, they become even sweeter.

CELERY

Celery has a unique shape and texture. It is enjoyable raw and gives crispness to salads. Diced celery balances raw onions and goes well with buckwheat in a salad. Celery can also be cooked for a short time with a touch of salt, which makes it sweeter. I enjoy celery boiled nishime-style with carrots and onions. The fiber of celery is good for digestion and strengthens the will and judgment. Celery leaves may be used for garnishing or for serving raw with a dip. The whole leaves are delightful in tempura.

ENDIVES

I first tried endive in Paris. It was sautéed and very delicious. While it can be sliced in various ways, I prefer to use it whole, sautéed in a little oil, adding a little diluted miso on top at the end. The miso helps to sweeten the endive and relieve the slightly bitter taste. Endives are a high-quality gourmet food and very enjoyable with a nice kuzu or tamari-ginger sauce.

Endive with Kuzu Sauce

1 to 2 small strips kombu
5 to 6 whole endives
2 teaspoons barley miso
Spring water
1 teaspoon kuzu
Tamari soy sauce
Grated fresh ginger
Parsley sprigs or sliced scallions for garnish

Put the kombu in a frying pan with the endives on top. Dilute the miso in a little water and spread it on top of the endives. Add about ¼ inch of water to the pan, cover, and bring to a boil. Turn the heat to low and cook until the endives turn transparent in color. Add a little diluted kuzu to the juice to thicken the liquid. Mix a little tamari soy sauce and grated fresh ginger in the remaining juice and pour over the endives in the serving bowl. Garnish with parsley sprigs or a few sliced scallions.

Variation: For a stronger taste, sauté the endives first in 1 to 2 tablespoons of dark sesame oil for a few minutes before adding the water and cooking as above. If you use the oil, the kombu is not needed.

SPROUTS

Sprouts grow easily at home and are readily available at most food stores. The soft ones, alfalfa, mung, or clover, are nice raw with a little brown rice vinegar or tamari soy sauce. The harder ones, like bean sprouts, can be sautéed quickly, Chinese-style, with other soft vegetables. Be careful not to overcook the sprouts. Sprouted grains, such as wheat, are very sweet and enjoyable.

BAMBOO SHOOTS

Bamboo shoots are one of my favorite dishes. One of the things I miss most living in America is bamboo forests. Bamboo trees are also traditionally grown at the side of farm houses in Japan and assume many shapes and configurations depending on the rain, sun, snow, or wind. The leaves are tender and beautiful. From late April to early May the shoots come forth and grow very quickly. Our relatives often came to visit bringing large bamboo leaves the size of a small baby strapped on their backs. Bamboo shoots are fun to peel, and children enjoy taking off the outer skin. We used these more fibrous layers for wrapping food, as a lunch box, and for making folded cups to drink from. We usually sliced the tender young shoots and boiled them with a little miso. The soft part could also be sliced fine and sautéed. Bamboo shoots give strong energy and should be used only on special occasions.

CHAPTER 16

WILD VEGETABLES

Through melting snow,
Sweet coltsfoot buds appear,
Messengers of spring.
—*Noboku*

Foraging for wild foods is a traditional activity in Japan. In the *Manyoshyu*, a classic dating back about 1,500 years ago, there is a famous poem by the Emperor Tenji Teno that tells of his going out to the fields in the springtime to pick wild pansy. He says that the spring fields were so beautiful that he stayed out overnight.

Some of my fondest memories are of searching for watercress, mugwort, fiddlehead ferns, and other wild plants in the mountains. Even within the village itself we often went into the rice fields to gather edible weeds. There were no restrictions on picking wild plants in the paddies. With my basket and knife I would collect *seri*, a red-purplish plant known in the West as hemlock parsley, whose sweet, slightly sharp taste fell between regular parsley and watercress. Seri on the table marked the coming of spring, and we knew the sparrows would soon return from the south.

Once in a cooking class over here many years later, someone asked me how many wild foods we gathered. On the blackboard I was able to jot down from memory over thirty edible wild foods. Seven of these were traditionally cooked with soft rice on the Lunar New Year, which usually fell in early February. During the war, when food was scarce, we often picked wild foods.

Wild vegetables begin to appear in the early spring, often while the snow is still on the ground. They have a very strong upward energy and are traditionally good for diseases such as tuberculosis, which is most common in spring. Wild foods are much hardier than cultivated plants and should be eaten only occasionally and in very small amounts. Of course, as with any unfamiliar food, care must be taken to make sure the plants are edible and not poisonous.

Wild vegetables often have a strong acid taste, similar to the foam that sometimes comes up when cooking beans, so we generally discard the first boiling water. Then we add fresh water, boil again, and season at the end. Wild plants can also be steamed, sautéed, or prepared tempura-style. The native people of North America used many wild grasses, herbs, roots, and barks. Some macrobiotic friends here have studied and learned how to use some of these traditional foods.

WILD CHIVES

Chives are usually the first plants to shoot up in the early spring. They continue to grow year-round but by summer's hot heat are very limp. Like onions and scallions, chives offer a very strong warm energy. They are one of the items traditionally included in the Spring Seven Grasses ceremony. Usually we just cut off the green part, allowing a new shoot to form from the root. Chives make a nice garnish for fried rice or fried noodles. They can also be combined with miso to make a strong condiment.

MUGWORT

Mugwort is traditionally pounded with sweet rice to make green mochi. On March 3, Girls' Day, we always served this dish in Japan. The fresh young mugwort leaves were gathered at the side of the rice field or stream and brought home. There we cleaned them, dipped them in boiling water, cooled them off in cold water, squeezed out the remaining liquid, and allowed them to dry. Mugwort prepared in this way keeps all year. By late summer, the mugwort leaves have become very strong and are good for making mugwort tea. This beverage is customarily used to protect against intestinal worms. Like chrysanthemum leaves, choice mugwort leaves have small white hairs on the underside. Central Japan is famous for its mugwort which has a very nice, strong oil and is collected for *moxa*. *Moxa* is a dried herbal preparation that is placed on the skin and burned slowly like incense. Moxabustion is one of the techniques of traditional Oriental medicine and, like acupuncture, is based on controlling the flow of electromagnetic energy through the meridians of the body.

FIDDLEHEAD FERNS

Fiddleheads are one of the most common ferns in both the Japanese and American countrysides. They can be boiled ohitashi-style and served with a miso sauce, which neutralizes their slightly bitter taste and makes them sweet. In addition to fiddleheads, we picked many other ferns. After initial cleaning and boiling, we soaked them in water containing wood ashes, rinsed out the ashes very well with cold water, and left the ferns to dry. In general, we should be very sparing in our use of primitive foods such as ferns, bracken, mushrooms, and fungi.

DANDELION

Dandelion is the king of wild grasses. It has a nice, slightly bitter taste and gives very strong energy. It can be boiled and served with a miso sauce or sautéed with a slight miso or tamari soy sauce taste. Dandelion roots are very bitter and when dried and powdered make a nice grain coffee-like drink. The roots make a good condiment sautéed with a little oil and sweetened with miso. Dandelion greens are excellent in tempura, and the roots and flowers may be dipped in batter and deep-fried as well.

Dandelion Greens and Tempeh

8 ounces tempeh
1 to 2 teaspoons dark sesame oil
1 to 2 teaspoons miso
Spring water
2 handfuls fresh dandelion greens

Cut the tempeh into 1- to 2-inch-long by ¼-inch-thick rectangular shapes. Oil a frying pan and sauté the tempeh for 3 to 4 minutes over low heat. Purée the miso in a little water and pour it over the tempeh. Next add about 1 cup of water to the pan, cover, and cook for about 15 minutes. Meanwhile, wash the dandelion greens and slice them into 1- to 2-inch sections. Put the dandelion greens on top of the tempeh and miso. Steam the dandelion greens for a few minutes. Mix the dandelions and tempeh together and cook until all liquid has evaporated.

Variation: Tamari soy sauce may be used instead of miso.

MILKWEED

I learned to appreciate milkweed in this country. It grows in meadows in early spring, at which time its small tender tips are very sweet and delicious. I boil them and serve them with a miso sauce and a few sesame seeds for garnish. They are also very good in tempura. By summer, milkweed often becomes too hard and fibrous to cook.

LAMBSQUARTERS

Lambsquarters is a very popular wild vegetable. It grows in the city as well as the countryside. It can be boiled and seasoned with miso, tamari soy sauce, or sea salt.

WILD BURDOCK

Wild burdock is sweeter than cultivated burdock but it is cooked in the same way. Our family has often hunted for wild burdock here in New England. It is well worth searching for.

Fried Rice with Wild Vegetables

Fried rice is a good way to combine wild plants.

Dark sesame oil
4 cups cooked brown rice
Tamari soy sauce
2 tablespoons roasted sesame seeds
½ cup finely chopped chives
½ cup finely chopped dandelion leaves and stems
½ cup finely chopped chickweed

Heat a small amount of oil in a frying pan and add the rice. Sprinkle a little tamari soy sauce over the rice and cover. Cook over low heat until rice is warm. Stir occasionally to heat the rice evenly. If the rice is dry, add a few drops of water at the start to moisten it. Add the roasted sesame seeds to the hot rice and mix them in. At the very end of cooking, add the wild vegetables and mix them with the rice. Cover and cook for only a few minutes. Remove and serve.

PIGWEED

Pigweed or goosefoot was a very common wild plant in the Japanese countryside. We called it *aoza* and ate it as frequently as some garden vegetables. We preferred picking the younger plants, but the older ones were also edible. After collecting the buds, we washed them and cooked them ohitashi-style by dipping them briefly in boiling water, then sautéed them with oil and cooked them nishime-style with tamari soy sauce to make a condiment. Softly boiled pigweed can also be prepared as a side dish with a ginger-tamari sauce or with a tofu dressing.

KNOTWEED

Knotweed has a strong sour taste. We did not use it very often as a side dish but mostly for pickles. The outer skin is removed before using.

THISTLE

As children, we gathered thistle roots and cooked them kinpira-style. They are usually prepared by themselves and are said to be good for helping to relieve Parkinson's disease.

HORSETAIL

I loved to pick this wild grass and give it to my mother. Since it was a little bitter to the taste, she discarded the first cooking water after boiling. Prepared as a side dish, horsetail goes well with miso or a sour sauce. It may also be cooked with tamari soy sauce.

BRACKEN

Bracken is very popular in the Orient. It grows rapidly and we collected it on many occasions. Freshly cut, bracken is added directly to miso soup or cooked together with bamboo shoots. Bracken can also be boiled with a pinch of wood ashes for a short time, rinsed free of the ashes, and allowed to dry. Dried bracken kept the whole year, and we enjoyed it on New Year's and other holidays when it could be cooked nishime-style with a little tamari soy sauce.

SHEPHERD'S PURSE

This plant does not have a very strong taste. It can be cooked together with a sesame-tamari sauce or be served separately with a sauce at the table.

SWEET COLTSFOOT

We called this wild grass *fuki*. It grew everywhere in Japan, along the banks of rice fields and by streambeds. Its leaves are so big that they are often used by country people as umbrellas. For cooking, we used only the stem which resembled celery but was hollow inside. To reduce coltsfoot's bitter taste, the first boiling water is traditionally discarded. After peeling off the fibrous outer skin, we cut the stems into 1-inch pieces and cooked them in a little water with miso added to sweeten their taste. The stems can also be sautéed with a little oil or tamari soy sauce. We also made it into pickles with salt. These kept for a long time and were enjoyed on holidays and at other festive times. In the spring, coltsfoot's roots are very cute, sending forth small buds that flower. A popular condiment called *fuki-no-to* made with these roots, tamari soy sauce, and miso is traditionally enjoyed for its nice bitter taste and taken as an accompaniment to sake. I recently discovered fuki growing near our new retreat center in the Berkshire mountains.

PRICKLY ASH

Actually a young tree, prickly ash is one of my favorite wild plants. I was also happy to find it growing in western Massachusetts. Its leaves can be cooked with miso or tamari soy sauce to make a pungent condiment. It can also be sliced and cooked with fried tofu. The seeds of prickly ash are very knotty and spicy and may be used along with the leaves as a garnish for other dishes.

TREE BARK

In Japan we used to look for the young bark of the sansyo tree. We don't have this tree in this country. Sansyo had a nice pungent taste and could be used in sushi, cooked with bamboo shoots, or made into a condiment. I am not so familiar with North American trees and barks. I understand pine needles steeped in hot water make a soothing tea with a delightful forest fragrance. High in vitamin C, pine needle tea was given to European sailors by the Indians and healed them of scurvy.

MUSHROOMS

I have many fond memories of exploring for mushrooms with my family. In the autumn when the ginkgo leaves turned golden, we would troop out to the mountains with big bamboo baskets to hunt for wild mushrooms. As children we heard scary stories about people who had touched poison mushrooms and later became sick after eating rice balls with the same hand, and so we were always very careful; this is just common sense for anyone who forages.

After a day in the woods we would bring home many types of edible mushrooms. Some were good for miso soup. The most enjoyable ones we baked. After washing and cleaning them and cutting off the ends of the stems, we wrapped the mushrooms in wet rice paper and put them in hot wood ashes. Then we baked them and served them with a little tamari soy sauce, which made them nice and crispy. Wild mushrooms are an elegant food and how we enjoyed these mushroom feasts.

Shiitake is the most famous Oriental mushroom. *Shii* means oak, and these large golden fungi traditionally grow wild from fallen oak trees. Now they are also cultivated, and the spores have recently been introduced to this country. We grow some in the backyard, and native North American shiitake of high quality are now available in some natural foods stores. Imported dried shiitake are also available. Shiitake are very delicious, but like other primitive foods, including other fungi, ferns, and wild grasses, they should be eaten only occasionally and in very small amounts. Wild foods are much stronger than cultivated plants and should be used very carefully.

As a small condiment-size side dish, I enjoy cooking them nishime-style by boiling them for 10 to 20 minutes in a little water. Dried shiitake should be soaked for a few minutes and the stems removed before cooking. These savory mushrooms are used commonly as a base for kombu stock or clear soup. From time to time a few slices may be added to miso soup as well as other bean, grain, and vegetable dishes. Sautéed well in sesame oil, they give a unique crunchy taste. Medicinally, shiitake have many uses, from lowering body temperature to purifying the blood and protecting against hardening of the arteries and tumors.

Ordinary cultivated *white and brown mushrooms* are also nice on occasion, though I don't use them as much as shiitake. Cultivated mushrooms are very nice sautéed, alone or with other vegetables. I especially enjoy them with seitan. Although some people eat them raw, I prefer mushrooms cooked, marinated with tamari soy sauce and rice vinegar, or pickled for a short time after cooking. Cultivated mushrooms are delicious in mushroom soup, barley soup, or barley stew and go well with soybeans and other grains. Usually I sauté mushrooms very well before adding them to other vegetables in soups and stews. In a restaurant in Bologna, Italy, I once had some very delicious tempura-style mushrooms. I also enjoy mushrooms broiled in backyard barbecues.

CHAPTER 17

TEMPURA-STYLE AND DEEP-FRIED FOODS

Broiling mochi
On a cool spring evening,
I feel happy and warm inside.

—Tatako

Food dipped in batter and deep-fried in oil at very high temperatures is called tempura. This unique method makes for a very delicious, crispy meal. The ingredients cook quickly, have a light taste, and produce strong energy. Tempura originated in Portugal as a cooking method for meat and seafood. European sailors brought the technique to Japan in the sixteenth century. There more fancy styles evolved, including *shojin age*, a vegetable tempura cuisine perfected in Buddhist temples.

Almost all foods can be prepared tempura-style, including seafood, sea vegetables, vegetables, grains, and beans. The major exception is soft, watery vegetables, which turn soggy. This style of cooking creates distinctive, beautiful shapes and is wonderful for parties, feasts, or other special occasions. At our home we enjoy tempura about once a week; we make it with a variety of sliced root, round, and green leafy vegetables, as well as seitan, tofu, and, on very special occasions, fish or seafood. Although tempura is not oily to the taste when properly cooked, it is not for daily consumption. For those who need to limit their intake of oil, it is preferable to avoid tempura.

Tempura is traditionally served with a tamari-ginger sauce. The cooked morsels are dipped into this sauce at the table. A small amount of grated daikon is usually eaten with tempura as a condiment at the table in order to make the oil more digestible. A little mustard or horseradish is also served with fish or seafood tempura.

Deep-frying is similar to cooking tempura-style, except that no batter is used. The food is cooked directly in the hot oil. Leftover grains and beans can be formed into croquettes, and deep-fried. Tofu and seitan are also very delicious deep-fried, as are a variety of vegetables and sea vegetables. For soups, deep-fried bread cubes make a rich garnish.

Tempura Batter

- 1 cup whole wheat pastry flour
- 1 to 2 tablespoons kuzu or arrowroot flour
- Pinch of sea salt
- 1 cup spring water per cup of flour and kuzu

Combine the dry ingredients and then stir in the liquid. Do not mix too much. Ideally the batter should be kept cold until it is used. It should be neither too dry nor too wet. If too watery, add a little more flour. If too dry, add a little more water. If the batter sits too long, it tends to thicken, so don't prepare it too far in advance. The more kuzu mixed into the flour, the more transparent and crispy the tempura will be. Small amounts of batter keep their consistency better than large amounts. When cooking large amounts of food, I make additional batter as needed.

TEMPURA OIL

Sesame oil is traditionally used in Japanese tempura. I am very fond of dark sesame oil. It makes very delicious tempura, but if you find its flavor too strong, use light sesame oil instead. For making large quantities of tempura, you may use unrefined safflower oil, which is also less expensive. Corn oil is too volatile to use. Mixing different oils also brings out bubbles and increases the danger of splashing.

When making tempura, I keep the kitchen extremely orderly and concentrate carefully on each step. It is better for babies and children not to be in the kitchen at this time. I am also careful not to put my face too near the top of the cooking pot where it can get burned from splashing oil. If the oil should splash my hand, I put it under cold water. If it is more than a minor burn, I immediately cover the burnt area with cold tofu and wrap it in a cloth bandage. Green vegetables, such as cabbage leaves, may be used if tofu is not available. This helps relieve the pain.

Tempura oil can be saved and reused. I allow it to cool and then strain it into a glass bottle or jar, and keep it in a cool, dark place until needed. For tempura, fresh oil is ideal, but oil may be reused several times. Replenishing it each time with some fresh oil will make it last longer, but it should be discarded after 2 or 3 months.

SELECTING VEGETABLES

Many combinations of vegetables may be cooked tempura-style. Any style of cutting is fine, including small pieces, large slices, flowerets, and whole leaves. The vegetables need to be dry and should be lightly patted with a cloth if too moist. I usually select about two vegetables from each group of root vegetables, round and ground vegetables, and green leafy vegetables. For each person I allow 2 to 3 pieces of each vegetable. The exact amount depends on the size and thickness of the pieces, the season of the year, and the freshness of the produce.

Root vegetables, such as carrots, parsnips, lotus root, and burdock, are often sliced thinly for tempura. They may also be cut into small matchsticks, dipped together in batter, and deep-fried. I especially like to combine 1 carrot slice and 1 burdock slice. Watery root vegetables, such as daikon, turnip, and rutabaga, are not usually cooked tempura-style.

Round and ground vegetables, such as sliced onion rings, thinly sliced winter squashes, cauliflower and broccoli flowerets, finely minced cabbage, and string beans, snow peas, or thinly sliced zucchini, can be used for tempura.

Green leafy vegetables give tempura a beautiful shape. The leaves may be deep-fried whole or sliced. I especially like to tempura dandelion (roots and flower can be cooked whole along with the greens), celery (the leafy part), and carrot tops. (I save the carrot stems for mincing and cooking tempura-style with root vegetables.) I also am fond of parsley, watercress, kale, collards, milkweed, and lambsquarters. In my childhood, we enjoyed tempura-style chrysanthemum leaves, made by applying batter on only one side and dipping the leaves in the hot oil for only 1 to 2 seconds. The other side remained bright green. Watery greens, such as Chinese cabbage, bok choy, and lettuce, are not usually cooked tempura-style.

Corn on the cob cut into 1-inch rounds is very delicious as part of tempura. Mushrooms, whole or sliced, are also very tasty. Small pieces of seitan, tofu, or tempeh may also be cooked tempura-style and are very energizing.

FISH AND SEAFOOD TEMPURA

A small amount of fish or seafood may occasionally be included in the tempura along with the vegetables and makes for a very strong dish. White meat fish, cut into fillets of 1½ to 2 inches, is preferable to blue- or red-skinned varieties, which are more oily. Shrimp is very nice in tempura and should be cleaned, shelled, and deveined before it is used. The tails may be left on, and making a pair of small diagonal cuts on the bottom about an inch apart will prevent the shrimp from curling up.

If I am including fish or seafood, I wait until all the vegetables are cooked first. Fish leaves a strong flavor in the oil and can affect the taste of vegetables. To remove a fishy taste from the hot oil after use, I add an umeboshi plum to the hot oil in the pot and cook until the plum turns black.

PREPARING TEMPURA

The usual procedure is to slice all the vegetables and seafood first, prepare the batter and let it sit a few minutes, and then heat up the oil. A cast-iron pot, high-sided frying pan, or wok is ideal for making tempura. Cast-iron allows for more even control, and the oil doesn't evaporate as quickly as with other metals. A minimum of 1 inch of oil is needed in the pot, and 2 to 3 inches are often used. The oil needs to be between 345 and 355 degrees. The ingredients will burn at higher heats or become soggy at lower temperatures. If the oil smokes, the temperature is too high. To check for the right temperature, I drop a piece of batter into the hot oil. If the temperature is right, it will sink to the bottom and then rise quickly to the top. If it stays at the bottom for a minute or so before rising, the temperature of the oil is too low. If the batter stays at the top and doesn't sink, the temperature is too high. I normally keep the heat within the medium range.

When the correct temperature is attained, I begin coating the sliced ingredients with batter and dipping them one by one into the hot oil. It is important not to cover the pieces with too much batter or they will stick together or turn out too soft. I use chopsticks or my fingers to dip them in and out of the batter quickly but evenly. I usually cook only 4 to 5 pieces of food in the pot at a time. More than that lowers the temperature of the oil and makes the tempura soggy. If the batter separates from the morsels while they are cooking, it is too thin, and I add a little more flour to the batter. Sometimes I also dip the coated vegetables in a little dry flour before dipping them into the oil. This adds extra body and texture.

The ingredients should be deep-fried until golden brown. After about a minute in the hot oil, I turn them over with chopsticks to cook them evenly on the other side. Altogether the pieces will crisp up in from 1 to 3 minutes, depending on the type of vegetable and the way it is cut. When the morsels are finished, I allow them to drain of excess oil in a wire mesh tempura rack that fits over one side of the pot or on paper towels on the counter. After cooking each piece I also skim the top of the oil with a wire oil skimmer to remove any particles of burnt oil and batter. After the ingredients have cooked and drained, I keep them warm on a baking sheet in the oven at low temperature. When everything is ready, I arrange the tempura attractively on a large platter, with like ingredients grouped together. The sauces and garnish are usually served individually. Making tempura properly takes time. I usually allow about 30 to 60 minutes altogether for slicing ingredients, preparing the batter and oil, and deep-frying.

Tempura Sauce

This volume is per person, so multiply accordingly.

- 1 tablespoon tamari soy sauce
- 1 tablespoon dashi (kombu stock)
- A touch of grated ginger
- ½ teaspoon grated daikon
- 1 teaspoon mirin (optional)

Mix the ingredients together. If you do not have dashi stock on hand, use water. Mirin may be added to the basic sauce, if desired, for a slightly sweeter taste. The sauce is served individually in small cups or bowls. At the table each person dips the tempura in the sauce before eating.

Tempura Garnish

In addition to the dipping sauce, a little grated daikon or grated turnip is traditionally served with the meal. To prepare, finely grate raw daikon or turnip and add 1 to 2 drops of tamari soy sauce to each serving. One teaspoon to 1 tablespoon of garnish per person is plenty. This helps to make the oil more digestible. For fish or seafood, a stronger garnish of mustard or horseradish may also be served.

Grain and Bean Croquettes

Croquettes are a delicious, crispy way to prepare leftover grains and beans. Millet sticks together a little better than rice, but both are very tasty.

- ¼ cup carrots cut into matchsticks
- Spring water
- Pinch of sea salt
- 2 cups cooked rice or millet
- ¼ cup minced parsley
- Whole wheat flour, if needed
- Dark sesame oil

Boil the carrots with a pinch of sea salt in about ½ inch of water for 2 to 3 minutes, or until soft. Save the water for a sauce. Strain the carrots and mix them together with the cooked grain and parsley. Fashion into balls. Any round or oval shape is fine. If too dry, add a little whole wheat pastry flour with a little water to moisten to keep the shape of the ball. If too wet, roll the ball in dry wheat flour. After shaping, deep-fry the balls in hot oil for a few minutes following the basic tempura technique (but do not dip them into the batter). Cook the balls until they are golden brown and crunchy. Croquettes may be served covered with a sauce made from carrots and onions cooked with a little tamari soy sauce, grated fresh ginger, and kuzu to thicken, or they may be served with a dip.

Variations: Buckwheat is also excellent prepared in this way. Minced and boiled celery and rinsed and boiled arame are also commonly added to grains when making croquettes. Normally onions and scallions are not used when deep-frying because they become too watery. Leftover beans can also be cooked in this way. Lentils and chick-peas are best. Kidney and azuki beans usually become too dark when deep-fried.

Seitan Croquettes

For deep-frying, I use homemade uncooked wheat gluten. After deep-frying, I press out the excess oil with a dry towel or rinse well in hot water. If the seitan is not too oily, the croquettes can be simmered for 15 to 30 minutes after deep-frying in a little kombu soup stock with a mild tamari soy sauce taste and a little grated fresh ginger.

Tofu Croquettes

In Japan we call this dish *ganmodoki*. *Gan* means "crane" and *modoki* means "looks like." This name refers to a traditional Buddhist vegetarian tofu dish that looks and tastes like fried fowl. Traditionally, one ginkgo nut is inserted into the center of each croquette. These are boiled whole and are available dried in some Oriental markets. They need special processing before they are edible. Ginkgo trees grow in some parts of the United States and Canada. However, ginkgo nuts are slightly toxic, and should not be used very often, even if properly dried and prepared. Almonds roasted in a little tamari soy sauce and chopped or used whole may be used instead.

- 16 ounces hard tofu
- ¼ cup carrots cut into matchsticks
- ¼ cup arame
- Spring water
- 4 to 5 almonds
- Kuzu or arrowroot flour, if needed
- Dark sesame oil
- Sliced scallions for garnish

Squeeze out the water from the tofu and mash the tofu in a suribachi. Boil sliced carrots and arame separately in a little water until tender. Mix with the tofu and form into 4 to 5 croquettes. Insert an almond into the center of each croquette. Add a little kuzu or arrowroot flour to the mixture if the ingredients don't stick together. If still wet, roll in flour. Then deep-fry for a few minutes until golden brown and crispy.

Tofu croquettes may be served with a sauce made from onions and carrots cooked in dashi soup stock with a little kuzu to thicken the sauce, a mild tamari soy sauce to taste, and a little grated fresh ginger and daikon radish. The croquettes may be simmered in the sauce for 1 to 2 minutes and then served with the sauce on top. Garnish with sliced scallions.

DEEP-FRIED LOTUS BALLS

Lotus root croquettes are very sweet and delicious, and over the years I have made them frequently. Grate fresh lotus root and mix in a little arrowroot flour or pastry flour to give the croquettes shape. Then form the mixture into small 2-inch dumplings. Usually lotus root balls are made plain, though a little chopped parsley or chopped pumpkin seeds may be mixed in if desired. After deep-frying in dark sesame oil for a few minutes, simmer in an onion-carrot sauce for a short time and serve topped with this sauce.

Variation: Carrot balls can be made in the same way or combined half and half with lotus root.

Burdock Eel

This eel-shaped dish of burdock roots is very strong and delicious.

- 2 medium-sized burdock roots
- Spring water
- ½ cup uncooked seitan
- Dark sesame oil
- Kombu-tamari soy sauce soup stock

Slice the burdock into 1½- to 2-inch pieces and boil in a little water for a few minutes. Wrap each piece of burdock in uncooked seitan to form an eel shape. Deep-fry each "eel" for a few minutes in sesame oil until golden brown and crunchy. Then simmer in a kombu-tamari soy sauce soup stock for about 15 minutes. If the eels are too oily, remove the excess oil by rinsing them in hot water or patting them with paper towels before putting them into the soup stock. Serve two burdock "eels" per person.

Variations: Burdock eels may also be cooked tempura-style in a thick batter. After they are deep-fried, simmer them in a dashi stock for only a couple minutes before serving. Or bake the eels, after deep-frying, in a moderate oven for about 1½ hours, or until the batter separates from the vegetables and forms a thick, creamy sauce. Place the deep-fried eels in a casserole dish, add water to just cover, and sprinkle with a little tamari soy sauce. After baking, season with a little more tamari soy sauce to taste and let sit uncovered about 10 minutes in the oven before serving.

DEEP-FRIED VEGETABLES

Vegetables that are deep-fried without batter are called *kara age* in Japan and are similar to Western-style potato chips. Root vegetables make nice sweet chips. I am fond of carrots, thinly sliced and dried for about ½ day, lotus root in whole slices, parsnip in small rounds, and thinly sliced winter squash. Deep-fried sea vegetables go well with beer and make a great snack. In addition to kombu and wakame strips, I like whole mekabu, which opens up into a big flower shape when deep-fried. Carrot tops, dandelion greens, and other leaves are also good prepared in this way. If the greens are tough, deep-frying without a batter is better than cooking them tempura-style.

CHAPTER 18

SALADS

Overhanging boughs.
The reflection of green
Moving on the river.

—Tatako

Salads give a very light feeling and energy to a meal served as a side dish or as a main course. They can be made with grains, beans, vegetables, sea vegetables, and seafood. Nice garnishes for salads include toasted sesame seeds, dulse or nori flakes, or deep-fried bread cubes.

In addition to fresh salad, which we enjoy especially in the summertime, salads may be prepared in several other ways to modify their taste, texture, and energy. Marinated and pressed salads involve a short pickling technique, usually from a few minutes to just under an hour, which changes the look and flavor of the ingredients without cooking. Lightly boiled salad, dipped in bubbling water for a brief time, also removes the raw, bitter, or pungent taste of some fresh vegetables and makes for a more digestible dish.

FRESH SALAD

Fresh salad, right from the garden, has a light, upward energy. Nice soft lettuce or other soft green vegetables are wonderful prepared this way. To preserve their freshness, I usually tear soft vegetables, such as lettuce or cabbage, with my hands rather than cut them with a knife. Some of my favorite small fresh salads include:

- Grated carrots served alongside fresh greens
- Celery stalks served with a dip
- Sliced endive
- Shredded red cabbage mixed with a touch of sea salt
- Watercress served with raw or cooked vegetables, deep-fried tofu, tempeh, or seitan
- Finely chopped parsley
- Jinenjo sliced and served with a little tamari soy sauce and rice vinegar and sprinkled with roasted sesame seeds
- Fresh sprouts and greens

Garden Salad

Ideally a fresh garden salad is served whole, allowing the ingredients to keep their natural shapes as much as possible. At the table everyone can then take what they like. For variety a large salad may also be mixed together.

1 ear of corn, kernels removed
1 head lettuce
5 to 6 red radishes, sliced thin
1 cucumber, sliced into thin rounds
1 box alfalfa sprouts
1 carrot, shredded

Boil the corn kernels in about ¼ inch of water in a saucepan for 2 to 3 minutes. Set aside kernels to cool. Arrange the lettuce attractively on a serving plate. A nice soft variety, such as Boston lettuce, opens up easily and the leaves can be torn by hand. Distribute the sliced radishes and cucumbers evenly in a circle on the lettuce leaves. Place the sprouts in small groupings in the center of the circle on top of the lettuce or around the outside edge or both. Sprinkle corn kernels over the salad. Finally, add the shredded carrot to the very top of the salad and, if you like, in the cardinal directions. Serve with a separate sauce, such as umeboshi plum dressing with a little onion and sesame seeds, tofu dressing with a little umeboshi, a miso–brown rice vinegar dressing with a little mirin, or a tamari-ginger dressing with a little mirin.

GRAIN, BEAN, AND NOODLE SALADS

Grains, beans, and noodles go well in salads. In the summer, I am very fond of transparent noodles, mung bean noodles, kuzu noodles, somen, soba, or whole wheat pasta served cold with a variety of ingredients in salad form. Brown rice, millet, kasha, bulghur, and couscous each make wonderful salads, cooked fresh or used as leftovers. Chick-peas, kidney beans, small cubes of cooked tofu, seitan, or tempeh, and other cooked or fresh beans give salads a strong, rich taste and provide a colorful complement to leafy greens and other soft vegetables.

Brown Rice Salad

- 2 cups brown rice
- 1¼ to 1½ cups spring water per cup of rice
- Pinch of sea salt
- 1 cup diced carrots
- 1 cup shelled fresh green peas
- ½ cup cucumbers quartered and sliced
- ½ cup diced celery
- ¼ cup very finely chopped shiso leaves
- Sliced scallions or chopped parsley for garnish

Wash and pressure-cook the rice with the water and salt. When rice is done, transfer it to a bowl to cool. Fluff up the rice to remove the steam and lighten it. Boil the carrots and peas separately in a saucepan containing a little water until tender. Drain and allow to cool. Add the carrots and peas to the rice, along with the cucumber and celery, and mix together well. Mix in the chopped shiso leaves, which come pickled with umeboshi plums and may sometimes be obtained whole by themselves. Garnish the salad with sliced scallions or parsley and serve.

Variations: Instead of using shiso leaves, the salad may be served with a dressing made of brown rice vinegar, salt, and mirin or lemon and salt. Roasted sesame seeds make a nice garnish.

Buckwheat Salad

- 2 cups buckwheat
- 4 cups spring water or juice drained from the sauerkraut
- Pinch of sea salt
- 1 cup diced or sliced celery
- ½ cup sliced scallions
- 1 cup chopped drained sauerkraut
- Parsley sprigs or red radish slices for garnish

Wash the buckwheat and dry-roast in a dry frying pan over low heat for several minutes. Bring the water to a boil and add the roasted buckwheat and a pinch of sea salt. Cover, reduce the heat to low, and simmer for about 20 minutes. When the buckwheat is done, drain it and transfer it to a large bowl. Fluff it up with chopsticks or a spoon to cool it off and keep it from lumping. If desired, lightly steam the celery for about 1 minute, so it retains a slight crispness or use it raw. Mix the scallions, celery, and sauerkraut in with the buckwheat. Mix well so all the vegetables are distributed evenly. Garnish with sprigs of parsley and a few red radish slices in an attractive serving bowl.

Tempeh-Macaroni Salad

Spring water
1 pound tempeh, cut into 1-inch squares
Tamari soy sauce
Brown rice vinegar
1 pound whole wheat macaroni noodles or pasta shells made with artichoke flour
½ head lettuce
½ head cabbage
1 bunch watercress
Parsley sprigs for garnish

Put about 1 inch of water in a saucepan and add the tempeh squares. Bring to a boil, lower the heat, and cook 20 to 30 minutes until soft. Drain the tempeh and allow it to cool. Prepare a marinade of half tamari soy sauce and half brown rice vinegar using several tablespoons of each; pour the mixture over the tempeh. While the tempeh is marinating, boil macaroni until done. Slice lettuce and cabbage or tear by hand into bite-sized pieces. Dip watercress into boiling water for 20 to 30 seconds to remove its bitter taste or use raw and cut it into small pieces. Mix the pasta, tempeh, and vegetables together very well and garnish with parsley sprigs.

SEA VEGETABLE SALADS

Salads are an excellent way to present seaweed or combine it with other ingredients. Usually it is cooked, though fresh nori may be eaten raw. There is also a sea vegetable called *mozuku* that is eaten raw and was my father's favorite seaweed. Freshly cooked or leftover wakame, kombu, hiziki, and arame all lend themselves to salads. Toasted nori strips and dried dulse flakes or powder make wonderful garnishes. A delicious vegetable aspic can be made with agar agar, a gelatinous sea vegetable.

Wakame Cucumber Salad

1 to 1½ cups spring water
1 cup sliced soaked wakame
2 cups cucumbers, halved and sliced
Tamari soy sauce
Brown rice vinegar
Grated fresh ginger

Put the water in a pot and bring it to a boil. Add the wakame and simmer for 1 to 2 minutes. Drain the wakame and allow it to cool. If the wakame is hard, cook it for a total of 3 to 5 minutes. Put the cucumbers in a bowl, add the wakame, and mix. Prepare a sauce by mixing a small amount of tamari soy sauce, brown rice vinegar, and grated fresh ginger. Pour the sauce over the wakame and cucumbers and mix.

Hiziki Salad with Tofu Dressing

Spring water
1 ounce dry hiziki, soaked for 3 to 5 minutes and sliced
1 cup carrots, halved and sliced diagonally
½ cup diagonally sliced celery
3 umeboshi plums, pitted
1 medium-sized onion, chopped very fine or grated
16 ounces tofu
2 tablespoons chopped parsley plus parsley sprigs for garnish

Pour a little water into a pot and add the hiziki. Bring to a boil. Reduce the heat to low, cover, and simmer for about 30 minutes. Drain the hiziki and set it aside to cool. Pour a little water into a pot and bring it to a boil. Put the carrots in the water, cover the pot, and simmer for 1 to 2 minutes. The carrots should be slightly crisp. Remove the carrots, drain, and set them aside to cool. Put the celery into the same boiling water and simmer for about 1 minute. Drain the celery and let it cool. Mix the carrots and celery with the cooked hiziki.

Put the umeboshi plums in a suribachi. Add the chopped onion. Grind until the umeboshi are smooth. Add the tofu to the suribachi with the umeboshi and grind until smooth and creamy. Mix in the chopped parsley. Put the tofu dressing in a small serving bowl. Garnish with a little parsley in the center of the tofu dressing. Place the hiziki and mixed vegetables in a serving bowl. Mix in with the dressing or serve separately at the table.

MARINATED SALAD

Another way to prepare raw vegetables is to marinate them for a short time in sea salt or tamari soy sauce. Seasoning them in this way draws out the liquid from the vegetables, making them crispier and sweeter. Sometimes I add a little brown rice vinegar to the marinade for a sour taste or mirin for a sweet taste. Some of my favorite marinated salads are:

- Shredded carrots, sprinkled with a pinch of sea salt, and marinated for 5 to 10 minutes.
- Sliced cucumber, sprinkled and mixed with a pinch of sea salt, and left to sit for about 30 minutes. Cucumbers prepared in this way are very crunchy and sweet and go well with beans, wakame, or fish.
- Daikon, sliced in rectangles or matchsticks, sprinkled with sea salt, and left to soften for about 30 minutes. Then I squeeze out excess water from the daikon and marinate it for a short time with tamari soy sauce, brown rice vinegar, or mirin for a sweet taste.
- Red radish, sliced or cut into flower shapes, and marinated for a short time with umeboshi vinegar. This makes for a beautiful pink color.
- Turnips marinated with sea salt, brown rice vinegar, or tamari soy sauce for 30 minutes.
- Rutabaga quartered, thinly sliced, and marinated for 30 minutes with tamari soy sauce. This is my favorite way to enjoy this vegetable.
- Cooked mushrooms marinated with a little tamari soy sauce and served with sesame seeds and a touch of brown rice vinegar.

Marinated Daikon and Carrots

1 cup daikon cut into matchsticks
½ cup carrots cut into matchsticks
4 pinches sea salt

Mix the ingredients together and let sit for 30 minutes. Then squeeze out any remaining liquid by hand.

Variations: Instead of salt, the vegetables can be soaked in 1 tablespoon rice vinegar and 1 teaspoon tamari soy sauce, or with 1 tablespoon umeboshi vinegar and 1 tablespoon spring water. A drop of ginger juice may be added to the marinade, if desired.

Lotus Root Salad

1 cup fresh lotus root quartered or thinly sliced
1 tablespoon tamari soy sauce
1 tablespoon brown rice vinegar
Sliced scallions for garnish

Marinate the lotus in a mixture of tamari soy sauce and brown rice vinegar. Let sit for 15 to 30 minutes. Garnish with a few sliced scallions.

Variation: For a sweeter taste, use 1 teaspoon white miso and 1 teaspoon tamari soy sauce with ¼ teaspoon grated fresh ginger for the dressing instead of vinegar. The lotus root may also be boiled for 1 to 2 minutes and cooled before being marinated.

PRESSED SALAD

A stronger form of marinating is the pressed salad. This is made by layering sliced raw vegetables in a small pickle press with sea salt. If a press is not available, simply layer the food in a bowl, and sprinkle sea salt between the layers. Then put a flat dish inside the bowl on top of the vegetables and set a small bowl with water on top of the dish to add pressure. When several vegetables are combined, they may be sliced in small pieces, mixed together with salt by hand, and then pressed.

The salt and the weight will cause the vegetables to give up water. When the water rises above the pressure plate or dish, the pressure should be reduced or the vegetables will become fibrous rather than juicy. The vegetables should remain soaking in the water or brine for 30 to 60 minutes. (If sufficient water does not rise, there is not enough salt or pressure and the vegetables may spoil.) Ingredients may be kept longer under pressure, up to a couple days, if desired, for making light pickles. Some of my favorite pressed vegetables include:

- Mustard greens or radish greens, chopped finely, mixed with sea salt, and pressed for 30 minutes.
- Cabbage leaves, layered with sea salt, and pressed for 30 minutes.
- Carrots, grated, shredded, or cut into matchsticks, sprinkled with sea salt, and pressed for 30 minutes.

Mixed Pressed Salad

½ head medium-sized cabbage, shredded
2 carrots, sliced or shredded
1 bunch red radishes, sliced, plus radish tops, thinly sliced
2 tablespoons sea salt

Mix the vegetables and salt together and press for 30 to 45 minutes. The pressure may be reduced as the water starts to come out. Before serving, squeeze out the remaining water by hand and, if the mixture is too salty to the taste, rinse briefly.

Variation: Most common garden vegetables may be pressed in this way. However, some of the softer varieties press very quickly and will become too watery if combined with other vegetables.

BOILED SALAD

In boiled salads, the vegetables are usually dipped separately into simmering water but served together on the same plate. Vegetables with the mildest flavors are usually boiled first in order to preserve their distinctive taste. Stronger flavored ones, such as daikon, turnips, celery, and especially watercress, are cooked at the end. The cooking method is similar to ohitashi-style boiling, except the ingredients are usually just dipped in and out more quickly, about 20 to 30 seconds for greens and 1 to 2 minutes for root vegetables. Boiling removes the raw flavor and makes the salad more digestible. Rinsing vegetables in cold water after boiling stops the cooking and preserves their bright colors. Boiled salad may be enjoyed throughout the year, though it is especially balancing in the cooler seasons. Steamed salad has a similar effect and is also highly recommended. A tofu or umeboshi dressing is very delicious with boiled or steamed salad.

- Boiled parsley, watercress, or other greens become brighter after just touching with hot water. Boiling also takes out their strong raw, bitter, or pungent taste.
- Other vegetables I enjoy in boiled salads include carrots, daikon, burdock, red radish, cabbage, Chinese cabbage, bok choy, kale, mustard greens, collards, daikon greens, dandelion greens, red cabbage, lotus root, arame, and hiziki. Lettuce is not particularly good when it is boiled as its color quickly darkens.
- Some foods may be cut into large pieces and will become very crunchy when boiled. These include cauliflower, broccoli, endive, asparagus, snow peas, string beans, fresh corn, mushrooms, and wakame.

Boiled Onion, Celery, and Dandelion Salad

Spring water
2 cups onions cut into half moons
1 cup celery sliced thinly on the diagonal
1 cup fresh dandelion greens, washed and cut into 1- to 2-inch lengths
2 tablespoons tamari soy sauce
Spring water
¼ teaspoon grated fresh ginger
2 tablespoons roasted sesame seeds

Pour a small amount of water into a saucepan and bring it to a boil. Add sliced onions and boil for about 1 minute. Remove the onions and drain them. Put the onions in a bowl. Add the celery to the cooking water and boil it for about 1 minute. Remove the celery, drain, and mix it with the onions. Add the dandelion greens to the cooking water and boil for 1 minute. Remove, drain, and mix with the other vegetables. Prepare a dressing by combining the tamari soy sauce, 2 to 3 tablespoons spring water, and the grated ginger. Mix the ingredients together and pour over vegetables. Add the roasted sesame seeds and mix everything together before serving.

Fruit Salad

A salad of seasonal, locally grown fruit is very attractive and enjoyable on a hot summer day. I am fond of fresh strawberries and cherries, as well as apples, grapes, and melons. Adding a pinch of sea salt to the fruit will bring out its natural sweetness.

Lettuce leaves
½ cup cubed honeydew melon
½ cup cubed cantaloupe
½ cup seeded watermelon shaped in balls with a scoop
½ cup sliced unpeeled apples
Pinch of sea salt

Put a few fresh lettuce leaves in the bottom of a serving bowl. In a separate bowl mix the fruit with the salt. Then arrange it in the bowl on top of the lettuce leaves. Allow to sit about 15 minutes before serving.

CHAPTER

19

DRESSINGS, SAUCES, AND DIPS

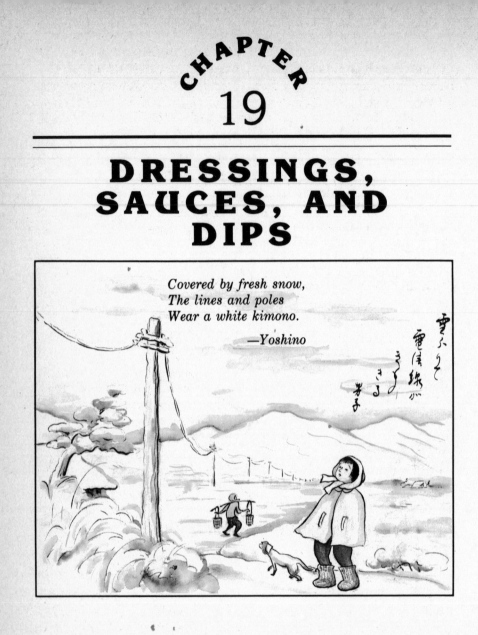

Covered by fresh snow,
The lines and poles
Wear a white kimono.
—Yoshino

Dressings and sauces are one of the keys to making balance in a meal. They offer color and variety to daily cooking and are an easy way to adjust and create the five basic tastes. Dressings and sauces add flavor and flair to the basic ingredients, stimulate the appetite, and offer many appealing styles and combinations. Some sauces may be put directly on top of the food, others to the side, and still others in a separate bowl for dipping into at the table. Dressings and sauces are an easy way to make adjustments for the personal needs of each family member as well as babies and children whose quality and quantity of food varies from older people. In addition to tamari soy sauce, vinegar, oil, and other liquids, a variety of solid ingredients, such as tofu, seitan, tempeh, nuts, small fish, and seafood, may be incorporated into sauces, gravies, or toppings. Whether simple or complex, dressings, sauces, and dips are an essential part of the meal and one of the keys to successful cooking.

CREATING DIFFERENT TASTES

Along with condiments, dressings and sauces are one of the basic ways to create a variety of different tastes at a meal.

Tamari soy sauce, sea salt, or miso produces a nice *salty* taste.

A *sour* taste can be created by making a dressing or sauce with a little umeboshi vinegar, brown rice vinegar, or sweet rice vinegar. I occasionally use apple cider vinegar for a more sweet vinegar taste but generally avoid spicy vinegars. A touch of freshly squeezed lemon or orange juice also produces a nice sour taste.

Grated daikon, sliced scallions, or grated fresh ginger may be used to create a hot *pungent* taste.

Carrots, onions, fall- and winter-season squashes, and other naturally sweet root and round vegetables can be cooked to produce a *sweet* sauce or gravy. Seasoning dressings or sauces with miso, mirin, apple juice, barley malt, a touch of maple syrup, or raisins also gives a nice sweet flavor.

Roasted sesame seeds give a slightly *bitter* taste and make rich savory dressings and sauces that everyone will enjoy. Tahini or sesame seed butter may also be used but they are much more oily.

THICKENING WITH KUZU

Kuzu is the main thickener I use for sauces, gravies, and stews. Kuzu grows wild in mountainous areas and has very deep roots. Its strong downward energy is traditionally recognized by Oriental medicine as good for helping to relieve intestinal troubles, diarrhea, constipation, or other lower stagnation. In the southeastern United States, kuzu grows abundantly and, as a vine, is known as *kudzu*. As a food, kuzu is dried and comes in the form of a white powder or chalky lumps. Kuzu cooks quickly, usually in 1 to 2 minutes. It should be diluted first in a little cold water and gradually mixed into the sauce or gravy at the very end of the cooking time. Kuzu is done when it becomes transparent. When cooking with kuzu, I continually stir the ingredients and broth to prevent lumps from forming. To keep its clear natural color, I season it with a touch of sea salt. For a brown sauce, tamari soy sauce or miso may be added. If kuzu is not available, arrowroot flour may be substituted. This soft white powdered root of the arrowroot plant is used widely in Chinese cooking as a thickener. Ordinarily I do not use cornstarch or other refined thickeners. One tablespoon of arrowroot equals about 1 teaspoon of kuzu.

TAMARI SOY SAUCE DRESSINGS

The natural salty taste of tamari soy sauce may be combined with vinegar or lemon for a lightly sour taste or with ginger for a more pungent flavor.

Tamari-Vinegar Dressing

- ¼ to ½ teaspoon sesame oil (optional)
- 1 tablespoon tamari soy sauce
- 4 tablespoons brown rice vinegar
- 1 tablespoon grated fresh onion
- ½ cup spring water

If using the oil, heat it for about 1 minute over a low heat. Purée all the ingredients together in a suribachi and serve.

Tamari-Lemon Dressing

- 2 to 3 tablespoons tamari soy sauce
- ½ cup spring water
- 2 to 3 teaspoons freshly squeezed lemon juice

Combine all the ingredients and mix well. For variety, a little minced onion and ½ teaspoon of heated sesame oil may be added.

Tamari-Ginger Dressing

- 2 tablespoons tamari soy sauce
- 2 to 3 tablespoons spring water
- ¼ teaspoon grated fresh ginger
- 2 tablespoons roasted sesame seeds, coarsely crushed

Combine all the ingredients and mix well.

UMEBOSHI DRESSINGS

Umeboshi plums make excellent dressings and sauces, combining a slightly sour and salty taste. If whole plums are unavailable, or for the sake of convenience, umeboshi paste may be used. Use 1 teaspoon of paste for each plum in the recipe.

❧ Umeboshi Dressing ❧

2 umeboshi plums
¼ to ½ teaspoon minced onion
½ teaspoon sesame oil
½ cup spring water

Purée the umeboshi and onion in a suribachi. Heat the oil for about 1 minute and add it to the other ingredients. Add the water and mix well.

❧ Scallion-Parsley Dressing ❧

½ cup sliced scallions
1 tablespoon chopped parsley
1 cup umeboshi juice (see Note), or 2 umeboshi plums and 1 cup spring water
½ teaspoon sesame oil

Mix ingredients together in a jar or a bowl.

Note: Umeboshi juice is made by placing 3 to 4 umeboshi plums in a glass jar, adding 1 cup spring water, shaking, and letting the mixture sit for about 30 minutes. Save plums for another recipe and use juice in making the dressing.

MISO DRESSINGS

Miso combines a nice sweet and salty taste. To add a sour, pungent, or bitter taste, mix together with a little vinegar, grated fresh ginger, or tahini as in the following recipes.

❧ Miso–Rice Vinegar Dressing ❧

2 tablespoons miso
½ cup spring water
2 tablespoons brown rice vinegar

Purée the miso in a little water in a suribachi; then add the vinegar and the rest of the water and blend.

Variations: Umeboshi vinegar, sweet rice vinegar, or lemon juice may be substituted for the brown rice vinegar. I also like this dressing with 1 teaspoon of grated lemon rind or grated fresh ginger.

Miso-Ginger Sauce

- 1 teaspoon barley miso
- ½ teaspoon grated fresh ginger
- Spring water

Put the miso in a suribachi and add the grated ginger. Purée with a small amount of water to make a smooth, creamy sauce.

Miso-Tahini Dressing

- 1 teaspoon miso
- 3 teaspoons tahini
- 1 teaspoon grated onion
- ½ cup spring water

Mix all the ingredients together in a suribachi.

TOFU DRESSINGS AND SAUCES

Buddhist temple cuisine is very famous for its creamy tofu dressings and sauces. In monasteries, it was the traditional job of novices to mash the tofu in giant suribachis. This task takes some time and is good for developing concentration. In this country, I notice many friends like to prepare tofu crumbly cottage cheese–style rather than smooth. That is fine, too. Or they use an electric blender, which is all right for parties. But for daily cooking, slowly stirring the tofu by hand gives the most peaceful, steady vibration.

When making tofu dressings or sauces, I usually squeeze out the excess water from the tofu by hand at the beginning. Ordinarily, liquid is not added to the suribachi when mashing. For a more digestible sauce and an interesting texture, I also usually dip the tofu in boiling water before preparing it. When it rises to the surface, I take it out of the pot and put it in the suribachi for mashing. After grinding the tofu for 10 to 15 minutes to the desired consistency, I season it with a little sea salt. This keeps the tofu's nice white color. Tamari soy sauce or miso will darken it. For a lovely pink dressing, however, I will combine the tofu with several pitted umeboshi plums or umeboshi paste. When the tofu has been puréed, I serve it on top of the salad, grain, or vegetable dish, or serve it in a small bowl at the table. Vegetables may also be marinated in the tofu sauce for 10 to 15 minutes before serving for a more distinctive flavor.

Tofu Dressing

1 cake tofu
1 tablespoon grated onion
1 teaspoon sea salt
½ teaspoon sesame butter or tahini

Purée all the ingredients together in a suribachi.

Sour Tofu Dressing

3 umeboshi plums
Spring water
1 cake tofu
¼ cup sliced scallions or chives for garnish

Put the pitted umeboshi in a suribachi and purée to a smooth paste. Add the tofu and purée until smooth and creamy. (Add a little spring water to moisten, if necessary.) Put the dressing in a serving dish and garnish with the sliced scallions or chives.

Variation: Add a little tamari soy sauce for a different flavor.

SESAME DRESSINGS AND SAUCES

Whole sesame seeds are an ideal way to consume oil. For sauces I usually mash roasted sesame seeds in a suribachi. For a garnish, I chop them with a knife. In addition to whole sesame seeds, sesame butter or tahini may also be used. The recipe for creamy tofu-sesame dressing is given in the tofu section above, and there is a tahini dressing in the tamari soy sauce group.

Sesame Dressings

½ cup roasted sesame seeds
½ cup dashi soup stock
1 teaspoon sweet rice vinegar
2 teaspoons tamari soy sauce

Dry-roast the sesame seeds in a frying pan for a few minutes until they turn brown and release a nice aroma. Half crush in a suribachi and mix the seeds well with the soup stock and combine with the other ingredients.

Variations: A little grated fresh ginger or mirin may be added to the basic recipe for a pungent or sweet flavor, respectively. Instead of sweet rice vinegar, brown rice vinegar, umeboshi vinegar, or 2 umeboshi plums may be used.

GRAVIES AND SAUCES

There are many gravies and sauces that go well on top of whole grains, noodles, beans, or vegetables. Some of my favorites are:

- Carrots and onions, finely diced, cooked until creamy in a little water, thickened with a little kuzu, and seasoned with tamari soy sauce and a little grated fresh ginger.
- Onions thinly sliced and cooked for a few minutes, then seasoned with a little diluted miso, and garnished with sesame seeds or a drop of sesame oil.
- Fall- or winter-season squash, sliced and cooked in a little water until creamy, mashed very fine, and thickened with kuzu.
- Carrots, burdock, onion, and celery sautéed together and seasoned with a little diluted miso at the end to make a creamy mixture. Dry tofu and seitan are also nice with this gravy.

Sweet and Sour Sauce

This sauce is delicious on seitan, tempeh, noodles, rice, baked onions, or other grains and vegetables.

½ cup finely minced onion
½ cup grated carrots
½ cup thinly sliced celery
1 cup dashi soup stock
Pinch of sea salt
1 to 2 tablespoons kuzu
3 tablespoons tamari soy sauce
1 to 2 teaspoons brown rice vinegar
½ cup apple juice

Cook the vegetables in the soup stock with a pinch of sea salt until soft, about 5 to 10 minutes. When the vegetables are almost done, add the kuzu diluted in a little cold water and stir for about 1 to 2 minutes to prevent lumping. When the mixture has thickened and the kuzu is transparent, add the tamari soy sauce, vinegar, and apple juice and cook for about 1 minute more.

Variations: Instead of apple juice, 2 tablespoons of mirin or 1 tablespoon of maple syrup may be used.

Seitan and Mushroom Gravy

½ cup thinly sliced fresh mushrooms
½ cup finely minced onions
1 tablespoon dark sesame oil
Pinch of sea salt
½ cup seitan, sliced into ¼-inch squares
1 cup dashi soup stock
1 tablespoon kuzu
3 tablespoons tamari soy sauce

Sauté mushrooms and onions in the oil with a pinch of sea salt over low heat for about 5 minutes. Add the seitan and cook for another 5 minutes. Add the dashi soup stock. Dilute the kuzu in a little cold water and stir it into the gravy. Cook for 1 to 2 minutes, or until the kuzu becomes transparent. Season with tamari soy sauce, mix, and serve over grains, noodles, or vegetables.

Béchamel Sauce

I used to make this sauce frequently for millet, kasha, and other dry grains. In recent years, I have switched to kuzu as a thickener instead of flour, but this rich gravy is nice on occasion.

1 medium-sized onion, diced
Sesame oil
½ cup whole wheat pastry flour or brown rice flour
3 cups spring water or soup stock
1½ tablespoons tamari soy sauce

Sauté the onion in a lightly oiled frying pan until it turns translucent. Add flour and dry-roast for 2 to 3 minutes. Stir gently to coat each piece of onion with the flour and add the water gradually while stirring to avoid lumping. Add the tamari soy sauce, cover, bring to a boil, and simmer over low heat for 10 to 15 minutes. A flame deflector may be placed under the pan to ensure even, gradual cooking. Stir occasionally to prevent the gravy from sticking.

Kuzu-Raisin Sauce

This sweet sauce is nice on baked apples, other desserts, or occasionally a casserole or side dish.

1 cup apple juice
¼ cup raisins
Pinch of sea salt
1 tablespoon kuzu

Put the juice, raisins, and salt in a saucepan and bring to a boil. Reduce the heat to low and simmer, covered, for about 5 minutes. Dilute the kuzu in a little cold water and add it to the sauce. Stir constantly to avoid lumping. Simmer for 1 to 2 minutes and serve.

Cranberry Sauce

½ cup raisins
1½ cups spring water
2 cups cranberries
Pinch of sea salt
¼ cup barley malt
2 tablespoons kuzu

Cook the raisins in ½ cup of the water for 10 minutes. Add the cranberries, remaining water, salt, and barley malt. Simmer for 10 minutes. Dilute the kuzu in a little cold water and add it to the mixture, stirring constantly to prevent lumping. Simmer for 5 to 7 minutes, pour into a bowl or mold, and allow to set.

DIPS

Dips are sauces that are served at the table to be used with raw or lightly boiled vegetables or noodles, tempura, or other ingredients.

Ginger-Tamari Dip

This makes a nice dipping sauce for tempura, croquettes, tofu, or tempeh.

3 tablespoons grated daikon
1 teaspoon grated fresh ginger
½ cup dashi soup stock
3 tablespoons tamari soy sauce

Mix all the ingredients well in the soup stock and serve in individual cups or bowls.

Tofu Dip

This dip is nice for celery, cauliflower, or other fresh vegetables and canapés.

1 tablespoon minced onion
1 cake tofu, mashed very well
½ cup dashi soup stock
2 teaspoons sea salt
1 teaspoon freshly squeezed lemon juice

Put the minced onion in a suribachi. Add the tofu and purée until creamy. Add the soup stock, salt, and a little freshly squeezed lemon. Mix and serve.

Chick-Pea Dip

This dip made from chick-peas and tahini is very popular in the Middle East. There it is known as hummus. Chick-pea dip is wonderful with small slices of whole wheat pocket bread (pita) or crackers and it may also be used on salads or vegetable side dishes.

- 2 cups drained cooked chick-peas
- ¼ cup unsalted sesame butter or tahini
- 1 small onion, peeled and diced
- 2 umeboshi plums
- 1 tablespoon chopped chives
- ⅓ cup chick-pea cooking water or spring water for diluting
- Parsley sprig for garnish

Grind the chick-peas in a suribachi, if desired (because we make this dish very occasionally and then for parties rather than everyday cooking, it is all right to use a blender). Purée all ingredients together, adding the extra water if needed to achieve desired consistency. Remove and mix in the chives. Garnish with the parsley and serve.

CHAPTER 20

PICKLES

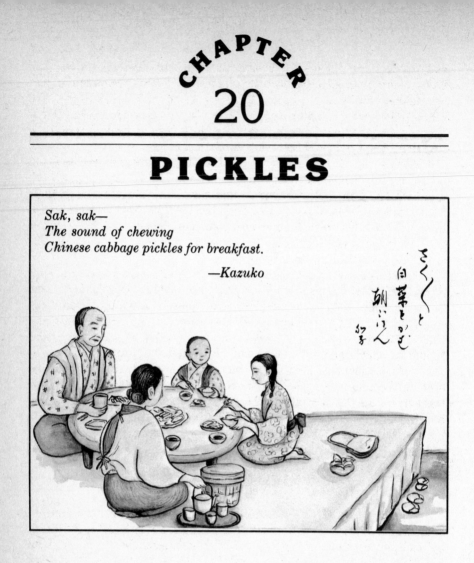

Sak, sak—
The sound of chewing
Chinese cabbage pickles for breakfast.

—Kazuko

Pickling is one of the traditional ways to preserve foods. Pickles increase the appetite, aid digestion, and strengthen the intestines. During the fermentation process, enzymes and bacteria change the sugar in pickled foods into lactic acid. Lactic acid strengthens the flora in the intestines, which assimilate metabolized foodstuffs into the bloodstream. While many modern people are familiar only with highly spiced cucumber pickles, an assortment of root, round, and green leafy vegetables may be pickled as well as some sea vegetables, fruits, fish and seafood, and even flowers. In addition to salt, pickles may be aged in tamari soy sauce, miso, bran, and other substances.

In Japan, almost every family made their own pickles and enjoyed them daily at each meal. We customarily ate pickles at tea time in the midafternoon as well as for breakfast, lunch, and dinner. In the Far East, where the principal food consists primarily of whole grains and vegetables that have a naturally sweet taste, salty pickles help to balance this predominant taste. In the West, where the main food is primarily meat, poultry, eggs, and dairy food high in sodium and other minerals, sour and spicy pickles provide balance.

Pickles come in several strengths. Short, quick pickles can be made in from a few hours to a few days or weeks. These light pickles are especially good in hot weather or for those who need to limit their consumption of salt. Strong, long-time pickles take from several weeks to several months to make and they can keep several years. They are good year-round but especially in the colder months and for those who are weak or lacking in vitality.

Pickles keep a long time without spoiling and are an excellent way to preserve food from one season to the next. Because they are so easy to carry, they make good food for traveling. If the pickles taste too salty, I soak them for about half an hour in cold water before using. Children require less salty food than adults, so their intake of pickles should be carefully watched.

Making pickles at home is a great adventure. Adjusting the salt or other seasoning, the pressure, the water level, and other variables takes some time to master, but once learned, the results are well worth the effort. The variety of wonderful pickles we can make is limited only by our own imagination.

PRESSED SALT PICKLES

In Japan, we regularly exchanged simple homemade salt pickles with friends and neighbors or gave them as gifts. Quick salt pickles may be made in the morning and eaten in the evening or left to ferment for 2 to 3 days. Long-time salt pickles can be aged for several weeks. A small pickle press (available at some natural foods stores or cooking suppliers) is useful for making these pickles. The food is placed inside, salted, and the pressure plate is screwed down. If a pickle press is not available, the ingredients may be placed in a small glass bowl. After layering with vegetables and salt, a small saucer that fits loosely inside the bowl may be placed on top of the food. On the saucer set a smaller bowl with water or a small weight, such as a stone, to supply pressure.

In making pickles, use fresh vegetables that are firm, crisp, and bright in color. Most pickles should be left to sit in a cool, dark place as warm temperatures or humidity can cause them to mold. If mold appears, I scrape it off at once as the whole batch will spoil if it spreads. Plastic pickle presses are all right for quick pickles, but this material should be avoided for long-time pickles as poisonous gases can be released during fermentation.

CHINESE CABBAGE PICKLES

Chinese cabbage pickles are very crunchy and delicious. While I was growing up, we made them every morning and ate them in the evening. Other soft vegetables, such as daikon, cucumber, red cabbage, and onion, may also be prepared in this way. There is also a longer method for preparing pressed salt pickles. In the countryside, many farm families had their own pickling shed and pickled Chinese cabbage or daikon greens in large quantities. The vegetables were layered in large wooden kegs about 2 feet in diameter and covered with lids with several heavy 10- to 15-pound stones.

Short Method

- 2 cups thinly sliced Chinese cabbage
- 1 to 2 teaspoons sea salt

Put the sliced cabbage in a pickle press or bowl. Sprinkle the salt and mix it in with the cabbage. Press the cabbage with the pressure plate or with a saucer and a small weight. Let sit all day until dinner. They are even more delicious if aged for 2 to 3 days. When done, like most salt pickles they will keep about 1 to 3 weeks if stored in a cool place.

Long Method

- 1 head Chinese cabbage
- Sea salt

Remove the cabbage leaves individually and wash them. Put them in a colander or allow to drain in a dish drainer by the sink. When the vegetable has dried, sprinkle a thin layer of sea salt in the bottom of a wooden keg or ceramic crock. Layer the whole cabbage leaves and several pinches of sea salt in the keg or crock, alternating between the salt and cabbage. The bottom and top layers in the keg or crock should always be salt. Rotate each layer of leaves 90 degrees from the previous layer, for example, from 12 o'clock to 3 o'clock to 6 o'clock to 9 o'clock. A whole strip of kombu may be added to the bottom of the keg or crock. The kombu absorbs water, adds minerals, and gives its flavor to the pickles.

Place a wooden disc or plate on top of the last layer of cabbage and sea salt. Set several clean heavy rocks or other heavy weights on top of the plate or disc to press the leaves down. If water doesn't start to come out of the cabbage leaves within 10 to 20 hours, more sea salt is needed. The pickles will spoil if not enough salt or pressure is used. Check the pickles daily for signs of spoilage. When the water rises up to the level of the disc or plate, remove some of the rocks or weight. The water should always just slightly cover the disc or plate. However, don't discard surfacing water or mold will form and the pickles will spoil if it spreads. The pickles should be ready to eat in 3 to 4 days or may be left for several more days for a more sour taste. Store in a cool, dark place. If too salty, rinse under cold water and slice before using. Refrigerated, pickles will keep 1 to 2 months.

Turnip-Kombu Pickles

2 cups quartered and *very thinly* sliced turnips
1 strip kombu, 6 to 8 inches long, soaked and *very thinly* sliced
1 teaspoon sea salt

Put the sliced turnips in a pickle press or bowl. Add the kombu to the turnips and mix in. Add sea salt and mix it in well with the turnips and kombu. Place the top on the press and screw down or place a saucer and weight on the vegetables in a bowl. Let the pickles sit for 1 to 2 days or more. If the water from the pickles rises above the pressure plate or saucer, release some of the pressure. When done, these pickles will keep for about 2 to 3 weeks if stored in a cool place.

Mustard Green Pickles

10 whole mustard green leaves
Sea salt

Wash the mustard greens, drain, and place 3 leaves in a pickle press or bowl. Sprinkle a pinch of sea salt on the leaves. Make another layer of 3 to 4 leaves and sprinkle with salt. Finally add the remaining leaves and salt. Place the top on the press or press down with a saucer and small weight. Let sit for 1 to 2 days.

Daikon Green or Turnip Green Pickles

1 cup daikon greens or turnip greens, washed and shredded very fine
½ teaspoon sea salt

Put the sliced greens in a pickle press or bowl. Add the sea salt and mix it well with the greens. To test for saltiness, taste the greens. They should have a mild salt flavor, not a heavy one. If not salty enough, add a little more seasoning. If too salty, add a few more finely chopped greens. Screw down the press or place a saucer and weight on the mixture. When water rises to the level of the pressure-plate or saucer, reduce pressure a little. Let sit for 3 to 4 hours or overnight.

Dill Cucumber Pickles

- ¼ to ⅓ cup sea salt
- 10 to 12 cups spring water
- 2 to 3 pounds cucumbers
- 1 large onion, halved and quartered
- 1 to 2 sprigs fresh or dried dill

Add the salt to the water, bring to a boil, and simmer for 2 to 3 minutes, or until the salt dissolves. Let cool. Wash the cucumbers and put them and the sliced onion and dill in a large glass jar or a ceramic crock. Pour the cooled salt water over the vegetables. Store covered with a cheesecloth or bamboo mats in a cool, dark place for 3 to 4 days, when they should be ready to eat. The pickles will keep for about 1 month in a covered container in the refrigerator.

Variation: Cauliflower, broccoli, carrots, and watermelon rinds may be pickled in the same way.

TAMARI SOY SAUCE PICKLES

Light quick pickles may also be made by aging vegetables in tamari soy sauce. This is especially good for soft vegetables, such as watercress, celery, or mustard greens, as well as harder ones like broccoli, cauliflower, daikon, carrots, and many others. Ingredients are pickled in a mixture of 50 percent tamari soy sauce and 50 percent spring water. The vegetables may be pickled raw or first dipped in simmering water. Dipping them in boiling water or pouring hot water over them removes the raw flavor, brings out a sweeter taste, and makes them crispier. Soup stock may be used instead of water, and a touch of mirin may be added for a sweet taste. Tamari soy sauce pickles are aged from several hours to several days. When done, remove the pickles, rinse off the excess tamari soy sauce under cold water for a less salty taste, and put in a container in the refrigerator until ready to use.

Rutabaga-Tamari Pickles

- 2 cups rutabaga, quartered and thinly sliced
- Tamari soy sauce
- Spring water

Put the sliced rutabaga in a pickle press, small ceramic crock, or bowl. Prepare a mixture of half water and half tamari soy sauce, enough to half-cover the rutabaga. Place the top on the pickle press and screw down or place a saucer and small weight on top of the rutabaga. Let sit for 4 hours or overnight. These pickles will keep about 1 week in a cool place.

Variation: Apple cider may be used instead of water.

❧ Broccoli and Cauliflower Pickles ❧

- 1 cup broccoli flowerets and stems
- 1 cup cauliflower flowerets and stems
- ½ cup tamari soy sauce
- ½ cup spring water or apple juice

Put the broccoli and cauliflower flowerets and stems in a pickle press or bowl. Mix the tamari soy sauce and water together and pour over the vegetables. Screw down the pickle press or place a small saucer and a weight on top. Let sit for several hours or overnight.

Variation: The vegetables may be dipped in hot water before pickling. A touch of ginger or other herb may also be added.

❧ Onion-Tamari Pickles ❧

- 2 cups onions, thinly sliced into half moons
- 2 to 4 tablespoons tamari soy sauce

Put the sliced onions in a strainer and dip quickly in hot water to take out the onions' strong pungent taste. (Usually red onions are mild and can be pickled raw.) Put in a bowl and pour the tamari soy sauce over the onions. Mix very well to coat each slice. Let sit for 2 hours or overnight.

Variation: The onions may be pickled whole if small. For variety, use 50 percent apple cider vinegar and 50 percent tamari soy sauce for a sweeter taste.

MISO PICKLES

Miso pickles are salty but have a nice sweet taste and give a strong touch to the total meal. They should be eaten only in small amounts. Root vegetables, such as burdock, carrots, daikon, kohlrabi, turnips, ginger, lotus, parsnips, and celery root, are excellent prepared this way. Traditionally they are first dried in a shady, warm place for about a day until they can be bent in a semicircle. Most of the time, I press them first with a little bit of salt for several hours or a day or two to take out excess water; or I boil them for a few minutes ohitashi-style before putting in the miso.

Aging will vary depending upon the type of vegetable and the way it is cut. Thinly sliced ingredients will be done in from 3 days to 1 week. Whole vegetables inserted in miso with slits cut in their skin will usually pickle in 1 to 2 weeks. Vegetables cut into thick rounds will take 3 to 4 months, while whole uncut, unslitted vegetables can be kept a year or more.

To prepare, wash and scrub the vegetables thoroughly with a brush. Slice to desired thickness and put them in a jar or crock containing miso. The miso should completely cover the ingredients. No weight on the cover is necessary. Store in a cool place until ready.

Green leafy vegetables are difficult to pickle in miso because of their high water content. Too much water spoils the miso. Quick boiling or pressing in salt first improves soft varieties. Sometimes I pickle cucumbers or summer squash in miso after first pressing them in salt and waiting for the water to come out. Then I put them in a jar filled about seventy percent with miso and let sit for a couple days before using. Watercress and broccoli stems may also be pickled in miso if dipped first in hot water ohitashi-style, then submerged in miso. (Peel the broccoli skin after dipping.) They will be ready in about 1 week.

Quick Lemon-Miso Pickles

10 lemon peels
½ cup spring water
½ cup dark sesame oil
1 cup miso
1 teaspoon grated fresh ginger

Mince the lemon peels and put them in a pot with the water. Cook, uncovered, for 5 minutes. Heat a frying pan and add the oil. Sauté the cooked lemon peel, miso, and ginger. Mix thoroughly and cook for 2 to 3 minutes. Cool and store in a jar for 1 week. Serve with rice or salad.

Scallion-Miso Pickles

1 bunch scallions
Miso

Wash the scallions and put them in a jar so they are completely covered with miso. Let sit for 1 to 2 days. Remove, scrape off most of the miso, and save it for cooking. Slice the scallions, rinse if too salty, and serve.

Tofu Pickled with Miso

Pickled tofu has a soft cheese-like texture and sweet taste and makes a delicious appetizer.

1 pound cake of tofu
1 to 1½ pounds of miso

Spread about a 1-inch layer of miso in bottom of a small bowl or container. Place tofu cake (raw and uncut) on top and spread another 1-inch layer of miso on top and around the sides. Cover bowl with cheesecloth or light towel and let sit 5 to 6 hours or overnight. Just before serving, scrape off miso (and save for other uses) and slice tofu into small cubes or rectangles.

Variation: For a sharper taste, mix 1 tablespoon of grated fresh ginger with the miso before spreading around the tofu.

UMEBOSHI PICKLES

For a nice sour taste, vegetables may be pickled with umeboshi plums. Sometimes I also pickle vegetables with shiso leaves. These nice leaves are customarily pickled together with umeboshi plums and are often available in the natural foods store or Oriental market in whole leaf form. They are also called beefsteak leaves.

RED RADISH PICKLES

Umeboshi or shiso leaves give red radish a lovely pink color inside. There are two ways to make this pickle.

Short Method

1 cup sliced red radishes
2 to 3 umeboshi plums

Put the radishes in a pickle press or bowl. Break apart the umeboshi with your hands and add them to the radishes. The pits are very strong and may be included but be sure to remove them before serving. Let sit for 3 to 4 days.

Variation: Instead of whole plums, 2 to 3 teaspoons of umeboshi paste or 1 tablespoon of umeboshi vinegar may be used.

Long Method

5 to 6 umeboshi plums
2 to 3 shiso leaves
1 bunch red radishes, washed and ends removed
1 quart spring water

Put the umeboshi plums, shiso leaves, and radishes in a quart jar. Pour the water over the radishes to fill the jar. Cover with cheesecloth and put the jar in a cool place for 2 to 3 days. Slice thin and serve.

Variation: Instead of umeboshi plums, shiso leaves, and water, the radishes may be covered with umeboshi vinegar.

Ginger Pickles

These pickles are spicy but very delicious. I enjoy serving them in very small amounts with rice, noodles, or placed inside of sushi rolls.

2 pieces fresh ginger, about 2½ to 3 inches long
Several shiso leaves

Peel the skin from the ginger and slice the ginger thinly on the diagonal. Then cut each diagonal into thin, short matchsticks. Wrap the ginger in shiso leaves and put it in a small bowl and cover it with a small weight. The shiso leaves should surround the ginger completely. Let sit in a cool, dark place for 3 days, or until the ginger turns dark pink.

NUKA PICKLES

During the Shogun era, when white rice started to be eaten in Japan, it was discovered that wonderful pickles could be made with rice bran. These are called *nuka* pickles. They are usually aged for a long time and give very strong energy. One type of dried daikon pickle prepared in bran is called *takuwan*. This very strong, salty pickle is named after a Buddhist monk who taught the Shogun and many feudal leaders. One of his pupils, Miyamoto Musashi, became one of the most famous samurai in Japan, and takuwan pickles, often aged for 1 to 3 years or more, are often called samurai pickles.

Instead of rice bran, wheat bran may be used for pickling and gives a slightly different flavor. In macrobiotic food preparation, we often use brown rice flour instead of nuka. Unlike most pickles, long-time nuka pickles may be cooked as well as eaten raw. To prepare, soak in cold water until soft, slice, and sauté in a little sesame oil. Season with a little tamari soy sauce at the end of the cooking time and add to fried rice or sushi.

Bran Pickles

Short-time pickles can also be made with nuka or brown rice flour. For this purpose many macrobiotic households keep a big crock filled with bran and many different types of vegetables pickled together. When the ingredients are removed as needed, new ones are added. In this way, a constant supply of pickles is on hand. The smaller the vegetables, the sooner they will pickle. The basic way to begin a pickle crock is as follows:

- 5 pounds nuka or brown rice flour
- 10 cups spring water
- 1 to 2 cups sea salt
- Kombu
- 1 cup hatcho barley or miso

Dry-roast the bran (nuka) or rice flour over medium heat until the color changes slightly. Let cool. Boil the water, salt, and kombu; let cool. Then put the liquid and kombu in a wooden barrel or ceramic crock. An enamel bucket will also work. Mix well with the nuka or flour and the miso. This is now the basis of the pickle barrel.

Unused portions of vegetables, such as onion skins, tied in a cloth sack and placed in the keg, will help stimulate fermentation more quickly. The sack may be removed 3 or 4 days later and the contents composted. Also a few egg shells may be added to the sack. These will add calcium to the barrel and help neutralize excess acidity.

To the barrel add vegetables that have been thoroughly scrubbed to prevent any undesirable bacterial growth. Firm vegetables, such as burdock, carrots, turnips, and daikon, seem to work best. The smaller the slices, the sooner the vegetable will pickle. Large root vegetables can be quartered or halved. Leaves, because they contain more water, should be allowed to dry for half a day before being put into the barrel. A small slice of carrot will be ready to eat in 2 to 3 days, while a larger piece may take 1 week to pickle. Add only enough vegetables so that the vegetable surfaces do not touch each other. Lighter vegetables, such as summer squash, zucchini, or celery, should be added whole to the mixture. The kombu may be eaten when it is soft.

Place a wooden cover or plate on top of the mixture and weight it with a heavy stone. After water rises to the top, remove the heavy weight and stir the mixture. Place a lighter weight (or none at all) whenever you remove a pickle, which should be daily, and stir the mixture to blend flavors and prevent mold. If no liquid has surfaced in 2 days, more weight is needed. If the liquid comes out in less than a day, there is too much pressure and it should be reduced.

When removing vegetables, shake excess bran back into the barrel and rinse the vegetables under cold water before serving. If the nuka or rice flour becomes too soft, add fresh roasted nuka or flour and some sea salt. Add only a little at a time or the taste will be affected.

With this method, the pickling mixture will remain good for a couple of years. The barrel should be kept in a cool, dry place. Covering the inside of the crock with a layer of cheesecloth will help keep the dust out. If traveling away from home for a few weeks, place the crock with the cheesecloth in the refrigerator or in a very cool place. No weight is necessary at this time. If you are going to be gone for several months, take the vegetables out and keep them unwashed in a container in a cool place and put them back in the bran or flour mixture when you return.

Variation: In the beginning, vegetables may also be layered in the barrel. A layer of bran should be on the bottom and the top, as well as in between each different type of vegetable, when following this method.

❧ Sauerkraut ❧

This delicious way of preparing cabbage is believed to have originated in Mongolia and spread west. Like nuka pickles, sauerkraut may be prepared in large quantities in a wooden keg or ceramic crock.

- 5 pounds cabbage, very finely shredded
- ⅓ cup sea salt

Put the shredded cabbage in a wooden keg or ceramic crock. Add the sea salt and mix well. Place a wooden disc or plate on top of the cabbage. Place several well-cleaned rocks or a heavy weight on top of the plate or disc to supply pressure on the cabbage. Cover the keg with a piece of clean cheesecloth or a cotton towel to keep out the dust. The water level in the keg should rise up to or above the plate or disc within 10 to 20 hours. If the fluid level exceeds the disc, reduce some of the pressure. If not enough water comes out, add a little more salt or increase the weight on top. Keep in a cool, dark place for 1½ to 2 weeks. Check the sauerkraut every day. If mold starts to form on top, remove and discard it at once before it spreads and spoils the whole batch. Before using, rinse the sauerkraut with cold water. It will keep stored in a container with its juice for a week or more in the refrigerator.

SAKE LEES PICKLES

Sake lees are the sediment remaining from brewing sake or Japanese rice wine. It is similar to cheese but made from naturally fermented grains. Sake lees have a sweet, slightly pungent taste and may be used to make pickles as well as soups, sauces, and other delicious dishes. In pickling with sake lees, we usually press the vegetables in a little salt first and then insert them in the sake lees as when making miso pickles. They are usually left to sit for a couple of weeks before eating. Since sake lees spoil quickly, they must be kept in a cool place or in the refrigerator during summer. In Japan, sake lees pickles are often served during midafternoon tea. In this country, sake lees are sometimes available packaged in the natural foods store or in Oriental markets.

CHAPTER 21

BEANS

A peaceful mountain sunset,
A plume of smoke
Rises over burnt grass stalks.

—Kinuyo

Beans are seeds that grow inside pods. After harvesting, beans are removed from the pod and dried, which accounts for their hardness. Beans developed in a warmer evolutionary era prior to cereal grains are relatively higher in protein and fat and lower in complex carbohydrates. Prepared in soups, as side dishes, or cooked with other foods, beans provide a slow, steady source of energy midway between the quick, rapid growth of vegetables and the calm, peaceful strength of whole grains. In macrobiotic cooking, beans make up about 10 percent of the diet, especially azuki beans, lentils, and chick-peas, which are smaller in size and contain less fat and oil than other beans. Moderate-sized beans, such as pintos, kidneys, and soybeans, are used occasionally and large beans, such as limas, less frequently.

SELECTING AND STORING BEANS

At the natural foods store, I look for beans that are well formed, uniform in size, smooth skinned, and full and shiny in color. Spots, streaks, flecks, wrinkles, and pitting indicate beans that have lost their vitality. Fish-eyes are beans that are open at the seams; this indicates oxidation from drying too quickly. A batch of quality beans has no more than one or two percent broken skins and surface chips.

To test for sufficient dryness, bite into a bean. Properly dried beans will crackle and shatter. Improperly dried beans will show only a dent.

At home I keep the beans in closed, airtight containers and store them in a cool, dark place. Preserved in this way, they should retain their energy almost indefinitely. It is not a good idea to store different beans together in the same jar or container. Even batches of the same type of bean will have dried slightly differently and mixing may result in uneven cooking. Cooking time varies with dryness. The drier the bean, the longer it needs to be soaked and the more time is required on the stove or in the oven.

WASHING AND SOAKING BEANS

Prior to cooking, I pour the beans onto a plate a little at a time and sort through them for stones and dirt. Then I put them in a large pot, cover them with cold water, and quickly rinse them with my hand in a gentle circular motion. The light dust will come out with the water during straining. Scooping the beans by hand into the strainer will leave a residue of heavy dust on the bottom of the pot. Depending on how clean they are, I rinse and strain the beans two or three times until the rinse water is clean.

Except for lentils, split peas, and other light beans, most beans are hard and require soaking in order to improve their digestibility. Intestinal gas, which is commonly experienced eating beans, results from lack of soaking, cooking that is either too short or too quick, insufficient chewing, or overeating. To soak, put the beans in a pot, cover them with cold water, and let them sit from several hours to overnight (see chart). The soaking water may be used as part of the cooking water and will contribute a richer taste to the final dish.

I recently began soaking beans with hot water. Beans prepared in this way become much softer and more digestible. They also require about 25 percent less soaking time than beans soaked in cold water. For example, in preparing black soybeans, I heat up 2½ cups of spring water (per cup of uncooked beans) to just below boiling. In a bowl I cover the beans with this hot water, adding a pinch of sea salt to prevent the skins from separating. Then I let the beans soak 5 to 6 hours or longer (instead of the usual 6 to 8 or more in cold water) and cook them very slowly. I have also begun experimenting using this method with other soybeans and azuki beans and produced excellent results.

After soaking, the beans are ready to cook. There are four basic ways to prepare beans: 1) the traditional shocking method; 2) boiling; 3) pressure-cooking; and 4) baking.

THE TRADITIONAL SHOCKING METHOD

This method of boiling is used throughout the Orient and in many traditional societies. It is the method I most prefer. Put the soaked beans in a cast-iron pot, add 2½ cups of water per cup of beans. Leave the pot uncovered to start and cook slowly over low heat until the water boils. Allow the water to bubble for a few minutes but do not let it boil strongly. Then put a small lid on top of the beans that fits down inside the pot. In Japan we had light wooden lids for this purpose but a metal one also will do, just so the pot is not tightly covered. The drop top keeps the beans from jumping around and lessens their cooking time. As the beans cook over the low heat, they will expand in size and the lid will jiggle as the water comes back to a boil. At this time, remove the lid and gently add just enough cold water down the side to stop the boiling. Put the lid back on. Continue to add cold water in this way each time the liquid boils until beans are about 80 percent cooked (see the chart for approximate times). At this point, add ¼ teaspoon of sea salt per cup of uncooked beans or other seasoning. After seasoning the beans, remove the cover, and cook until done, adding more cold water when necessary. When the beans are soft, turn up the heat to boil off any excess liquid. The result should be perfect beans, smooth, delicious, and easy to digest. The long, slow cooking, low heat, and alternations of hot and cold water will bring out the beans' natural taste better than any other method.

COOKING TIME FOR THE SHOCKING/BOILING METHODS*

Type of Beans	Soaking Time	Add Seasoning	Total Cooking Time
Soft Beans Green lentils, red lentils, mung beans, split peas	None	45 to 50 minutes	1 hour
Medium Beans Small, light azuki, pinto, kidney, navy, lima, black, turtle, and other medium-sized beans	2 to 4 hours	1½ to 1¾ hours	2 hours
Hard Beans Big, dark azuki, chick-peas, black, white, and yellow soybeans, and other hard beans	6 to 8 hours or overnight	3¼ to 3½ hours	4 hours

*Times are approximate and may vary according to climate, soil conditions, season, altitude, etc. Soaking times are using cold water. For soaking with hot water and a pinch of salt, soaking time may be reduced about 25 percent.

PRESSURE-COOKING

Type of Beans	Soaking	Add Seasoning	Total Cooking Time
Soft	None	30 minutes	45 minutes
Medium	1 hour	45 minutes	1 hour
Hard	2 hours	1 to 1¼ hours	1½ to 2 hours

BOILING BEANS

The ordinary boiling method calls for 3½ to 4 cups of cold water per cup of dried beans. Bring the beans to a boil, lower the heat, cover the pot, and simmer until beans are eighty percent done. Uncover, season with about ¼ teaspoon of sea salt per cup of uncooked beans or equivalent miso or tamari soy sauce. Cover the pot and cook until the beans are soft. When done, remove cover, turn up the heat, and boil off any excess water. Transfer the beans to a serving bowl and serve.

PRESSURE-COOKED BEANS

Except when cooking beans with rice or other grains, ordinarily I do not pressure-cook beans by themselves. As a side dish to the daily meal, beans are better shocked or boiled. However, on those occasions when the beans need to be cooked more quickly and there isn't as much time to soak them, pressure-cooking may be used and creates a strong energy. Simply wash the beans, soak them as long as possible, put them in a pressure cooker, and add two cups of water per cup of beans. Bring the beans and water to pressure, reduce the heat to low, and cook until the beans are nearly done. Let the pressure come down, uncover, and season with ¼ teaspoon of sea salt, ½ tablespoon of miso, or 1½ teaspoons of tamari soy sauce. Continue to simmer the beans until any excess liquid has evaporated.

BAKED BEANS

Beans baked in a ceramic pot or crock are very delicious. Total cooking time is usually 3 to 4 hours for traditional favorites such as navy beans or pintos. To prepare, clean and soak the beans, put in an ordinary pot, and cover with 4 to 5 cups of cold water per cup of beans. Put the pot on top of the stove and boil for 15 to 20 minutes to loosen the skins. Pour the beans and cooking water into a crock or baking dish, cover, and put in the oven. Bake the beans at 350 degrees until 80 percent done; then season them with about ¼ teaspoon of sea salt or ½ tablespoon of miso. Add more water if necessary and continue to cook until the beans are soft and creamy. At the very end, remove the cover to allow the beans to brown on top. Diced carrots, onions, and other vegetables may be added when beans are 50 to 60 percent done. Raisins, dried apples, or other fruit may also be added at the beginning for a sweeter dish.

SEASONING

Beans are seasoned toward the end of cooking to allow the insides and outsides to cook evenly. Seasoning beans at the beginning of cooking hardens the skins and makes for uneven cooking. As a rule of thumb, ¼ teaspoon of sea salt is used to season each cup of uncooked beans. Instead of sea salt, the beans may also be seasoned with 1 to 1½ teaspoons tamari soy sauce or 1½ to 1⅔ teaspoons of miso for each cup of uncooked beans. When cooking beans in large quantities, I reduce the seasoning slightly.

I prefer azuki beans cooked with sea salt, soy beans with tamari soy sauce or miso, kidney beans with tamari soy sauce or miso, chick-peas with a touch of tamari soy sauce, black soybeans with a touch of tamari soy sauce, and lima and other beans either with sea salt or occasionally a mild herb, such as bay leaves. For a sweet taste, a touch of barley malt may be added.

COOKING BEANS WITH KOMBU

A strip of kombu sea vegetable is traditionally added to beans in the Far East. The combination improves the flavor of the beans and adds minerals from the sea, making for a more balanced dish. To any of the four basic methods, simply add one 3- to 6-inch-long strip of kombu that has been rinsed and soaked for a few minutes in cold water. Put the strip on the bottom of the pot and the beans on top.

AZUKI BEANS

In the part of Japan where I grew up, azuki beans were cultivated in the mud banks in between the paddies and harvested after the rice. Small and compact in size, azukis are lower in fat and oil than other beans and are considered an honorary grain in the Far East. In the chapter on rice, we described how these beautiful shiny red beans are cooked with rice on holidays and special occasions to make Red Rice. They are also frequently eaten plain and occasionally sweetened as a dessert.

Prior to cooking, azukis need to be thoroughly washed and rinsed. Once, while teaching grammar school in the mountains, I cooked azuki beans for a school board meeting, and everyone made a face after tasting my dish. I was not very experienced as a cook and had not washed the beans very well. The bean dish I served contained sand and grit, and I was very ashamed before the president of the school and the other teachers. Like lentils and other light beans, azukis do not need soaking, but I prefer to soak them for several hours, because doing so improves their digestibility.

The azukis imported to the United States and Canada are superior in quality. Usually they are grown in Hokkaido, the cold northernmost island of Japan, and selected by hand. Macrobiotic and natural foods farmers are now growing organic azukis on various parts of this continent. Their quality is also very high. At home we prepare azuki beans regularly, two or three times a week. Usually I soak them for 6 to 8 hours, put a 3- to 6-inch piece of kombu on the bottom of the pot, and cook with the shocking or boiling method explained above. I am also very fond of azukis and wheat berries, mixed fifty/fifty, pressure-cooked. Azuki bean juice, the liquid in the pot from cooking, is rich-tasting and I enjoy it over mochi, creamy-style.

Azuki Beans and Squash

This makes a nice sweet dish for the autumn.

1 cup azuki beans
Spring water
1 strip kombu, 6 to 8 inches long
1 cup buttercup squash or other winter squash, cubed but not peeled
¼ teaspoon sea salt

Wash the beans, cover them with water, and soak for 6 to 8 hours. Put the kombu in the bottom of a pot and cover with the squash. Next add the azuki beans. Add water to just cover the squash layer. Do not cover the beans at the beginning. Place the bean mixture over low heat and bring to a boil slowly. Cover after about 10 to 15 minutes. Cook until the beans are 70 to 80 percent done, about 1 hour or more. The water will evaporate as the beans expand, so add cold water occasionally to cover to keep the water level constant and make the beans soft. When the beans are 70 to 80 percent done, add sea salt and cook until done and most of the liquid has evaporated, another 15 to 30 minutes. Transfer to a serving bowl and serve.

Variation: This dish may also be pressure-cooked. First pressure-cook the kombu and beans for 15 to 20 minutes. Bring down the pressure, uncover, and add the squash. Continue to cook without pressure until the beans are 70 to 80 percent done. This makes for a less bitter taste. Then season and continue to cook until done. If you add the squash at the beginning of pressure-cooking, it will melt too much.

Azuki Beans with Lotus Seeds

Lotus seeds are traditionally said to contribute to vitality and longevity.

1 cup azuki beans
½ cup lotus seeds
1 8-inch strip kombu
2½ cups spring water
¼ teaspoon sea salt or 1½ teaspoons tamari soy sauce

Wash and soak the azuki beans and lotus seeds together for 3 to 8 hours. Put the kombu in the bottom of a pot. Next put the seeds on top of the kombu, followed by the azuki beans and lotus seeds. Add water to almost cover the beans. Bring to a boil. Cover, reduce the heat to medium-low, and simmer until beans are about 70 to 80 percent done, about 1½ hours, adding cold water when necessary as the beans expand and original water evaporates. When the beans are 70 to 80 percent done, add approximately ¼ teaspoon sea salt or 1½ teaspoons tamari soy sauce and simmer for 30 minutes longer, or until the beans are done. Total cooking time is about 2 hours.

Variation: Add 1 cup fresh lotus root or dried soaked lotus root, cut into ½-inch rounds. In Japan, this dish is called "cousins-style azuki beans."

Omedeto

Omedeto is a porridge made from azukis and roasted brown rice. It takes its name from the Japanese word meaning "congratulations" and "happy holidays." This sweet-tasting porridge was a breakfast favorite at George Ohsawa's dormitory outside Tokyo.

1 cup brown rice
1 6- to 8-inch-strip kombu
1 cup azuki beans
2½ cups water per cup of rice and beans
Pinch of sea salt per cup of rice and beans

Dry-roast the rice in a frying pan. Combine the beans and rice in a pot with kombu underneath. Add the water and cook, following the basic shocking or boiling method. Season with sea salt when the beans are 70 to 80 percent done and cook for another 30 minutes, or until they are done.

Azuki Beans and Chestnuts

This dish is especially good for strengthening tight kidneys and provides warming energy in the winter.

- ½ cup dried chestnuts
- 1 cup azuki beans
- 3 cups spring water
- ¼ teaspoon sea salt

Dry-roast the chestnuts in a frying pan until a nutty aroma is released. Cook following the basic shocking or boiling method.

Variation: Instead of dry-roasting, the chestnuts and azukis may be soaked together several hours or preferably overnight.

For an especially sweet dish or for a dessert, add a small amount of dried apple, fresh apple, or raisins at the start of cooking.

SOYBEANS

Soybeans contain more protein and fat than other beans. They are usually easier to digest in naturally processed form as miso, tofu, tempeh, natto, or tamari soy sauce rather than in whole form. But if cooked properly, they are very sweet prepared whole and give no problem with intestinal gas. Yellow soybeans should be soaked overnight with a strip of kombu and cooked slowly. I often pressure-cook them for 20 minutes and then let them boil uncovered for 10 to 15 minutes longer. Yellow soybeans go well with hiziki sea vegetable.

❧ Colorful Soybean Casserole ❧

This is my favorite casserole. It is very delicious, creates strong energy and attraction between man and woman, and may also be taken medicinally by those who are chronically ill.

- 2 cups yellow soybeans
- Spring water
- 2 3-inch pieces kombu
- 1 shiitake mushroom
- 5 large pieces dried lotus root
- 6 pieces of dried tofu, 2 by 2¼ inches thick
- 1 celery stalk, sliced
- 1 dried daikon, shredded
- 1 carrot, sliced
- 1 burdock, sliced
- Pinch of sea salt
- 1½ tablespoons tamari soy sauce
- 1 teaspoon kuzu
- Grated fresh ginger
- 1 to 2 tablespoons mirin (optional)

Soak the soybeans in cold water overnight in 2½ cups of water per cup of soybeans. Next day, put the beans and the soaking water in a pressure cooker. Boil the soybeans uncovered for 15 minutes. Remove the beans and skim off the hulls. Then put beans back in pressure cooker, cover, and bring up to pressure.

Soak kombu, shiitake, lotus root, and dried tofu for 10 minutes. After beans have cooked about 70 to 80 percent, approximately 20 minutes, reduce the pressure, open the pot, and layer the kombu, shiitake, lotus root, and dried tofu on top of the beans. Bring back to pressure and cook for 10 more minutes. Reduce the pressure, open the pot, and remove the beans and vegetables and put them on separate plates.

Slice the cooked kombu and put it in the bottom of a large saucepan. Add a little water. On top of the kombu lay the soft vegetables, such as celery, shiitake, daikon, and tofu. Then add the root vegetables and the lotus root. Finally on top, place the partially cooked soybeans, add a pinch of sea salt, and any original water remaining in the pressure cooker. Cover, cook for 30 minutes, or until the carrots and celery are soft. Then add the tamari soy sauce. Finally add 1 teaspoon of kuzu to make a creamy sauce and a little grated fresh ginger for flavoring. For a slightly sweeter taste, the mirin may be added, if desired. The soybeans should be very tender and sweet when this dish is done.

Variation: Depending on availability, some vegetables may be omitted or added. Seitan makes this dish especially delicious. If not using a pressure cooker, boil the beans in a pot with a drop top for about 1 hour prior to cooking with the soft vegetables.

BLACK SOYBEANS

These nice shiny beans are also called Japanese black beans. They have a strong, delicious taste. Their juice is said to make the voice clear and beautiful. Throughout Japan, mothers prepare their children for music tests and singing lessons with this dish. Black soybeans are also used medicinally to help discharge animal toxins from the body.

They may be prepared plain or cooked together with rice. When cooked with rice, black soybeans are cleaned in a special way and then roasted. To clean the beans, moisten a clean dish towel with cold water. Put the beans on a damp towel and rub to clean them. If you wash these beans under water, the skins will loosen and fall off. After washing, dry-roast for several minutes and then cook with rice. When cooked by themselves, I sometimes sweeten the beans with a little barley malt, rice syrup, mirin, or maple syrup. The basic recipe for preparing black soybeans follows.

Basic Black Soybeans

- 2 cups black soybeans
- 3 cups cold spring water per cup of beans
- ¼ teaspoon sea salt per cup of beans
- 1¼ to 1½ tablespoons tamari soy sauce

Wash beans with cold water very quickly and put them in a bowl. Cover with about 6 cups of water in total. Add sea salt and let the beans soak for several hours or overnight. Put the beans in a pot with the salted soaking water and bring to a boil. Reduce the heat to medium-low and simmer until the beans are about 90 percent done. During the simmering, add water when necessary as the liquid evaporates. As the beans cook, skim off and discard any skins that float to the surface, as well as any gray foam that surfaces. When the beans are about 90 percent done, add the tamari soy sauce. Shake the pot gently up and down to evenly coat the beans with the juice and tamari. Do not mix with a spoon. Shaking gives the skins a very shiny black appearance. Cook until almost all the remaining liquid has evaporated. Total cooking time for this dish is 2½ to 3 hours.

Brown Rice with Black Soybeans

In some regions of the country, because of the combination of black and white, this dish is served as a traditional mourning dish, whereas in other regions, it is used to mark a joyous occasion. This is one of my favorite dishes.

- 2 cups brown rice
- 4½ cups spring water
- 1 cup black soybeans
- 3 pinches of sea salt
- 2 teaspoons tamari soy sauce

Wash the rice and put it in a pressure cooker. Add the water. Put a clean moist towel on a countertop and put the soybeans on the towel. Fold the towel over the beans and pat the beans gently with the towel to remove any dust. Put the cleaned beans in a preheated cast-iron frying pan and dry-roast, quickly but gently, stirring with a wooden paddle or spoon. When the beans begin to crack and the insides turn slightly golden, add the soybeans to the rice in the pressure cooker. Add the salt and tamari soy sauce. Cover the pressure cooker and cook over low heat for 10 minutes; then raise the heat until pressure is reached. As soon as pressure is achieved, reduce the heat to low and cook for 45 to 50 minutes. Remove the pot from the heat and let sit for 5 minutes; then release the pressure. Let the pot sit for 10 minutes longer. Then open the pot and transfer the rice and soybeans to a wooden bowl.

❧ Kidney Beans ❧

Along with azukis and soybeans I grew up on kidney beans. They are sweet to the taste when seasoned during cooking with sea salt, miso, or tamari soy sauce. I usually prepare them as a side dish. Along with brown rice and tempeh, a tasty chili-style meal can be prepared using kidney beans.

- 1 cup kidney beans
- Spring water
- 1 strip kombu, 6 to 8 inches long
- 1½ teaspoons miso per cup of beans, preferably barley miso

Wash and soak the beans for 6 to 8 hours. Put the kombu in the bottom of a heavy pot. Set the beans on top of the kombu and add water to just cover the beans. Bring to a boil. Reduce the heat to medium-low and cover. Simmer until the beans are about 80 percent done, or about 1 hour. Add cold water following the basic shocking method as needed. When the beans are 80 percent done, add the puréed miso. (Barley miso is best to use with this dish.) Just add the miso on top of the beans and do not mix in. The miso will filter down into the beans as they continue to cook. Continue to cook until the beans are soft and creamy, another 20 to 30 minutes. Transfer to a serving bowl and serve.

Variation: Pressure-cook the beans for 45 minutes. Then add the puréed miso and cook, *not* under pressure, about 20 to 30 minutes longer.

❧ Chick-Peas ❧

The first time I had chick-peas was in a summer salad at a friend's in New York. They were combined with celery, carrots, and corn and very delicious. I now use them regularly, cooked plain, mixed together with rice or other grains, prepared with vegetables as in the Colorful Soybean Casserole recipe, in soup, with salty seitan, or in the form of pan-fried patties, mashed and mixed with scallions, parsley, and celery. Chick-peas are also a main ingredient of hummus, the traditional spread made from cooked chick-peas and tahini popular in the Middle East. The basic recipe for chick-peas follows:

- 1 cup diced chick-peas
- 3 cups spring water
- 1 6- to 8-inch strip kombu, soaked and diced
- 1 cup diced onions
- 1 cup diced carrots
- 1 cup cooked diced seitan
- ¼ to ½ teaspoon sea salt per cup of beans

Soak the chick-peas for 6 to 8 hours or overnight. Drain, but reserve soaking water. Lay the kombu in the bottom of a pressure cooker. Place the drained beans on top and add reserved water. Cover and cook over low heat at less than full pressure for 30 to 40 minutes. Bring down the pressure and remove the beans from the pot. Put the onions, carrots, and seitan in the pot. Then add the cooked beans and kombu on top. Bring to a boil, cover, and reduce the heat to medium-low. Simmer until the beans are about 80 percent done, approximately 1 hour, and add the sea salt. Cook until beans are very well done but not mushy and most of the liquid has evaporated. Transfer to a serving dish and serve.

Lentils

I also discovered lentils in the United States. They are soft, soothing, easy to cook, and go well together with root vegetables. Cooked with burdock, they create an especially strong taste. I also enjoy them mixed with carrots and onions or with winter squash. For occasional variety, try red lentils. They completely dissolve when cooked, turn an olive green in color, and produce a rich creamy soup, somewhat like split peas.

- 1 cup dried lentils
- 2 to 2½ cups spring water per cup of lentils
- 1 cup diced onion
- ½ cup diced celery
- 1 cup diced carrots
- ¼ cup diced burdock
- ¼ teaspoon sea salt, or 1½ teaspoons tamari soy sauce
- Parsley for garnish

Wash the lentils. Make layers of the onions, celery, carrots, and burdock in a pot. Put the lentils on top and add the water. Bring to a boil, reduce the heat to medium-low, and cover. Simmer for 40 to 45 minutes. Season and simmer for another 10 to 15 minutes. Transfer to a serving bowl and garnish with parsley and serve.

LIMA BEANS

Limas are native to Central and South America and are higher in fat and oil than other beans. In modern Japan, lima beans are sweetened with sugar and make a popular snack. Of course, we don't use sugar. Just seasoning with a little sea salt brings out their naturally sweet taste during cooking. Like other beans, I enjoy them from time to time served with burdock, carrots, corn, or other vegetables.

CHAPTER 22

TOFU, TEMPEH, AND NATTO

Koro, koro—
Tumbling the beans at night,
Mother's hands move very quickly.

—Kinuyo

Tofu, tempeh, natto, and other soybean products are traditional staples in the East. Macrobiotic cooking has popularized these high-protein foods in the West. They are now available in most natural foods stores, as well as a growing number of supermarkets, and are enjoyed as a nourishing alternative to meat, poultry, dairy products, and other items high in saturated fat and cholesterol. As a complement to whole grains, soy products may be eaten daily or every other day in small amounts in place of or in addition to beans in whole form.

TOFU

Tofu, the most versatile of the soy products, originated several thousand years ago in China, and its discovery is attributed to a Taoist alchemist. By the early centuries of this era, tofu reached Japan with Buddhist monks and formed an important part of Buddhist temple cooking *(shojin-ryori)*, as well as finding enthusiastic acceptance among all strata of society.

Bland tasting in itself, tofu readily absorbs the flavors and subtle aromas of the foods it is cooked with and lends itself to hundreds of recipes and styles of preparation. It can be added to soups, cooked with grains, noodles, and vegetables, marinated in salads, or used in pickles, sauces, and spreads. Quick and easy to prepare, tofu can be made at home in several hours or purchased ready to eat and prepared in a few minutes. Depending on the form, tofu can be stored for a week to several months or longer. The most familiar form of tofu consists of square or rectangular white cakes, weighing from about ½ pound to 1½ pounds and kept covered in cold water. In the kitchen, these cakes are cut and sliced in a variety of ways and boiled, steamed, sautéed, broiled, baked, deep-fried, or occasionally served raw.

In Japan, fresh tofu was traditionally made daily in small neighborhood tofu shops. By 5 or 6 A.M., tofu makers would be out on the streets with their pushcarts, somewhat like milkmen in the West. From open windows housewives in their early morning kimonos would buy fresh tofu to put in miso soup for their families' breakfast.

The special tofu dish I remember most was prepared at New Year's. Mother pan-fried sliced tofu on top of dried bamboo leaves in a big ceramic fry pan. Earlier we had gathered the large bamboo leaves from the mountains, especially the tender, lower-growing leaves. The bamboo was dried at home and could be heated in the pan without oil and without sticking. After pan-frying for a few minutes, the tofu would be boiled in kombu and shiitake mushroom stock for 10 to 15 minutes with a mild taste of tamari soy sauce. Then the tofu would be sliced diagonally, cooked in any style, and served. The bamboo lent a delicious taste to the meal.

TOFU QUALITY

Tofu is traditionally solidified with *nigari* in the way that dairy cheese is curdled with rennet. Nigari is the concentrated residue that remains after sea salt is extracted from sea water. It is very rich in magnesium, iron, and other minerals. Another natural solidifier used in making tofu is calcium sulfate, obtained from gypsum in the mountains. Today, most of the tofu sold in Japan and Oriental markets around the world is made with vinegar, alum, refined calcium sulfate, or other chemicals that are very low in quality. When I first came to the United

States and made tofu at home, I could not obtain natural nigari. Instead I used lemon juice, which is the next best alternative. However, high-quality tofu is now available from hundreds of community and regional soy dairies. Where I live in Boston, even the supermarkets now stock organic tofu made with nigari.

SOFT AND FIRM TOFU

Fresh tofu is usually sold in cakes labeled as either soft or firm. In Japanese, we call soft tofu *kinugoshi dofu*, meaning silk strain, and we call firm tofu *momengoshi dofu*, meaning cotton strain. Silk and cotton refer not only to the comparatively smooth or rough texture of the tofu but also to the traditional manner of preparation. A cotton cheesecloth is used to strain the firm variety, while a silken cheesecloth is used for the soft style. Silky tofu is used primarily for miso soup, salad dressings, and for short-time cooking. Cottony tofu is used more for deep-fried tofu, nishime-style tofu, scrambled tofu, pickled tofu, fermented tofu, and other long-time preparations.

COOKING TOFU

Tofu has a natural cooling energy and for proper digestion is preferably eaten cooked. In summer when it is very hot, I occasionally prepare raw tofu on a bed of ice, with a tamari and ginger sauce. Otherwise, I always cook it, even boiling the tofu for salad dressings for 2 to 3 minutes before puréeing it.

Also, because tofu is high in protein and oil, its natural balance is a salty taste, such as miso or tamari soy sauce. In the United States, tofu desserts, sweetened with barley malt, maple syrup, or honey, are very popular. However, sweetening tofu is unknown in the Far East and only intensifies the original cooling energy of the tofu. Except for those in transition from dairy food, please be very careful in making desserts with sweetened tofu. For a sweet taste, a touch of mirin, a condiment made from liquefied sweet rice, may occasionally be added in cooking.

For miso or clear soup, I add soft tofu cut into small cubes about ½ inch square at the end of cooking. The pieces of tofu will initially sink to the bottom. When they rise to the surface, I add the seasoning to the soup and after 2 to 3 minutes stop cooking. If boiled too long, the tofu will become hard and rubbery.

For short-time cooking, I enjoy tofu scrambled egg-style. After crushing the tofu by hand, I sauté it for a few minutes in a little sesame oil, adding fresh corn or chopped greens, and seasoning with tamari soy sauce. Tofu can also be added to fried rice or noodles and cooked in this way.

For long-time cooking, I use firm tofu cut in big slices and cooked over a low flame with vegetables in nishime or sukiyaki styles. The tofu will taste better in combination with other vegetables if it is pan-fried first for a few minutes. This allows the moisture to escape and prevents a rubbery taste.

Deep-fried tofu is good with vegetables sautéed kinpira-style. It also goes well with *hiziki*, arame, and kombu sea vegetables prepared nishime-style. After deep-frying I usually rinse out the excess oil with hot water, then cook with shiitake and kombu stock a few minutes before cooking in one of the above ways. In the sushi section, I described another of my favorite tofu dishes, kitsune (fox-style) sushi, consisting of triangular-shaped pouches of deep-fried tofu stuffed with vegetables.

STORING FRESH TOFU

Fresh tofu is perishable and will keep about one week. To store, place in a container, cover with cold water, and either refrigerate or keep in a cool, dark place. In cold weather, I change the water every 2 or 3 days and in warm weather I change the water daily. Tofu that has spoiled turns moldy, is filmy to the touch, and has a sour taste and smell. If only the surface and edges are affected, scrape or slice off, discard, and use the inside portion which is still edible. You may also cook it with umeboshi or umeboshi vinegar. However, if the spoilage is extensive and there is any doubt about the taste being off, discard and prepare a new batch.

FROZEN TOFU

Frozen tofu has a smoother and finer texture than fresh tofu and keeps longer. According to legend, frozen tofu was discovered when a Buddhist monk dropped a bucket of tofu in the snow after being frightened by a fox. The next day he retrieved the frozen tofu and brought it back to the temple, where its unique qualities were enjoyed by all. At home, frozen tofu can be made by pressing the water out of fresh tofu and freezing it. To do this, place fresh tofu cakes on a cutting board and cover with a light dish towel. On top of tofu, place another board and a stone or weight on top. Tilt the boards at a slight angle by placing a chopstick underneath and allowing the water to drain off. After 1 hour the moisture should be reduced. Next, slice the tofu into large ½-inch-thick slices and place them, without touching each other, on a platter in the freezer. After freezing anywhere from 12 to 24 hours, place the tofu slices in a plastic bag and keep in the freezer until ready to use. Frozen tofu will keep for about 3 months. To thaw, place the frozen tofu in boiling water for about 10 minutes, rinse under cool water, and press out the excess water gently with the palm of your hand. Frozen tofu can also be thawed by soaking in cold water for 10 minutes, rinsing, and squeezing.

DRIED TOFU

Another popular form of tofu is dried tofu. It has a completely different texture from either fresh or frozen tofu. Dried tofu goes extremely well with thinly sliced root vegetables. In Spain we once had a delicious dish of dried tofu cooked with carrots and a miso sauce. Traditionally, dried tofu is made in the wintertime by pressing out the water from frozen tofu, wrapping the slices in straw mats, and leaving for one week in a cold shady place. The tofu slices are then tied in groups of five with rice straw and hung from poles under the eaves of farmhouses out of the sunlight. During the day they thaw, and at night they freeze. After several weeks of alternating temperatures, the result is a dry, crisp, light beige tofu that is similar in appearance, weight, and longevity to dehydrated camping food. Modern dried tofu is made commercially with ammonia gas. To wash out the gas and reconstitute the dried tofu, add hot water to cover, soak 3 to 5 minutes but not too long, pour off hot water and add lukewarm or cool water, and press with the hands to eliminate excess liquid. Repeat rinsing with cool water and pressing several times. Use instead of fresh tofu in any of the recipes.

❧ Homemade Tofu ❧

---

3 cups organic yellow soybeans
Spring water

4½ teaspoons natural nigari or lemon juice

Soak the beans overnight, strain, and grind in an electric blender. Put the ground beans in a pot with 6 quarts of spring water and bring to a boil. Reduce the heat to low and simmer for 5 minutes, stirring constantly to avoid burning. Sprinkle cold water on the beans to stop bubbling. Gently boil again and sprinkle with cold water. Repeat a third time. Place a cotton cloth or several layers of cheesecloth in a strainer and pour this liquid into a bowl. This is soy milk. Fold the corners of the cloth to form a sack or place cloth in a strainer and squeeze out the remaining liquid. Pulp in sack is called *okara* and may be saved for other recipes. In a suribachi or blender, grind the nigari. If unavailable, use lemon juice. Sprinkle the powdered nigari over the soy milk in the bowl. With a wooden spoon carefully make a large X-shaped cut with two deep strokes in this mixture and allow to sit for 10 to 15 minutes. During this time it will begin to curdle. The next step calls for a wooden or stainless-steel tofu box (available in many natural foods stores) or a bamboo steamer. Line the box or steamer with cheesecloth and gently spoon in the soy milk. Cover the top with a layer of cheesecloth and place a lid on the box or steamer so it rests on the cheesecloth and curdling tofu. Place a small stone or weight on the lid and let stand for about 1 hour, or until the tofu cake is formed. Then gently place the tofu in a dish of cold water for 30 minutes to solidify. Keep the tofu covered in water and refrigerate until used. One pound of soybeans makes about 3½ to 4 pounds of tofu.

Note: A tofu box can be made at home with wood 4½ inches to a side or 6½ by 3½ by 4½ inches deep. Drill holes 1½ inches apart in the bottom and sides of the container and make a lid with several holes that fits inside the top rim.

Boiled Tofu with Ginger-Parsley Sauce

Spring water
16 ounces tofu, sliced into 5 pieces about ½ inch thick
Tamari soy sauce
Grated fresh ginger
Chopped parsley or scallions for garnish

Put about ¼ inch of water in a pot and bring to a boil. Put the tofu slices in the water and cover the pot. Reduce the heat to low and simmer for 1 to 2 minutes. Keep the heat low or the tofu will become hard. Remove the tofu, drain, and put the slices on individual serving plates. Prepare a sauce by mixing a small amount of water, tamari soy sauce, and grated fresh ginger together. Pour a teaspoon of the sauce over each slice of boiled tofu and garnish with chopped parsley or scallions.

Broiled Tofu

This dish is especially good served with sauerkraut.

16 ounces soft tofu, sliced
Tamari soy sauce

Drain the tofu and slice it into 8 equal slices. Lay the tofu on a baking sheet and sprinkle a few drops of tamari soy sauce over each piece. Put the tofu under the broiler and broil for 2 to 3 minutes. Turn the tofu over and sprinkle a couple drops of tamari on the other side. Broil for 1 to 2 minutes longer. Remove and serve individually.

Scrambled Tofu and Corn

Only a short time is needed to cook this delicious dish.

- 3 tablespoons dark sesame or corn oil
- 16 ounces firm tofu
- 3 cups fresh sweet corn kernels, removed from cob
- ½ to 1 teaspoon sea salt
- Sliced scallions for garnish

Heat the oil in a pot. Crumble the tofu and add it to the pot. Put the sweet corn on top of the tofu. Cover and cook over low heat for 3 to 4 minutes, or until the tofu becomes hot and the corn is done. Sprinkle a small amount of sea salt on top of the corn. Mix and serve hot. Just before serving, add scallions as a garnish but don't cook them to retain their bright green color.

Variations: The tofu, corn, and scallions may also be sautéed in 2 to 3 tablespoons of water for those who need to limit their oil. Other vegetables may be added or substituted including cabbage, onions, carrots (cut into matchsticks), mushrooms, and occasionally a slice of green pepper. The colors of the vegetables should be bright and the texture slightly crispy.

Sautéed Tofu and Vegetables

This is a variation of the previous recipe.

- 2 to 3 tablespoons dark sesame oil
- 1 celery stalk, sliced ¼ to ½ inch thick
- 2 carrots, sliced ¼ to ½ inch thick
- Scallion roots, chopped fine
- 16 ounces firm tofu
- 1 teaspoon sea salt, or 2 tablespoons tamari soy sauce
- 2 scallions, sliced for garnish

Heat the sesame oil in a frying pan. Add the celery and carrots. Add scallion roots and sauté for 1 to 2 minutes. Crumble tofu and mix it into the sautéed vegetables. Season with sea salt or tamari soy sauce to taste. Cover and cook for 3 to 5 minutes. Garnish with sliced scallions and serve.

Baked Tofu with Miso Sauce

- 1 tablespoon barley miso
- 2 to 3 teaspoons freshly squeezed lemon juice
- ¼ to ⅓ cup spring water
- 16 ounces firm tofu, sliced into ½-inch by 3-inch-wide slices
- 1 tablespoon roasted and chopped sesame seeds
- ¼ cup sliced scallions or chopped chives

Put the miso and lemon juice in a suribachi. Add the water, and purée until the sauce is smooth and creamy. Put the tofu in a shallow baking dish, leaning the slices against one another so they are slightly tilted like this: / / / / /. Spoon the sauce over the tofu so that the sauce covers the center of each slice. About one inch on each side of the tofu slices should be left free of sauce. Bake the tofu in a preheated 350-degree oven for 15 to 20 minutes. Remove the dish and sprinkle a few sesame seeds and a few scallions or chives on top of the miso sauce. Return to the oven and bake for 2 minutes longer. Remove and serve hot.

Baked Tofu Sandwich

This is one of the most popular dishes in my cooking classes. It is a nourishing alternative to the grilled cheese sandwich.

- 16 ounces firm tofu, cut into slices 3 by 2 by ¼ to ½ inch
- Barley miso
- 1 sheet nori, toasted

Take 4 to 5 slices of tofu and spread a thin layer of puréed miso on each slice. Place the other 4 to 5 slices on top of the miso layers to create a sandwich effect. Slice the nori into 1-inch-thick strips. Wrap a nori strip around each tofu sandwich. Place the sandwiches on a baking tray or dish. Bake in a preheated 350-degree oven for 15 to 20 minutes.

Variations: This sandwich may also be pan-fried in a little sesame oil. Or, cook each side over a medium-low heat with 50 percent miso and 50 percent tahini; miso with ginger; or miso with scallion, onion, chopped almonds, walnuts, or roasted sesame seeds.

Oden

Oden is a traditional Japanese stew, enjoyed especially during the colder months. It is cooked family-style on the table and eaten from the pot. Oden consists of tofu, daikon, and a wide variety of other ingredients in a broth and is frequently accompanied by hot sake. It is prepared both in the countryside and in the cities, where it is associated with taverns and spicy toppings and seasonings.

- 2 strips kombu, soaked and sliced into 3- to 4-inch-long strips
- 2 cups daikon, sliced into ½-inch-thick rounds
- 4 to 5 shiitake mushrooms, soaked, stemmed, and halved
- Dark sesame oil
- 5 to 6 slices firm tofu, 3 by 2 by ½ inch thick
- Spring water
- Tamari soy sauce

Tie each kombu strip into a bow, with the knot in the center of the kombu strip. Place the kombu in one section of a pot. Add the daikon rounds in the pot next to the kombu bows and the shiitake next to the daikon. Place a little oil in a skillet and lightly pan-fry each of the tofu slices on both sides for a few minutes. Add the tofu slices to the pot next to the shiitake and kombu. Each of the ingredients should have its own separate section in the pot. Do not mix or layer the ingredients. Add water to half cover the ingredients. Bring to a boil, reduce the heat to medium-low, cover, and simmer for 30 to 45 minutes, until the daikon is soft and translucent. Season with a little tamari soy sauce to taste and cook until there is only about ¼ cup of liquid left. Transfer to a serving dish and serve.

Yudofu

Yudofu means hot water tofu. Its delicate simple flavors are very popular. Most Japanese restaurants carry this dish.

- 2 cups spring water
- 1 strip kombu
- 2 shiitake mushrooms
- 1 pound fresh tofu, sliced into 1-inch-thick slices
- 1 bunch watercress, washed
- Tamari soy sauce
- Sliced lemon
- Gingerroot juice
- Finely sliced scallions for garnish

Place water, kombu, and mushrooms in a saucepan and bring to a boil. Reduce the heat to low and simmer for several minutes. Remove shiitake and kombu and set aside for use in another recipe. Return water to a boil and add the sliced tofu. When tofu becomes hot, add the watercress and let sit for a few seconds. Make a sauce in a small pan: For each person combine 1 tablespoon of tamari soy sauce, 1 tablespoon of hot shiitake stock, a drop of squeezed lemon, and 1 to 2 drops of gingerroot juice. At the table serve sauce individually to each person, garnished with the scallions. The tofu is then picked up, dipped in the sauce, and eaten.

Deep-Fried Tofu with Kuzu Sauce

In Japan, deep-fried tofu is called *aburage*. There are tales of mountain folk traveling home with a recent purchase of aburage on their back who find it missing when they arrive. It was said that a crafty fox had stolen it because, as every child knows, foxes love aburage. At Shinto shrines today, offerings of aburage are still offered to fox guardian spirits.

- 1 strip kombu, 6 to 8 inches long
- 3 cups spring water
- Tamari soy sauce
- 1 pound firm tofu
- 3 tablespoons arrowroot or whole wheat flour
- Light sesame oil
- 1 cup diced onion
- 4 tablespoons kuzu
- ½ cup sliced scallions
- 1 teaspoon grated daikon

Wash the kombu and put it in a pot with the water. Bring to a boil, cover, and reduce the heat to medium-low. Simmer for about 10 minutes. Remove the kombu and set aside for another recipe. Season the water with a little tamari soy sauce to taste. Drain the tofu and slice into 1-inch-thick slices and cover with arrowroot or whole wheat flour. This prevents the oil from splashing and keeps the tofu soft. Deep-fry each slice until golden brown in at least 1 inch of light sesame oil. Remove and drain the excess oil from the tofu on paper towels. Place the deep-fried tofu and the diced onions in the tamari-seasoned water and simmer for 15 to 20 minutes. After the onions are soft and the tofu has cooked sufficiently, remove the tofu and place it in a serving dish. Then, dilute a little kuzu in cold water and add it to the tamari-seasoned broth. Add the sliced scallions to the kuzu sauce and pour the hot sauce over the deep-fried tofu. Serve immediately, before the aburage vanishes! Serve with a teaspoon of grated daikon.

Dried Tofu, Carrots, and Onions

- 2 tablespoons dark sesame oil
- 1 cup onions, sliced into half moons
- 1 cup carrots, cut into matchsticks
- Spring water
- 1 cup dried tofu, soaked and sliced
- 1 tablespoon tamari soy sauce

Heat the sesame oil in a frying pan and add the onions. Sauté for 1 to 2 minutes. Add the carrots and enough water to cover the bottom of the pan. Add the sliced tofu and sauté for 1 to 2 minutes. Bring to a boil. Add a little tamari soy sauce. Reduce the heat to low and cover. Simmer for several minutes, or until the carrots and onions are done. Season with a little more tamari soy sauce, mix, and sauté until all liquid has evaporated. Transfer to a serving bowl and serve.

Sautéed Okara and Vegetables

Okara is the soybean pulp left over from making tofu. Beige in color, okara has a fine-grained texture and is high in fiber. It is traditionally used to flavor and give body to soups, casseroles, croquettes, and vegetable and grain dishes.

- 1 celery stalk, cut in half and thinly sliced
- 1 bunch scallions and scallion roots, chopped
- 3 to 4 tablespoons dark sesame oil
- ½ cup burdock, quartered and sliced
- 3½ to 4 cups okara
- 1½ tablespoons tamari soy sauce, or ¾ teaspoon sea salt
- 1 handful tamari roasted almonds, chopped

Sauté the celery and finely chopped scallion roots in the oil for about 1 to 2 minutes. Add the burdock and sauté for 5 to 10 minutes. Add the okara and sauté for about 10 minutes. Stir constantly to avoid burning. Add the tamari soy sauce for a richer flavor or sea salt, which gives the dish a natural color. Add the almonds and scallions. Sauté and mix just for a few more seconds. The vegetables should be a little crispy.

Variations: Other vegetables, such as dried daikon, shiitake mushrooms, or carrots, may be substituted. Also arame sea vegetable is especially good cooked with okara—the arame is cooked first and the okara is added at the end.

YUBA

Yuba is the skin that forms on the surface of soy milk in the making of tofu. In Japan yuba has a cuisine all its own, and there are many specialty shops serving only dishes made with yuba. It is usually prepared in large flat sheets about 12 to 15 inches to a side. To prepare yuba, follow the basic recipe for homemade tofu on page 265.

Pour the soy milk into a cast-iron pot to a level about 1 to 1½ inches deep. Skim off the foam. Heat the soy milk to steaming but not quite boiling. It takes about 5 to 10 minutes for a film to form on the surface. With a knife trim the skin around the edges of the pot and gently lift off entire sheet with a long moistened chopstick. Drain for a few seconds over the pot and set over another pot to drain and cool for about 5 minutes. Transfer the yuba to a plate. Continue lifting yuba in 5 to 10 minute intervals until nearly all the soy milk has evaporated. The residue in the bottom of the pot is especially delicious as a drink. Serve the yuba hot and season with a little tamari soy sauce.

Yuba can also be cut and folded into rolls, dumplings, and cutlets and stuffed with cooked vegetables, sea vegetables, or miso.

TEMPEH

Tempeh is a whole fermented soy food that is traditionally eaten in Indonesia. I first tasted it in Amsterdam, where there are many Indonesians, and found it chewy, delectable, and satisfying. It gives great energy, especially to vegetarians, and is very appealing to those in transition from animal food. Its taste and texture are somewhat similar to pork or chicken. Tempeh is easy to digest and is appropriate for any age, even for just-weaned babies. Tempeh, like miso and other fermented soy products, is a natural source of vitamin B_{12} and other important nutrients.

Tempeh can be made at home using a special tempeh starter. It is also increasingly available in natural foods stores. At our home we use it regularly with vegetables, sea vegetables, and grains. Tempeh should always be cooked, not eaten raw. It can be cooked for a short time or long time, pan-fried or steamed, or deep-fried or broiled. For little children it should be very well cooked with kombu until soft and served without salt or tamari soy sauce. Tempeh keeps well in the refrigerator for a week or more. It may also be frozen for considerably longer periods. On my travels I have carried it wrapped in plastic, and it has kept fresh for several days. Even if it turns a little moldy and sour, the spoiled part can be scraped off and the remainder eaten. Medicinally, Michio recommends tempeh for restoring energy and vitality. I highly recommend this wonderful food, a little of which can be eaten every day.

Homemade Tempeh

This is the basic method of making tempeh adapted for a modern urban home. After the initial preparation of the soybeans, the mixture needs to incubate for 22 to 28 hours, so plan accordingly. Tempeh starter is available in many natural foods stores, or it can be ordered from The Farm, 156 Drakes Lane, Summertown, TN 38483.

2½ cups organic yellow soybeans
Spring water
1½ tablespoons rice vinegar
1 teaspoon tempeh starter

Wash and drain the soybeans. Then put them in a pot with 7½ cups water and bring to a boil. Simmer for 20 minutes, remove from heat, cover, and let sit for 2 hours. Drain the water from the pot; then rub the beans briskly between your palms for 3 minutes to remove hulls. Fill the pot with fresh water and stir gently in a circular motion until hulls rise. Pour off the water and hulls into a colander or strainer. Refill the pot with water and repeat the process 3 to 5 times, until all the bean skins are discarded. Add 10 cups of hot water and the vinegar to the drained beans. Bring to a boil and cook, uncovered, over medium-high heat for 45 minutes. Pour the beans into a colander and drain in the sink for several minutes. Shake well to reduce the moisture and transfer the beans to a baking pan or tray lined with cotton cloth or a dish towel. Spread the beans out evenly and allow to sit for 20 to 30 minutes. Stir occasionally until the beans have cooled to body temperature and their surface is almost dry. Fan or pat the surface of the beans with a towel to reduce moisture and transfer beans to another baking pan, large bowl, or plastic bag.

Sprinkle the tempeh starter evenly over the beans and mix for 2 minutes with a large spoon or shake vigorously if using a bag. Lay two 7- by 8-inch self-locking plastic bags on top of each other on a wooden board or four thicknesses of clean, soft cheesecloth. Poke holes through bags with a clean nail or a large sewing needle at ½- to ¾-inch intervals to form a perforated pattern of holes. This will allow mold to breathe during incubation. Fill the bags half full with the beans and close or seal. Place the bags on a flat surface and with the palm of your hand or a spatula press the upper surface of bag to distribute the beans uniformly in layer ½ to 1 inch thick. (The beans may instead be put in a baking pan, frying pan, or pie plates rather than bags and covered with aluminum foil and perforated as before.) Place the tempeh containers in an incubator which can be made from a Styrofoam cooler (available at the hardware store for a couple of dollars). Poke a small hole in one side and insert a thermometer. Poke 1-inch-diameter hole in the top of cooler and insert a lamp dimmer (also available at the hardware store) and connect it to a wall plug. Insert a 20-watt light bulb into the dimmer. (You can also use a plastic ice chest and rather than poking holes run the cord in beneath the lid and set the thermometer inside. A small night light can be used instead of a dimmer and bulb, but it is more difficult to regulate the light and thus the temperature in this way.) Set tempeh containers on a rack of any kind (steamer, bowl, dish) in the incubator to facilitate air circulation.

Place the incubator near the oven, hot water heater, woodstove, or other warm area. In winter, cover the incubator with blankets. Incubate the tempeh at exactly 86 to 88 degrees for 22 to 28 hours. Monitor the temperature and adjust the dimmer or light accordingly, especially every two hours toward the end.

Tempeh cakes should have a dense uniform white mycelium when ready. Good tempeh has a clear, pleasant, sweet, or mushroomy aroma and can be lifted as a single cake and held without crumbling. Gray mycelium or black sporulation near the pinholes or edges indicates overincubation, but tempeh is still all right to eat if the aroma is fresh. The main cause of failure is overheating which results in a rotten smell or an odor similar to strong ammonia or alcohol. This tempeh is inedible and should be discarded. Undercooked tempeh is wet, slimy, sticky, or crumbles easily when picked up. For further information on the ins and outs of making tempeh consult *The Book of Tempeh* by William Shurtleff and Akiko Aoyagi (Harper & Row, 1979).

TEMPEH IN SOUP

Cut tempeh into small cubes and boil with daikon, cut into rounds, and wakame, which has been soaked until soft. When tender, add the miso and cook for several minutes longer. For a clear soup, cook tempeh with carrots, onions, and burdock. Add tamari soy sauce or sea salt and kuzu diluted in cold water at the end of cooking and cook for 5 minutes longer. Garnish with chopped scallions and serve.

TEMPEH WITH VEGETABLES

Cut the tempeh into small cubes and pan-fry it in a little sesame oil with scallions or with vegetables for a short time so that they remain crisp. To make a sauce, pan-fry the tempeh and vegetables with a little tamari soy sauce, dissolve 1 tablespoon kuzu in 1½ cups water, and add it to the mixture. Boil until the kuzu is transparent. Watercress, celery, or tofu cooked with tempeh in this way is very delicious. Another method is to pan-fry or boil tempeh with tamari soy sauce. Slice many different vegetables, such as cabbage, carrots, celery, kale, or collards, on the diagonal. Put the vegetables in a pot (with a little oil if desired) and put the tempeh on top. Quickly cook with a small amount of water, mix, and serve.

FRIED RICE OR NOODLES AND TEMPEH

Cut the tempeh into cubes and pan-fry on each side for 5 to 10 minutes over low heat. Slice a variety of vegetables into small pieces and pan-fry briefly. Add cooked rice or noodles and cooked tempeh. Cover, cook for 5 to 10 minutes, adding a small amount of water if necessary. At the end of cooking, add tamari soy sauce to taste, cook a few more minutes, mix, and serve.

Cabbage-Roll Tempeh

This is one of my favorite tempeh dishes.

5 to 6 green cabbage or Chinese cabbage leaves, lightly steamed
5 to 6 slices tempeh, 2 by 3 inches
Spring water
Tamari soy sauce
Grated fresh ginger
5 to 6 strips *kampyo* (dried gourd strips), soaked and cut into 5- to 6-inch lengths; if not available, toothpicks will suffice to fasten the cabbage leaves
2 strips kombu, 6 to 8 inches long, soaked
Kuzu
Sliced scallions for garnish

Green cabbage leaves are often hard to remove. Steam the entire head of cabbage several minutes, remove leaves and allow to cool slightly. If using Chinese cabbage leaves, remove from stem and boil in water for 2 to 3 minutes. Place the tempeh in a saucepan. Add water to just cover the tempeh. Add tamari soy sauce for a mild salt taste. Add ½ teaspoon of grated fresh ginger. Bring to a boil, cover, and reduce the heat to low. Simmer for 15 to 20 minutes. Remove and drain. Wrap each piece of tempeh in a cabbage leaf. Tie a strip of kampyo squash around each cabbage roll or fasten the cabbage leaf with a toothpick. Place the kombu in the bottom of a frying pan and set the cabbage rolls on top of the kombu. Add water to half or three-quarters cover the cabbage rolls. Bring to a boil, cover, and reduce the heat to low. Simmer a short time if you like the rolls slightly crisp and bright green. For elderly people, sick persons, or children cook a long time until cabbage rolls are very soft and tender. Remove the cabbage rolls and place in a serving dish. Thicken the remaining cooking water with diluted kuzu, stirring constantly to avoid lumping. Season with a little grated ginger and tamari soy sauce to taste. There should be a mild but not strong salt taste. Pour the sauce over the cabbage rolls. Garnish with a few sliced scallions and serve.

Barley Stew with Tempeh

1 cup barley
Spring water
Dark sesame oil
2 celery stalks, sliced
2 cups sliced cabbage
1 carrot cut into matchsticks
4 ounces tempeh
1 strip kombu or wakame, soaked
Tamari soy sauce or miso
Sliced scallions for garnish

Soak the barley in 4 cups of water overnight and then boil for 1 hour. Set aside. In another pot, add some oil and sauté quickly in sequence the celery, cabbage, carrots, and tempeh. Add the soaked and cut sea vegetables. Add the barley and simmer for up to 30 minutes, adding more water, if desired. Add tamari soy sauce or miso to season and garnish with scallions.

Tempeh Kinpira

4 medium-sized burdock
Dark sesame oil (optional)
8 ounces tempeh, cubed
Spring water
Tamari soy sauce
Grated fresh ginger or ginger-root juice

Cut the burdock into very thin matchstick pieces. Sauté over low to medium heat with or without oil. Place the cubed tempeh on top. Add a little water and tamari soy sauce. Cover and steam until soft. When almost done, add more tamari soy sauce to taste. Grated ginger or ginger juice can also be added for greater digestibility.

Variations: Carrots cut into matchsticks can be sautéed after the burdock in the same pan or eliminate the burdock and cook carrots and thinly sliced onions. This makes a very sweet dish, especially suitable for children.

Tempeh with Arame

8 ounces tempeh
2½ ounces arame
1 onion, thinly sliced
½ to 1 carrot, cut into matchsticks
Tamari soy sauce

Cut the tempeh into small cubes. To make a strong dish, pan-fry the tempeh until brown or just leave plain. Soak the arame for 10 minutes, then put the arame and soaking water into a pot. Add the onion and carrot and place the tempeh on top. Add tamari soy sauce to taste. The water should cover the vegetables but it's not necessary to cover the tempeh. Boil over medium heat for 30 minutes.

Tempeh Paella

Paella is a traditional Spanish dish made with rice, vegetables, and various combinations of meat, poultry, and seafood. Tempeh paella is very popular among macrobiotic families in Europe.

- 1 to 2 strips kombu
- 2 cups brown rice
- Dark sesame oil
- 1 cup cubed celery
- 1 cup cubed onion
- 1 cup cubed carrots
- ½ cup cubed burdock
- 8 ounces tempeh
- Tamari soy sauce
- 2 to 2½ cups spring water
- Ginger juice

Soak the kombu for 2 hours. Dry-roast the brown rice in a dry frying pan or with a little oil until lightly brown and fragrant. Set aside. Pan-fry the vegetables in a little oil over high heat, starting with the celery, then adding onion, carrots, and finally the burdock. Cut the kombu into small squares and add it to the vegetables. Pan-fry the tempeh until dry with a little tamari soy sauce. Layer the vegetables in the above order in a pressure cooker, followed by the kombu, tempeh, and rice on top. Add tamari soy sauce to taste. Pressure-cook for 30 to 40 minutes with 2 cups water or boil in 2½ cups water until water is absorbed. At the end of cooking, mix all the ingredients together. Season with a little juice squeezed from freshly grated ginger.

Tempeh Shish Kebab

This is a favorite for parties or summer barbecues. Quantity of ingredients will vary with number of people served and how items are arranged on skewers.

- Carrots
- Burdock
- Red radishes
- Umeboshi plums
- Broccoli flowerets
- Cauliflower flowerets
- Tempeh
- Tamari soy sauce

Cut the carrots and burdock into chunks and lightly boil until soft but not falling apart. Boil the small red radishes with 1 or 2 umeboshi plums for 15 minutes, or until water has boiled away. Boil the broccoli so that it is still bright green and crunchy. Boil the cauliflower similarly. Pan-fry or boil tempeh with a little tamari soy sauce until soft but still crispy. Arrange the ingredients attractively on skewers and serve hot.

NATTO

Natto is a fermented soybean product that looks like baked beans connected by long sticky strands. It is very famous in northern Japan where it was traditionally prepared by soaking, steaming, and wrapping soybeans in rice stalks and hanging them over the kitchen stove to ferment naturally. In the region where I grew up, natto was not so very popular and the first time I tasted it was in New York. Natto is high in protein, calcium, iron, and niacin and aids in the smooth functioning of the intestines. Its strong odor may take some getting used to. About 50 percent of macrobiotic people come to love it, while the other 50 percent can't stand it. Natto is traditionally eaten as a small side dish with a little tamari soy sauce, grated ginger, grated daikon, horseradish, mustard, sliced scallions, jinenjo mountain potato, or raw egg yolk. It is also enjoyed mixed with brown rice, served on top of buckwheat noodles, or spread on mochi. Natto can be made at home with *koji,* a grain starter also used in making miso, tamari soy sauce, and sake. Both koji and ready-to-eat natto are available in select natural foods stores. Natto will keep fresh in the refrigerator several weeks and can be frozen indefinitely. It does not need to be recooked when eaten by itself or placed on top of grains or noodles. However, for more elaborate dishes, it may be lightly sautéed or deep-fried.

Homemade Natto

4 cups organic soybeans
Spring water
3½ ounces koji starter

Wash the soybeans and soak for 4 to 6 hours. Discard the soaking water. Put the beans in a pressure cooker and cover with water. Cooking without the cover, bring to a boil, reduce the heat to low, and simmer until a white foam floats to the top. Skim and discard foam and any skins that float to the surface. Boil and skim several times until foam stops forming. Put the cover on and bring to pressure. Cook for 30 to 45 minutes. Bring the pressure down by running cold water over the outside of the pressure cooker. Drain, cool, and place beans in pot. Mix the koji with cooked beans. Cover the pot with a tight-fitting lid and place in a 102- to 104-degree oven. (This is the usual temperature produced by a pilot light.) Let the natto ferment for 22 to 24 hours without uncovering the pot or opening the oven door. Remove from the oven, place in a container, and put in the freezer or beans will continue to ferment and become inedible. This recipe makes twelve 7½-ounce containers of natto. Remove the natto from the freezer as needed, thaw, and serve.

CHAPTER 23

SEA VEGETABLES

Plucking water grasses,
In the field—
A frog startles me.

—*Kimie*

せりつみや
びっくりさせる
蛙かな
きみ子

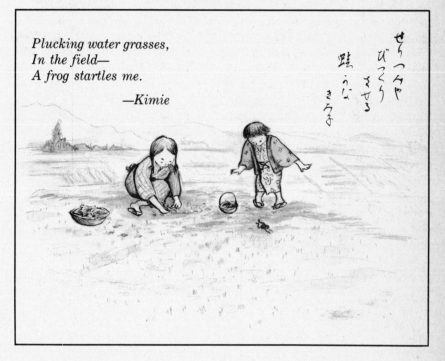

Each spring a fisherman's wife from Oki Island on the Sea of Japan would journey to our mountain village and go door to door selling sea vegetables. Strapped on her back was dried *wakame,* a chief ingredient used in making miso soup. Wakame usually comes in long thin strips, but this wakame (*izumo-wakame*) was specially dried in large sheets like nori, the sea vegetable used in wrapping sushi. My mother bought sufficient quantity to last the coming year. The wakame was so nice and tender that it didn't need cooking. We cut it with scissors, roasted it briefly over an open flame, and used it in teas, for snacks, in miso soup, as an addition to daikon pickles, crushed as a condiment on top of brown rice, or as wrapping for rice balls. There is also a type of nori (*fu-nori*) that we used in making a wonderful hair shampoo. We soaked it in a bucket, squeezed out the starch with a cheesecloth, and mixed it in soapy water.

In my youth I took seaweeds for granted, and it wasn't until I was unable to get them in later life that I fully appreciated their value. Once in 1952, during my first pregnancy, I was in Paris and craved sea vegetables but couldn't find any. While trooping around the streets, I came upon a fish market and discovered a bunch of clams sitting in a bed of giant kelp. I offered to buy the kelp, but the shopkeeper, surprised at my desire to devour the seaweed instead of the clams, readily gave me the slimy green substance. The kelp was very tough, but I cooked it a long time, and it satisfied my body's need for extra minerals.

For optimal health, we need to balance foods that grow above the ground with those that grow below the sea. The deep ocean, from which primordial life evolved, has a salty composition similar to human blood. Sea vegetables are high in iron, calcium, iodine, vitamins A, B_{12}, C, and other nutrients and are a perfect complement to whole grains, beans, and vegetables growing on land. The fiber in sea plants is softer than in land plants and more digestible. Wild bears, deer, foxes, and domesticated horses and cattle along coastal regions all naturally nibble seaweed and algae on the rocks and shore. By eating a small amount of this ancient form of life each day, we strengthen our bodies, experience more of the energy of the earth as a whole, and develop toward universal consciousness.

ORIGIN AND BENEFITS

In the mid-1960s, after Erewhon started, a wide variety of sea vegetables became available in natural foods stores across the United States and Canada. Some people had the impression that because these foods were imported from Japan that they were unique to Far Eastern cuisine. Actually, nearly all traditional societies harvested algae, grasses, and edible plants from the sea, including Indians in both North and South America, the Celts, Vikings, Russians, Mediterranean cultures, the Chinese, Africans along the coastline, the original Australians, and islanders of the Pacific. For example, from colonial days through the nineteenth century, dulse gathered from the Atlantic Ocean was widely consumed as a snack and added to breads and stews in the towns and cities of New England. Seaweeds have also been used the world over for fertilizer, as a source of salt, and for soda used in making glass. In the twentieth century, sea vegetables have been used extensively for industrial purposes, in cosmetics, and as fillers, stabilizers, and emulsifiers for processed foods. Happily, with the advent of the modern natural foods movement, whole sea vegetables, including alaria, laver, and kelp (similar to wakame, nori, and kombu respectively), are once again being harvested off the coasts of North America in Maine, Nova Scotia, and California.

In the Orient the health benefits of sea vegetables are well known. The dark black and purple seaweeds give a unique rich taste, flavor, and color to meals. They are traditionally taken to strengthen the kidneys, intestines, digestive system, and sexual organs, as well as to improve the power of the will and provide clear judgment. Seaweeds are also taken medicinally to dissolve excess fat and cholesterol deposits resulting from past consumption of meat and other animal food. The inhabitants of Oki Island—where my family's special wakame came from—enjoy the greatest longevity of any region of Japan. The therapeutic value of sea vegetables was recognized in the West in the 1960s and 1970s when scientists at McGill University reported that common seaweeds helped eliminate nuclear radiation and fallout from the body. Medical researchers in Japan have recently confirmed folk tradition and found that seaweeds help reverse hardening of the arteries, bring down high blood pressure, and regress tumors.

GETTING STARTED

Most Westerners who are not accustomed to sea vegetables at first find their flavor, smell, and texture foreign. However, properly cooked and introduced into the diet gradually, these vegetables become truly appetizing and are soon viewed as an integral part of the new way of eating.

In the beginning I recommend starting with arame, nori, and dulse, which are milder tasting, and then moving on to kombu, wakame, and hiziki, which are stronger and more flavorful. Arame has a naturally sweet taste and light texture which lends itself to serving as a small side dish and is the seaweed most commonly enjoyed by newcomers. Nori comes in sheets which can be lightly toasted for a few seconds over an open flame and can be used in wrapping sushi or rice balls or crushed and sprinkled on soups, salads, grains, or vegetables. Dulse usually comes in thin strips or in powder form and also can be roasted and used as a condiment.

Wakame, kombu, and hiziki may be introduced in small amounts, especially in miso soups and in combination with root vegetables or whole soybeans. Long-time cooking changes their aroma, and their fishy taste and smell disappear. It also makes them tender and more digestible. In previous chapters, I have described how a little kombu enhances the taste of grains and beans and shortens their cooking time. Simply place a 3- to 6-inch piece of kombu beneath the other ingredients in the pressure cooker or pot. This is a simple way to make the acquaintance of this savory sea vegetable as is kombu stock, the basic broth for noodles and stews, described in the soup chapter.

Over time, as your taste for these special foods develops, you can try the more complex recipes as well as experiment with other, lesser-known varieties you may find in specialty stores or harvest yourself. Unlike mushrooms, there are no toxic varieties of seaweed, so you don't have to worry about exploring and sampling unfamiliar underwa-

COOKING SEAWEED

Sea Vegetable	Cleaning	Dry Weight	Cooked Volume	Cooking Time	Cooked Appearance	Main Uses
Agar agar	see package instructions			5 to 10 minutes white	translucent white	kanten fruit gelatin; vegetable aspic
Arame	rinse 1 to 3 times	1 ounce	2 cups	30 to 40 minutes	dark brown	side dish with sautéed root vegetables, tofu, or beans; in salads
Dulse	rinse			5 to 10 minutes	red/purple	dry-roasted as a garnish for soups and salads
Hiziki	rinse 1 to 3 times or soak 5 minutes	1 ounce	5 cups	45 to 60 minutes	black	side dish with sautéed root vegetables; baked or boiled; in salads
Irish Moss	soak 20 to 30 minutes			30 minutes	translucent white	gelatins, tea

Kombu	rinse and soak 3 to 5 minutes	1 ounce	2 to 3 cups	35 to 40 minutes	green/black	dashi broth; side dish; condiment; cooked with grains and beans
Mekabu	rinse and soak 3 to 5 minutes	1 ounce	2 to 3 cups	35 to 40 minutes	green/black	side dish
Nori	none			toast 1 minute or less	green	sushi; rice balls; garnish for soups, salads, noodles; casseroles
Wakame	rinse and soak 3 to 5 minutes	1 ounce	3 cups	5 to 10 minutes	translucent green	miso soup; side dish; in salads

ter plants. Some varieties may be foul-smelling, tough, and disagreeable to the taste, but they will not harm you. Using sea vegetables harvested from polluted water, however, should be carefully avoided because it can affect the quality. A clean shore away from industrial areas is best.

As the physical and mental benefits of sea vegetables are noticed, you will find yourself including a little bit in some form at nearly every meal. As with beans, it is preferable to limit consumption to only a small amount at a time. In addition to the recipes that follow, sea vegetables are also included in some of the soups, salads, vegetable dishes, grain dishes, condiments, pickles, and desserts described elsewhere in this book. Basic information is summarized on pages 282 and 283.

COOKING SEA VEGETABLES

Washing and, in some cases, soaking sea vegetables are very important to remove dust, sand, and dirt and prevent a gritty taste. Cleaning methods are explained below for each variety. Please master these thoroughly and your enjoyment of seaweed will be much enhanced.

Usually we use no oil in cooking kombu and wakame, which are naturally oily, and these plants are generally boiled or cooked in some other way. Hiziki and arame, on the other hand, go very well with oil and are commonly sautéed. Nori and dulse toast up quickly and do not need further cooking. Wakame, arame, and other thinner sea vegetables need only moderate cooking, while kombu, hiziki, and thicker varieties require longer time cooking to become tender.

Although harvested from sea water, sea vegetables do not have a high sodium content or naturally salty taste. Even so, seasoning them with sea salt usually makes for too sharp a taste and too salty a flavor. Instead, a little tamari soy sauce is usually added to sea vegetables at the beginning of cooking and brings out their natural sweetness. Occasionally, I will soften a very tough variety with a little rice vinegar or mirin.

Beans and root vegetables, such as burdock, carrots, onions, lotus root, and daikon, go especially well with sea vegetables. When cooking, wakame is usually prepared on one side of the vegetables, while other seaweeds are usually layered on the bottom of the pot and topped with other vegetables. The colors of these versatile foods from the ocean range from black to deep brown, olive, bright green, purple, and red and, when attractively presented, contribute to the aesthetic enjoyment of the meal. Hiziki's black tresses are especially beautiful nestled in an array of colorful vegetables, beans, and grains.

Dried sea vegetables will keep almost indefinitely, at least a century. While they do not need to be tightly covered, it is a good idea to keep them in a cool, dark place in a jar or crock. Roasted sea vegetables that have been ground in a suribachi or bowl into powder for condiments should be tightly sealed to maintain their freshness. Cooked sea vegetables will keep about a week in the refrigerator and should be kept in closed containers until heated as leftovers.

ARAME

Arame grows on both coasts of the Pacific, including regions of Japan and Peru. Its fronds resemble big, very tough oak leaves, and in the West arame is known as *Sea Oak*. After harvesting, shredding, and drying in the sun and wind, arame shrinks down to a clump of wiry black threads. When cooked it turns dark brown and has a sweet, delicate taste. Arame is commonly sautéed with root vegetables, tofu, or soybeans and can be substituted in any recipe calling for the stronger, thicker, and slightly longer-cooking hiziki. High in complex carbohydrates, fiber, niacin, calcium, iron, and iodine, arame is traditionally used to help relieve female disorders and to bring down high blood pressure.

Arame, like kombu, is a firm sea vegetable. It is parboiled, shredded, and diced by the time you purchase it. Accordingly, it does not usually have heavy dust as other seaweeds may. Its cooking time is shorter than that of hiziki, although it is cooked in the same manner.

To clean arame, place a handful or the amount to be cooked on a white plate and pick or shake out any loose dust. Transfer the sea vegetable to a pot, cover and rinse quickly with plenty of cold water from one to three times depending on how clean the arame is. Don't use warm water which depletes minerals. Swish completely with your hands and pour out each rinse water. The last time, scoop out the seaweed by hand and transfer it to a strainer. A residue of sand and grit should remain at the bottom of the pot. The final rinse water is customarily saved for cooking. For a strong, rich taste arame should not be soaked. After the final rinse, the sea vegetable may be left in the strainer to drain while the other beans or vegetables to be cooked are cut. One ounce of dried arame will expand to about 2 cups when cooked.

Arame with Onions

- 1 ounce dried arame
- 1 tablespoon dark sesame oil
- 2 medium-sized onions, sliced
- Spring water
- 2 to 3 tablespoons tamari soy sauce

Wash and drain the arame. Brush a frying pan with the oil and heat it. Add the onions and sauté for 2 to 3 minutes. Place the arame on top of the onions and add water to just cover the onions. Bring to a boil, turn the heat to low, and add a small amount of tamari soy sauce. Cover and simmer for about 40 to 50 minutes. Add more tamari soy sauce to taste.

The mixture should have a mild salt taste but not be overly salty. Simmer for another 15 to 20 minutes and then mix and stir until the liquid has evaporated.

Variations: For those who need to limit their oil intake, the arame may be sautéed with 3 tablespoons of water. One carrot cut into matchsticks may be added to the basic recipe. Lotus root or dried daikon also go well with arame and onions. For an especially rich taste, add 1½ cups of cubed tempeh. Roasted sesame seeds, chopped very fine, make a nice garnish.

Arame with Sweet Corn

- 1 ounce dried arame
- 1 tablespoon dark sesame oil
- 1 cup onions, sliced in half moons
- Spring water
- 2 to 3 tablespoons tamari soy sauce
- 2 cups fresh sweet corn kernels

Clean the arame and put it in a strainer to drain. Oil a frying pan and heat it. Sauté the onions for 1 to 2 minutes, stirring to ensure even cooking. Add the arame on top and enough water to just cover the onions. Add a little tamari soy sauce. Cover and bring to a boil, then turn flame to medium-low, and simmer for about 20 minutes. Add the corn and a little more tamari soy sauce to taste. Simmer for 10 to 15 minutes and then mix until the liquid has evaporated.

Arame with Dried Tofu and Carrots

- 1 ounce dried arame
- 2 pieces dried tofu, soaked and cubed
- 1 teaspoon dark sesame oil
- 1 cup carrots, cut into matchsticks
- Spring water
- 2 to 3 tablespoons tamari soy sauce

Wash the arame and put it in a colander to drain. Put the dried tofu in a bowl and soak it for 2 to 3 minutes in boiling water until soft. Rinse the tofu under cold water, squeeze out the liquid, and slice into cubes. Heat the oil in a frying pan. Add the arame and carrots and sauté for 1 to 2 minutes. Add the dried tofu and water to cover the arame and carrots. Add a little tamari soy sauce. Bring to a boil, cover, and reduce the heat to low. Simmer for 40 to 45 minutes. Season with a little more tamari soy sauce to taste and simmer for 10 to 15 minutes longer. When nearly all the all the liquid has evaporated, mix and serve.

HIZIKI

Hiziki (or hijiki) is a pine-needle-shaped sea vegetable that is found in East Asian waters stretching from Japan along the China coast to as far south as Hong Kong. It is harvested at low tide in the spring and sun-dried and packaged. Hiziki has a strong ocean flavor and is highly valued for its nutty aroma. Its coarse black strands become very tender when properly cooked, and its crispy texture improves any meal.

High in minerals, hiziki contains ten times more calcium than a comparable volume of milk, cheese, or other dairy food. It is also high in iron, protein, vitamins A, B_1, and B_{12}. In traditional Oriental medicine, hiziki is recommended for strengthening the intestines, producing beautiful shining hair, and purifying the blood. When cooked it swells to five times its original volume, so plan accordingly. Hiziki can be prepared in a large batch and keeps well under refrigeration. As a side dish it is usually sautéed in sesame oil but it can also be boiled, steamed, baked, or deep-fried in combination with other foods. In summertime it is popular in salads.

Hiziki is cleaned in a way similar to arame (see p. 285). The final rinsing water is customarily saved for cooking unless the hiziki is too strong tasting. If the hiziki, however, is too tough, it may be soaked for no more than 5 minutes. Soaking in this way usually gives it a strong, rich taste.

Hiziki with Onions

1 ounce dried hiziki
1 teaspoon dark sesame oil
2 onions, sliced
Spring water
2 to 3 tablespoons tamari soy sauce

Wash and drain the hiziki. Brush a frying pan with oil and heat it. Add the onions and sauté for 2 to 3 minutes. Put the hiziki on top of the onions and add water to just cover the onions. Bring to a boil, turn the heat to low, and add a small amount of tamari soy sauce. Cover and simmer for about 45 to 60 minutes. Add more tamari soy sauce to taste. The mixture should have a mild salty taste. Simmer for another 15 to 20 minutes, or until the liquid has almost evaporated.

Variations: Sliced carrots, fresh lotus root, and deep-fried tofu or dried tofu go well with this basic preparation.

Hiziki with Soybeans

1 ounce dried hiziki
½ cup soybeans
Spring water
2 to 3 tablespoons tamari soy sauce

Wash hiziki, drain, and slice the strands into 1- to 2-inch pieces. Wash the soybeans and dry-roast them over low heat until golden brown, watching carefully to prevent burning. The beans may also be soaked overnight to soften instead of roasting. Stir constantly to roast the beans evenly and avoid burning. Put the hiziki in a pot. Put the soybeans on top but don't mix them together. Add enough spring water to cover the top of the hiziki. Bring to a boil, cover, and turn the heat to low. Simmer until the beans are 80 percent done, about 40 to 50 minutes. Season with tamari soy sauce to taste and simmer until beans are done, about another 10 minutes. Remove the cover, raise the heat slightly, and evaporate most of remaining liquid. Mix and serve.

Hiziki with Fried Tofu

1 cup tofu, cut into 1-inch cubes or 2-inch rectangles
Light sesame oil
1 ounce dried hiziki
1 cup onions cut into half moons
1 cup carrots cut into matchsticks
Spring water
3 to 4 tablespoons tamari soy sauce

Cut the tofu and deep-fry it in a deep pot filled with 1 inch of oil until it is golden brown. Put on paper towels to drain off any excess oil. Wash the hiziki and put it in a pot; add the onions and carrots. Put the tofu on top. Add water to cover the hiziki but not the vegetables and tofu. Add a little tamari soy sauce and bring to a boil. Cover, reduce the heat to low, and simmer for about 45 minutes. Add a little more seasoning to create a mild salt taste and simmer until almost all the remaining liquid has evaporated. Mix and serve.

Hiziki Rolls

These delicious rolls are cut up into spiral rounds like sushi. They are a great way to eat sea vegetables while traveling and make attractive hors d'oeuvres for a party.

- 1 ounce dried hiziki
- 1 medium carrot, cut into matchsticks
- 1 small onion, cut into half moons
- 1 teaspoon dark sesame oil
- 1 to 2 tablespoons tamari soy sauce
- Spring water
- 1 large pie crust

Cook the hiziki, carrot, and onion together following the basic hiziki with onions recipe until all the liquid has evaporated, and let cool. Roll the pie crust out as in making a pie. Place the cooked mixture evenly on the crust. Leave about one inch around the outer edge of the crust uncovered by hiziki and vegetables. Roll up the crust, seal the edges with water, and press with a fork as in making strudel. Bake in a preheated 350-degree oven for about 30 to 35 minutes. After cooling, slice into 1-inch rounds and arrange on their sides on a platter.

Variation: Vegetables may be cooked separately from the hiziki and spread in thin layers on top of the seaweed after laying out the dough. Other vegetables may be substituted for carrots and onions, as well as tofu, though in baking tofu tends to lose moisture and may produce a soggy crust.

KOMBU

The *Laminaria* family of sea vegetables includes kombu, some kelps, tangle, oarweed, and other deep-ocean varieties. Japanese kombu is blackish-brown in color, has wide, thick celery-like leaves, and is gathered in cold seas off southern Hokkaido. The kelp most similar to kombu contains numerous rhizomes and roots and is found in abundance off the Pacific coast between British Columbia and San Francisco. Other edible varieties of kelp and Laminaria grow on rocks at low water levels in colder regions all around the world.

In Japan, kombu is harvested between July and September by boatmen with long poles. It is then dried on the ground by sun and wind. Some kombu washes up on shore and other kombu is cultivated, but their quality is not so good. After drying in a dark place for two to three years, kombu is packaged and sold in a variety of grades and forms. The city of Osaka is known for its superior kombu and there are said to be large warehouses stocking over 100 different kinds.

Without kombu, Japanese cuisine would not exist. Its distinctive taste is the basis for dashi, the traditional broth used as a stock for soup and noodles. It is enjoyed as a side dish or as an accompaniment to grains, beans, and root vegetables. Kombu is also made into teas, pickles, condiments, snacks, and candy. High in vitamins A, B_2, C, calcium, and iodine, kombu is therapeutic and protective against degenerative disease.

The Japanese kombu available in North American natural foods stores is usually called dashi kombu and is high in quality. It consists of dried flat strips about 3 to 18 inches long. To clean, wipe off the dust with a dry or moist towel. Do not, however, scrub the tiny white flecks off its outer surface. These are mineral salts and complex sugars that appear when the sea vegetable loses moisture and they contribute to its delicious taste and energy. Soak the kombu in cold water for 3 to 5 minutes or wash it thoroughly under cold running water. After soaking it will double or triple in size. Soak only long enough for the kombu to soften. If soaked too long, it becomes slippery and hard to cut.

There are many ways to cut kombu, including very fine, small cubes or squares, large slices, and long strips used to tie around other vegetables. Kombu is thick and requires a minimum of about 30 minutes to cook and become tender, and it can stand to be cooked even longer. Dashi kombu is traditionally saved and cooked after using in soup stock. After using kombu in making stock, remove it from the pot and cut it into small pieces and cook them with tamari soy sauce until the liquid has evaporated. For a stronger side dish, boil the kombu nishime-style until it is soft and thin, about 30 to 60 minutes. To make a nice condiment, clean the kombu, cut with scissors, soak in tamari soy sauce for 1 to 2 days, and cook for 3 to 5 hours very slowly until the tamari has evaporated. This is eaten in very small amounts.

Wakame, which is thinner and cooks much more quickly, may be substituted in any recipe calling for kombu. North American kelp and oarweed cook a bit more quickly than kombu and also can be used in any of the following recipes. The *Laminaria* plants are usually seasoned during cooking with tamari soy sauce. There are also two other forms of kombu available in selected natural foods stores. *Natto kombu,* prepared from a tougher plant, is precut into strands and can be cooked like hiziki except that it doesn't need washing. *Tororo kombu* is a finely shaven, paper-thin form that has been soaked in brown rice vinegar. It can be used to wrap rice balls or sushi, or used as a condiment over other dishes.

Boiled Kombu

1 strip kombu, 10 to 12 inches long
Spring water
1 onion, peeled and quartered
1 carrot cut into triangular shapes
1 teaspoon tamari soy sauce

Wash and soak the kombu for 3 to 5 minutes. Slice it in half, then cut it diagonally into 1-inch-long pieces. Put the sliced kombu in a pot. Add the onions, carrots, and enough soaking water to half cover the vegetables. Bring to a boil, reduce the heat to low, and simmer for 30 minutes. Add the tamari soy sauce and cook for 10 minutes longer.

Pressure-Cooked Shio Kombu

Shio kombu is a heavy thick dashi kombu. This condiment makes for a very strong dish.

- 1 ounce dried kombu
- 3 tablespoons tamari soy sauce
- ½ cup spring water

Wash and soak the kombu for 3 to 5 minutes. Cut with scissors into ¼-inch squares. Put the kombu in a pressure cooker and add the tamari soy sauce and water. Bring up to pressure and cook for 10 minutes. Let the pressure come down naturally, uncover, and simmer until all the liquid has evaporated.

Baked Kombu and Vegetables

- 1 3-inch strip kombu
- 2 onions, peeled and quartered
- 2 carrots cut into triangular shapes
- ½ cabbage sliced into ½-inch strips
- ½ cup spring water
- 1½ tablespoons tamari soy sauce

Wash and soak the kombu and put it in a baking dish. Arrange the onions in one side of the dish, the carrots in the center, and cabbage at the other side. (The vegetables should be separate to prevent the flavors from mixing.) Pour the water into a dish and add the tamari soy sauce. Cover and bake in a preheated 375-degree oven for 30 to 40 minutes, or until all the ingredients are tender.

Kombu, Carrots, and Burdock

- 2 to 3 strips kombu, 6 to 8 inches long
- 1 cup burdock cut in thick diagonals
- 2 cups carrots cut in large chunks
- Spring water
- 1 to 2 tablespoons tamari soy sauce

Soak the kombu and slice it into cubes. Put the kombu in the bottom of a pot, then cover it with the burdock and carrots. Add water to about half cover the carrots. Bring to a boil, reduce the heat to low, cover, and simmer until the carrots and burdock are soft. Season with a little tamari soy sauce, cover, and simmer until liquid has nearly evaporated. At the end of the cooking time, mix ingredients together to coat them with the juice and seasoning.

Kombu Carrot Rolls

2 strips kombu, 12 inches long
Spring water
8 strips kampyo (gourd strips)
4 medium-sized carrots

Soak the kombu in 2½ to 3 cups of water until it is soft enough to slice. Slice into 6-inch lengths. Soak the kampyo about 5 minutes and cut into 6-inch lengths. (Kampyo can be found in some natural foods stores or Oriental markets. If unavailable, simply soak another 6-inch strip of kombu several minutes and slice it into 8 thin strips about ¼ to ⅓ inch wide for tying.) Put a piece of kombu on a cutting board. Place one carrot on the strip. Roll up the carrot inside the kombu. Make sure you roll them as tightly as possible. Tie the kombu roll with the kampyo strips in three places spaced evenly apart. Continue to roll and tie the remaining kombu and carrots until ingredients are used up. Pour the soaking water from the kombu into a pot. Put the kombu rolls in the water and bring to a boil. Cover and reduce the heat to medium-low. Simmer for about 45 to 60 minutes, or until the kombu and carrots are very tender. Remove the rolls from the water and slice each roll into three 2-inch sections. Be sure each section is tied together. Arrange the sections on a platter and serve.

Variation: Burdock may be substituted for the carrots or combined with a piece of carrot inside each section of kombu.

To save time, this dish may be pressure-cooked. Put the water and kombu rolls in a pressure cooker. Bring to pressure. Reduce the heat to medium-low and cook for about 5 to 10 minutes. Usually this dish is made without additional seasoning, though a little tamari soy sauce may be added at the very end of cooking if desired.

Kombu and Dried Daikon

2 strips kombu
3 to 4 shiitake mushrooms, soaked, stemmed, and sliced
½ cup dried daikon, soaked and sliced
Vegetable soaking water
Tamari soy sauce

Wash, soak, and thinly slice the kombu. Put the kombu in a pot with the shiitake. Set the dried daikon on top. Add the soaking water to just cover and bring to a boil. Cover and turn the heat to low. Simmer for 40 to 45 minutes, or until the kombu is very soft. Season with a little tamari soy sauce to taste and simmer until remaining liquid has almost evaporated.

WAKAME

Wakame is harvested off Hokkaido Island and along the coasts of Korea and China. In appearance, texture, and taste it is similar to alaria, a sea vegetable that is found worldwide and is part of the traditional cuisine of Scotland, Ireland, and northern Europe. Wakame is extremely high in calcium and contains large amounts of iron, vitamins A and C, niacin, and protein. Medicinally, it is noted for its antibacterial properties and is used to cleanse the blood after childbirth.

To clean, wash wakame quickly under cold water to remove surface dust, then soak for 3 to 5 minutes. When softened, unfold wakame and rinse. The last soaking water may be kept and used in cooking, but in pouring it off be careful to leave behind any particles of sand at the bottom of the pot. However, if the soaking water is too salty, do not use it in cooking seaweed but save it for cooking beans or grains. After soaking, wakame turns a beautiful translucent green. To cut, slice down the center along the thick vein. Cut the soft outer portions into bite-sized pieces and then chop the harder central vein itself very finely to make sure of even cooking. Wakame cooks more quickly than most other seaweeds. In addition to miso soup, it is enjoyed prepared as a side dish with ground vegetables, baked and ground into a condiment, and deep-fried as a snack.

Wakame with Onions

---

1 ounce dried wakame
2 medium-sized onions, peeled and sliced
Soaking water
Tamari soy sauce, about 2 teaspoons

Wash, soak, and slice the wakame into 1-inch pieces. Put the wakame and onions in a pot side by side. Add enough soaking water to almost cover the seaweed. Bring to a boil, reduce the heat to low, and simmer for 30 minutes, or until tender. Some varieties take longer to cook than others. Add tamari soy sauce to taste and cook for 10 to 15 minutes longer.

Wakame with Sour Tofu Dressing

1½ ounces dried wakame
Spring water
3 umeboshi plums
16 ounces tofu
¼ cup sliced scallions or chives for garnish

Wash and soak the wakame. Pour a small amount of water into a pot and bring to a boil. Add the wakame and boil for 3 to 5 minutes. If the wakame is very tender just dip it in boiling water and remove. After cooking, slice the wakame into small pieces. Place in a serving dish. Purée the umeboshi in a suribachi into a smooth paste. Add the tofu and purée until creamy. Place the dressing in a serving dish and garnish with the sliced scallions or chives. Place a spoonful of tofu dressing on top of each serving of wakame.

Wakame and Scallions with Miso–Rice Vinegar Sauce

- 1 ounce dried wakame
- Spring water
- ½ cup sliced scallions
- 2 teaspoons puréed barley miso
- 4 teaspoons brown rice vinegar

Wash, soak, and slice the wakame into small pieces. Put the wakame in a saucepan with a little water. Bring to a boil, reduce the heat to low, and cover. Simmer several minutes. Remove, drain, and let cool. Transfer the wakame to a bowl and mix in the sliced scallions. Put the puréed barley miso and brown rice vinegar in a suribachi and purée. Add a little water and further purée until smooth and creamy. Mix the miso–rice vinegar sauce in with the wakame and scallions.

Wakame and Carrots

- ½ ounce dried wakame
- 2 cups carrots cut into large chunks
- 1 cup spring water
- 2 teaspoons tamari soy sauce
- Parsley sprigs for garnish

Wash, soak, and slice the wakame into large pieces. Put the carrots in a heavy pot, add water to half cover the carrots, and bring to a boil. Cover, reduce the heat to low, and cook until the carrots are 70 to 80 percent done. Then add the wakame to one side of the carrots and simmer until the carrots are soft, another 5 to 10 minutes. Add a little tamari soy sauce to taste and cook for several minutes longer. Garnish with parsley sprigs and serve.

Variation: Cauliflower, parsnips, burdock, celery, daikon, and cabbage also go well with wakame. Just adjust the time of cooking for each vegetable.

NORI

Unlike most sea vegetables that are harvested wild, *nori* is primarily cultivated. From late autumn to early spring, fresh nori is gathered from nets strung on bamboo poles in islets along the Japanese coast.

These nets contain special spores and fertilizers that promote attachment and growth. Before industrialization, Tokyo Bay was famous for its superior nori. Nori-makers competed to produce the most delectable nori and found that nori picked just before sunrise in the spring was the softest and most tender. The highest grades of nori are expensive and used only for very special occasions. After harvesting, the nori is washed and dried into thin sheets which are commonly folded in half and sold ten to a package.

Nori is a member of the *Porphyra* family of red algae and in Scotland is known as laver and in Ireland as sloke. In Europe it was traditionally harvested wild and boiled down into a gel and fried with oatmeal to produce laver bread. Natural foods stores here have recently begun to sell some native laver harvested off the coast of Maine. Nutritionally, the most outstanding features of nori or laver are its high carotene (vitamin A) content (from two to four times the amount of an equal volume of carrots), high protein content (twice as high as beefsteak), and high amount of vitamin B_{12}. It is also high in B vitamins, vitamin C, calcium, and iron. Medicinally, nori is associated with relieving beriberi and reducing serum cholesterol.

In the kitchen, dried nori does not need to be washed or soaked before using. However, to increase its digestibility, it is usually toasted by holding the shiny side about 6 inches over low heat and twirling for about 15 to 30 seconds until the sheet turns from purple to green. It may also be baked for 4 to 5 minutes in a 300-degree oven. As a garnish for soups, salads, fried rice, noodles, or casseroles, nori is delicious toasted and cut into thin strips with a scissors, crushed by hand, or ground into a powder. In the chapter on brown rice dishes, the way to use nori to wrap rice balls and make sushi is described (page 62).

Toasted Nori Squares

4 sheets nori
Grated fresh ginger
Tamari soy sauce
Mirin

Toast the sheets of nori and cut them into small squares. Place several squares of nori on each individual serving plate. Place a pinch of grated ginger and 2 to 3 drops of tamari soy sauce and mirin on each serving.

Fresh Laver

This recipe is for fresh laver (nori) foraged at the seashore. The best time to go is at low tide. Take some wood ashes along to dip your fingers in. Laver is very slippery and the ashes will improve your grip. At home, fresh laver should be washed in water thoroughly many times to remove all the sand.

6 to 7 cups fresh laver (nori)
3 tablespoons tamari soy sauce
Sesame seeds, roasted and chopped for garnish

Wash, soak, and slice the nori into bite-sized pieces. Put it in a pot. For a salty taste, use only tamari soy sauce to cook in as the nori will give off water as it cooks. Cook over low heat until the liquid has almost evaporated, about 30 to 40 minutes. Garnish with roasted and chopped sesame seeds and serve.

DULSE

Dulse was a traditional staple in Scotland, Wales, Ireland, Canada, and New England through the early part of this century. Though moderate in flavor compared to most other sea vegetables, it adds zest to dishes. In Japan, dulse is called *darusu.* Tufted in appearance, dulse has a purplish-red hue and is harvested in the warmer months of the year. It does not require soaking but should be inspected for tiny seashells and salt crystals. Raw, its taste is rather salty. Washing and soaking for a few minutes reduce its saltiness. Commonly, dulse is prepared by dry-roasting for about 5 to 10 minutes in a frying pan. Then it is crushed or ground into a powder and sprinkled on salads, soups, or vegetables, added to breads, fritters, and casseroles, or steeped to make a tea. Dulse may also be sautéed and deep-fried.

Dulse, Carrots, and Celery

Spring water
2 cups carrots halved and sliced on a diagonal
1 cup celery sliced on a diagonal
½ ounce dried dulse

Pour a little water into a pot and bring to a boil. Reduce the heat to medium-low. Add the carrots and cook until soft. Remove, and put carrots in a bowl. Add the celery to the boiling water and simmer until done. Wash the dulse and soak it for 2 to 3 minutes. Remove and cut into small pieces. Remove the celery from the heat and drain it. Add the celery and the dulse to the carrots. Mix and serve.

AGAR-AGAR

Agar-agar is a processed sea vegetable product used to make *kanten,* a delicious gelatin that can be prepared with pieces of fruit, vegetables, or beans or enjoyed plain. Originally derived from a smelly red algae growing along the Japanese coast, agar-agar is transformed into odorless light-weight translucent bars, shaved into fine flakes, or powdered. The bars, flakes, or powder are dissolved in hot water and poured over cooked ingredients, cooled, and allowed to gel.

Other members of the *Gelidium* family to which agar-agar belongs are found on both sides of the Atlantic and along the Pacific rim from Baja California to British Columbia. Agar-agar is high in calcium, iodine, and trace minerals and is a healthful alternative to commercial Jell-O or gelatins made with animal products.

To prepare, rinse 1 bar (or part of bar, following the directions on the package) in water until spongy and add to 1 quart of simmering hot water. Cook for 10 minutes, skim off any foam that surfaces, pour into molds or cups containing several pieces of cooked fruit or vegetables. In the refrigerator, the mixture will solidify in about 45 to 60 minutes. If using agar flakes or powder instead of bars, follow the directions on the package. The proportion of flakes to liquid varies from about 1 teaspoon to 2 tablespoons per quart of liquid. The flakes are cooked in the same way as the bars. Add to hot water, stir until dissolved, and cook for about 10 minutes. Pour over other ingredients and allow to cool. By itself, agar-agar is tasty topped with a sweet-and-sour miso sauce, grated fresh ginger and tamari soy sauce, or chopped scallions or other greens. Agar-agar is good for the intestines but taken in excess can lead to diarrhea. The following recipe is for a bean aspic. The recipe for fruit kanten is in the dessert chapter.

Azuki Bean and Raisin Aspic

- 1 cup azuki beans
- ⅛ cup raisins
- 4 cups spring water
- ½ teaspoon sea salt, or 1 tablespoon tamari soy sauce
- 1 bar agar-agar or equivalent flakes or powder

Wash the beans and combine them with the raisins in a pot. Add the water. Bring to a boil, reduce the heat to low, cover, and simmer until the beans are soft, about 1½ hours. Add the seasoning and mix in the agar-agar until thoroughly dissolved. Cook for another 10 minutes and pour into individual molds or a large serving bowl. Refrigerate until jelled and serve cool.

Variations: Other good combinations are split peas and fresh peas; lentils and celery; and carrots and onions.

IRISH MOSS

Irish moss is native to both sides of the north Atlantic and comes in many shapes, sizes, and colors including white. It is primarily used as a gelatin or thickening agent and can be used in any recipe calling for agar-agar, though it produces a slightly softer gelatin. As the jelly carrageenin, Irish moss is used in modern food processing to give bulk and stabilize a wide range of foodstuffs. High in vitamin A, iodine, and minerals, Irish moss is said to relieve coughs and urinary disorders. It is also combined with other ingredients for external use as a skin lotion and burn cream.

To prepare, soak 1 cup of dried Irish moss in 1 quart of water for 20 to 30 minutes. Discard the soaking water and cook with other ingredients to be included in the gelatin, for about 30 minutes. After cooking, take out the Irish moss, squeeze out excess liquid, pour mixture into a mold or dish, and chill in the refrigerator. Irish moss may also be tied in a small cheesecloth after soaking and cooked and squeezed out in the same way.

MEKABU AND NEKABU

Mekabu is the flowering sprout of the wakame plant and has a strong, sweet, and creamy taste. It is customarily drunk as a tea. Cooked thoroughly, it also goes well with grains, beans, soups, or vegetable dishes and may be deep-fried without batter. Clean in the same way as wakame but cook considerably longer. The wakame root is known as *nekabu* and is even tougher. It is used primarily for teas.

CORSICAN SEAWEED

This foxtail-like plant grows beneath the warmer waters of the Atlantic and Pacific. It is traditionally prepared in a tea to relieve intestinal parasites. In Japan it is known as *makuri*. We were given makuri tea at school once a month to safeguard our health. Modern medicine has synthesized some of the ingredients in Corsican seaweed to overcome the effects of harmful microorganisms. To prepare, add one-quarter ounce of Corsican seaweed to two cups of spring water. Cook down slowly until one cup of liquid remains. Drink before breakfast or on an empty stomach and wait at least 2 hours before taking any food.

CHAPTER 24

CONDIMENTS AND GARNISHES

Sparrows on the rooftop.
The melting snow
Makes them very happy.
—*Noboko*

Condiments and garnishes are very important to balancing the meal as a whole, and provide variety to simple cooking. Garnishes are added at the very end of cooking or just before the food is served at the table. Garnishes provide a touch of color and beauty, stimulating the appetite and contributing to the aesthetic enjoyment of the meal. Condiments are seasonings, usually served separately for use at the table. Condiments satisfy one or more of the five tastes and allow each person to make individual adjustments during the meal, according to taste and condition of health. Condiments may also be used medicinally. Almost all foods can be used as condiments in small amounts, including fresh chopped leafy greens, dried and powdered sea vegetables, long sautéed root vegetables, slivered nuts, citrus rinds, seasonings, and sauces.

Condiments may be used daily in small amounts. I'm careful not to use too much, especially those with a salty or pungent taste. We generally do not give condiments to infants, as small children require much less salt than adults. During pregnancy, condiments are a good source of minerals but salty ones should not be overconsumed.

Most of the following recipes are for condiments traditionally used in Japan. Macrobiotic friends in the United States, Canada, and Europe have incorporated some mild traditional herbs as condiments into their diet, including bay leaves, sage, and mint. In preparing condiments we should be governed by the principles of ecological balance. If we live in a temperate climate, it is preferable to avoid strong curries, chili, hot peppers, and other tropical spices. In the following chart, note that some condiments provide two or more tastes.

SOUR	BITTER	SWEET
Vegetable pickles	Gomashio	Miso
Sauerkraut	Tekka	Tekka
Umeboshi plums	Green nori	Green nori
Shiso leaves	Dried parsley	Dried parsley
Brown rice vinegar	Wakame powder	Scallion miso
Sweet rice vinegar	Dandelion	Sigure miso relish
Apple cider vinegar	Sigure miso relish	Carrot tops with miso
Lemon		Green peppers with miso
Lime		Amasake
		Applesauce
		Barley malt

PUNGENT	SALTY
Gingerroot	Miso
Scallions	Umeboshi plums
Watercress	Shiso leaves
Onions	Gomashio
Grated daikon	Shio kombu
Scallion miso	Wakame powder
	Tamari soy sauce

GARNISHES

I often put a sprig of bright green parsley or watercress or a few sliced scallions in the center of a large bowl of freshly cooked rice. Roasted sesame seeds, green nori, or other powdered sea vegetables may also be sprinkled on rice or other dishes before serving.

Bread cubes are delicious in soups. Cut the bread into small cubes and add them fresh, dried, or, for more texture, deep-fried.

Scallions are one of the most versatile garnishes. They can be cut into slivers, sliced, or cut on the diagonal. You can use either the white part or the green part or both parts together along with the roots. I wash out the scallions' strong taste with cold water and I may also soak them to remove the fine dirt from the roots (which are very nourishing and should always be saved for another dish). For an even less raw taste, I boil the scallions for 1 minute before using them as a garnish.

Lemon rind, chopped fine or grated, and cooked with a little miso to reduce its sour taste, makes a sweet and sour combination.

Fresh gingerroot, grated very finely or in long strips, adds zest to a wide variety of dishes.

CONDIMENTS

Some of the principle condiments in macrobiotic cooking are described below.

Gomashio

Gomashio, or roasted sesame seed salt, is the most popular macrobiotic condiment. Its salty-bitter taste balances the natural sweetness of rice and other grains and vegetables. Gomashio's tiny seeds also make the dish more chewy. Sesame seeds are an excellent source of oil, and they are high in calcium and other nutrients. The seeds are better when they are roasted because raw oil is not easy to digest. However, the seeds should not be overroasted. Each seed should puff up.

We used to raise black sesame seeds in our garden in Japan. They have a stronger, nuttier taste than white (brown) sesame seeds. They are also a little larger and better formed. Either variety is fine for regular use. Most sesame seeds in natural foods stores come from Central America and are unhulled. Some organic sesame seeds are grown in California. Generally, the more convex-shaped seeds are higher in quality than the concave-shaped ones. Hulled varieties processed with chemicals and stripped of nutrients should be avoided.

The proportion of salt to sesame seeds depends on age and level of physical activity. Too much salt overstimulates the appetite leading to excess consumption of liquids, fruits, and sweets. In Japan, the proportion is usually one part salt to four parts sesame seeds. However, in Japan the climate is very moist, and the Japanese generally grow up with less animal food consumption (high in sodium). Moreover, traditional sea salt has less sodium and more minerals than either refined sea salt or most natural sea salt available in the West. For Americans and others native to the West, as well as those living in dry climates, we recommend about one part salt to ten to twelve parts sesame seeds for ordinary adults. For extremely active adults, such as those engaged in manual labor, one part salt to eight to ten parts sesame seeds may be used for a stronger condiment. For small children, one part salt to sixteen to twenty parts sesame seeds makes a lighter, less salty side dish. Separate batches of gomashio should be made and clearly labeled for adults and children, since too much salt will make children overactive. Half a teaspoon to 1 teaspoon of gomashio on a bowl of rice is plenty.

Adult Gomashio

1 cup sesame seeds

2½ to 3 tablespoons sea salt

Very Active Adult Gomashio

1 cup sesame seeds

3½ to 4 tablespoons sea salt

Children's Gomashio

1 cup sesame seeds

1½ to 2 tablespoons sea salt

Wash seeds in a very fine mesh strainer as in preparing rice and let them drain. Any seeds that float to the top while they are being washed should be discarded. Dry-roast the sea salt in a frying pan for a short time. For both sea salt and sesame seeds, stainless steel is lighter, easier to handle, and heats up and cools off more quickly than cast-iron. However, cast-iron cooks more evenly and may be used instead, if desired. Roasting the sea salt releases moisture in the salt and helps to make fluffy gomashio. Roasting also releases a strong chlorine from the salt. The salt is roasted when it becomes shiny.

Roast the sesame seeds after the salt has been roasted, ground, and set aside. Always roast the sesame seeds when they are wet. They will cook more evenly. Dry seeds will burn easily. Use medium heat to roast the seeds. Do not roast too many seeds at once or some will burn, while others will not be roasted enough. Add only enough seeds to cover the bottom of the frying pan. While roasting, push the seeds back and forth in the pan with a rice paddle or wooden spoon. Shaking the pan occasionally will also help to roast seeds evenly and avoid burning. The seeds are done when they crush easily between the thumb and index finger, about 5 to 10 minutes. Do not overroast the seeds as they tend to become a little darker from their internal heat after they have been removed from the frying pan. The seeds will also begin to pop and give off a nutty fragrance when done.

Place the roasted sea salt in a suribachi and grind until it becomes a fine powder and all small lumps are dissolved. Add the hot roasted sesame seeds to the roasted, ground sea salt. Hot seeds grind more easily and should always be added after the salt has been ground. If seeds are ground first, they will turn darker when the salt is added. Slowly grind the seeds in an even circular motion with a wooden pestle, making sure to use the grooved sides of the suribachi to grind against instead of the bottom of the bowl. Grind until each seed is half-crushed and thoroughly coated with salt. Do not grind into a powder. If you grind gently, the gomashio will taste sweeter. More powerful or quicker grinding crushes the seeds and makes them saltier to the taste. Allow the gomashio to cool when you have finished grinding and transfer it to an airtight glass or ceramic container to store. If you put warm gomashio in a container, moisture will collect on the top and sides of the jar causing it to spoil quickly. Gomashio will keep fresh for several weeks and may be roasted again if it begins to dry out. I avoid making too much at a time and so prepare it fresh at least once a week.

Variation: For variety, sesame seeds may be prepared with miso, tamari soy sauce, roasted umeboshi plums, roasted powdered kombu or wakame, or shiso leaves. Roasted sesame seeds may also be used as a condiment or garnish without salt or other seasoning.

Scallion Miso Condiment

The pungent taste of scallions goes very well with miso, creating a warm energy. Use on rice, other grains, noodles, boiled vegetables, or as a spread for bread.

- 2 to 3 bunches of scallions with scallion roots
- 1 tablespoon dark sesame oil
- 3 teaspoons miso
- 3 teaspoons spring water

Wash the scallions and roots very well. Soak the roots in cold water, if necessary, to loosen any soil. Layer the roots and then the scallions in an oiled frying pan. Form a little hollow in the center of the scallions. Purée the miso with a very small amount of water and pour the mixture into the hollow. Cover and simmer for about 5 minutes. Mix very well when done and serve.

Variations: Five tablespoons of roasted and mashed sesame seeds may be substituted for the oil. A touch of brown rice vinegar, mirin, or maple syrup may also be added.

Carrot Tops with Miso

- 2 cups finely chopped carrot tops
- ¼ to ½ cup spring water
- 1 teaspoon miso mixed with 3 teaspoons spring water

Put the carrot tops and water into a pot. Add the puréed miso in the center of the greens. Cover and cook over low heat for about 5 to 10 minutes, depending on the hardness of the tops. The miso will filter down through the greens.

Roasted Soybeans and Miso

- 1 cup roasted yellow or black soybeans
- Spring water
- 1 cup sliced celery
- 1 cup diced onion
- 1 cup sliced lotus root
- ½ cup diced carrots
- ¼ cup burdock, thinly sliced
- 1 to 2 tablespoons sesame oil
- 1 tablespoon miso
- ½ to 1 teaspoon grated fresh ginger for garnish

Dry-roast the soybeans, and after roasting soak in 1 cup of warm water for 10 minutes. Meanwhile, slice the vegetables. In a pot, warm up the sesame oil and add the vegetables in layers, beginning with the celery, then the onion, lotus root, carrots, and burdock. Strain the roasted soybeans from the water and put them on top. Add the strained soaking water to the pot gently, being careful not to disturb the order of the layers. Dilute the miso in ½ cup of water and place on top of the soybeans. Cover the pot and cook for 10 to 20 minutes. The carrots and burdock should become soft but not too soft. When done, garnish with grated ginger, mix well, and serve.

Green Peppers and Miso

- 3 green peppers, sliced into half moons ¼ inch thick
- 1 tablespoon dark sesame oil
- 1 teaspoon barley miso
- Spring water

Sauté the peppers in the oil for several minutes over low heat. Dilute and purée the miso with 1 to 2 tablespoons of water. Pour the puréed miso into the center of the peppers but don't mix it in. Cover and simmer over low heat for about 30 minutes. Mix and serve.

SEA VEGETABLE POWDERS

Dried and powdered sea vegetable condiments are a good way to introduce seaweed into a meal. They are high in calcium, iron, and other minerals besides strengthening to the heart, kidneys, and nervous system. Nori and dulse are the lightest, kombu and kelp are stronger, and wakame condiment has the saltiest taste.

To prepare, roast either nori, kombu, wakame, dulse, or kelp in a 350-degree oven for about 10 to 15 minutes, or until they are dark and crisp but not burnt. Crush and grind the seaweed in a suribachi until it becomes a fine powder. Use as you would gomashio.

Ground sea vegetable powders may be combined with roasted sesame seeds to make a slightly different condiment. Use about 60 percent seeds and 40 percent seaweed. Be careful to grind the seaweed before adding the seeds or the seeds will be ground too much.

Nori Condiment

5 to 6 sheets nori, torn or cut into 1-inch pieces

Spring water

Tamari soy sauce

Put the nori in a saucepan and cover it with water, about ½ cup. Bring to a boil, cover, and reduce the heat to low. Simmer until most of the water evaporates and the nori forms a thick paste, about 30 minutes. Add several drops of tamari soy sauce a few minutes before the end of the cooking time. The nori should have a light salt taste. Cool and store in a glass jar.

Variation: For a saltier condiment, use 1 to 3 tablespoons of tamari soy sauce.

SHIO KOMBU

Shio kombu means salty kombu and is a popular condiment in Japan. It is traditionally made by rinsing the dust off kombu strips, cutting with scissors into small squares, and soaking in tamari soy sauce for 1 to 2 days. After soaking, the kombu is put in a pot with just enough tamari soy sauce to cover and cooked over a slow heat without a cover. It is cooked until nearly all the juice has evaporated, 1 to 2 hours, and care is taken to prevent burning. At the end, each piece of kombu is mixed very slowly to coat it with the remaining juice. A few roasted sesame seeds are mixed in at the end. The salty kombu will keep unrefrigerated for over a year. Only one or two small pieces are eaten each time.

For a faster method, soak 5 to 6 strips of kombu, 8 to 12 inches long, for several minutes, or until they are soft enough to cut. Slice into 1-inch squares. Place in a saucepan and cover with a mixture of ½ cup of tamari soy sauce and ½ cup of spring water. Bring to a boil. Cover and reduce the heat to low. Simmer until all the liquid evaporates, about 30 to 40 minutes. Cool off and store in a glass jar.

Wakame Condiment

- 1 cup soaked wakame, sliced
- 2 tablespoons brown rice vinegar
- 2 tablespoons tamari soy sauce
- 2 tablespoons spring water (optional)
- 1 tablespoon sesame seeds, washed and roasted

Put the wakame into a pot. Add the vinegar and tamari soy sauce. Add 2 tablespoons of water, if desired, and bring to a boil. Cover, reduce the heat to low, and simmer until almost all the liquid has evaporated, about 10 to 20 minutes. Garnish with sesame seeds.

Tekka Root Vegetable Condiment

Tekka is a root vegetable condiment made of miso and various root vegetables that have been sautéed together for a long time and cooked down into a concentrated black powder. Tekka combines a variety of strong tastes and makes for strong blood. Since it is so strong, it should be used only in small amounts.

Traditionally, tekka is cooked over low heat in a cast-iron pot for about 16 hours, or until it is dry and very black. In this country, we use a shorter method. The same amount of oil and miso should be used but the proportion of the other ingredients may vary. Hatcho miso is preferred since it is less salty than other miso, less watery, and easier to make into powder. Imported tekka is available in select natural foods stores, and some of them are good quality.

- ½ cup dark sesame oil
- ⅔ cup finely minced burdock
- ⅔ cup finely minced carrots
- ⅔ cup finely minced lotus root
- ½ teaspoon grated fresh ginger
- ½ cup hatcho miso

Heat a cast-iron frying pan and add ½ cup of sesame oil. Sauté the burdock for several minutes. Add the carrots and lotus root and sauté for several minutes. Add the ginger and miso. Reduce the heat to low and sauté for about 4 hours. During the cooking, stir frequently until all liquid has evaporated and the tekka is dry and very black. Cool completely and store in a glass jar.

Variation: Onions may be added to make a slightly sweeter taste.

Sigure Miso Relish

Sigure means late autumn quiet rain. This soft-style tekka was named by Lima Ohsawa who introduced it to me in my home in New York.

½ cup minced onion
½ cup minced carrot
½ cup minced lotus root
3 tablespoons dark sesame oil
A small amount of spring water
1 heaping tablespoon miso
⅛ teaspoon grated fresh ginger

Sauté onion, carrot, and then lotus root in the oil. Add just enough water to cover vegetables and simmer until soft. Blend in the miso and cook for 3 minutes. Stir in the grated fresh ginger and remove from the heat. This relish is good on grains, vegetables, bread, or noodles.

Grated Daikon

A small amount of grated daikon is traditionally served with fish or seafood. It helps to neutralize the effects of animal food. Horseradish may also be used instead of grated daikon for this purpose. Mustard is customarily used with red-meat fish.

1 cup grated daikon
Tamari soy sauce
Sliced scallions for garnish
Grated fresh ginger (optional)

Put the grated daikon in a serving bowl. Pour several drops of tamari soy sauce in the center of the daikon. Garnish with a few scallion slices. When served, each person can take a tablespoon of daikon and put 1 or 2 more drops of tamari soy sauce on it when eating. A tiny bit of grated ginger may also be added.

UMEBOSHI PLUMS

Umeboshi plums are customarily used in rice balls, with plain rice or soft rice, or lightly rubbed on sweet corn. I always carry them as a condiment when traveling.

TAMARI SOY SAUCE

Tamari soy sauce is not usually used as a condiment at the table. Rather it is added as a seasoning during cooking. Occasionally, though, a few drops may be added at the table to soups, noodle dishes, or boiled green vegetables.

SHISO LEAVES

Shiso are pickled beefsteak leaves. They are customarily prepared with umeboshi plums. Whole pickled leaves are available in some natural foods stores and make a delicious condiment for grains, vegetables, and soups. They may also be used for wrapping squares or rectangles of tofu. They look and taste somewhat similar to grape leaves.

SWEETENERS

Applesauce, barley malt, or amasake may be used as a condiment to provide a sweet taste. Children are especially attracted to sweet flavors while growing up and these are of good quality. Adults enjoy them, too, occasionally on morning cereal or other dishes.

CHAPTER

25

FISH AND SEAFOOD

A rice field cat
Approaches.
The smell of broiling fish.

—*Fusako*

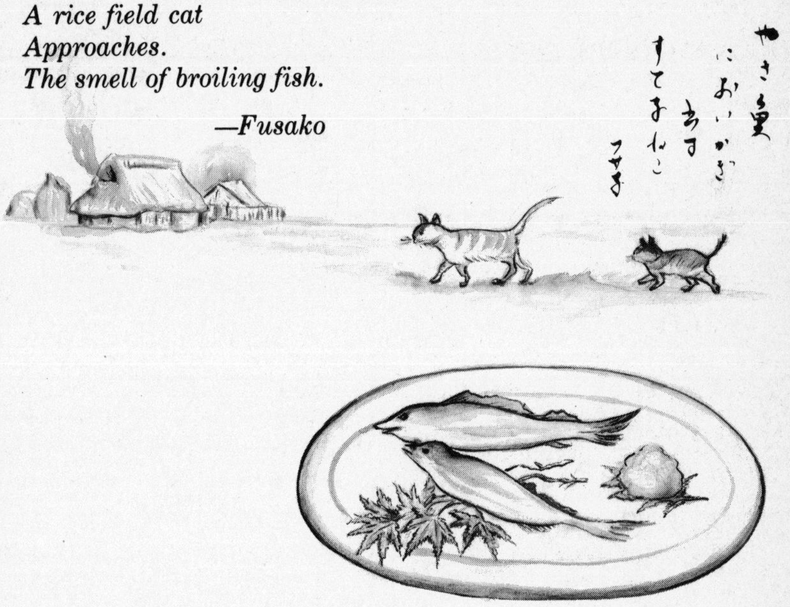

Because I grew up in the mountains where transportation to and from the sea was slow, we did not have fresh fish very often. Mostly we ate salted cod. During rice planting season, farmers would often place it on soft oak leaves and eat it with rice balls for lunch in the fields. Like many farm families, my family had a small outdoor pond in which we kept carp. Carp are very delicious cooked with miso, and we picked them out of the pond for special occasions. Even in cold weather, they were available and could be used for making *koi koku*, an energizing soup made with carp, burdock, miso, and bancha tea and traditionally eaten for strength and vitality. Cold carp blood was used medicinally to reduce fever.

In the old days there were also many tiny fishes in the rice paddies. We would catch them by hand with a cloth and bucket or a mesh strainer. Along the sandy banks of clear mountain streams we gathered small freshwater clams called *shizimi-gai.* They were very plentiful and after boiling for 1 minute they would open up and make a nice base for miso soup. Small clams were said to be good for relieving jaundice and other liver problems. Nowadays we must be careful to obtain shellfish from unpolluted waters. My father and brother used to go out with a friend at night to hunt salmon and eel. Broiled eel on a hot summer day is very good for restoring energy and weight loss on account of the weather. I also have memories of a wonderful fish called *ayu.* One year while I was teaching in a remote mountain district one of the junior high school boys brought me a fresh ayu. I broiled it and was so surprised to find that its taste and energy were more like vegetables than fish. It was the most delicious fish I ever ate. Nowadays, most freshwater fish, mountain fish, and rice field fish have died out in Japan because of chemical sprays and pollution. It is very sad.

PREPARING ANIMAL FOOD

After starting macrobiotics, I stopped eating almost all animal food. Prior to the early 1950s, meat was very rare in rural Japan. Sometimes we enjoyed rabbit stew. One of the big occasions of the year fell once each winter when the grammar school served rabbit stew to the students. The older boys and teachers would catch wild rabbits and bring them back to prepare the stew. Families also often raised rabbits for food on holidays and special occasions. Usually rabbit meat was cut up in small pieces and cooked with taro, carrots, and daikon. Some farmers also kept chickens for food, but mostly they were prized for their eggs. After serving oily or animal food, mother would always clean the dishes thoroughly with wood ashes before using them again for vegetable-quality food.

My college was situated on the Sea of Japan, and I ate considerably more fish and seafood during those years than when I grew up in the mountains. Once a senior roommate took me aside and solemnly told me that I was smiling too much. I had placed first in the entrance examination and was always elected chairman of my class. Apparently my simple and relaxed country ways didn't sit too well with some of the city people. Years later I realized that many modern persons lose their smiles from eating too much animal food, including fish and seafood. In any event, after Pearl Harbor, everyone became tense and lost their smiles completely.

After the war ended and the Americans came, red meat became more widely available. Once I visited a friend and her family in a distant city, and she asked me to cook a steak. I had never eaten beef before and assumed it was cooked like rabbit. I cut it into small pieces, and when I served it rabbit style they were very upset. That was the first and last time I ever cooked beef.

PREPARING FISH

In macrobiotic cooking, we serve fish and seafood as an optional side dish two or three times a week for those who are in good health. Fish should always be as fresh as possible and not frozen, prestuffed, or prebreaded. Generally, deep-ocean fish are preferable to clear-water fish which absorb more pollutants in the food chain. White-meat fish are less fatty than either red-meat or blue-skinned varieties and may be used much more frequently. When cooking fish, I prepare it as a side dish to the meal rather than as the main course. Usually it should be consumed with a regular serving of whole grains and two to three times the usual amount of hard leafy green vegetables. These foods help to balance the strong contractive energy of fish and seafood. To neutralize possible toxic side-effects, from 1 teaspoon to 1 tablespoon per person of grated daikon with a few drops of tamari soy sauce and a touch of grated fresh ginger is customarily served at the meal. For stronger red-meat fish, a little mustard or *wasabi* (the Japanese mustard) may be prepared to further aid in digestion. Parsley sprigs and lemon slices give a nice taste and bright color to fish dishes and may be used as garnishes.

The following fish recipes have been specially selected for this book by Mayumi Nishimura, a young lady from Japan who has cooked in my home and who now, with her husband Jinn, is in charge of cooking at our new seminar center in the Berkshire mountains. Mayumi comes from an island in the sea where her family had a hotel and served their guests many traditional fish dishes. She must be a very good daughter who helped her mother as her way of handling fish is really excellent. These are some of her favorite recipes. The grain, soup, salad, and tempura chapters contain a few other recipes utilizing fish and seafood.

Baked Halibut with Miso

The sweet marinade gives this dish a rich flavor and delicious taste.

1 cup barley miso or hatcho miso
1 cup white miso
½ cup mirin
2 tablespoons sake
1½ to 2 pounds halibut fillets
Grated daikon

Purée the miso, mirin, and sake together thoroughly in a suribachi. Spread half this marinade over the bottom of a shallow baking dish. Lay the fish fillets on top of the miso spread. (The fish may be wrapped in cheesecloth to preserve its shape.) Then spread the remaining marinade on top. Let sit for 4 to 5 hours. Remove the fish from the marinade.

Save the mixture for marinating another fish or, if you don't mind the fishy taste, use it for soup. Put the marinated fish in a baking dish and bake in a preheated 475-degree oven for 15 to 20 minutes. Serve with grated daikon.

Variations: The fillets of other tender white-meat fish, such as red snapper, scrod, and cod, can be prepared in this way. Flounder is often too thin. Instead of the marinade, the fish may be seasoned just prior to baking with plain salt sprinkled on both sides. Tamari soy sauce, a little mirin, and a touch of grated fresh ginger may also be combined and sprinkled on the fish just prior to cooking.

Baked Trout

Prepared in just a few minutes, baked trout makes a very appetizing dish.

3 tablespoons barley miso or white miso
2 tablespoons mirin
3 tablespoons kombu stock or spring water
1 medium-sized trout, about 10 ounces
Grated daikon

Mix the miso, mirin, and kombu stock or spring water together in a suribachi. Put the trout, either whole or cut in half, in a baking dish and make shallow diagonal slices along the top like this: / / / / /. Bake in a preheated 475-degree oven for 7 to 10 minutes. When the fish is 70 percent done, open oven and spread the miso sauce on top of the fish between the head and tail. Bake for another 5 minutes. Serve with grated daikon.

Steamed Sole

In Japanese this delicate dish is called *saka mushi*. It cooks quickly and has a nice tender texture and mellow flavor. Served with bright colored mushrooms, broccoli, and lemon slices in an attractive ceramic bowl, steamed sole is a true work of art.

1 medium-sized sole, about 6 ounces
1 6-inch strip kombu
2 tablespoons sake
2 shiitake mushrooms, fresh or dried
4 to 5 broccoli flowerets
Lemon slices for garnish
Tamari-ginger sauce for dipping

Make shallow crosscuts on both sides of the fish with a sharp knife. Soak the kombu for 5 minutes and put it on the bottom of a small heat-proof ceramic bowl. Put fish on top of the kombu and season with the sake. Nestle the whole shiitake mushrooms next to the fish. (If using dried mushrooms, first soak for a few minutes and remove and discard the stems.) Bring about ½ inch of water to boil in a large kettle. When the steam is up, gently place the ceramic dish containing the sole inside the kettle and cover the kettle. Steam for 10 to 15 minutes. During the last few minutes of cooking the broccoli can be added, but it shouldn't be cooked too long in order to retain its crispness and bright green color. When the fish is done, remove the ceramic dish from the kettle, and garnish with several slices of lemon. Serve with a tamari-ginger sauce for dipping.

Variation: Other white-meat fish may be prepared in this way as well as salmon, mackerel, and tuna.

❧ Baked Scrod ❧

This fish dish, prepared with skewers, is very soft and tender. Grated fresh ginger gives the marinade a slightly spicy flavor.

1 cup tamari soy sauce
½ cup mirin
½ cup kombu stock
1 tablespoon grated fresh ginger
1½ to 2 pounds scrod fillets, sliced into 6-inch-long pieces
Grated daikon

Combine a marinade of the tamari soy sauce, mirin, kombu stock, and grated ginger in a container which will hold the fish. Insert fillets and marinate for 30 to 60 minutes. After marinating, remove the fillets and pierce each one with two thin wooden skewers. Suspend the skewered fillets over the bottom circular stand on which a wok rests or other object with raised sides. The wok stand should rest on a baking sheet to catch any drippings. Bake the fish in a preheated 475-degree oven for 15 to 20 minutes. Serve with grated daikon.

❧ Deep-Fried Red Snapper ❧

Deep-frying is called *kara age* in Japanese, and fish are traditionally prepared in this way for holidays and special occasions. Red snapper, a favorite on New Year's Day, is very crispy and delicious.

Dark sesame oil
1 whole red snapper, about three pounds
Whole wheat pastry flour or kuzu powder
Grated daikon

Dipping Sauce

½ cup kombu stock
2 tablespoons tamari soy sauce
3 tablespoons brown rice vinegar
3 tablespoons mirin
1 tablespoon kuzu
1 teaspoon grated fresh ginger

Fill a deep-sided frying pan with a couple of inches of dark sesame oil and heat it to about 300 degrees. For deep-frying or tempura-style food, this temperature is very low. The fish should be cooked at this heat for a long time in order to soften the bones and increase its digestibility. Before frying, roll the fish in pastry flour or kuzu powder, and then deep-fry in the hot oil for 30 minutes. Meanwhile, prepare the sauce. Dissolve the kuzu in a little of the kombu stock, then mix in with the other ingredients. Serve in small individual dipping dishes with grated daikon on the side.

Variation: Carp, sole, smelt, and other white-meat fish can be prepared in this way.

BROILED FISH

In contrast to baking, which cooks fish with dry heat, broiling brings out the fish's inherent juiciness. To broil, sprinkle fish with a little sea salt and place under the broiler for about 5 minutes, or until it is browned on top. The fish does not need to be turned over in the broiler. Broiled fish may also be marinated with equal amounts of tamari soy sauce and spring water with a touch of grated fresh ginger or sprinkled with fresh lemon juice and a few drops of tamari soy sauce.

PICKLED FISH

Herring, mackerel, sardines, and other red-meat varieties may be pickled by sprinkling with sea salt for 30 to 60 minutes and then marinating with brown rice vinegar. Let sit for 1 hour in the vinegar before using. The pickled fish will keep for 1 week in the refrigerator.

SASHIMI

Sashimi or small slices of fresh raw fish is a famous Japanese delicacy. Only fish caught the same day are usually suitable for use. Mastering the intricate removing of the bones takes experience and very sharp knives. If not properly prepared, sashimi can produce serious digestive troubles. Sashimi is one of the few dishes I do not prepare at home but prefer to enjoy at a good restaurant.

Koi Koku (Carp and Burdock Soup)

This delicious, invigorating soup is excellent for restoring strength and vitality and opening the electromagnetic channel of energy in the body. It is usually enjoyed even by those who ordinarily don't like fish and by those with sicknesses who otherwise should not have animal products. The whole fish, including bones, scales, head, and fins, becomes soft and digestible. Koi koku is traditionally prepared for mothers who have just given birth or who are breastfeeding. In cold weather it is particularly warming but may be enjoyed all year-round. Be careful to eat only a small amount at a time (1 cup or less), otherwise you will become overly attracted to liquids, fruits, and sweets. Koi koku will keep for a week in the refrigerator or several months in the freezer where it can be taken out from time to time, thawed, and used as needed.

- 1 fresh carp, approximately 5 pounds
- Burdock in weight at least equal to the fish
- ½ to 1 cup used bancha tea twigs and leaves wrapped in a cheesecloth
- Bancha tea and spring water
- Miso to taste
- 1 tablespoon grated fresh ginger
- Chopped scallions for garnish

Select a live carp at a fish market and express your gratitude for taking its life. Ask the fishmonger to carefully remove the gallbladder and yellow bitter bone (thyroid) and leave the rest of the fish intact. This includes the scales, bones, head, and fins. At home, cut the entire fish into 1- to 2-inch-thick slices. Remove eyes if you wish. Meanwhile, cut at least an equal amount of burdock root (ideally 2 to 3 times the weight of fish) into thin slices or matchsticks. This quantity of burdock may take a while to prepare so plan accordingly. When everything is chopped, place fish and burdock in a pressure cooker. Tie old bancha twig leaves and stems from your teapot in a cheesecloth. It should be the size of a small ball. Place this ball in the pressure cooker on top or nestled inside fish. The tea twigs will help soften the bones during cooking and make them more digestible. Add enough liquid to cover fish and burdock, approximately one-third bancha tea and two-thirds spring water. Pressure-cook for 1 hour. Bring down the pressure, take the cover off, add miso to taste (½ to 1 teaspoon per cup of soup), and grated fresh ginger. Simmer for 5 minutes. Garnish with chopped scallions and serve hot.

Variation: The burdock may be sautéed for a few minutes in dark sesame oil prior to cooking with the fish. Koi koku may also be made by boiling in a heavy lidded pot for 4 to 6 hours, or until all the bones are soft and almost dissolved. As the liquid evaporates, more water or bancha tea should be added. If carp is unavailable, substitute another light fish, such as perch, red snapper, or trout. If burdock is scarce, use carrots instead, or use half burdock and half carrots combined.

SEAFOOD

In addition to fish, mollusks, shellfish, and other seafood may be prepared on occasion. The slower moving varieties, such as clams and oysters, contain less fat and cholesterol than faster moving ones like lobsters and crabs. Squid is good for tempura or may be boiled quickly and served in a salad with wakame and cucumber. Used whole, squid may also be stuffed with sweet rice or sushi rice after removing the skins and taking out the insides. Clams, mussels, and other small shellfish are good in soups. Oysters can be included in nabe-style dishes and be prepared together with rice, gomoku-style. Once I accompanied my family on a trip to Hiroshima which was renowned for its oysters. We enjoyed several oyster dishes at a restaurant. Some were cooked together with rice and seasoned with tamari soy sauce, while others were baked in the shell and served with a dipping sauce or prepared tempura-style. Shrimp are traditionally used in dishes such as shrimp cocktail, Spanish paella, and seafood tempura, to name a few. However, shrimp are said to affect the voice. My Noh drama master once told me that he never touched shrimp because he would lose his ability to sing beautiful songs.

In moderation, fish and seafood can be enjoyed by those who wish variety in their cooking, a quick source of energy, or strong flavor and taste.

CHAPTER
26

DESSERTS AND SNACKS

Red persimmons
All wear white caps
After the snowfall.
—Yoshiko

Desserts are served much more commonly in the West than in the East. In Japan, our daily diet of whole grains and vegetables provided a naturally sweet taste. We rarely had special dishes prepared with concentrated sweeteners. Ordinarily we would finish the meal with tea and pickles. Occasionally we ate fruit between meals. We usually consumed it in whole form and always in season.

When I grew up, we used unrefined black sugarcane. White sugar was expensive and never eaten at home. Mother would buy white sugar as a gift to the doctor or for other special occasions. I remember that very often for daily cooking she would send me to the grocery store to buy barley malt or rice syrup. During the war sugar was not available.

Right afterwards I noticed that under government rationing, each family received a big basketful of sugar. Thanks to American influence, people started cooking Western-style desserts and began incorporating sugar into their cooking much more than before. At George Ohsawa's dormitory near Tokyo I was introduced to apple pie. They made it with all natural ingredients at Christmas and for birthdays, and it was very delicious. In the United States I learned from my students how to make pies, cakes, puddings, cookies, and other desserts. My students made them by the methods their mothers used but with whole wheat flour and natural thickeners and sweeteners instead of white flour, dairy products, and sugar. In exchange I taught them traditional sweet dishes using kanten, chestnuts, azuki beans, and amasake.

Whole grains, beans, vegetables, and fruits contain complex carbohydrates, such as starch, cellulose, gums, and pectin. These complex sugars, or polysaccharides, are an ideal way to consume sugar. They are digested slowly in the intestines and release sugar into the bloodstream at a slow gradual rate. In contrast, simple sugars, such as white sugar, honey, and molasses, enter the digestive system in the mouth, esophagus, and stomach. Premature absorption of sugar can create elevated swings in mood, cause insulin flooding, raise blood sugar levels, and overwork the adrenal glands. By definition, sweeteners are concentrated products, not whole foods. Even good-quality natural sweeteners, such as barley malt or rice syrup, taken in excess can lead to imbalanced health.

As much as possible we try to satisfy a sweet taste in daily cooking. Naturally sweet vegetables may be served often, including winter-season squashes, carrots, parsnips, rutabagas, and onions. Adding a pinch of sea salt to vegetables during cooking makes them even sweeter. Long-time nishime-style boiling and baking also make foods richer and sweeter to the taste. Thorough chewing of each mouthful also makes foods sweeter, especially brown rice and other grains. When food is properly chewed, an enzyme in the saliva begins to turn the starch into sugar in a similar way to the fermentation of malt.

A craving for sweets and snacks is often an indication that we are eating too few whole grains and vegetables or that our food is too salty or strongly seasoned. Animal food consumption and overeating in general will also make one eat and drink sweet foods and beverages in an attempt to create balance and compensate for overstimulation.

NATURAL DESSERTS

On the Standard Macrobiotic Diet, delicious desserts made with all natural ingredients may usually be served two to three times a week. Whole foods and their products can be used imaginatively to make these items in the following ways:

Whole Grains—Grains and grain products can be used to make cakes, puddings, sweet breads, and cookies. Whole grain flour makes nourishing, crispy crusts for pies, strudels, and other pastries. Sweet rice mochi is very delicious and may be made into waffles or served with a light sweet sauce or fruit topping. Popcorn is an excellent, healthful snack.

Beans—Azuki beans are naturally sweet and may be used often in preparing sweet dishes. They go especially well with chestnuts, squash, or mochi and can be served plain or sweetened with a few raisins, fresh or dried apple, barley malt, or maple syrup. In Japan, women especially like juicy azuki beans with barley malt and served with soft mochi.

Sea Vegetables—A delicious natural gelatin called *kanten* can be made with agar-agar seaweed. A variety of sliced fruit, nuts, beans, and seeds can be mixed into the kanten, chilled, and served. Deep-fried kombu chips and other sea vegetable and vegetable chips make crunchy snacks. Seaweed candy, sweetened with barley malt or rice syrup, is available in many natural foods stores.

Nuts and Seeds—Chestnuts, walnuts, pecans, almonds, and other nuts can be added to cakes, pies, puddings, and cookies. Roasted seeds, seasoned with a little sea salt or tamari soy sauce, make wonderful snacks. Tahini and other nut or seed butters can be added to puddings and custards for thickening and texture. Nut milks, made by boiling and purëeing nuts, are very creamy and delicious and may be used as a base for many desserts.

Fruit—Fruit may be served fresh, dried, or cooked and, ideally, is grown in a similar climate. Apples are the most balanced of the fruits, though berries, melons, pears, plums, peaches, apricots, grapes, and other temperate-climate varieties may also be used.

In preparing desserts, I do not use eggs, dairy foods, chocolate, carob, honey, refined sweeteners, tropical spices, or baking powder. Nor do I use tofu, which becomes too weakening when combined with sweets and served cold. For baking, I use sesame oil whenever its taste will not conflict with the other ingredients. For a lighter, crispier taste unrefined corn oil is often more satisfactory. Kuzu or arrowroot flour thicken nicely instead of cornstarch or egg whites. For garnish or a slight spicy taste, I use a little grated fresh ginger.

NATURAL SWEETENERS

To supplement the naturally sweet taste of whole foods, I use small quantities of several natural sweeteners for desserts. Processed naturally from whole cereal grains and other plants, they include:

Amasake—Amasake is a fermented beverage made from sweet rice and a grain starter called *koji*. Amasake is creamy, thick, and delicious. It is white or light beige in color, and may be used as a sweetener for pies, cakes, puddings, and other desserts; in addition it may be served warm or chilled as a beverage. When combined with other ingredients and cooked, amasake firms up and gives a wonderful taste and texture. I use it often. (Please see the beverage section for recipe for making amasake at home.)

Barley Malt—Barley malt has a rich toasted flavor, is a dark opaque color, and has a thick consistency. It may be used in pies, cakes, puddings, and other desserts. When shopping, I am careful to obtain 100 percent barley malt rather than that which has been mixed with refined corn syrup.

Rice Syrup—Rice syrup (also known as rice malt) has a lighter, more delicate flavor than barley malt and is golden-amber in color. It is usually made with a small amount of barley. One brand of rice syrup, called yinnie syrup, is more pearly colored and has a more bittersweet taste.

Mirin—Mirin is a traditional cooking wine made from fermented sweet rice. Like sake, it is used primarily as a seasoning in regular cooking but may be added, in small amounts, to frostings, sauces, and other sweet toppings.

Maple Syrup—Maple syrup, processed from maple sugar trees, is very sweet and delicious. However, it is a very concentrated product. Forty gallons of sap are needed to produce one gallon of syrup. One hundred percent Grade A maple syrup contains about 65 percent sucrose compared to white sugar with 99 percent sucrose. Grades B and C have only slightly lesser amounts. Maple syrup should be used very sparingly. Just a touch in cooking or desserts is usually plenty.

REFINED SWEETENERS

None of my five children was brought up on sugar or other refined sweeteners. Once in high school a friend of my daughter Lilly insisted she try ice cream. She put a single teaspoon into her mouth but the ice cream was so strong and strange that she couldn't swallow and had to spit it out. That day she came home with a purple, swollen nose. She hadn't noticed it, but when I pointed it out she looked in the mirror and recalled her experience at lunch. Several years later, while in Japan, Lilly visited some friends and unknowingly ate some sweet ohagi that had a little sugar in it. She became disoriented and on the way home had an accident involving a train. Fortunately it was nothing serious.

During the Middle Ages, when refined sugar first became processed and entered Europe, it was locked away in apothecary shops for centuries as a dangerous drug. The widespread availability and consumption of sugar in the modern world is a primary cause of degenerative disease and mental and emotional disorders. In addition to the natural sweeteners mentioned above, there are a variety of other sweeteners available in the natural foods store that some people use as an alternative to white sugar. However, in my experience even these are too refined for even occasional use.

These include *honey*, which is a natural food, but one that is refined by the bees and has the highest sucrose content next to white sugar. The nectar from flowers is primarily sucrose and is broken down by the bees into fructose and glucose, two simple sugars that are assimilated rapidly into the bloodstream. *Carob* and *date sugar* are also high in fructose and should be avoided.

Molasses is a by-product of the refining of sugarcane into white sugar and is extremely high in sucrose. *Blackstrap molasses* is slightly less high in sucrose than regular molasses, as is *Barbados molasses*, which is made by boiling the sugarcane down directly into a syrup. *Sorghum molasses*, made from sweet sorghum, a cereal grain similar to millet, has a light, more fruity taste and about two-thirds the sucrose of the other types of molasses. *Brown sugar* is simply white sugar combined with a little molasses to give it a dark color and flavor. *Blond, turbinado* and *raw sugars* are white sugar minus the final bleaching process. They contain about 96 percent sucrose.

Corn syrup is made from chemically processed cornstarch mixed with sucrose for additional strength. *Fructose* is highly refined corn syrup or sucrose broken down to simple sugars. Fructose occurs naturally in fruits but the type sold as a sweetener is usually synthesized. *Xylitol* is a sweetener chemically extracted and processed from birchwood trees. *Sorbitol* is made from industrially refined glucose. *Saccharine* is an artificial sweetener processed from coal tar. *Aspartame* is a chemically synthesized sweetener recently introduced into soft drinks.

Whether processed naturally or artificially, all highly refined sweeteners should be strictly avoided.

Kanten

Kanten is a delicious all-natural gelatin made with fruit, beans, nuts, or seeds dissolved in a seaweed gel made from agar-agar. Any seasonal fruit, such as strawberries, raspberries, blueberries, melons, peaches, pears, and apples, may be used. Azuki beans and raisins make an excellent combination. A few nuts or seeds may also be added for variety and a crunchier dessert. When mixed with vegetables or soup stock agar-agar makes a vegetable aspic.

Agar-agar is available packaged in bars, flakes, or powder. I am always careful to read the directions on the package since the amount used varies with the batch. Here is a typical recipe for kanten.

2 cups spring water
2 cups apple juice
Pinch of sea salt
1 bar or 6 tablespoons agar-agar (follow package instructions)
3 medium-sized apples, sliced and cored

In a pot bring liquids and salt to a boil, gradually stirring in the agar-agar until it dissolves. Reduce heat to low and simmer for about 15 minutes. Add apple slices the last 5 minutes, stirring occasionally. Pour mixture into a large dish or into several small molds; refrigerate until jelled. Kanten is usually ready to serve in 45 to 60 minutes.

Variations: Instead of apple juice, water may be used with about ½ cup of raisins added to the apples for sweetness. Do not cook melons; just let the hot liquid cook and cool about halfway, then pour over the melon pieces and refrigerate. When using azuki beans and raisins, cook them together about 1½ hours before adding to other ingredients.

Applesauce

5 or 6 apples, sweet or tart or combined
Pinch of sea salt
Spring water
Raisins for garnish

Core and slice the apples. Place apples and a pinch of sea salt in a pot. Add enough water to slightly cover the bottom of the pot. Bring to a boil, cover, and reduce heat to low. Simmer until the apples are soft. Purée the apples in a hand food mill or in a suribachi. Serve in individual dishes and garnish with several raisins.

Variation: Naturally sweet fruits and vegetables can be prepared in this way to make nice sauces. For example, onion sauce is even sweeter than applesauce. To prepare, slice 4 to 6 medium-sized onions very thinly, bring to a boil with a pinch of sea salt in a little water, and simmer for about 30 to 40 minutes. The onions should turn dark in color and almost melt to the touch when they are done.

❧ Glazed Pears ❧

- 4 to 6 ripe pears, cut in half
- 1 cup apple juice
- 1 tablespoon kuzu
- Pinch sea salt
- ½ teaspoon grated fresh ginger

Place pears in a baking dish facing up. Pour juice over the pears, cover the baking dish, and cook in a 350- to 400-degree moderate oven until soft. When done, drain the liquid from the pears into a small pot, add the kuzu dissolved in a little cold water, and stir thoroughly. After 30 minutes, add the salt and the ginger to the pot. Stir occasionally and cook until the mixture thickens and becomes transparent, usually only several minutes. Pour topping over the pears and bake for 15 minutes more until glazed. Be careful pears don't burn.

❧ Baked Apples with Kuzu-Raisin Sauce ❧

- 1 cup apple juice
- ¼ cup raisins
- Pinch of sea salt
- 1 tablespoon kuzu
- Spring water
- 5 to 6 baking apples

Place the apple juice, raisins, and sea salt in a saucepan and bring to a boil. Reduce heat to low, cover, and simmer for about 5 minutes. Dilute the kuzu in a little water and add to the apple juice and raisins, stirring constantly to prevent lumping. Set aside. Wash apples, core, and put in a baking dish with a little water and bake in a 375-degree oven for about 30 to 40 minutes. Remove apples and place in individual serving dishes. Spoon sauce over the apples and serve hot.

Variation: Apples may be cored and filled with a mixture of tahini, raisins, and a small amount of puréed miso.

❧ Fruit Compote ❧

- ¼ cup raisins or currants
- Pinch of sea salt
- 4 cups spring water
- 2 cups sliced apples
- 1 cup sliced pears
- 2 tablespoons kuzu

Place raisins or currants in a pot and add some sea salt. Add the water, bring to a boil, cover, and simmer for about 5 minutes. Add the apples and pears, and simmer until they are soft. Dilute kuzu with a little water. Reduce heat to low and add the kuzu to the cooked fruit. Stir constantly until thick, simmer for 2 to 3 minutes, and serve.

Variation: Practically any fruit can be prepared in this way. For dried fruit, soak 30 minutes or longer and slice before cooking. Dried fruits usually take at least 20 minutes to cook and soften.

Fresh Watermelon

Fresh watermelon is cooling and delicious on a hot summer day. It may be cut in a variety of ways. I sometimes quarter and slice it, cut it into small cubes, or use a metal scooper to fashion beautiful watermelon balls. A little sea salt sprinkled on the melon makes it sweeter tasting and juicier.

Amasake Pudding

1 quart amasake
6 tablespoons kuzu
1 lemon slice for garnish
A few celery or parsley leaves for garnish

Place amasake and kuzu diluted in a little water in a pot. Stir and slowly bring to a boil. Continue to stir constantly to avoid lumping and burning. Simmer for 2 to 3 minutes, remove from heat, and pour into a serving dish. Smooth the amasake and garnish with a slice of lemon and a few fresh green leaves in the center of the dish. Allow to set before serving. If enough kuzu is used to thicken the amasake, it will harden and can be cut into squares.

Variation: For a different pudding, raisins, apples, pears, peaches, strawberries, and other sliced fresh fruit may be cooked with the amasake before adding the kuzu. Squash purée or chestnut purée also goes well in this dessert.

Rice Pudding

½ cup whole almonds
Spring water
3 to 4 tablespoons tahini
3½ cups cooked brown rice
1½ cups apple juice
¼ teaspoon sea salt

Boil almonds in ¾ cup water and add the tahini. Purée the almond-tahini mixture in a blender until smooth. Add all ingredients to pressure cooker, stir to combine, and cook for 40 to 45 minutes. After pressure-cooking, put rice mixture in a baking dish and bake in a 350-degree oven for 45 to 60 minutes. Just before end of cooking, remove cover to brown the top.

Tahini Custard

- 3 apples
- ½ cup raisins
- 2 cups apple juice
- 2 cups spring water
- 2 to 3 tablespoons tahini
- Pinch of sea salt
- 5 tablespoons agar-agar flakes or 1 bar (follow package instructions)

Wash apples, core, and slice. Place the apples and raisins in a pot with the liquids, tahini, sea salt, and agar-agar. Mix well, bring to a boil, reduce heat to low, and simmer for 2 to 3 minutes. Chill in a shallow bowl until almost hardened. Place cooled mixture in a blender and blend until smooth and creamy. Place custard back in serving bowl and chill once more before serving.

Chestnut Purée

- 2 cups dried chestnuts
- 5 cups spring water
- Pinch of sea salt

Wash chestnuts and dry-roast in a skillet over low heat for several minutes. Stir constantly to ensure even roasting. Remove and place in a pressure cooker. Add the water and salt and pressure-cook for about 40 to 50 minutes. Mash or grind in a hand food mill until smooth and creamy.

Variation: One tablespoon of the chestnut purée may be wrapped around a teaspoon of cooked mochi dough to make chestnut *ohagis*. The purée may also be put in different molds to make nice shapes and be decorated with seeds, nuts, and vegetable slices. Instead of roasting, chestnuts may be soaked overnight or for several hours. They become very sweet this way.

Chestnut or Squash Twists

This beautiful and delicious dessert is traditionally served on holidays in Japan and is known as *chakin-shibori*. It is customarily made with a *chakin*, a tea napkin used to wipe the tea bowl in the Japanese tea ceremony. At home it may be made instead with a few layers of twisted cheesecloth.

- 2 cups dried chestnuts or baked squash
- 5 cups spring water
- Pinch of sea salt

If using chestnuts, prepare as for chestnut purée and mash until smooth and creamy (see previous recipe). If using squash, cut butternut or buttercup squash in half and place, cut side down, on a baking sheet and bake in a 350- to 375-degree oven, until tender enough to purée. Remove skin and mash pulp well. To sweeten the squash even more, boiled currants or raisins may be mixed in or the squash may be combined with the chestnut purée.

Take 2 tablespoons of either mixture and place in the cheesecloth. Draw up the ends and twist tightly. When you remove it from the cheesecloth, you will have a round shape with a design from the twist of the cloth around the top. The twists will keep for one day unrefrigerated, then store remainder in refrigerator. Serve 2 to 3 pieces to each person.

Azuki Beans, Chestnuts, and Raisins

This nice dish needs no additional sweetener other than the beans and fruit. It is traditionally served over hot baked or dry pan-fried mochi.

- 1 cup azuki beans
- 1 cup dried chestnuts
- 5 cups spring water
- 1 strip kombu, about 6 inches long
- ½ to ¾ cup raisins
- ½ to 1 teaspoon sea salt

Soak beans and chestnuts together for 5 hours in the water. When finished soaking, place kombu in the bottom of a pot. Add the azuki beans, chestnuts, and raisins. Add the soaking water to cover the mixture and bring to a boil. Cover, reduce heat to low, and simmer for about 3 hours. Add extra cold water if necessary from time to time. Season with a little sea salt and simmer several more minutes before serving.

Note: To prepare more quickly, mixture may be pressure-cooked for about 40 to 45 minutes instead of boiled. Add salt at the end of cooking.

❧ Sweet Rice Cookies ❧

This recipe makes about 12 to 15 large, thin cookies.

- 1 cup sweet rice flour
- 1½ cups whole wheat pastry flour
- ½ cup roasted sesame seeds
- ½ cup roasted sunflower seeds
- ¼ teaspoon sea salt
- 2 tablespoons sesame or corn oil
- 1 cup raisins or currants
- 1½ cups apple juice

Mix the dry ingredients together in a large bowl. Add oil and mix well with your hands. Add raisins or currants and apple juice and mix well again. Spoon a heaping tablespoon of batter at a time ½ inch apart on a well-oiled baking sheet. Spread out batter very thin and bake in a 350-degree oven for 25 minutes or until done.

❧ Oatmeal Cookies ❧

This recipe will make about 1 dozen cookies.

- 1½ cups rolled oats
- ¾ cup whole wheat pastry flour
- 1½ tablespoons corn oil
- ½ cup chopped walnuts
- ½ cup rice syrup
- ½ cup spring water
- ⅛ teaspoon sea salt

In a large bowl combine the oats, salt, and flour, add the oil, and mix together well. Add the walnuts, rice syrup, and water. Mix and spoon batter onto a lightly oiled baking sheet. Smooth batter with the back of a spoon. Bake in a 350-degree oven for 20 to 25 minutes or until cookies are golden brown.

❧ Apple Pie ❧

- 10 to 12 baking or cooking apples, sliced and cored
- ¼ cup rice syrup or barley malt
- ¼ cup spring water
- 2 tablespoons arrowroot flour
- Pinch of sea salt

Combine all of the ingredients in a saucepan and bring to a boil. Mix well and stir to prevent lumping or burning. Reduce heat to low, cover, and simmer until apples are soft and desired consistency. Remove from heat and cool. Meanwhile, prepare pie dough (see recipe below). After the bottom shell has baked, add the fruit filling and cover with the top crust. Seal edges. Make several holes with a fork in top crust for steam to escape. Bake in a preheated 350- to 375-degree oven for about 35 to 45 minutes or until golden brown.

Basic Pie Crust

For a light flaky crust, I use whole wheat pastry flour. For variety, a little brown rice flour, sweet rice flour, or corn flour may be mixed in (¼ to ½ cup per 3 cups of pastry flour). The following recipe makes one double crust or two 9-inch crusts.

- 3 cups whole wheat pastry flour
- ¼ to ½ teaspoon sea salt
- ⅓ to ½ cup corn oil
- ½ cup cold spring water

Combine flour and salt in a large bowl. Add the oil and with a fork stir it into the flour until the flour is coated and has a pebble-like consistency. Add spring water, mix with a fork, and form dough into a ball. Divide into two equal pieces. Roll out one half of the dough between two sheets of wax paper. A little water may be put under the bottom paper to prevent sliding and a little dry flour on the surface to prevent sticking. Roll out dough, starting with light short strokes, ending with longer strokes and more pressure. Peel back the top piece of wax paper and turn rolled-out dough upside-down into pie plate. Peel off the other layer of wax paper. Press down edges with your thumb or with a fork. Then, with a fork, prick the bottom and sides of the dough. Bake for about 10 minutes in a preheated 375-degree oven. Meanwhile, prepare top crust, rolling out the same way. Set aside.

Peach Pie

- 4 cups sliced, unpeeled fresh peaches, about 2 pounds
- 2 to 3 tablespoons spring water
- Pinch of sea salt
- 2 to 3 tablespoons rice syrup
- 1 to 2 tablespoons kuzu or arrowroot flour

Place peaches and water in a saucepan, add salt, and bring to a boil. Reduce heat to low, cover, and simmer for 2 to 3 minutes. Add the rice syrup and mix. Dilute kuzu or arrowroot flour in a little water and mix in with the peaches. Stir well to avoid lumping. Cook for several minutes until thick. Allow to cool slightly before placing in a pie shell. (See recipe for pie crust above. Bake as for apple pie.)

Variations: Other fruit pies can be made in this way, including blueberry pie, cherry pie, and other berry pies. Depending on the natural sweetness of the fruit, a little more rice syrup may need to be added.

Squash Pie

Squash pie is very sweet and delicious and one of the most anticipated treats in autumn and winter. I am especially fond of buttercup squash but other winter squashes, including pumpkins, may be used.

- 1 medium-sized buttercup squash, about 2½ to 3 pounds
- 1 cup spring water
- Pinch of sea salt
- ¼ to ½ cup barley malt
- 1 tablespoon kuzu
- 1 cup chopped walnuts

Wash squash and remove skin and seeds (the seeds may be saved for roasting). Cut squash into chunks and place in a pot with the water. Add a pinch of salt, bring to a boil, reduce heat to medium-low, and cover. Simmer until the squash is soft, about 20 minutes. Purée the squash in a hand food mill until smooth. Return the puréed squash to the pot and add the barley malt. Simmer for about 5 minutes. Dilute the kuzu in a little water and add it to the puréed squash, stirring constantly to avoid lumping. Simmer for 2 to 3 minutes. Remove from the heat and allow to cool. Prepare pie dough for 1 crust, following recipe for basic pie crust, page 328. Bake the bottom crust in a preheated 350-degree oven for about 10 minutes. Fill with the squash mixture, smooth out the top of the filling, and sprinkle with the chopped walnuts. Bake in a 350-degree oven for 30 to 35 minutes or until the crust is golden brown.

Cherry Strudel

- 3 cups fresh cherries, washed and pitted
- Spring water
- Pinch of sea salt
- 1 teaspoon kuzu
- ½ cup chopped almonds
- Pastry dough (½ Basic Pie Crust, page 328)

Place the cherries in a pot and add about 2 tablespoons of water and a pinch of sea salt. Gently bring to a boil and simmer for 3 to 5 minutes. Place the kuzu in a little cold water and dilute, making sure to dissolve all lumps before using. Add the diluted kuzu and mix well to coat the cherries thoroughly. Simmer until a thick sauce is formed. Remove from the heat and stir in the chopped nuts. Let cool.

Prepare pastry dough for 1 crust, roll out, but do not turn into a pie plate. When the cherries have cooled, spoon the cherry mixture onto the rolled-out dough and spread evenly to cover, leaving the edges of the pastry uncovered. Roll filled pastry into a log or cylinder shape. Seal the ends by pressing with a wet fork. Poke several holes in the top of the roll with a fork to let steam escape while cooking and to keep the strudel from splitting in half. Put the strudel on a lightly oiled baking sheet. Bake in a preheated 375-degree oven for about 30 minutes or until the crust is golden brown. Remove and allow the strudel to cool. Slice into 1½- to 2-inch rounds and serve attractively arranged on a platter.

Pear Crisp

- 2 tablespoons arrowroot flour
- Pinch of sea salt
- ¼ cup spring water
- 5 to 6 ripe pears, washed, sliced, and cored (peel, if desired)
- ½ cup roasted walnuts
- 1 cup rolled oats
- 2 tablespoons rice syrup or barley malt

Combine the arrowroot flour, sea salt, and water in a bowl. Add the pears and gently toss to coat well. Transfer to a greased baking dish and spread out evenly. Separately dry-roast walnuts and oats until golden brown. Chop the walnuts and mix them together with the roasted oats and the rice syrup or barley malt. Spread this topping evenly over the pear mixture, cover, and bake in a preheated 375-degree oven for about 20 minutes. Remove cover and let bake another 5 to 10 minutes until top is brown.

Variations: Other fruits may be made in crisps in this way. Berries can be baked for slightly less time and apples slightly longer.

Apricot-Couscous Cake

Couscous cake is a mild sweet cake made with a fluffy whole wheat product popular in the Middle East. Couscous cake has become a standard feature at most macrobiotic parties, weddings, and holiday celebrations. Instead of the apricot topping below, strawberries, apples, cherries, and other fresh fruits may be used.

- 2 cups couscous
- 2 cups apple juice
- 1½ to 2 cups spring water
- Pinch of sea salt

Topping

1 cup spring water
2 cups apple juice
Pinch of sea salt
4 to 5 tablespoons agar-agar flakes or 1 bar (follow package instructions)
2 cups fresh apricots, pitted and sliced but not peeled

Wash the couscous and place it in a fine mesh steamer or line the bottom of a steamer with cheesecloth to keep the couscous from falling through. Steam for about 5 minutes. Remove and put in a bowl. Fluff up couscous to help it cool. Bring the apple juice, water, and salt to a boil. Boil for 1 to 2 minutes; pour the hot liquid over the couscous and mix well. Put the couscous in a glass cake pan or baking dish and press it down so that it occupies about half the height of the pan and is fairly compact. Cover and let sit for a few minutes while you prepare the topping. Place the water, juice, sea salt, and agar-agar in a sauce pan and bring to a boil. Reduce heat to low and simmer for 2 to 3 minutes. Add the apricots and remove the pan from the heat. Let liquid cool a little, then pour it over the couscous. Place the cake in a cool place or refrigerate and let sit until the topping jells. When done the cake should be firm and cover the bottom half of the pan. The apricot topping also should be firm and cover the top half of the pan. Slice into squares and serve.

Strawberry Shortcake

2 cups yellow cornmeal
1 cup whole wheat pastry flour
½ teaspoon sea salt
3 tablespoons light or dark sesame oil
½ cup rice syrup
½ cup barley malt
1 cup spring water

Topping

2 quarts fresh strawberries
¼ to ½ cup spring water
½ cup rice syrup
Pinch of sea salt
½ cup arrowroot flour

To prepare the shortcake, combine the dry ingredients in a large bowl. Mix in oil very well. Add the rice syrup, barley malt, and water and mix together. Put the batter in a lightly oiled cake pan or in muffin tins. You should have about 12 muffins. Bake in a preheated 250-degree oven for 15 minutes; then raise the heat to 375 degrees and continue to bake for another 15 to 20 minutes.

Meanwhile, prepare topping. Wash strawberries, remove stems, and cut berries in half. Put the fruit, water, rice syrup, and salt in a pan. Add the arrowroot flour and mix gently but well. Bring to a boil, reduce heat to low, and simmer until sauce thickens and strawberries are soft. Stir to prevent sticking and lumping. When the cake is done, remove from oven. Slice it into squares and serve with the strawberry topping.

Variation: Instead of strawberries, peaches, blueberries, pears, applesauce, and other fresh fruits may be used to make fruit sauces.

SNACKS

For in between meals and for light desserts, there are a variety of snacks that may be prepared with natural ingredients. Like other foods containing high amounts of fat, oil, or natural sweeteners, they should be used only occasionally and then in small volume.

DRY-ROASTED SEEDS

Dry-roasted sesame, sunflower, pumpkin, or squash seeds are very delicious. To prepare, first gently rinse the seeds; then place a handful or two (but not too many seeds at a time) in a dry skillet. Adjust heat to medium-low and gently stir the seeds using a wooden roasting paddle or wooden spoon for 5 to 10 minutes, shaking the pan from time to time. When done, seeds will have darkened in color, become crisp, and will have a fragrant aroma. Seeds may be lightly seasoned with sea salt or tamari soy sauce toward the end of roasting to make them more digestible and tasty.

POPCORN

Popcorn is a traditional native American food. Oil is not necessary for cooking, and without it salt is not needed afterward to make balance. To prepare popcorn, take three kernels of popcorn and put them in a pot or saucepan. Cover lightly and turn heat to medium-low. When the three kernels have popped, the pot is hot enough to cook the kernels. One tablespoon of popcorn kernels makes about 2½ cups of popcorn, so judge accordingly. After adding the corn kernels, place a flame deflector beneath the pot, cover lightly, and cook until nearly all the kernels have popped and there are no more popping sounds. For storage, popcorn kernels should be kept in tightly sealed containers in a cool dark place. Loss of internal moisture will cause popcorn to lose its fluffiness and crispness. To restore moisture, fill a jar about three-quarters full of popcorn kernels, add one tablespoon of spring water, and shake every few minutes until the liquid is absorbed. Let sit a couple of days before using and moisture should be restored.

Cracker Jacks

¼ cup popcorn kernels
Sea salt
½ cup barley malt
½ cup rice syrup

Prepare popcorn as described above and put it in a large bowl. Season with several pinches of sea salt. Heat barley malt and rice syrup either separately or combined. Bring the sweeteners to a boil, reduce the heat, and simmer for 1 to 2 minutes. Pour the hot sweetener over the popcorn and mix well to coat the popcorn. Put the sweet popcorn in an ungreased baking pan and bake in a preheated 375-degree oven for several minutes. The sweetener will darken when done. Be careful not to burn the syrup which heats quickly. Remove from oven and let cool. The sweetener will harden as it cools.

Variation: Instead of popcorn, sweet rice can be used. It puffs up like popcorn. First soak the sweet rice overnight, then dry-roast it; sweeten and bake it as in this recipe.

RICE CAKES

Made from puffed brown rice and sea salt, rice cakes are a tasty, crunchy snack. They are available ready-made in most natural foods stores and may be eaten plain or enjoyed with sesame or peanut butter, natural fruit jellies and jams, or spreads made with miso, tofu, or other ingredients. In addition to regular brown rice cakes, there are varieties made with sesame seeds, buckwheat, millet, oats, or other grains mixed in. Rice cakes store well but they will dry out with age. To restore their crispness, heat them in a slow oven for a few minutes.

Miso-Tahini Spread

This spread makes a delicious snacktime food. It may be served with crackers and bread or combined with some chopped onion and can be used as a sandwich filling.

3 tablespoons tahini
1 tablespoon miso

In a skillet dry-roast the tahini over medium heat until it begins to turn golden. The tahini cooks quickly and requires constant stirring and watching to prevent burning. When roasted, remove the tahini and blend with the miso. For a thinner mixture, dilute with a little cooled, boiled water.

Variation: For a little different taste, add ½ teaspoon freshly grated orange rind with the miso.

Walnut-Miso Spread

1 cup walnuts, shelled
2 tablespoons miso
¼ cup spring water

Dry-roast the walnuts in a skillet over medium heat until lightly toasted. Remove from heat, let cool, and cut into slivers. Put the walnut slivers in a suribachi and grind to a paste. Purée miso and water and blend with walnuts to make a smooth cream.

Variations: Instead of walnuts, pecans, peanuts, or sunflower seeds may be used. A nice salad dressing may be made by doubling the amount of water. This spread goes well on celery sticks and on lightly boiled ohitashi-style vegetables.

Apple Butter

Apple butter makes a nice smooth spread for rice cakes, bread, or crackers.

2 pounds of cooking or baking apples
Pinch of sea salt
½ cup spring water

Peel the apples, core, and slice. Put apple slices in a pot with a little salt and a small volume of water, about ½ cup. Bring to a boil, cover, and reduce heat to very low. Place a flame-deflector beneath the pot and stir the apples from time to time to prevent burning. Simmer on a low heat until the apples have thickened and turned brown. Store in a tightly covered jar in the refrigerator.

Squash-Apple Butter

1 small buttercup squash, about 1½ pounds
2 to 3 apples
½ cup spring water
Pinch of sea salt

Peel the squash, remove seeds (save for roasting), and cut squash into cubes. Peel the apples, core, and cut into chunks or thin slices. Put the squash and apples in a pot and add a little water and sea salt. Bring to a boil, reduce heat to low, cover, and simmer until squash is soft. Purée mixture in a food mill until creamy. Return to pot and cook on a low heat, stirring occasionally, for about 30 to 45 minutes. The butter is done when it has thickened. Store in a tightly covered jar in the refrigerator.

Kombu Chips

These deep-fried seaweed chips can be served for snacks or parties. They are salty and are usually eaten with a beverage.

4 to 5 medium-sized kombu strips
Light sesame oil

If very salty dust off the kombu with a wet sponge. Break the kombu into 1-inch pieces. Heat at least 1 inch of oil to 375 degrees in a pot. When the oil is hot, but not smoking, add several of the kombu pieces to the hot oil. Deep-fry for 1 to 2 minutes or until crispy. Remove, and drain the seaweed of excess oil on a paper towel. Serve in a basket or bowl lined with a napkin to absorb oil.

Variations: Other vegetables can be deep-fried this way. Carrots make especially good chips.

CHAPTER

27

BEVERAGES

Red bees,
Have you come to fetch nectar
In the tea bushes?
—Tsuroyo

Beverages are essential to our health. Yet sometimes we drink out of habit rather than necessity. It is ideal to drink only when thirsty. If we are constantly thirsty, we need to reflect on our way of eating. Animal foods are extremely high in sodium and other mineral salts and can lead to retention of excessive fluid in the body. Overeating can cause frequent thirst as can cooking that uses too much salt.

In hot weather and in warm climates we naturally tend to drink more and enjoy our beverages cool. However, even in hot environments it is best to avoid icy cold beverages. Cold foods and drinks can shock the digestive system, producing a paralyzing effect on the intestines. Warmth is the symbol of life. Our bodies need to remain at a certain temperature. Even slight fluctuations above or below our normal individual body temperature can result in very serious illness. Warm or hot foods and beverages contribute to maintaining this inner fire. Very young and old persons must be particularly careful about consuming cold fluids and other chilled items.

In macrobiotic households, we generally serve bancha twig tea as the main beverage after or in between meals. Bancha is a mild, soothing, naturally processed tea that may be taken by young and old alike. Other regular beverages include spring or well water, roasted grain teas, grain coffee, and amasake. Less frequently we enjoy a glass of apple juice, apple cider, or other organic high-quality fruit juices for a temperate climate, vegetable juice, green tea, herbal teas, or mineral water. Aromatic and stimulating beverages, such as coffee, black tea, and mint tea, are generally avoided. Brown rice sake, unsweetened grape or plum wine, or beer made without sugar or preservatives may be enjoyed in small portions at parties or other special occasions.

WATER

Good quality water is essential for daily food preparation. Natural spring water or deep well water is best. Chemicalized tap water or distilled water is less satisfactory. Mineral water is not recommended for regular consumption but may be enjoyed occasionally at parties instead of alcohol or soft drinks. The less bubbly ones and those without sodium bicarbonate or other additives are preferred. As with other beverages, water should not be served cold or iced.

TEA

Tea originated in India, in the region of Assam, and accompanied Buddhism to China and Japan. In the Far East, tea bushes commonly serve as hedges around temples. As a child I often climbed with my playmates in the tea bushes around the village temple and picked the beautiful white flowers in spring.

All tea comes from the tea plant, but not all tea is alike. Tea may be made from the buds, leaves, twigs, or stems of a tea bush. The season when these are harvested and the way they are processed determine the quality of the tea. *Black tea*, also known as red leaf tea, is most popular in the West. It is fermented, highly processed, often dyed, and high in caffeine and tannin, the reddish substance which gives the tea its strong, astringent flavor. Common types of red leaf tea include Orange Pekoe and Souchong. *Green tea* is unfermented, steamed, and much less processed but also very high in caffeine. Typical types include Gunpowder, Young Hyson, and Imperial. *Oolong tea* is a combination of black and green tea and usually is scented with gardenia or jasmine. *Twig tea*, made from the stems and twigs of the tea bush, is known as bancha or kukicha tea in Japan. It is picked at the end of the summer or fall when the caffeine has naturally receded from the tea plant. *Bancha* means "late growing tea." Unlike black, green, or oolong teas, which are acidic, bancha twig tea is slightly alkaline. Twig tea is very good for digestion, serves as a buffer to acids in the stomach, and has many medicinal uses.

Bancha Tea

Place 1½ to 2 tablespoons of roasted twigs in 1½ quarts of spring water and bring to a boil. Keep unused twigs in an airtight jar until needed. When the water boils, reduce heat to low and simmer for several minutes. For a light tea, simmer 2 to 3 minutes. For a darker, stronger tea, simmer for 10 to 15 minutes. To serve, place a small bamboo or metal tea strainer in each cup and pour out the tea. Twigs in the strainer may be returned to the teapot and reused several times. Bancha tea may be served hot year-round as well as cool in the summer. It is usually drunk plain, though for medicinal purposes a drop of tamari soy sauce, kuzu, or other ingredients may be mixed in.

Green Tea

Green tea has a nice mild natural flavor. In Japan, we customarily served it at tea time in the afternoon along with pickles. A special grade of green tea, made from the first buds of the tea plant, is used in the tea ceremony. In the natural foods store, green tea is sometimes labeled as "Bancha Green Leaf Tea" and should not be confused with "Bancha Twig Tea." Because of its high caffeine content, green tea should be used very sparingly.

Roasted Barley Tea

In Japan we call barley tea *mugi cha*, and it is commonly available under this name in the natural foods store. Roasted barley tea is very cooling to the body, and we enjoyed it often during the summer while growing up. It may be served cool as well as warm. To make at home, dry-roast unhulled barley over medium heat for about 10 minutes or until a fragrant aroma is released. Stir and shake pan occasionally to prevent burning. Add 2 to 3 tablespoons of roasted barley to 1½ quarts of spring water. Bring to a boil, lower heat, and simmer for 5 to 15 minutes, depending on how mild or strong you like it.

Roasted Brown Rice Tea

Roasted brown rice tea has a wonderful nutty flavor and is made similar to roasted barley tea. Other grain teas, such as oat tea, millet tea, or buckwheat tea, may also be made in this way. All whole grain teas are suitable for daily use. For variety, grain tea may be mixed with bancha twig tea.

Corn Silk Tea

Native peoples in North America traditionally enjoyed a beverage made from the golden silk strands of fresh corn. To prepare, place a half cup of fresh corn silk in a quart of spring water and bring to a boil. Reduce heat and simmer for several minutes. Corn silk tea is good in hot weather and is beneficial to the kidneys and heart.

Umeboshi Tea

Umeboshi tea has a nice sour taste. It helps cool the body in summer and prevent loss of minerals through perspiration. It can be made by boiling 2 or 3 pitted umeboshi plums in a quart of spring water, reducing the heat, and simmering for about 20 to 30 minutes. It may also be made by cooking 3 or 4 leftover umeboshi pits. A few shiso leaves may be added to enhance flavor. Umeboshi tea is usually served cool in the summertime, though it also may be prepared hot. The taste should not be overly salty or it will contribute to thirst rather than quench it.

Mu Tea

Mu tea is a special tea named by George Ohsawa and prepared from 9 or 16 herbs. It contains a little ginseng, a very strong root that we do not otherwise use in macrobiotic cooking. Mu tea is traditionally used for medicinal purposes to strengthen the stomach and reproductive organs, but it may occasionally be taken in the colder months for strength and vitality. It is slightly sweet tasting and very soothing. Mu tea is available prepackaged in most natural foods stores.

Herbal Teas

There are many types of herbal teas made from the flowers, leaves, or roots of different plants. I enjoy herbal teas on occasion, especially those that are not too strong or spicy. Many herbal teas are aromatic or stimulating, and I find that it is easy to become imbalanced if using them for any length of time. Herbal teas also have many medicinal uses, but we should be very careful about experimenting with them. In macrobiotic home care, we use special medicinal teas for specific conditions, for a short period of time, and usually under the guidance of an experienced counselor. Traditional Chinese herbal teas are especially strong and in my view should be taken only in consultation with an herbal specialist.

Dandelion Tea

I enjoy the strong bitter taste of dandelion root tea. This is made by washing and drying the roots, steeping them in hot water, and preparing like bancha twig tea.

GRAIN COFFEE

Grain coffee makes a healthful alternative to regular coffee or decaffeinated coffee which is usually prepared by a chemical process.

Homemade Grain Coffee (*Yannoh*)

A recipe for grain coffee popularized by George Ohsawa is called *Yannoh.* It is available prepackaged in Japan and Europe. Here's how to make it at home.

3 cups brown rice
2½ cups winter wheat
1½ cups azuki beans
2 cups chick-peas
1 cup chicory root

Separately dry-roast each ingredient in a skillet until dark in color, stirring to prevent burning. Mix roasted grains, beans, and chicory together and grind to a fine powder in a grain mill. Brew coffee using 1 teaspoon of yannoh per cup of water. If left to boil, the yannoh tends to foam, so quickly reduce the heat and simmer for 5 to 10 minutes. Store the powder in an airtight container.

Many delicious grain coffees may be made combining chicory with different roasted grains and beans. Several ready-made grain coffees are available in the natural foods store. I prefer those that contain no molasses, honey, dried tropical fruits, spices, or other strong ingredients.

VEGETABLE AND FRUIT JUICE

The first time I tasted fresh carrot juice was at a farmers market in Los Angeles. It was very delicious. Usually in preparing macrobiotic meals, we minimize the use of vegetable or fruit juices because they are too highly concentrated for regular consumption. However, in very hot weather, an occasional glass of good-quality juice is enjoyable. Among fruit beverages, organic apple juice or apple cider is the most balanced, though grape, cranberry, apricot, pear, and other temperate-climate fruit juices may also be enjoyed in small volume. A nice punch for summertime parties can be made by combining 1 quart of apple juice with ½ quart of mineral water and garnishing with several slices of lemon, lime, or orange. In the autumn, warm or hot apple cider may be served occasionally to those in good health or used as a sweetener in cooking.

AMASAKE

Amasake is a beverage made from fermented sweet rice. It is thick and delicious, and traditionally given to nursing mothers, babies, and others requiring strength and vitality. Amasake may also be used to sweeten pies, cakes, puddings, breads, and other baked products. Served warm on a cold winter day amasake is very nourishing. In summer it may be served chilled. Amasake is usually served with a touch of grated ginger. In the natural foods store, amasake is now available in quart or half-quart containers. It may also be made at home using rice koji as a starter. The basic recipe follows.

Homemade Amasake

4 cups sweet brown rice
8 cups spring water
½ cup koji

Wash rice, drain, and soak in the water overnight. Place rice and soaking water in a pressure cooker and bring to pressure. Lower heat and cook for 45 minutes. Turn off heat and allow to sit in pressure cooker for another 45 minutes. When cool enough to handle, mix the koji into the rice with your hands. Then transfer the mixture to a glass bowl (do not use metal), cover with a wet cloth or towel, and place near an oven, radiator, or any other warm place. Allow to ferment 4 to 8 hours. During the fermentation period, occasionally stir the mixture to melt the koji. After fermenting, put the amasake in a pot and bring to boil. When bubbles appear, turn off the heat. Allow to cool. Refrigerate in a glass bowl or jar and tightly seal. When fermentation has stopped, it will keep for a couple of weeks. To serve as a beverage, first stir the amasake and put it in a saucepan with a pinch of sea salt and enough spring water to achieve the consistency desired. Bring to a boil and serve hot or allow to cool and serve chilled. When used as a sweetener in puddings or pastries, amasake may be added directly or blended first until smooth.

CHAPTER 28

SEASONAL AND HOLIDAY MENUS

謹賀新春
Happy New Year!
In the attic
Even the mice celebrate.
—Yoshiko

This chapter contains a week of daily menus for each of the four seasons. These daily menus give some idea of how to balance meals with the changing environment as well as typical combinations of foods in the Standard Macrobiotic Diet. Our daily food is ideally like a melody with a basic theme and many variations. Pressure-cooked brown rice, miso soup, a few basic vegetable and sea vegetable dishes, and beans and bean products are the theme, while other whole grains, bean and vegetable soups, salads, occasional fish or seafood, fruit, and desserts are the variation. Principal food can take many forms too, depending upon the cooking method, whether it is cooked alone or in combination with other ingredients, seasoning, garnishes, and condiments and pickles accompanying the meal. Variety is very important to balanced meals, but novelty should complement order, never replace it.

Following the seasonal recipes are suggested menus for holidays, birthdays, and other special occasions when more festive foods are traditionally served.

Information on how to prepare all of the dishes listed in this chapter can be found by consulting the index.

SPRING MENU

	Breakfast	Lunch	Dinner
SUNDAY	Soft Rice Celery Miso Soup Bancha tea	Udon and Broth Marinated Daikon and Carrots Grain Coffee	Pressure-Cooked Brown Rice Tamari Broth Tofu with Arame Boiled Carrots and Onions Steamed Kale Quick Lemon-Miso Pickles Oatmeal Cookies Bancha tea
MONDAY	Whole Oats Rice Kayu Bread Bancha tea	Miso Soup with Wakame and Daikon Brown Rice Sweet-and-Sour Seitan Bancha tea	Pressure-Cooked Brown Rice and Wheat Berries Red Lentil Soup Broccoli with Tofu Cream Dressing Boiled Kombu Onion-Tamari Pickles Dandelion tea
TUESDAY	Miso Soft Rice with Chives Bancha tea	Baked Tofu Sandwich Tamari Broth Boiled Salad with Dandelions Bancha tea	Pressure-Cooked Brown Rice Steamed Tempeh and Sauerkraut Boiled Mustard Greens with Tamari-Ginger Sauce Boiled Wakame and Onions Amasake Pudding Bancha tea

WEDNESDAY	Miso Soup with Onion and Wakame Toasted Mochi Grated Daikon with Nori Strips Grain Coffee	Rice Ball Chinese Cabbage with Tamari-Lemon Sauce Bancha tea	Pressure-Cooked Rice and Barley Clear Soup Chick-peas Nishime Vegetables Broccoli and Cauliflower Pickles Bancha tea
THURSDAY	Miso with Wakame Soft Millet Sprouted Wheat Bread Bancha tea	Fried Soba Natto Dulse, Carrots, and Celery Grain Coffee	Brown Rice with Wild Vegetables Carrot Soup Hiziki Carrot Tops with Sesame Seeds Kanten Bancha tea
FRIDAY	Brown Rice Cream Miso Soup with Scallions Bancha tea	Seitan and Sauerkraut Sourdough Bread Small Garden Salad with Sprouts Bancha tea	Pressure-Cooked Brown Rice Azuki Beans and Wheat Berries Clear Broth Wakame with Sour Tofu Dressing Chinese Style Sautéed Vegetables with Kuzu Sauce Bancha tea
SATURDAY	Miso Soup Creamy Buckwheat Dumplings Mustard Green Pickles Grain Coffee	Boiled Millet Tamari Broth Tempeh with Watercress Bancha tea	Pressure-Cooked Rice and Rye Fu and Broccoli in Broth Kombu, Carrots, and Burdock Nori Condiment Fruit Compote Bancha tea

SUMMER MENU

	Breakfast	Lunch	Dinner
SUNDAY	Miso with Wakame and Daikon Boiled Tofu with Ginger-Parsley Sauce Bancha tea	Boiled Millet Fresh Corn Soup Boiled String Beans and Almonds Watermelon Corn Silk tea	Brown Rice Salad Black Beans Wakame with Scallions Rutabaga Tamari Pickles Bancha tea
MONDAY	Soft Rice with Nori Flakes Red Radish Pickles Bancha tea	Cold Somen Noodles Steamed Cabbage, Celery, and Carrots Grain Coffee	Brown Rice with Corn Kernels Cool Chick-pea Soup Sautéed Snowpeas and Chinese Cabbage Hiziki Salad with Tofu Bancha tea
TUESDAY	Scrambled Tofu and Corn Sourdough Bread Bancha tea	Miso Soup with Sesame Seeds and Broccoli Corn on the Cob with Umeboshi Boiled Onions Grain Coffee	Chirashi Sushi Clear Broth Kombu, Carrots, and Burdock Baked Zucchini with Miso-Lemon Sauce Strawberry Shortcake Barley tea
WEDNESDAY	Soft Barley with Scallions and Nori Strips Chinese Cabbage Pickles Bancha tea	Barley Stew Arepa Bancha tea	Buckwheat Salad Lentils Celery Soup Boiled Cabbage with Sesame and Umeboshi Sauce Bancha tea

THURSDAY	Creamy Onion Miso Soup Whole Oats Rice Kayu Bread Bancha tea	Udon and Broth Wakame Cucumber Salad with Tamari-Vinegar Sauce Grain Coffee	Pressure-Cooked Brown Rice Corn on the Cob Cauliflower Soup Arame with Tempeh and Onions Quick Lemon-Miso Pickles Steamed Kale Fruit Salad Bancha tea
FRIDAY	Soft Rice with Scallions Corn on the Cob Bancha tea	Bulghur Sautéed Tofu and Vegetables Parsley with Ginger Sauce Brown Rice Tea	Brown Rice and Lotus Seeds Boiled Carrots, Onions, and Chinese Cabbage Red Radishes and Kuzu Sauce Shio Kombu Barley tea
SATURDAY	Soft Millet with Sweet Corn Tamari-Onion Pickles Bancha tea	Rice Ball Tempeh Shish kebab Sliced Cucumber Bancha tea	Polenta Barley Soup Hiziki with Soybeans Boiled Turnip Greens with Sesame-Tamari Sauce Fresh Cantaloupe Bancha tea

AUTUMN MENU

	Breakfast	Lunch	Dinner
SUNDAY	Whole Oats Miso Bread Bancha tea	Wild Rice Miso Soup with Daikon and Wakame Broiled Tofu Bancha tea	Pressure-Cooked Brown Rice Clear Broth Nishime Daikon and Vegetables Chinese Cabbage with Tamari-Lemon Sauce Hiziki Tamari Turnip Pickles Applesauce Bancha tea
MONDAY	Soft Rice with Corn and Umeboshi Daikon Tamari Pickles Bancha tea	Roasted Rice Creamy Onion Miso Soup Bancha tea	Millet with Squash Barley Soup Boiled Cauliflower and Broccoli Kombu Carrot Rolls Ginger Pickles Bancha tea
TUESDAY	Soft Barley with Scallions Miso Soup with Squash and Millet Bancha tea	Fried Noodles and Tempeh Pressed Mixed Salad Grain Coffee	Pressure-Cooked Brown Rice Azuki Beans and Chestnuts Baked Butternut Squash and Onions Boiled Cabbage with Sesame Seeds and Umeboshi Sauce Shio Kombu Daikon Green Pickles Bancha tea

	Bancha tea	Steamed Mustard Greens Bancha tea	Clear Soup Lotus Root Stuffed with Miso Boiled Collard Greens with Tamari-Vinegar Sauce Arame with Onions Chinese Cabbage Pickles Squash Pie Grain Coffee
THURSDAY	Soft Barley Rice Kayu Bread Grain Coffee	Rice Ball Onion Wakame Soup Sautéed Tofu and Vegetables Bancha tea	Pressure-Cooked Brown Rice Squash Soup Seitan Kinpira Parsley with Ginger Sauce Dulse, Carrots, and Celery Bancha tea
FRIDAY	Soft Buckwheat with Scallions Sauerkraut Bancha tea	Whole Wheat Sourdough Bread Broccoli with Tofu Dressing Lotus Root Salad Roasted Brown Rice Tea	Sweet Brown Rice and Azuki Beans Clear Soup Endive with Kuzu Sauce Steamed Kale with Tamari Ginger Sauce Kombu and Dried Daikon Bancha tea
SATURDAY	Soft Millet with Squash Tamari-Onion Pickles Bancha tea	Rye and Vegetables Chick-pea Soup Boiled Salad Grain Coffee	Fried Rice Corn Soup Watercress Rolls Baked Carrots Wakame with Scallions Rutabaga Tamari Pickles Sweet Rice Cookies Bancha tea

WINTER MENU

	Breakfast	Lunch	Dinner
SUNDAY	Miso Soup with Wakame and Cauliflower Soft Rice with Parsley Chinese Cabbage Pickles Bancha tea	Fried Soba Boiled Carrots and Onions Grain Coffee	Brown Rice and Sesame Seeds Azuki Bean Soup Sautéed Cabbage, Celery, and Carrots Boiled Kombu Bran Pickles Glazed Pears Bancha tea
MONDAY	Whole Oats with Dulse Rice Kayu Bread Bancha tea	Baked Tofu Sandwich Tamari Broth Bancha tea	Pressure-Cooked Brown Rice Oden Colorful Soybean Casserole Turnip Greens with Sesame-Tamari Dressing Arame with Dried Tofu and Carrots Bancha tea
TUESDAY	Soft Millet with Squash Jinenjo Miso Soup Bancha tea	Nori-Maki Sushi Seitan Croquettes Grated Daikon Bancha tea	Brown Rice and Azuki Beans Clear Daikon Soup Burdock Kinpira Boiled Watercress Salad Wakame with Scallions and a Miso-Vinegar Sauce Turnip Green Pickles Baked Apple with Kuzu-Raisin Sauce Bancha tea

WEDNESDAY	Miso Soft Rice Pickled Daikon Greens Bancha tea	Buckwheat Soup Cabbage Roll Tempeh Grain Coffee	Gomoku Sweet-and-Sour Seitan Steamed Kale and Carrots Hiziki Broccoli and Cauliflower Pickles Bancha tea
THURSDAY	Buckwheat Pancakes with Apple-Kuzu Sauce Grain Coffee	Seitan Stew Sauerkraut Roasted Brown Rice Tea	Fried Rice Black Soybeans Baked Buttercup Squash Boiled Collard Greens with a Tamari-Ginger Sauce Wakame and Onions Takuwan Pickles Amasake Pudding Bancha tea
FRIDAY	Miso Soup with Wakame and Onion Toasted Mochi Grated Daikon and Nori Strips Bancha tea	Rice Ball Azuki Beans with Lotus Seeds Onion-Tamari Pickles Bancha tea	Sweet Brown Rice and Chestnuts Cauliflower Soup Burdock Eel Daikon Greens and Kombu Ginger Pickles Grain Coffee
SATURDAY	Rice Cream Creamy Onion Miso Soup Bancha tea	Pressure-Cooked Brown Rice Yudofu Boiled Broccoli Bancha tea	Boiled Brown Rice Vegetable Tempura Grated Daikon and Ginger Kidney Beans Steamed Kale Amasake Bancha tea

HOLIDAY MENUS

New Year's Day (January 1)

Zoni—Miso or clear soup with mochi
Red Rice—Pressure-cooked brown rice with azuki beans
Kinpira Burdock and Carrots
Black Soybeans—Boiled, sweetened or unsweetened
Kombu Knots—Strips of boiled kombu tied in knot shapes
Nishime Vegetables—Pan- or deep-fried tofu, daikon, carrots, taro, seitan boiled nishime-style
Kara Age Sliced Lotus—Deep-fried lotus root
Kara Age Whole Red Snapper—Deep-fried white-meat fish decorated with sliced lemon, parsley, and grated daikon
Shredded Daikon and Carrots—Marinated with tamari soy sauce, mirin, and brown rice vinegar
Kale and Watercress with Ginger-Tamari Sauce—Greens boiled separately and mixed together with a sauce
Chestnut Twists with Raisin or Dried Apple
Daikon Pickles
Sake, Beer, or Wine
Bancha Tea

Girls' Day (March 3)

Green and White Mochi—Pounded sweet rice made with mugwort and made plain, and served with azuki beans, dried apple, and raisins and with almonds and tamari soy sauce
Clear Soup with Tofu and Carrots
Seitan in Cabbage Rolls with Kuzu Sauce
Boiled Watercress Salad with Tamari Soy Sauce and Sesame Seeds
Arame with Dried Tofu and Carrots
Sauerkraut and Quick Red Radish Pickles
Amasake
Bancha Tea

Boys' Day (May 5)

Mochi Wrapped with Oak Leaves or Cherry Leaves—Served with tamari soy sauce and grated ginger; nori may be substituted for the leaves
Miso Soup with Cherrystone Clams
Sweet-and-Sour Seitan
Red Rice—Pressure-cooked brown rice with azuki beans
Carrots Rolled Up in Kombu
Boiled Celery with Tamari Soy Sauce and Brown Rice Vinegar
Boiled Mustard Greens with Tamari Soy Sauce
Pressed Cabbage and Daikon Salad
Strawberry Shortcake
Apple Juice, Grain Coffee, or Bancha Tea

Family Birthday

Clear Soup with Watercress and Fu
Fried Rice with Vegetables and Tofu
"Pig" in a Blanket—Rolled up burdock and carrots, cooked with raw seitan and served with an onion-kuzu sauce
Boiled Broccoli and Cauliflower—Served with tamari soy sauce, mirin, and tahini or sesame seeds
Arame with Lotus Root and Sesame Seeds
Takuwan Pickles
Apricot-Couscous Cake
Bancha Tea or Grain Coffee

Midsummer Picnic (July 4)

Celery Soup with Wakame, Cauliflower, and Dulse
Tempeh Shish Kebab with Broccoli, Daikon, Seitan, Tofu, and Green Pepper
Boiled Corn Kernels, Tofu, and Onion
Buckwheat Salad with Sauerkraut and Parsley
Boiled Cabbage and Red Radish
Hiziki with Almonds and Garnished with Scallions
Cherry Strudel
Cool Umeboshi Drink

Peace Day (August 6 or 9)

Carrot Soup
Nori-Maki Sushi—Made with fresh cucumbers, boiled carrots, and pickles
Nigiri Sushi—Seitan, pan- or deep-fried tofu, and broccoli placed on top of rice and wrapped with nori strips
Corn on the Cob with Umeboshi
Chinese Cabbage Rolls with Carrots and Watercress
Chick-pea Salad with Black Olives
Wakame and Cucumber Salad
Fruit Kanten—Cherries, strawberries, and slices of watermelon and cantaloupe cooked with apple juice and agar-agar in a gelatin
Spring Water

Thanksgiving (Fourth Thursday in November)

Parsnip Soup Garnished with Parsley
Black Bean Rice
Hubbard Squash Stuffed with Kasha and Celery
Walnut Sourdough Bread
Cranberry Sauce
Whole Onions with Seitan and Kuzu Sauce
Boiled Scallions and Celery with Miso Sauce
Vegetable and Seafood Tempura Served with Grated Daikon and Ginger
Carrot and Daikon Pickles
Arame with Carrots and Tofu Dressing
Pumpkin or Squash Pie
Apple Cider, Amasake, or Bancha Tea

Christmas (December 25)

Squash Soup
Seitan Stew—Made with daikon, mushrooms, burdock, lotus, taro, and kombu
Gomoku Rice—Served with shellfish, if desired
Vegetable Tempura—Squash, onions, carrots, broccoli, parsnips, and other vegetables deep-fried in batter
Kale with Tamari Soy Sauce and Grated Ginger
Daikon Marinated with Umeboshi
Shio Kombu and Green Olives
Apple Pie or Baked Apples
Apple Cider
Beer, Sake
Bancha Tea

New Year's Eve (December 31)

Hot Soba—Buckwheat or other noodles garnished with kinpira burdock and carrots, grated daikon, grated ginger, boiled watercress, nori slices, or raw scallions
Baked Millet and Squash—Served in squares
Quick Rutabaga Pickles
Apple Juice, Sake, Beer, Wine, or Champagne

CHAPTER 29

SPECIAL COOKING

An empty nest.
The baby swallows
Have all gone.
—Mieko

The Standard Macrobiotic Diet is recommended for generally healthy adults and older children. For babies, infants, and smaller children, as well as the old, it can be modified to take into account different needs and levels of activity. For adults, too, the volume and content of meals may be slightly adjusted depending on sex, lifestyle, and personal orientation. In this chapter, we shall consider these special needs as well as cooking for single people, preparing lunches for school and office, and food for traveling.

BABY FOOD SUGGESTIONS

Our diet should change in accordance with the development of our teeth. The ideal food for the human infant is mother's milk, and all of the baby's nourishment should come from this source for the first six months. At about that age, the quantity of breast milk can gradually be decreased over the next six months while soft foods, containing practically no salt, are introduced and proportionately increased. Mother's milk should usually be stopped around the time the first molars appear (usually 12 to 14 months) and the baby's diet by then should consist entirely of soft mashed foods.

Harder foods should be introduced around the time the first molars appear and gradually increase in percentage over the next year. By the age of 20 to 24 months, softly mashed foods should be replaced entirely by harder foods which constitute the mainstay of the diet.

At the beginning of the third year, a child can receive one-third to one-fourth the amount of salt used by an adult depending upon his or her health. A child's intake of salt should continue to be less than an adult's until about the seventh or eighth year.

At the age of four, the standard diet may be introduced, along with mild sea salt, miso, and other seasonings, including ginger.

The following dietary recommendations may be followed:

Whole Grains—Cereal grain milk can be introduced after eight months to one year as the baby's main food. The grain milk may also be given earlier to the baby as a replacement for mother's milk if the mother cannot breast-feed. Brown rice is the principal ingredient in cereal grain milk, and its nutrients come very close to mother's milk. Different tastes appeal to us at different periods of our development. A natural sweet taste particularly nourishes babies and children. In order to simulate the sweet taste of mother's milk and provide enough protein and fat for the baby's growth, sweet rice, which contains more of these factors, may be included as may barley or other whole grains.

Cereal grain milk should be in the form of a soft whole grain porridge consisting of 4 parts brown rice (preferably short grain), 3 parts sweet brown rice, and 1 part barley. Preferably, the cereal is cooked with a piece of kombu, although this sea vegetable does not always have to be eaten. Millet and oats can be included from time to time. However, buckwheat, wheat, and rye are usually not given.

The cereal may be prepared by pressure-cooking or boiling. To pressure-cook, soak the grains overnight or for 24 hours if the weather is very cold. Pressure-cook with five times more water than grain (using the soaking water as well). Cook for about 1½ hours until the cereal is soft and creamy in consistency. Cook over a medium-low heat once the grain comes to pressure. To boil, soak the cereals in the same way and boil with ten times more water until one-half the original volume of water remains. When the cereal comes to a boil, turn the heat to medium-low and simmer.

When preparing grain milk cereal for a newborn or very small baby, place the cooked mixture into a cheesecloth sack and strain it to remove the bran. Then it can be sweetened by adding 1 teaspoon of barley malt or rice syrup to one cup of grain milk. Heat the sweetened mixture and simmer several minutes before use.

When preparing the grain milk for an older baby, after the mixture has finished cooking, put it into a suribachi or a hand food mill and mash it very thoroughly. Do not use a blender or electric device for grinding. After mashing the mixture, add a small amount of barley malt or rice syrup.

Once the grain milk has been prepared—having the proper consistency and seasoned to taste—heat the mixture to about body temperature and put it in a baby bottle. Store cereal grain milk in a glass jar in the refrigerator for a couple of days; reheat it before subsequent feedings.

If either of the above cereal grain milks do not flow smoothly through the nipple, they can be further diluted with water and strained several times through cheesecloth. You may also enlarge the opening of the nipple with a large darning needle. To do this, first sterilize the tip of the needle by holding it over a flame before using it to enlarge the opening. Special orthodontic nipples are preferably used as these tend to foster natural development of the teeth and jaws.

The ingredients and proportions of the grain milk can be varied slightly, depending also on the age and needs of the baby. Grain milk can be one of the first soft foods that a baby is given once foods in addition to breast milk are introduced. In general, a more watery grain milk is recommended for younger babies, while older infants can receive a thicker mixture. Depending on the age of the baby, the proportion of water to cereal can range from 10:1 to 7:1 to 3:1.

Sesame seeds may be added to the grain milk, if desired. The seeds should be well-roasted and thoroughly crushed in a suribachi before being added. About 5 to 10 percent crushed seeds can be cooked along with the grains.

Babies may also be given special rice cream from time to time. To prepare, pressure-cook brown rice with 3 to 6 parts water and a 1-inch piece of kombu for at least 2 hours. (Do not add salt.) Squeeze the cooked rice and liquid through a strainer lined with sanitized cheesecloth into a bowl. Put the resulting thick liquid into a baby bottle, diluting and straining it again, if necessary. On occasion, the rice can be dry-roasted prior to pressure-cooking.

Be careful to avoid giving babies ready-to-eat creamy cereals or porridges made with mucus-forming flour products.

Soup—Soup can be introduced after five months, especially broth. The contents may include vegetables that have been mashed until creamy. No salt, miso, or tamari soy sauce should be added before an infant is 10 months old. Thereafter, a slightly salty taste may be used for flavoring. However, in special cases, if the baby's stool is green or the baby experiences digestive troubles, a salty taste may need to be used, but then only in small amounts and for a short period.

Vegetables—In addition to grain milk, very young babies can be given the juice from cooked vegetables. To prepare, bring vegetables, such as carrots, squash, cabbage, broccoli, or corn, to a boil. A small, 1-inch piece of soaked kombu may be added. Simmer the ingredients over a low heat for 30 to 45 minutes. Strain the liquid from cooking the vegetables through a strainer lined with sanitized cheesecloth. Place in a bottle, cool, and give to the baby. Whole vegetables may be introduced after the baby is five to seven months old, usually when teeth come in and after grains have been given for one month. When introducing vegetables to children, start by giving them sweet vegetables, such as carrots, cabbage, winter squash, onions, daikon, and Chinese cabbage. These may be boiled or steamed and should be cooked well and thoroughly mashed. Because it is usually difficult for children to eat greens, parents should make a special effort to see that they are eaten. Sweet greens, such as kale and broccoli, are generally preferred over slightly bitter-tasting greens, such as watercress and mustard greens. Very mild seasoning may be added to vegetables after 10 months to encourage the appetite. When the baby's teeth start coming in, a raw carrot may be given as a toy to stimulate teething.

Beans—Naturally processed soy milk may be given to babies as a supplement to cereal grain milk. To prepare, soak about 3 cups of soybeans overnight, strain, and discard the soaking water. Grind the beans in an electric blender (this is one of the rare instances in which electric devices are used in macrobiotic cooking). Or if you have the time and patience, a hand food mill can be used. Add about 6 quarts of water and a 1-inch piece of kombu to the bean mash and bring to a boil. Reduce heat to low and simmer for about 5 minutes. Stir continuously to prevent burning. Sprinkle cold water on the mash to stop bubbling and bring gently to a boil again. Sprinkle cold water once more on the mash and again bring to a boil. (Don't cover the mash as it will bubble over the top of the pot.) Line a strainer with a cotton cloth or cheesecloth and pour the liquid—the soy milk—through the strainer into a bowl. Fold the corners of the cloth together to form a sack and squeeze out the remaining liquid. (The pulp, known as okara, can be saved and used in other dishes.) Put the soy milk in a bottle, cool, and feed to the baby. If the soy milk does not flow smoothly, dilute it with some water and strain it once more through a cheesecloth until the desired consistency is obtained. Soy milk is usually very sweet, but if additional sweetener is desired, barley malt or rice syrup can be added as in the grain milk recipe. Soy milk can be stored for 1 or 2 days in a glass jar in the refrigerator and reheated to body temperature prior to use.

Whole beans can be introduced after 8 months,. but only small amounts of azuki beans, lentils, or chick-peas, cooked well with kombu and mashed thoroughly, are recommended. Other beans such as kidney beans, whole soybeans, and navy beans can also be cooked occasionally provided they are cooked well until very soft and mashed thoroughly.

After about 10 months old, beans may be seasoned with a tiny amount of sea salt or tamari soy sauce or sweetened with squash, barley malt, or rice syrup.

Sea Vegetables—Kombu is generally cooked with cereal grain milk, but taken out after cooking. If mashed until very soft, a tiny amount of kombu may be given to babies, as well as a touch of nori or a taste of hiziki and arame. Generally, seaweeds can be introduced as a separate side dish after the child is 1½ to 2 years old.

Seasoning—Ordinarily, no salt, miso, or tamari soy sauce should be given babies before they are 10 months old. After that age, a slightly salty taste may be used for flavoring depending on the baby's condition, especially the color and texture of the bowel movements. At the beginning of the third year, a child can receive from one-third to one-fourth the amount of salt used by an adult. Seasoning can gradually be increased until age 7 or 8 years when seasonings for older children and adults become the same. During the time when seasoning levels are being increased, food for children and adults may be cooked together; however, before the final seasoning is added, the children's portion may be taken out and served separately. Or, dishes may be seasoned minimally, with additional seasoning used by adults at the table in the form of gomashio and other condiments. Generally young children should not be given very much tempeh, seitan, tofu, and other foods high in salt or sodium. Small amounts, with very soft consistency, may be given from time to time.

Animal Food—Ideally, infants younger than 4 years old should not have any animal food, including fish, except in special cases where the child is weak, slightly anemic, or lacks energy. Then feed your child about one tablespoon of white-meat fish or seafood that has been boiled well with vegetables and then mashed. At the age of four, if desired, a small amount of white-meat fish or seafood may be included from time to time for enjoyment.

Fruit—Fruit may be given to babies and infants occasionally. Temperate-climate fruit, in season, can be introduced in small amounts, about 1 tablespoon, in cooked and mashed form, after 1½ to 2 years of age. However, in some special cases, cooked apples or apple juice may be used temporarily to balance overly tight conditions.

Pickles—Traditionally made pickles that are briefly aged and light in seasoning can be introduced after a child is 2 to 3 years old.

Beverages—Daily drinks may include spring or well water (preferably boiled and then allowed to cool), bancha twig tea, cereal grain tea, apple juice (warm or hot), and amasake (which has been boiled with twice as much water as usual and cooled).

For further information on baby and childhood nutrition and health, please refer to our book, *Macrobiotic Pregnancy and Care of the Newborn*, or contact a qualified macrobiotic counselor.

COOKING FOR THE ELDERLY

With age we begin to lose some of our teeth, and our chewing ability is not as strong as when we were younger. Usually food for older persons may be prepared a little softer to aid in chewing and digestion. Salt, miso, tamari soy sauce, and other seasoning levels may be reduced in cooking. To aid circulation and warm the body, one or two cooked dishes using oil, such as sautéed vegetables, may be prepared each day. However, if there is any serious illness, oil may need to be reduced or avoided until the condition stabilizes. Since the health and activity level of the elderly vary so considerably, few other general principles can be recommended. Each case needs to be considered separately.

COOKING FOR MEN AND WOMEN

Generally, men need slightly stronger cooked foods than women, tend to eat more volume of total food, and enjoy a wider variety of dishes. Dynamic foods, such as seitan, tempeh, and stews, and dynamic cooking styles, such as tempura and deep-frying, may be used more frequently for men, while lighter dishes such as salads may be prepared more often for women. Fish or seafood may be served to boys and men two to three times a week. Ideally, it is better for girls and women not to eat any animal food. However, if desired, a small volume of fish or seafood may be eaten once or twice a week. Similarly, females are better able to metabolize fruits and sweets than males and may enjoy them more frequently.

During menstruation, women must be very careful to avoid extremes. Both salty and sweet foods, including all fish and other animal food and fruit, should be reduced during these times to prevent menstrual cramps and heavy discharges. The total volume of food consumed may also be reduced during menstruation. During pregnancy it is important to eat a well-balanced variety of foods. If cravings arise, they should be satisfied with good quality foods. Meat and sugar should strictly be avoided; fish and fruit are better for women at this time.

COOKING FOR VARYING ACTIVITY LEVELS

People who are physically active, work outdoors, or are involved in sports or heavy exercise usually require stronger cooking, more food, and more variety in their meals than people who work indoors or are less physically active. In general, food for active people can be prepared having a saltier taste or more miso, and slightly more oil and other seasonings may be used in cooking. Buckwheat is an especially energizing grain and may be served more often, as well as fried noodles, tempeh, seitan, fish and seafood, and deep-fried and tempura-style foods. While everyone should have a balance of root, round, and green leafy vegetables each day, active people may be served relatively more root and hard green leafy vegetables. Long-term pickles, sometimes lightly spiced, may also be consumed more regularly.

Mentally active people can follow the Standard Macrobiotic Diet. Supplemental foods, such as fish, seafood, fruits, sweets, juice, herbal teas, and other stimulants, should be either avoided, reduced, or taken only in condiment-sized portions. Cooking should not be too salty, and oil should be taken only in small quantities, especially tempura-style and deep-fried foods. More round vegetables may be included, and vegetables may be frequently cooked in a simple nishime style. Boiled salad is also good for less active individuals. Sea vegetables are very important to help stabilize the mind and emotions but should not be taken in excessive amounts. Slightly less beans and bean products can be prepared. In general, the volume of food will be less than for physically active persons, and for mental clarity and focus it is important that all food be chewed very, very well.

COOKING FOR SPIRITUAL DEVELOPMENT

Cooking for spiritual development and insight represents a further refinement of cooking for mental development. Meals should consist entirely of grains and vegetables and animal food should be strictly avoided. For meditation and self-reflection, all spices, stimulants, and strong pungent foods, such as garlic, should be discontinued. Daily food should be prepared very simply. For example, in traditional Buddhist cooking, daily food consisted of brown rice, miso soup, a small amount of land and sea vegetables, pickles, and tea. Excellent festive cuisine utilizing a variety of cooking styles was served on holidays and special occasions. In addition to brown rice and millet, whole corn and barley are especially good for opening the spiritual channels and may be prepared frequently. Wild grasses, roots, berries, and other foraged foods also may be prepared, but because of their strong energy they should be taken sparingly and then only occasionally. In general, the volume of total food prepared should be less than usual, and from time to time those in good health may wish to eat only brown rice and other whole grains for seven to ten days. However, grain fasts, which are very energizing, should be done only under the guidance of a qualified macrobiotic counselor. Regular bancha tea and roasted grain teas are good beverages for spiritual development.

COOKING FOR SINGLE PEOPLE

When pressure-cooking small amounts of brown rice or other grains, a very low heat should be used until the pressure comes up. Also, grains should definitely be soaked to improve digestibility. Grains and beans can be made in sufficient quantities to last for several days; they keep well and can be reheated quickly. Vegetables should be prepared fresh for each meal and ideally, so should soups, especially miso soup. Some sea vegetables, such as hiziki and arame, keep for several days and can be prepared in quantities, but others, such as wakame, kombu, and nori, should be prepared fresh rather than used as leftovers. Some items, including tofu, mochi, and natto, can be frozen until needed. The key to cooking for yourself is variety, as meals tend to become repetitious and uninteresting. Having on hand a good supply of different condiments and pickles can make the same ingredients taste and feel completely new and fresh.

WHOLE GRAIN LUNCHES TO GO

Rice balls are the all-purpose food for school or office lunches. They can be made in various sizes and shapes, and their ingredients and coatings changed frequently to give variety and appeal. Rice balls require no utensils, they keep for several days unrefrigerated, and are always appetizing. Naturally fermented whole wheat or sourdough bread can be used to prepare delicious sandwiches. Seitan or tempeh make great sandwiches, cooked well and cooled, sliced, and combined with lettuce, sprouts, and a dressing or spread. Fresh corn on the cob, either whole or cut into 2- to 3-inch rounds, as well as large chunks of boiled carrots, daikon, or other vegetables, can be packed in sandwich bags. Fresh or dried fruit, nuts and seeds, rice cakes or cookies can be included for dessert. For office lunches, an attractive lacquerware lunch box is ideal. Its compartments will hold a complete meal consisting of cooked whole grains, vegetables, and sea vegetables. Beans tend to spoil, so be careful if using them. Lunch boxes are usually not so good for school since children prefer to carry as little as possible. A lunch prepared in a disposable brown paper bag is better. Thermoses of hot miso or bancha tea can also be taken to work.

MACROBIOTICS ON THE ROAD

Traveling challenges us to make harmony with new and often very different environments. It is important to eat as well as possible, balancing our usual foods with our natural curiosity for new and exotic fare. There are many macrobiotic and natural foods restaurants all over the world, and we try to eat at them or at the homes of friends as much as possible on our travels. Still, there are many times when we find ourselves at regular restaurants, on the plane during mealtime, or at airport or train coffee shops. On these occasions, I order as best I can, usually plain salads without dressing, boiled vegetables, plain spaghetti, or if available grains cooked without any oil, butter, or chemicals. In my bag I always carry a small supply of condiments, and with a little creativity a fairly decent meal can be improvised. The condiments include gomashio, tekka, umeboshi plums, tamari soy sauce (in a little dispenser), barley malt, and sometimes sea vegetable powders or green nori flakes. I also carry a little *ume* extract, which is a concentrated and very powerful form of umeboshi plums, for intestinal troubles, airsickness, or discomfort arising from inadvertent consumption of foods containing sugar or chemicals.

For traveling, rice balls, quality whole grain bread, rice cakes, whole grain crackers, quality sesame or peanut butter, amasake, apple juice, and homemade pickles all keep for several days or more. Full-strength miso travels well and keeps indefinitely, though instant miso is also available and is very convenient. Packaged fu and noodles, especially ramen, heat up quickly. There are also some new instant brown rice dinners that need only a few minutes to cook. I don't recommend these instant or precooked natural foods for regular home use, but on the road they can come in handy. Some friends have devised homemade traveling cooking kits for more extended journeys, including small portable propane stoves or burners and a variety of cookware and utensils. With a little forethought, eating away from home can be a pleasant and healthy experience.

CHAPTER 30

MEDICINAL COOKING AND HOME CURES

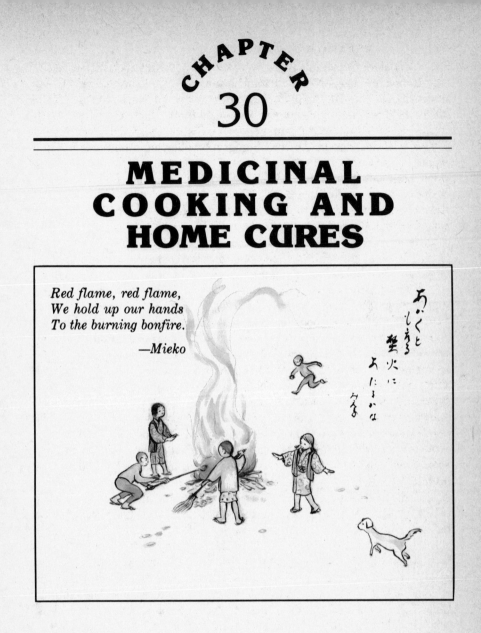

Red flame, red flame,
We hold up our hands
To the burning bonfire.

—Mieko

Food is our best medicine, and all food has medicinal effects. This was demonstrated to me during a household crisis in 1964. We were living in Cambridge, Massachusetts, at that time. One beautiful autumn day, my five-year-old son Yoshio was taking a nap upstairs. Michio and I were downstairs when we heard Yoshio wailing. We rushed upstairs and found Yoshio bouncing up and down in pain. We had never seen anyone behaving like this before and thought he must have stuck himself with a pin.

Taking off his clothes, we found to our shock that part of his intestine was protruding. A finger-length segment was poking out his lower left side. We didn't know what to do, but I instinctively raced to the kitchen and prepared some bancha tea with a teaspoon of tamari soy sauce, half an umeboshi plum, and a little grated fresh ginger. While Michio held Yoshio's mouth open, I spooned him some tea. Just as one or two drops of tea touched his tongue, the intestine retracted. It happened so fast, like speeded-up flower photography showing a bud opening and closing. There was still most of the tea left in the spoon! Michio and I were totally amazed at this powerful energy. Yoshio immediately stopped crying, fell asleep, and the hernia never returned. I was so thankful and bowed in appreciation to the ginger. In Japan this drink is called *ume-sho-bancha* and is commonly used to stimulate circulation and relieve disorders of the digestive system. Applied externally in the form of a compress, ginger is often used to relieve stagnation and smooth blockages in the lower abdomen. Because of its naturally warming effects, ginger directs energy to the whole body. But we had never seen such a powerful internal effect in as brief a moment of time.

A balanced whole foods diet will strengthen our digestive, circulatory, and nervous systems and provide mental and emotional stability as well as physical health and vitality. On the Standard Macrobiotic Diet, colds, headaches, or the flu are rare and the more serious diseases of modern society almost unknown. However, from time to time, especially during the changing of the seasons, fevers, coughs, and minor ailments may occasionally arise when the excess foods and beverages consumed in the previous season begin to be discharged from the body as it adjusts to changing weather conditions and a slight change in patterns of food consumption. At this time a medicinal tea or other special side dish may be taken to help relieve discomfort and restore balance.

Medicinal beverages or specially cooked side dishes may also be taken by those who are new to macrobiotics. In the transition from a modern refined diet to a more natural way of eating, the body begins to rid itself of past excess, including the accumulation of surplus fat, protein, and refined carbohydrates resulting from many years of eating meat, dairy food, eggs, refined salt, sugar, excess liquid, refined flour, chemicals and additives, and taking drugs and medications. The elimination of these substances may take the form of colds, fever, headaches, sore throats, constipation, diarrhea, and various aches and pains. The appearance of these symptoms is a positive sign indicating that the body is beginning to heal itself. However, to make the transition more comfortable and control the rate of discharge, medicinal preparations may be beneficial.

In the case of seriously ill patients, a modified form of the Standard Macrobiotic Diet may need to be followed until vitality is regained, blood quality has changed, and the inner organs have healed. If symptoms are experienced in a particular organ, slightly more whole foods associated with that organ may need to be taken. In addition, salt and oil intake may need to be very carefully regulated and many supplemental foods reduced or avoided entirely. These often include flour products and baked goods, including quality whole grain bread and noodles; fish, seafood, and other animal products; fats and oils, including quality unrefined vegetable oil; nuts and nut butters; fruits, juices, and desserts, including those made with natural sweeteners.

In addition to dietary adjustments, compresses or other external treatments may be applied to help relieve stagnation and control the discharge process. For specific dietary guidelines for digestive and circulatory disorders, please see the books *The Cancer-Prevention Diet* and *Diet for a Strong Heart.* For baby and childhood illnesses, see *Macrobiotic Pregnancy and Care of the Newborn,* and for other conditions *Natural Healing through Macrobiotics.* We recommend that persons with a serious illness seek guidance in proper cooking and implementation of home care remedies from a qualified macrobiotic counselor. In some cases, medical attention from health care professionals may also be necessary.

MEDICINAL TEAS

Ume-Sho-Bancha Tea

Strengthens the blood and the circulation through the regulation of digestion. Also helps relieve headaches in the front part of the head caused by excessive consumption of sweets, fruits, liquids, and other expansive substances. Pour one cup of bancha tea over the meat of ½ to 1 umeboshi plum and 1 teaspoon of tamari soy sauce. Stir and drink hot.

Variation: To further increase blood circulation, add ¼ teaspoon of grated and squeezed fresh ginger juice to this drink.

Tamari Bancha Tea

Neutralizes an acidic blood condition, promotes blood circulation, relieves fatigue, and generally calms and soothes. Pour one cup of hot bancha tea over one to two teaspoons of tamari soy sauce. Stir and drink hot.

Ame-Kuzu Tea

Relieves overly tight conditions and headaches in the back of the head from excess consumption of salt or animal food. Dissolve one teaspoon of kuzu in a little cold water. Add more water to make one cup of liquid. Add one tablespoon of rice syrup. Put in a saucepan, turn heat to medium, and slowly bring tea almost to a boil. Reduce heat to low and cook for 10 to 15 minutes, stirring constantly to avoid lumping. Serve hot.

Kuzu Drink

Strengthens digestion, increases vitality, and relieves general fatigue. Dilute one teaspoon of kuzu in a little cold water, then add enough cold water to make one cup. Put in a saucepan and bring the mixture to a boil. Then reduce the heat to a simmer, and stir constantly to avoid lumping until the liquid becomes a transparent gelatin. Stir in one teaspoon of tamari soy sauce and drink while hot.

Variation: A slightly stronger tea can be made by adding the meat of ½ to 1 umeboshi plum and ⅛ teaspoon of grated fresh ginger.

Umeboshi Tea

Neutralizes an acidic condition and relieves intestinal problems, including those caused by microorganisms. Also good for nausea, anxiety, and travel sickness. Take ½ to 1 umeboshi plum with one cup bancha tea. The plums may also be baked whole or powdered. If you are using powder, add one tablespoon powder to one cup of hot water.

Lotus Tea

Helps relieve coughing, sinus blockages, upper respiratory problems, and helps dissolve excess mucus in the body. Grate one-half cup of fresh lotus root, squeeze the juice into a pot, and add a small amount of water. Cook for 5 to 8 minutes, add a pinch of sea salt or tamari soy sauce, and drink hot.

Variation: A powdered form of this tea is available in many natural foods stores. If available, fresh lotus root makes a stronger, more soothing tea.

Burdock Tea

Gives strength and vitality. To one portion of fresh burdock shavings, add ten times the amount of spring water. Bring to a boil, reduce heat, and simmer for ten minutes.

Dandelion Root Tea

Strengthens the heart and small intestine function and increases vitality. Use one tablespoon of dandelion root to one quart of water. Bring to a boil, reduce heat, and simmer 10 minutes.

Kombu Tea

Strengthens the blood. Use one 3-inch strip of kombu to one quart of water. Bring to a boil, reduce heat, and simmer for 10 minutes.

Variation: Another method is to dry kombu in a 350-degree oven for 10 to 15 minutes, or until crisp. Grate ½ to 1 teaspoon of dried kombu into a cup and add hot water.

Shiitake Mushroom Tea

Relaxes an overly tense, stressful condition and helps to dissolve excessive animal fats. Soak a dried black shiitake mushroom cut in quarters. Cook in 2 cups of water for 20 minutes with a pinch of sea salt or 1 teaspoon of tamari soy sauce. Drink only a half-cup at a time.

EXTERNAL APPLICATIONS

Ginger Compress

Stimulates blood and body fluid circulation, helps loosen and dissolve stagnated toxic matter, soothes and relieves various internal organs, aches, and pains. Especially good for the kidneys, stomach, and intestines. Do not use for appendicitis. Place a handful of grated fresh ginger in a cheesecloth and squeeze the ginger juice into a pot containing 1 gallon of very hot water. Keep the water below boiling or the power of the ginger will be diminished. Let simmer for about 5 minutes. Then dip the middle part of a cotton hand towel into the ginger water by holding both ends. Wring the towel to squeeze out excess water and apply, very hot but not uncomfortably hot, to the area of the body needing treatment. A second, dry towel can be placed on top of the wet towel to reduce heat loss. When the wet towel cools, remove and replace with a fresh hot towel. Repeat this every few minutes for about 20 minutes, or until the skin becomes very red.

Salt Pack

Used to warm any part of the body. To relieve diarrhea, for example, apply the pack to the abdominal region. Dry-roast sea salt in a pan until hot and then wrap in a thick cotton linen pillowcase or towel. Tie with a string or cord as for a package to hold the salt in place. Apply to the troubled area and change when the pack begins to cool.

Dentie

Helps to prevent tooth problems, promotes a healthy condition in the mouth, and stops bleeding anywhere in the body by contracting expanded blood capillaries. Bake an eggplant, particularly the calix or cap, until charred black. Crush into a powder and mix with 30 to 50 percent roasted sea salt. Use daily as a tooth powder or apply to any bleeding area—even inside the nostrils in case of a nosebleed—by inserting squeezed, wet tissue dipped in dentie into the nostril.

CHAPTER

31

COOKING CLASSES AND RESOURCES

Deep snow ahead,
We climb in the footsteps
Of our elder brother.
—Fusako

Macrobiotics International in Boston and its major educational centers in the United States and Canada offer ongoing classes for the general public in macrobiotic cooking and traditional food preparation and natural processing. They also offer instruction in Oriental medicine, shiatzu massage, pregnancy and natural childcare, yoga, meditation, science, culture and the arts, and world peace and world government activities. Macrobiotics International Educational Centers also provide dietary counseling services with trained and certified consultants, referrals to professional health care associates, and cooperate in research and food programs in hospitals, medical schools, prisons, drug rehabilitation clinics, nursing homes, and other institutions. In scores of other cities and communities, there are smaller Macrobiotics International learning centers, residential centers, and information centers offering some classes and services.

There are also several hundred Macrobiotics International centers in Central and Latin America, Europe, the Middle East, Africa, Asia, and Australia. There are also friendship and professional associations such as the United Nations Macrobiotics Society.

Most of the foods in this book are available at natural foods stores, health food stores, and a growing number of supermarkets around the world. Macrobiotic specialty items are also available by mail order from various distributors and retailers.

Please contact the Boston headquarters or some of the regional centers for further information on any of the above services or whole foods outlets in your area.

Boston Headquarters:

Macrobiotics International and
East West Foundation
17 Station St.
Brookline, MA 02146
800/MACRO-17
Toll-free Hotline on Macrobiotic Programs and Services in the United States, Monday-Friday 12 noon to 4 p.m., E.S.T. (at other times or in Massachusetts call 617/738-0045).

For those who wish to study further, the Kushi Institute, an educational institution founded in Boston in 1979 with affiliates in London, Amsterdam, Antwerp, and Florence, offers full- and part-time instruction for individuals who wish to become certified macrobiotic cooking instructors, teachers, and counselors. The Kushi Institute publishes the *Macrobiotic Teachers and Counselors Directory* and makes referrals to graduates who are qualified to give cooking instruction and offer guidance in the macrobiotic approach to health. The Cook Instructor Service is an extension of the Kushi Institute and comprises specially qualified graduates of the Kushi Institute's advanced cooking program. These men and women are available to assist individuals and families in learning the basics of macrobiotic food preparation and home care in their home. For information, contact:

Kushi Institute and Cook Instructor Service
Box 1100
Brookline, MA 02147
617/731-0564

GLOSSARY

Aburage	Deep-fried tofu.
Agar-agar	A white gelatin processed from a sea vegetable into bars, flakes, or powder, and used in making kanten and vegetable aspics.
Amasake	A sweet, creamy beverage made from fermented sweet rice.
Arame	A thin, wiry black sea vegetable similar to hiziki.
Arepa	An oval-shaped corn ball or cake made from whole corn dough and baked or pan-fried.
Arrowroot flour	A starch flour processed from the root of an American plant. Used as a thickening agent for sauces, stews, gravies, or desserts.
Azuki bean	A small, dark red bean originally from Japan but now also grown in the West.
Bake	To cook with dry heat, especially in an oven.
Bancha tea	The twigs, stems, and leaves from mature Japanese tea bushes, also known as *kukicha*.
Barley	A whole cereal grain; the traditional staple of the Middle East and Southern Europe.

Barley malt	A natural sweetener made from concentrated barley that has a rich, roasted taste.
Boiled salad	A salad whose ingredients are lightly boiled or dipped in hot water before serving.
Bok choy	A leafy green and white vegetable popular in Chinese cooking.
Bollos polones	Boiled corn balls made from whole corn dough.
Bonito flakes	Flakes shaved from dried bonito fish. Used in soup stocks or as a garnish.
Bran	The outer coating of the whole grain removed together with the germ during refining to produce white flour or white rice. May be used in pickling or as a garnish.
Broil	To cook by direct radiant heat such as over a grill.
Brown rice	Whole unpolished rice. Comes in three main varieties: short, medium, and long grain. Brown rice contains an ideal balance of nutrients and is the principal staple in macrobiotic cooking.
Brown rice miso	A fermented soybean paste made from brown rice, soybeans, and sea salt. A nice sweet miso usually preferred for light cooking. In Japanese called *genmai miso*.
Buckwheat	A hardy cereal grass eaten in the form of kasha (whole groats) or soba noodles.
Bulghur	A form of whole wheat that has been cracked, partially boiled, and dried.
Burdock	A hardy wild plant that grows throughout the United States and abroad. The long, dark root is valued in cooking for its strengthening qualities.
Carbon steel	Iron with carbon and other elements added. Used for quality knives and cooking utensils.
Cast-iron	A hard, brittle, nonmalleable iron-carbon alloy used for making heavy cookware.

Chakin shibori	Chestnut or squash twists.
Chirimen iriko	Very small dried fish.
Cholesterol	A waxy constituent of all animal fats and oils, which can contribute to heart disease, cancer, and other sicknesses. Vegetables do not contain cholesterol. The liver naturally produces all the serum cholesterol needed by the body.
Churashi sushi	Rice and cut-up vegetables served salad-style.
Cold-pressed	Pertaining to oils processed at low temperatures to preserve their natural qualities.
Couscous	Partially refined cracked wheat.
Cracked wheat	Whole wheat berries that have been processed and cut into small pieces.
Crumb	The soft inside portion of a loaf of bread.
Crust	Hard outer part of a loaf of bread.
Daikon	A long white radish used in many types of dishes and for medicinal purposes.
Dashi	Traditional Japanese soup stock made from kombu broth.
Dentie	A black tooth powder made from sea salt and charred eggplant.
Diastatic malt	A leavening agent made from dried and pulverized barley sprouts.
Disaccharide	A type of simple sugar such as sucrose that enters the bloodstream rapidly and may cause imbalance.
Dried tofu	Dried type of tofu that is beige in color and very lightweight.
Drop top	A loose fitting lid that rests on the contents in the pot rather than on the rim.

Dry-roast	To toast grains, seeds, or flour in an unoiled frying pan. To prevent burning, ingredients are stirred gently until brown or golden and a nutty aroma is released.
Dulse	A red-purple sea vegetable used in soups, salads, vegetable dishes, or as a garnish.
Empanada	A deep-fried tortilla filled with beans or vegetables.
Endive	A succulent vegetable native to Belgium.
Endosperm	Starchy inner part of the whole grain or seed surrounding the germ or embryo.
Fiber	The part of whole grains, vegetables, and fruits that is not broken down in digestion and gives bulk to wastes.
Fish-style	Cooking vegetables lengthwise in long fish shapes. For decoration fin-like slits and eyes may be made.
Flame deflector	A round metal disc that is placed under a pot or pressure-cooker to distribute heat evenly and prevent burning.
Food mill	A small hand mill operated by a crank to make purées, sauces, and dips.
Fu	Dried wheat gluten cakes or sheets.
Gandomaki	Tofu croquettes.
Genmai miso	Miso made from brown rice, soybeans, and salt. (See also brown rice miso entry.)
Germ	Embryo of the whole grain, removed in modern refining.
Ginger	A spicy, pungent golden-colored root used in cooking and for medicinal purposes.
Ginger compress	A compress made from grated gingerroot and water. Applied hot to an affected area of the body, it serves to stimulate circulation and dissolve stagnation.
Ginkgo	Tree native to the Orient with fan-shaped leaves.

Gluten	The protein factor in grain. The higher the gluten, the lighter the bread. In making seitan, gluten is the sticky substance that remains after the bran has been separated from whole wheat flour.
Gomashio	Sesame seed salt made from dry-roasting and grinding sea salt and sesame seeds and crushing them in a suribachi.
Gomoku	Casserole style of cooking combining five or more ingredients.
Grain mill	A small hand mill used to grind grains, beans, seeds, and nuts into various forms, including flour.
Green rice	Rice cooked with green mugwort leaves.
Groats	A hulled, usually crushed grain such as buckwheat or oats.
Haiku	A traditional three-line Japanese poem consisting of 5, 7, and 5 syllables.
Hatcho miso	A fermented soybean paste made from soybeans and sea salt and aged at least two years.
Hiziki	A dark brown sea vegetable which when dried turns black. It has a wiry consistency and may be strong tasting. Native to Japan and the North Atlantic.
Hokkaido pumpkin	A round dark green or orange squash that is very sweet and harvested in the fall. Native to New England, it was introduced to Japan and named after the island of Hokkaido.
Hull	The dry outer covering of a grain, seed, or fruit.
Hummus	A combination of chick-peas and tahini puréed into a smooth thick mixture and used as a dip or sandwich filling. A Middle Eastern favorite.
Husk	Outer sheath of the seed, grain, or fruit. Similar to *hull*.
Hydrogenation	Process of solidifying oils at room temperature so that they won't melt. Hydrogenating saturates vegetable oils.

Iriko	Small dried fish.
Irish moss	A seaweed found in the Atlantic and valued for its natural gelatinous properties.
Ito soba	A very thin type of soba noodle.
Jinenjo	A light brown Japanese mountain potato that grows to be several feet long and two to three inches wide.
Jinenjo soba	Noodles made from jinenjo and buckwheat.
Kanpyo	Dried gourd strips, used to tie cabbage rolls and other special vegetable dishes.
Kanten	A jelled fruit dessert made from agar-agar.
Kara age	Deep-fry style of cooking.
Kasha	Roasted buckwheat groats.
Kayu	Cereal grain porridge that has been cooked with 5 to 10 times as much water as grain for a long time until soft and creamy.
Kelp	A large family of sea vegetables similar to kombu that grows in northern ocean latitudes.
Kernel	A grain or seed enclosed in a hard husk or the inner, usually edible part of a nut or fruit.
Kim-chi	A hot spicy Chinese cabbage pickle popular in Korea.
Kinako	Roasted soybean flour.
Kinpira	A style of cooking root vegetables first by sautéing, then adding a little water, and seasoning with tamari soy sauce at the end of cooking.
Knish	A piece of dough stuffed with vegetables or other ingredients and baked or fried. Traditional Jewish dish.
Koi koku	A rich thick soup made from carp, burdock, bancha tea, and miso.

Koji	A grain inoculated with bacteria and used in making fermented foods such as miso, tamari soy sauce, amasake, natto, and sake.
Kojiki	An ancient Shinto classic.
Kombu	A wide, thick, dark green sea vegetable that grows in deep ocean water. Used in making soup stocks, condiments, candy, and cooked as a separate dish or with vegetables, beans, or grains.
Kukicha	Bancha tea. The older twigs, stems, and leaves of the Japanese tea bush.
Kuzu	Also called *kudzu.* A white starch made from a prolific wild vine. Used in thickening soups, gravies, sauces, desserts, and for medicinal beverages.
Laver	Scottish seaweed, similar to nori.
Lotus root	Roots of the water lily. Brown-skinned with a hollow, chambered off-white inside, lotus root is used in many dishes and for medicinal preparations.
Macrobiotics	From the traditional Greek words for Great Life or Long Life. The way of life according to the largest possible view, the infinite order of the universe. The practice of macrobiotics includes the understanding and practical application of this order to daily life, including the selection, preparation, and manner of cooking and eating, as well as the orientation of consciousness.
Maifun	Rice flour noodles.
Maki sushi	A style of sushi in which rice is rolled up in nori with vegetables, pickles, fish, tofu, or other ingredients inside and sliced into small spiral rounds.
Marinate	To let foods such as salads or fish soak in seasoning.
Masa	Dough made from whole corn. Used in making arepas, tortillas, and other traditional South American dishes.
Mekabu	Root of the wakame sea vegetable.

Meridian	One of the channels of electromagnetic energy circulating in the body in traditional Oriental medicine.
Millet	A small yellow grain that can be prepared whole, added to soups, salads, and vegetable dishes, or baked. A staple in China and Africa.
Mirin	A sweet cooking wine made from sweet rice.
Miso	A fermented paste made from soybeans, sea salt, and usually rice or barley. Used in soups, stews, spreads, baking, and as a seasoning. Miso has a nice sweet taste and gives a salty flavor.
Mochi	A cake or dumpling made from cooked, pounded sweet rice.
Monosaccharide	Simple sugar such as glucose, fructose, and galactose that enters the bloodstream rapidly and may lead to imbalance.
Moxa	Dried mugwort preparation placed on the skin and burned to stimulate energy in the meridians.
Mugi cha	Roasted barley tea.
Mugi miso	Also known as barley miso. Soybean paste made from barley, soybeans, sea salt, and water. A nice sweet miso used frequently for miso soup and daily cooking.
Mugwort	A wild plant that can be dried and made into a tea, used in cooking, or prepared into moxa.
Mu tea	A tea made from a variety of herbs that warm the body, strengthen the female organs, and have other medicinal properties.
Nabe	A traditional Japanese one-dish meal, prepared and served in colorful casserole dishes and accompanied with a dipping sauce or broth made of tamari soy sauce or miso and various garnishes.
Natto	Soybeans that have been cooked and mixed with beneficial enzymes and fermented for 24 hours. A sticky dish with long strands and a strong odor. Good for improving digestion.

Natto miso	A spicy condiment made from shortly fermented soybeans, grain, ginger, and kombu.
Natural foods	Whole foods that are not processed and have not been treated with artificial additives or preservatives.
Nigari	Hard crystallized salt made from liquid droppings of dampened sea salt. Used in making tofu.
Nigiri sushi	Small pieces of vegetables or seafood served on top of clumps of rice and wrapped with thin strips of nori.
Nishime	Long, slow style of boiling in which vegetables or other ingredients cook primarily in their own juices. Gives strong, peaceful energy.
Nitsuke	An intermediate style of boiling between quick and slow cooking.
Noh	Classical Japanese drama with music and dance.
Nori	Thin sheets of dried sea vegetable. Black or dark purple, they turn green when roasted over a flame. Used as a garnish, to wrap rice balls, in making sushi, or cooked with tamari soy sauce as a condiment.
Nuka	Rice bran. Used to make a type of pickle.
Oden	Stew made with tofu or deep-fried tofu simmered with a variety of other ingredients.
Ohagi	A rice cake made from cooked pounded sweet rice and coated with azuki beans, chestnuts, sesame seeds, roasted soybean flour, and other ingredients.
Ohitashi	A style of light boiling in which vegetables are cooked in a small volume of bubbling hot water for up to a few minutes or just dipped in and out to take out their raw or bitter taste and preserve their bright fresh color.
Okara	Coarse soybean pulp left over when making tofu. Used in soups or cooked with vegetables.
Omedoto	A porridge made from azuki beans and roasted brown rice.

Open-pollinated Traditional Indian corn that is pollinated by the wind as opposed to hybrid corn. Also known as standard corn.

Organic foods Foods grown without the use of chemical fertilizers, herbicides, pesticides, or other artificial sprays.

Origami The art of folding colored paper into decorative objects.

Paella A traditional Spanish dish made with rice, vegetables, and seafood or other ingredients.

Pan-fry To sauté with a little oil over a low to medium heat for a moderate to long time. Ingredients may occasionally be stirred or turned over but not so often as compared to stir-frying.

Parboil To partially boil for a short time before adding to other ingredients.

Pearl barley A small white barley valued for its cosmetic properties.

Pearled barley A polished form of barley.

Pickle press A small enclosed glass or plastic container with a screw-plate for making pressed salad or light, quick pickles.

Polenta A traditional Latin or Mediterranean dish made with corn, and sometimes also with beans and vegetables.

Polysaccharides Complex sugars that gradually become absorbed during digestion. They include starch and cellulose found in whole grains and vegetables.

Polyunsaturated fats Essential fatty acids found in high concentration in grains, beans, seeds, and in smaller quantities in fish.

Pressed salad Salad prepared by pressing sliced vegetables and sea salt in a small pickle press or with an improvised weight.

Pressure cooker An airtight metal pot that cooks food quickly by steaming under pressure at a high temperature. Used primarily in macrobiotic cooking for whole grains and occasionally for beans and vegetables.

Proofing	Stage in bread-making in which the dough sets and rises to proper lightness.
Purée	To mash food in a suribachi, bowl, mill, or food processor until smooth and even in consistency.
Ramen	A Chinese-style noodle that has been deep-fried and dried before reheating.
Red miso	A short-time fermented miso made from rice koji, soybeans, and sea salt.
Red rice	Rice cooked with azuki beans and having a nice red color.
Refined oil	Cooking oil that has been chemically processed to alter or remove its natural color, taste, and aroma.
Rice cake	A light round cake made of puffed brown rice, popular as snacks and eaten plain or with a spread.
Rice kayu bread	A whole grain bread made from baking soft cooked rice with a little whole wheat flour, and occasionally other ingredients such as raisins.
Rice paddle	Flat spatula used for toasting grains, seeds, and flour, and for serving foods.
Rice syrup	A natural sweetener made from malted brown rice.
Rolled oats	Oats that have been rolled and flattened. Common oatmeal.
Saifun	A clear noodle made from mung beans.
Saka mushi	Steamed sole.
Sake	A wine made from rice. In Japan, traditionally served warm in small cups.
Sake lees	Fermented residue left from making sake. Used in soups, with vegetables, or making pickles.
Sakura	Cherry blossom leaves.
Samurai	Member of the feudal Japanese military caste.

Sashimi — Raw sliced fish.

Saturated fats — Found primarily in meats, poultry, eggs, dairy food, and a few vegetable oils such as coconut and palm tree oil; these fats elevate serum cholesterol and may accumulate in and around arteries and organs.

Sauté — To fry lightly in a skillet or shallow pan.

Scotch oats — Oats that have been coarsely cut with sharp steel blades.

Sea salt — Salt obtained from the ocean. Unlike refined table salt, unrefined sea salt is high in trace minerals and contains no chemicals, sugar, or added iodine.

Seasoning — Something used to flavor food such as salt, tamari soy sauce, miso, or vinegar.

Sea vegetable — An edible seaweed such as kombu, wakame, arame, hiziki, nori, or dulse.

Seed — A fertilized and ripened plant with an embryo capable of germinating.

Seitan — Also known as wheat gluten or wheat meat. A whole wheat product cooked in tamari soy sauce, kombu, and water. Used for stews, croquettes, grain burgers, and many other dishes. High in protein and gives a strong, dynamic taste.

Shiitake — A mushroom native to Japan but now cultivated in the United States as well. Used widely dried or fresh in cooking, for soups and stews, and in medicinal preparations. Scientific name is *Lentinus edodes*.

Shio kombu — Salty kombu. Pieces of kombu cooked for a long time in tamari soy sauce and used in small amounts as a condiment.

Shio nori — Salty nori. Pieces of nori cooked for a long time in tamari soy sauce and water and used as a condiment.

Shiso — Also known as beefsteak leaves. Leaves customarily pickled with umeboshi plums. Also available whole.

Shocking	Traditional style of cooking noodles or beans by adding some cold water to the pot each time the water comes to a boil.
Shogun	Any of a line of feudal Japanese rulers who exercised absolute sovereignty under nominal allegiance to the emperor.
Shojin ryori	Traditional vegetarian Buddhist temple cuisine.
Shoyu	Soy sauce.
Sloke	Irish sea vegetable similar to nori.
Soba	Noodles made from buckwheat flour or buckwheat combined with whole wheat.
Sobagaki	Buckwheat dumplings.
Somen	Very thin whole wheat or white noodles.
Sourdough bread	Bread made with a sour starter of whole wheat flour and water or other sour food that has naturally fermenting properties.
Soy milk	A liquid residue from cooking tofu. Used as a beverage or replacement for milk.
Soyfoods	Products made from soybeans such as miso, tofu, tempeh, natto, and tamari soy sauce.
Sprout	A bud, shoot, or young plant, often edible and tender.
Stainless steel	Steel alloyed with chromium to resist corrosion, oxidation, or rusting. Used to make quality cookware and utensils and may be lined or combined with another substance such as enamel.
Steam	To cook by exposing to hot steam.
Stir-fry	To quickly cook food in a wok or skillet using a small amount of oil, high heat, and with continuous stirring.
Stone-ground	Unrefined flour that has been ground in a stone mill that preserves the germ, bran, and other nutrients.

Sukiyaki — A one-dish Japanese meal prepared in a large cast-iron skillet with a variety of vegetables, noodles, sea vegetables, seitan, tofu, or seafood and fish.

Suribachi — A serrated, glazed clay bowl or mortar. Used with a pestle, called a *surikogi,* for grinding and puréeing foods.

Sushi — A traditional Japanese dish consisting of rice served with various vegetables, sea vegetables, seafood, or pickles. In addition to spiral rounds, sushi can be prepared in several other styles including deep-frying or as a salad.

Sushi mat — A small bamboo mat used to roll up nori-maki sushi or to cover bowls and dishes to keep food warm.

Sweet rice — A glutinous type of rice that is slightly sweeter to the taste than regular rice and used in a variety of regular and holiday dishes.

Taco — A tortilla folded up and filled with beans, vegetables, or sea vegetables.

Tahini — A thick, smooth paste made from ground sesame seeds.

Takuwan — A daikon pickle made with rice bran and sea salt. Very strong like the famous Buddhist monk it is named after.

Tamari soy sauce — Traditional, naturally made soy sauce as distinguished from refined, chemically processed soy sauce. Also known as organic or natural shoyu. A stronger, wheat-free soy sauce called real or genuine tamari, a by-product of making miso, is used for special dishes. Tamari soy sauce is used for daily cooking.

Taro — Also called *albi.* A potato that has a thick, hairy skin. Used occasionally in soups or stews and for medicinal purposes.

Tekka — Condiment made from hatcho miso, sesame oil, burdock, lotus root, carrot, and gingerroot. It cooks down to a black powder when sautéed on a low heat for several hours.

Tempeh — A traditional Indonesian soyfood made from split soybeans, water, and a special bacteria. Tempeh can be made at home by fermenting for about one day or it may be purchased ready-made in many natural foods stores. High in protein and with a rich dynamic taste, tempeh is used in soups, stews, sandwiches, casseroles, and a wide variety of dishes.

Tempura — To deep-fry sliced vegetables, sea vegetables, and fish dipped into batter in oil until golden brown and crunchy. The tempura is customarily served in a tamari-ginger dipping sauce and eaten with a little grated daikon.

Tendon — A one-dish meal consisting of rice served with tempura-style vegetables and covered with a light tamari broth.

Tofu — Soybean curd made from soybeans and nigari. High in protein and usually prepared in the form of cakes that may be sliced and cooked in soups, vegetable dishes, salads, sauces, dressings, and many other styles.

Tostada — Tortilla served open with beans or vegetables.

Trivet — A short three-legged stand used under a hot dish on a table or at the stove.

Udon — Japanese whole wheat noodles.

Umeboshi — A salted pickled plum usually aged for several years. Its nice zesty sour taste and salty flavor go well with many foods; it is used as a seasoning, in sauces, as a condiment, in beverages, and in many medicinal preparations.

Umeboshi vinegar — Also known as *ume-su*. The liquid that umeboshi plums are aged in. Used for sauces, dressings, and seasoning and making pickles.

Unrefined oil — Vegetable oil that has been naturally processed to retain its natural color, taste, aroma, and nutrients.

Vegetable brush — Small hand brush made from natural ingredients. Used to clean vegetables without bruising the skin.

Wakame — A long, thin green sea vegetable used in making miso soup. Also used in salads and vegetable dishes.

Wasabi — Japanese mustard.

White miso — A sweet, short-time fermented miso.

Whole foods — Foods in their natural form that have not been refined or processed, such as brown rice or whole wheat berries.

Whole grains — Unrefined cereal grains to which nothing has been added or subtracted in milling except the inedible outer hull. Whole grains include brown rice, millet, barley, whole wheat, oats, rye, buckwheat, and corn.

Whole wheat — A whole cereal grain that may be prepared in whole form or made into flour. Whole wheat products such as noodles, seitan, fu, bulghur, couscous, and cracked wheat make a wide variety of dishes.

Wild rice — A wild cereal grass native to North America.

Wok — A deep round Chinese skillet excellent for stir-frying and tempura.

Wood ashes — Residue of burnt hardwood used to soften and flavor corn, mushrooms, and other food, and as a natural cleanser.

Yang — One of the two fundamental energies of the universe. Yang refers to the relative tendency of contraction, centripetality, density, heat, light, and other qualities. Yang energy tends to go down and inward and in the vegetable kingdom predominates in small compact grains such as brown rice, millet, and buckwheat; in root vegetables; and in sea salt, miso, and tamari soy sauce. Its complementary and antagonistic energy is yin.

Yannoh — A natural grain coffee made from five different grains and beans which have been roasted and ground into a fine powder.

Yellow miso — A short-time fermented miso, very mellow in flavor.

Yin — One of the two fundamental energies of the universe. Yin refers to the relative tendency of expansion, growth, centrifugality, diffusion, cold, darkness, and other qualities. Yin energy tends to go up and outward and in the vegetable kingdom predominates in large whole grains such as corn, oats, and barley; leafy green vegetables; and oils, nuts, fruit, and most liquids. Its complementary and antagonistic energy is yang.

Yuba — The film that develops from heating soy milk. Commonly available dried and used in many tofu-style dishes.

Yudofu — A traditional tofu dish prepared by simmering tofu with other vegetables and served with a sauce.

Zoni — Miso or clear soup made with mochi.

BIBLIOGRAPHY

Books

Aihara, Cornellia. *The Do of Cooking*. Chico, Calif.: George Ohsawa Macrobiotic Foundation, 1972.

Dietary Goals for the United States. Select Committee on Nutrition and Human Needs, U.S. Senate, Washington, D.C.: 1977.

Dufty, William. *Sugar Blues*. New York: Warner Books, 1975.

Esko, Edward and Wendy. *Macrobiotic Cooking for Everyone*. Tokyo: Japan Publications, 1980.

Esko, Wendy. *Introducing Macrobiotic Cooking*. Tokyo: Japan Publications, 1978.

Fukuoka, Masanobu. *The One-Straw Revolution*. Emmaus, Pa.: Rodale Press, 1978.

Heidenry, Carolyn. *An Introduction to Macrobiotics*. Florence, Italy: Aladdin Press, 1984.

I Ching or *Book of Changes*, trans. Richard Wilhelm and Cary F. Baynes. Princeton: Bollingen Foundation, 1950.

Jacobson, Michael F. and Letitia Brewster. *The Changing American Diet*. Center for Science in the Public Interest, Washington, D.C.: 1978.

Kohler, Jean and Mary Alice. *Healing Miracles from Macrobiotics*. West Nyack, N.Y.: Parker, 1979.

Kushi, Aveline. *How to Cook with Miso*. Tokyo: Japan Publications, 1978.

——— and Michio Kushi, *Macrobiotic Pregnancy and Care of the Newborn*. Tokyo: Japan Publications, 1984.

——— and Wendy Esko. *The Changing Seasons Macrobiotic Cookbook*. Wayne, N.J.: Avery Publishing Group, 1984.

Kushi, Michio. *The Book of Macrobiotics*. Tokyo: Japan Publications, 1977.

——— *Natural Healing Through Macrobiotics*. Tokyo: Japan Publications, 1978.

——— *The Book of Do-In: Exercise for Physical and Spiritual Development.* Tokyo: Japan Publications, 1979.

——— *How to See Your Health: The Book of Oriental Diagnosis.* Tokyo: Japan Publications, 1980.

——— *Cancer and Heart Disease: The Macrobiotic Approach to Degenerative Disorders.* Tokyo: Japan Publications, 1982.

——— *Your Face Never Lies.* Wayne, N.J.: Avery Publishing Group, 1983.

——— *The Era of Humanity.* Brookline, Mass.: *East West Journal* (1980).

——— and Alex Jack, *The Cancer-Prevention Diet.* New York: St. Martin's Press, 1983.

——— *Diet for a Strong Heart: Michio Kushi's Macrobiotic Dietary Guidelines for High Blood Pressure, Heart Attack, and Stroke.* New York: St. Martin's Press, forthcoming.

——— and the East West Foundation. *The Macrobiotic Approach to Cancer.* Wayne, N.J.: The Avery Publishing Group, 1982.

Lloyd, G.E.R., ed. *Hippocratic Writings,* trans. J. Chadwick and W. N. Mann. New York: Penguin Books, 1978.

Mendelsohn, Robert S., M.D. *Confessions of a Medical Heretic.* New York: Warner Books, 1981.

——— *Male Practice.* Chicago: Contemporary Books, 1980.

Ohsawa, George. *Cancer and the Philosophy of the Far East.* Oroville, Calif.: George Ohsawa Macrobiotic Foundation, 1971.

——— and William Dufty. *You Are All Sanpaku.* New York: University Books, 1965.

Ohsawa, Lima. *The Art of Just Cooking.* Brookline, Mass.: Autumn Press, 1975.

Sattilaro, Anthony, M.D., and Tom Monte. *Recalled By Life: The Story of My Recovery from Cancer.* Boston: Houghton-Mifflin, 1982.

Shurtleff, William and Akiko Aoyagi Shurtleff. *The Book of Kudzu.* Lafayette, Calif.: The Soyfoods Center, 1977.

——— *The Book of Miso.* New York: Ballantine Books, 1981.

——— *The Book of Tempeh.* New York: Harper & Row, 1979.

——— *The Book of Tofu.* New York: Ballantine Books, 1979.

Yamamoto, Shizuko. *Barefoot Shiatsu.* Tokyo: Japan Publications, 1979.

The Yellow Emperor's Classic of Internal Medicine, trans. Ilza Veith. Berkeley: University of California Press, 1949.

Periodicals

East West Journal, Brookline, Mass.

George Ohsawa Macrobiotic Foundation News, Oroville, Calif.

Infinite Gates, Pejepscot, Maine

Le Compas, Paris, France

MacroMuse, Rockville, Md.

Nutrition Action, Washington, D.C.

The People's Doctor, Evanston, Ill.

Index

The true cook . . . holds in his or her palm the happiness of mankind, the welfare of generations yet unborn.

—N. Douglas, *An Almanac*